W. E. B. DU BOIS and *The Souls of Black Folk*

The John Hope Franklin Series in African American History and Culture

Waldo E. Martin Jr. and Patricia Sullivan, editors

W. E. B. Du Bois

and *The Souls of Black Folk*

Stephanie J. Shaw

THE UNIVERSITY OF NORTH CAROLINA PRESS
Chapel Hill

This book was published with the assistance of the
John Hope Franklin Fund of the University of North Carolina Press.

The paper in this book meets the guidelines for permanence
and durability of the Committee on Production Guidelines for
Book Longevity of the Council on Library Resources.

The University of North Carolina Press has been a member
of the Green Press Initiative since 2003.

Frontispiece: W. E. B. Du Bois, Niagara delegate meeting, Boston, 1907;
courtesy of W. E. B. Du Bois Papers (MS 312), Special Collections and
University Archives, University Libraries, University of Massachusetts Amherst.

Library of Congress Cataloging-in-Publication Data

Shaw, Stephanie J. (Stephanie Jo), 1955–
W. E. B. Du Bois and *The Souls of Black Folk* / Stephanie J. Shaw.
pages cm. — (The John Hope Franklin series in African American history and culture)
Includes bibliographical references and index.
ISBN 978-0-8078-3873-0 (cloth : alk. paper)
1. Du Bois, W. E. B. (William Edward Burghardt), 1868–1963. *Souls of Black Folk*.
2. Du Bois, W. E. B. (William Edward Burghardt), 1868–1963—Criticism and interpretation.
I. Title.
E185.6.D797328 2013
323.092—dc23   2013008289

17 16 15 14 13   5 4 3 2 1

THIS BOOK IS DEDICATED TO THE BLESSED MEMORY OF

Jennie Lee Thompson Shaw,

Vera Louise Thompson, and Richard Thompson

There was joy in the South. It rose like perfume—like a prayer. Men stood quivering. Slim dark girls, wild and beautiful with wrinkled hair, wept silently; young women, black, tawny, white and golden, lifted shivering hands, and old and broken mothers, black and gray, raised great voices and shouted to God across the fields, and up to the rocks and the mountains.

A great song arose, the loveliest thing born this side of the seas. It was a new song. It did not come from Africa, though the dark throb and beat of that Ancient of Days was in it and through it. It did not come from white America—never from so pale and hard and thin a thing, however deep these vulgar and surrounding tones had driven. Not the Indies or the hot South, the cold East or the heavy West made that music. It was a new song and its deep and plaintive beauty, its great cadences and wild appeal wailed, throbbed and thundered on the world's ears with a message seldom voiced by man. . . .

. . . [And] it lived and grew; always it grew and swelled and lived, and it sits today at the right hand of God, as America's one real gift to beauty; as slavery's one redemption, distilled from the dross of its dung.

—W. E. B. Du Bois, *Black Reconstruction in America*

CONTENTS

ACKNOWLEDGMENTS

In 1995, I read *The Souls of Black Folk* from cover to cover for the first time in about twenty years. The farther I got into the book the stranger it seemed, and the more exhilarating it became even though I had read it before. Moreover, I had been reading *about* the book ever since I first read it. Yet it no longer seemed like the book I had previously read, nor did it seem to be quite the same book I had been reading about all those years since. Ultimately, I did what any curious person would have done—I began rereading all the things I had read about the book, and then some. This process was made infinitely easier because of the superb research skills of two (then) graduate students, Tiwanna Simpson and Stephen G. Hall, who spent a couple or more weeks conducting literature searches for me—in the library and without the assistance of Google(!). Their accomplishment gave me more than a good start on what ultimately became this book and was worth far more than the hourly rate they were paid. Even my deeply felt gratitude is not enough.

The more I read and reread, the more I talked about Du Bois' master-work. I might never have written a word about it had it not been for Julius Scott. For the next two or three years, almost every time we talked I ended up rambling on and on about *The Souls of Black Folk*. At some point Julius suggested that I write something. I was in the middle of another project, with five or six years' worth of research already behind it, but one day I took Julius's advice, and after two or three (or four or five) hours one weekend, I had written two paragraphs that became the opening of the *one* essay I intended to write about *Souls*. Thank you, Julius!

Several years later, while a fellow at the Center for Advanced Study in the Behavioral Sciences, I completed a reasonable draft of that essay. I am grateful to Tom Holt, Julie Saville, Evelyn Brooks Higginbotham, Elsa Barkley Brown, and Joe Reidy, who read and commented on it. Thanks also to Doug McAdam, who then directed the center, and Waldo Martin, Fred Cooper, and Sterling Stuckey, all fellows that year, for their comments on that draft. I met Nahum Chandler that year, and he immediately encouraged and promoted my efforts. Nahum shared his published and unpublished work and continued to support my efforts over the years that followed. Adolph Reed read that first essay in the form of an article manuscript for a journal and encouraged its publication. Later having the opportunity to talk with Reed, along with Kenneth Warren, about this work and others, and their subsequent critiques of new chapter drafts, helped me to improve my initial efforts and to extend them to what was slowly becoming a book. It might have remained "a becoming" had I not had the opportunity to meet David L. Lewis and to comment on his Distinguished Keynote Address at one of the events in the 2005–6 Buffalo State College yearlong centennial celebration of the meeting of the Niagara Conference. Although I had previously read both of Lewis's volumes on Du Bois' life, Lewis's paper pushed me to read more classical philosophy. His response to my comments and his subsequent comments on what had become three drafted chapters helped me immensely. My thanks also go to Pat Sullivan and Shelia Martin for reading a draft of the essay that began as that commentary, and to Shelia, Wanda Davis, and Felix Armfield for their roles in my receiving the invitation to participate in this important celebration.

Subsequent presentations at the American Historical Association meetings (2003) and the meetings of the Association for the Study of African American Life and History (2009) yielded very helpful comments from Ernest Allen, Jim Grossman, Earl Lewis, and the audience members at both sessions. In particular, a question from Robert Harris at the AHA session forced me to relate my conclusions to Du Bois' *international* concerns in *Souls*. My project was still in its early stages, and this single question was central to my rethinking everything. It led to my first efforts to tackle Hegel and, ultimately, to the one article's becoming *this* book. I will always be grateful for the question. Audience members at the 1999 and 2005 meetings of the Collegium for African American Research also provided important comments and raised useful questions. A presentation at the 2010 "History—Ancient to Modern" conference of the Athens Institute for Education and Research brought me face-to-face with another body of insightful scholars of the histories of states, societies, art, philosophy, and religion. Among these scholars, I especially thank Andrea Eis, a scholar of classical art, whose example is inspiring, and Christopher Phelps, then an OSU colleague on a different campus, who pointedly asked me to reconcile my own conclusions about Du Bois' work with his years of study with William James. I might not yet have a complete response, but the question alone (and much subsequent pondering of it) further convinced me of Du Bois' intellectual independence and yielded more insights that made their way into this book.

Many current and former colleagues at OSU have had a hand in the production of this book. Kenneth Hamilton read one of the first complete drafts of the book and provided me chapter-by-chapter (really, line-by-line) comments. I am surprised he still speaks to me after enduring this burden. Alamin Mazrui read the first chapters of this project and actively supported and encouraged my efforts. Greg Anderson directed me to important literature on Pythagoras and Pythagoreans. Kwaku Korang provided copies of his own related work, and Stephen Kern and Cynthia Brokaw provided copies of other related scholarship. Carole Fink not only provided copies of scholarship on Du Bois that turned up during her own unrelated research, but she read an early draft of the whole manuscript and always asked good, hard questions about it. She has contributed much to this volume. Les Benedict gave me more than enough to think about regarding constitutional history. His equally impressive understanding of Hegel and his detailed comments on parts of my manuscript began to ease the chronic headache that reading Hegel (over and over) had bequeathed me. Les also read those first two paragraphs, years earlier, and completely transformed one of them by changing one word. Bill Childs graciously read and commented on the entire manuscript and never stopped supporting it. Eugene O'Connor, because of his training in classical philosophy and literature, totally intimidated me. I am grateful that his comments, along with those of Kenneth Goings, on rough, early chapter drafts helped me to refine some of my discussions. Penny Russell patiently waited for years to read the entire manuscript and generously provided helpful comments. Jacqueline Royster also read one of those early drafts of the whole manuscript and engaged in long, helpful conversations with me about it. I am equally grateful to Ted McDaniel for reading and commenting on the manuscript and for assisting me in my education on various aspects of music history and theory. I am also thankful to Ted for introducing me to Gabriel Miller, whom I must thank for helping me with the piano work, for answering all my questions about the music, and for anticipating other, usually more important, questions. Pat Pannell Bullock and Kelly Eager completed some of the tedious work of proofreading and documentation checking. Long and regular conversations with Stephen Hall, on his work and mine, gradually (and fortunately) moved me toward thinking about this whole project in the context of intellectual history. I am especially grateful for those conversations and others about whatever we were reading at the time or had just read. Stephen always asked the question or made the observation that made me think about books and ideas in new and useful ways.

John C. Burnham read the first complete draft of this manuscript around 2008. Having served as my Ph.D. adviser, this historian of science and medicine probably never imagined that he would still be reading my draft work after these many years. One of the benefits of his also being a friend is that he has never been too busy (and he might be busier than any-body I know) to talk with me about it or to listen to me talk about things I was still trying to understand. And yes, John, I AM WORKING ON THE GRANDMOTHERS EVEN AS I AM WRITING THESE ACKNOWLEDGMENTS. I thank Marjorie Burnham for enduring all those Sunday brunches that were almost always accompanied (probably dominated) by my (often re-petitive) thinking out loud about this book, those (temporarily) neglected grandmothers, and stuff, in general. I am equally grateful for her insights on this work and everything else.

The support of other friends has been critical throughout this process. Robin Hailstorks has been an ace since graduate school. Carlton Wilson, also a long-timer, read and commented on an early, really rough draft of this book and pushed me to learn more about eighteenth- and nineteenth-century European political thought. Carlton, even if you don't see the evidence of it in this book, I really did read everything you suggested. Thank you for everything. Many thanks, also, to Lynda Morgan for reading this manuscript, for helping me to think about it, and for always lending a good ear. I am grateful for the friendship of Ross Bagby, Deborah Post, Chris Burton, Lynn Gale, Randy Roth, Jim Bartholomew, Colin Palmer, Susan Hartmann, Paulette Pierce, Jim Upton, and Lydia Lindsey, all of whom contributed to the completion of this book. Another former student, Keith Griffler, read, reread, commented on, and discussed several chapters of this study with me. Thank you, Keith. And thank you, Kenneth Andrien, for being a great friend and Julius Gordon for everything.

In the category of friends *and* family, Dianne, Aaronia, and Kevin, thank you. I love you. Jennie, Aaron, Vera L., Richard, and Vera A., we miss you.

I have incurred a huge debt to all the Du Bois scholars, living and dead, whose works have provided me an education that could never have come in school. I remain humbled by their work. I am equally indebted and grateful to the Hegel scholars, whose works helped me through the most difficult text I have ever read, and reread, and reread. I only wish I could have done more in both areas.

I finished the first reasonable draft of the first essay for this book (which now comprises parts of the first and second chapters) as a 2002–3 fel-low at the Center for Advanced Study in the Behavioral Sciences, and I finished the first complete draft of the final chapter as a 2008–9 Marta Sutton Weeks Fellow at the Stanford Humanities Center. In both cases, I was working primarily on something else. I am grateful for both fel-lowships, for the time and space they provided, and for the opportuni-ties they presented for meeting, listening to, and talking with so many fine scholars. As remote as some of their areas of study appeared to be from my own, all the talks I attended at the Stanford Humanities Center contributed directly to this project. In addition to the people I have already thanked from CASBS, I owe a special debt to István Bodnár, the first philosopher in whose care I entrusted that first, tentative essay draft. I am grateful to him for taking it seriously, providing helpful comments, and remaining interested in this project over many years. I am thankful to OSU for supplementing both fellowships and for a publication subvention grant. I am grateful to the University of North Carolina Press for taking a chance on this book and for all the work and patience of the staff. I will forever be grateful to Lucius Outlaw and to UNC Press readers Robin Kelley and Wilson Moses for their thoughtful comments and for the ways they helped make this book better.

INTRODUCTION

"It has been said that a great man lays the world under the obligation to understand him. The obligation is not easily fulfilled when a man of genius of the highest order produces a philosophical interpretation of experience so novel in its design, so subtle in the texture of its thought, so comprehensive in its range and penetrating in its vision. It is impossible to trace the stages in the construction of the system. He made his 'voyage of discovery' alone, and we are only made aware of his arrival at his destination. It has been customary to seek and to find the origins of his thought in his immediate predecessors. . . . At best, however, these provide merely clues. . . . The partial and formal similarity of principle does not account for the manner in which the principle was completely transformed. . . . His mind was much too original to remain under their influence; and the easy mastery of their doctrine in his . . . writings shows that he quickly passed beyond them."[1]

The above lines, written about Georg Wilhelm Friedrich Hegel and *Phenomenology of Spirit*, could just as easily have been written about William Edward Burghardt Du Bois and *The Souls of Black Folk* (hereafter, *Souls*). Ever since the book's publication, it has simultaneously captivated and confounded readers partly because of the complex and diverse world of ideas that informed its discussions. Classical philosophical concerns appear from the very beginning of the book—in its title. Biblical texts, occasionally paraphrased, make profound statements throughout the *Souls*. Well-known black writers of the nineteenth century deserve much credit for Du Bois' accomplishment: his chapter on the Sorrow Songs, for example, recalls Frederick Douglass's earlier discussion of them, and Anna Julia Cooper's *A Voice from the South* resonates throughout *Souls*.[2] Nor did Du Bois ignore mainstream scholars. Franz Boas' turn-of-the-century breakthroughs in cultural anthropology are evident in the book, and the ideas of Du Bois' Harvard teachers (William James, Albert Bushnell Hart, Josiah Royce, and George Santayana, in particular), and other important thinkers in and around Cambridge, filter into and out of *Souls*. Also making appearances are a variety of eighteenth- and nineteenth-century British and French scientists, philosophers, and political and economic theorists and nineteenth-century German materialists, including idealists, Hegel chief among them. Du Bois' intellectual foundation was broad and deep, and, like Hegel, he mastered the ideas of many of his intellectual forerunners, and he went beyond some of them.

Generations of scholars, from different disciplines and from interdisciplinary areas as well, agree that we would be hard pressed to point to more than a few intellectuals who exceeded the accomplishments of W. E. B. Du Bois. His appropriation of Plato's *Republic* in framing his theory of the Talented Tenth is probably flawless. And as a trailblazer in the not-yet-established field of sociology when he undertook and subsequently published his study of black life in Philadelphia's Seventh Ward, he was, as Aldon Morris and Amin Ghaziani have written, "a sociologist a century ahead of his discipline." Du Bois argued then what is now accepted as common knowledge: "that black people were not inferior biologically or culturally; that race was socially constructed; that race, class, and gender inequalities were interdependent and reinforcing; and that worldwide capitalism was the fundamental source of global racism. His work thoroughly integrated multiple methods." "Yet," Morris and Ghaziani continue, "Du Bois's seminal achievements remain understated, at best, given his academic marginality and the discrimination he encountered."[3]

Over the course of his long and storied life and career, Du Bois wrote poetry and plays, fiction and nonfiction. Many of his scholarly publications have become intellectual icons. Scholars generally recognize *The Philadelphia Negro* (1899) as the first major sociological study of race produced in the United States. *The Souls of Black Folk* is a foundational work in African American and African studies programs worldwide and also influenced the conceptualization of other area studies. The Atlanta University social studies produced under Du Bois' direction remain important sources for information on early twentieth-century black life. And despite Du Bois' lack of access to most major archives while researching *Black Reconstruction* (1935), it remains the most significant book ever produced on the subject; it sits at the foundation of *all* subsequent studies.

The recent one-hundredth anniversary of some of these achievements provided a perfect opportunity for extensive, critical reexaminations of Du Bois' work. In addition to celebrating the one-hundredth anniversary of the publication of *The Philadelphia Negro* and *The Souls of Black Folk* in 1999 and 2003, respectively, academics and activists commemorated the centennial of the meeting of the Niagara Conference, which Du Bois initiated, in 2005. Its descendant, the National Association for the Advancement of Colored People, reached that landmark anniversary in 2009. Each of these milestones resulted (worldwide) in special conferences, special sessions at conferences, symposia, new books, articles, and even journals, many of which focused on Du Bois and his work. None of this was unde-served. Du Bois and his work have served the public as symbols of intel-lectual accomplishment for more than a century.

Although it is true, as Stephen Jay Gould wrote, that "all the world loves a centennial," this book did not begin as an effort to commemorate any of these important anniversaries.[4] Instead, this book evolved from a simple interest in rediscovering *The Souls of Black Folk* as the major historical icon that it has always been. It has led to this effort to discuss the book as a momentous intellectual accomplishment not only for reasons now well known but for others not yet fully revealed and situated squarely in the era during which Du Bois wrote—when narrow, disciplinary boundaries were not clearly established, and when intellectuals were much more multidi-mensional than they are now and capable of seeing and addressing many aspects of a point in a variety of ways at once. In the chapters that follow, I hope to re-present *The Souls of Black Folk* as an even bigger and more important book than has heretofore been demonstrated. I also hope to do justice to a major American intellectual.

I seek, first and foremost, to examine *The Souls of Black Folk* as one whole, coherent text in which each part, whether an individual chapter or a single idea, though complete itself, relates to the larger story of the whole volume. While paying attention to Du Bois' discussion of Booker T. Washington, "veils," "double consciousness," and "the color line," I have moved the discussion of *Souls* significantly away from the heavy (and nar-row) emphases that most studies of the book place on them. As important and useful as these topics have been to scholarly analyses of *Souls*, I see them as the proverbial "trees." Consequently, here, while not ignoring the significance of these themes in Du Bois' volume, I have focused on what I see as "the forest"—Soul.

Thus, my second goal is to analyze *The Souls of Black Folk*, with all of its history, sociology, economics, politics, religion, music, anthropology, and psychology as, equally, a complete work of philosophy.[5] After all, the book is about the needs, desires, capacities, and, most important, the *striving* of the human soul. The other possible conclusion is that *Souls* is a work of re-ligion, which would not be far from the mark, either, if one should consider religion as more than theology.[6] This theme is clearly evident throughout my study, but, even there, my particular interest is in the great potential of reading *Souls* with more of Du Bois' formative and formidable training in philosophy in mind.

Reading *Souls* as a single text rather than a series of compiled essays yielded an unexpected result. It is a particularly risky one. I have, third, proposed reading *The Souls of Black Folk* in the context of Hegel's *Phenomenology of Spirit* (hereafter, *Phenomenology*), which philosophers have described as the most intensely studied work of philosophy at the turn of the twentieth century.[7] The biggest risk in doing this (beyond my not being a philosopher and the regularly noted difficulty of *Phenomenology*, even for philosophers) is that there is no proof of a direct relationship between the two texts. As J. B. Baillie reminded us of Hegel, Du Bois "made his 'voyage of discovery' alone," and we can only reflect upon the similarities between *Souls* and other texts. The closest we can get to "evidence" from Du Bois of a possible relationship between the two texts is an ambiguous statement he wrote during the 1950s to his good friend Herbert Aptheker: "For two years I studied under William James while he was developing pragmatism; under Santayana and his attractive mysticism; and under Royce and his Hegelian idealism. I then found and adopted a philosophy which has served me since; thereafter I turned to the study of history."[8] Most obviously, Du Bois could have been alluding, generally, to Hegel's influential philosophy of history, which, though published as a book after Hegel's death, certainly formed the foundation of *Phenomenology*. But beyond that important concession, most Du Bois scholars have concluded that Hegel does not figure in any significant way in Du Bois' work. An important exception is Shamoon Zamir, who argued for a direct relationship between *Phenomenology* and Du Bois' first chapter of *Souls*, a conclusion others have made but Zamir detailed. Zamir not only pointed to *Phenomenology* as a likely focus of Du Bois' course with Santayana, but also noted that the course Santayana took with Royce the previous year included a significant focus on *Phenomenology*. This study seeks, then, to add substantively to the works that have acknowledged more than a general influence of Hegel's philosophy of history. In particular, I show that we do not need to limit the relationship to one between *Phenomenology* and the first chapter of *Souls*, but that it should extend to the whole text.[9]

Louis Menand has described Hegel's theory of knowledge as "one of the most grandly architectonic answers to the question, How does the world hang together? ever formulated." To be sure, no turn-of-the-century student of philosophy could have avoided Hegel or the importance of his work. When Du Bois attended Harvard in the late 1880s and early 1890s, Hegel was at the center of many scholarly discussions and courses. And when Du Bois arrived at the university in Berlin in 1892, the school was under the influence of what others have described as a neo-Hegelian revival. But despite persistent scholarly conclusions that Du Bois' introduction to Hegel came at Harvard, and perhaps was solidified in Berlin, Du Bois had Hegelian idealism on his mind *before* either of these life-changing experiences in Massachusetts and Germany. His 1888 Fisk University commencement address on Bismarck, which scholars often point to as evidence of Du Bois' early fascination with or admiration of German nationalism was, rather, a serious reflection on "the power of purpose, the force of an idea." The meditation showed "what a man can do if he will." It was not a totally positive assessment. In Du Bois' view, Bismarck might have accomplished his goal of making "Germany a nation," but he created a nation "that knows not the first principle of self government." In the concluding paragraph of the address, which Du Bois apparently cut from the delivery, he summarized the important result: Bismarck "more than any other is responsible for making Germany a nation of theorists for the vagaries of Lasalle [*sic*], the pessimism of (Schopenhauer?), and the idealism of Hegel." Ferdinand Lassalle, often credited with being "the originator of the social-democratic movement in Germany," was a dedicated Hegelian; he famously adapted Hegel's "Lordship and Bondage" discussion to the German working class. And Schopenhauer was anti-Hegelian to an equal degree.[10] Hegel's example, his study of experience and knowledge, the physical and the metaphysical, and the relationship between them provided Du Bois a useful model—a model he encountered *before* his arrival at Harvard—for creating as complete a study as possible of black folks' effort to live their own (self-determined) lives.[11]

In *Phenomenology*, Hegel began his "system of philosophy" through a study of "the science of the experience of consciousness" and by exploring *both* the "experience of consciousness" *and* the "philosophy of spirit."[12] The Platonic concept of World Soul (*anima mundi*) as the spiritual principle that is the explanation for or the cause of all natural phenomena is central to Hegel's analysis. World Soul is, itself, a living being, an aspect of everything in the universe; and everything in the universe, though complete in itself, is an interdependent part of World Soul.[13] *Phenomenology* explores the history of the experience of consciousness's (or Du Bois' soul's) striving for freedom in this larger context. As a philosophy of spirit we see soul's/consciousness's persistent quest for knowledge. This process begins with conscious's recognition of an abstract (a particular) condition or factor. Eventually, however, a self-generated doubt (or skepticism) develops that questions whether that abstract object/condition is what it appears to be. Consciousness overcomes this negative through a process of reasoning during which it subsumes the useful parts of the negative and abandons the rest. Thus, consciousness becomes a new thing—what Hegel called the concrete—and has done so in part by recognizing its "other" in itself.[14]

As consciousness continues to seek greater knowledge, the process begins again and moves, potentially, from consciousness to self-consciousness to reason to spirit. Thus, in each stage of this teleological process, through reflection (reason), consciousness undermines the contradictions between its immediate (determinate) understanding of things (appearances) and what is real. For Hegel, true knowledge (science or philosophy) is achieved when the object as it appears (consciousness) and the object as it actually is coincide. Thus, consciousness must know itself as it actually is, not as it appears. "Absolute Knowledge" represents the highest possible understanding.

Using diverse historical contexts (evidence of "experience") from the ancient world to the end of the eighteenth century, Hegel's evidence comes from the histories of peoples he ultimately characterized as world-historical. My contention is that *Souls* adds black people to Hegel's queue in a way that makes it clear that the souls of these folks were no different from the souls of others. And, importantly, in the context of Hegel's (Plato's) World Soul, the striving of the souls of black folk was not simply comparable to that of Hegel's other peoples, but was part of the same struggle—the nineteenth-century American part—of Conscious's (Du Bois' soul's) striving for freedom, wholeness, and harmony, and spirit's quest for knowledge. I suggest here that with *The Souls of Black Folk*, Du Bois did more than write an important and moving history of the postemancipation world in which black Americans lived: his study added the nineteenth century and America to Hegel's philosophy, via the souls of black folk.[15]

Recent scholars have speculated on what "a sequel to the [*Phenomenology*] would look like were Hegel able to complete one."[16] When Hegel published *Phenomenology* in 1807, America had no history to speak of as a nation. But a century later and a century ago it was possible to add America and the *nineteenth* century to Hegel's discussion, and I propose that *The Souls of Black Folk* accomplished that. The extreme irony in this proposition relates less to *Phenomenology* and more to Hegel's subsequent *Philosophy of History*, which explicitly excluded Africa (black, sub-Saharan Africa) because of an apparent lack "of development [and] culture." Hegel wrote: "What we properly understand by Africa, is the Unhistorical, undeveloped Spirit, still involved in the conditions of mere nature, and which had to be presented here only as on the threshold of the World's History."[17] He recognized that both China and India had old civilizations and *culture*—visual and performing arts, literature, and poetry. But one had a form of government that inhibited freedom of thought/ideas, and the other was burdened by an "ossified" caste system that equally constrained the development of freedom. It is possible that Hegel would later have recognized, by his own definition, the ways these and/or other areas we now characterize as the new global South crossed "the threshold of world history" just as other groups and places about which he wrote had.[18] But what is more important here is what America would look like in this hypothetical study. America finally abolished slavery, one of the existing conditions that kept Africa out of Hegel's narratives of the philosophy of history, but created a color line that was nearly as effective as slavery at blocking the self-development of a group of its people (and, by extension, World Soul). But when Hegel wrote the lectures that later became part of *Philosophy*, he left America to "the future, where, in the ages that lie before us, the burden of the World's History shall reveal itself." He insisted that "we have to do with that which (strictly speaking) is neither past nor future, but with that which *is*, which has an eternal existence—with Reason; and this is quite sufficient to occupy us."[19] At the turn of the *twentieth* century, America was ripe for commentary in the context of consciousness's (soul's) constant striving for freedom/self-determination. But by Hegel's definition of philosophy, America remained outside the realm of reason. Du Bois' discussion of the experience of the souls of black folk provides the proof.

Although other scholars have recognized some of the philosophical aspects of Du Bois' study, acknowledgements of Du Bois' metaphysics rarely go beyond mentioning it. The general failure of scholars fully to consider Du Bois' engaging metaphysics has resulted in the most significant misunderstandings and misrepresentations of *Souls* and a major gap in analyses of it. Because metaphysics, a study of being as being (among other things), depends in part on the acceptance of a priori synthesis (*deductive* reasoning), and apriorities are anathema to empiricists who rely on a posteriori evidence (*inductive* reasoning) to explain phenomena, it became far too easy for critics, especially positivists, to treat aspects of Du Bois' discussion as romantic (sentimental) drivel, or to ignore them altogether. And so, fourth, I have tried to explain and to balance (perhaps to reconcile) the two types of evidence. *The Souls of Black Folk* is a study of both the material world (*phenomena*) and the spiritual world (*noumena*) in which the souls of black folk moved. Explaining both worlds sometimes involved different types of evidence. Du Bois clearly provided both types, and he never confused the two.[20]

Fifth, throughout this study are both implicit suggestions and explicit appeals for reading *Souls* as a discussion of the discord between the material and spiritual worlds. The extensive scholarly focus on Du Bois' discussion of the "double consciousness" of the American Negro—"two souls, two thoughts, two unreconciled strivings; two warring ideals in one dark body, whose dogged strength alone keeps it from being torn asunder"—has partly obscured the importance of the "two worlds," often limiting them to a manifestation and discussion of race relations. Both double consciousness and the color line were also aspects (evidence) of the dissonance that existed between the spiritual and material worlds—the inner world of the mind/soul where there was great potential and power, and the external, material world of diverse constraints (the color line among them) that constantly worked against a people's ability to discover/determine and to become who they "really" are. In this light, an important goal of *Souls* was to encourage real democracy—a material world that supported the freedom (self-determination) of consciousness (soul) for all its members to and for the good of the whole society—a unity that would reflect (and contribute to) the wholeness and harmony of World Soul.[21]

My smaller goals are in some ways related to the larger goals noted above and are no less significant. In each chapter in this volume I have attempted to provide new ways of thinking about other aspects of *The Souls of Black Folk*. My first chapter proposes that, in addition to the traditional characterizations of the three parts of *Souls* as history, sociology, and spirituality or culture, we would gain much by also seeing these parts as being about work, culture, and liberty—the objectives of the striving of the souls of black folk—and as an adaptation of the Aristotelian triumvirate of appetite or desire, reason or thought, and spirit. The chapter also proposes our seeing these objectives in light of the division between the material and spiritual worlds and as an explicit quest for freedom *and* liberty. The second chapter offers a new interpretation of Du Bois' chapter "Of the Coming of John" as a fable that encourages us to think not only about the preeminence of Soul in the book, but of its sovereignty and the importance of respecting and encouraging its striving, with severe consequences for not doing so.

It was *The Souls of Black Folk* that gave Du Bois' theory of the Talented Tenth its greatest exposure. Although his whole volume is a substantial commentary on the importance of self-determination, the sovereign right to be whatever one's aspirations and abilities encourage and allow, Du Bois' discussions of the Talented Tenth made that case most clearly. Other scholars have noted parallels between Du Bois' Talented Tenth and Plato's Philosopher Rulers. In my third chapter, I have illustrated the parallels fully. My interests, however, go beyond that specific illustration. In addition to demonstrating further the utility of connecting Du Bois' scholarship to his foundational study in philosophy, this chapter shows that Du Bois' theory of the Talented Tenth was neither elitist nor conservative, which have been the prevailing views until very recently. Instead, it was a thoroughly radical proposition put forth at a time when many thinkers, writers, and activists were proposing alternatives to what people regularly described as a "Gospel of Wealth."[22]

My fourth chapter focuses on Du Bois' chapter on Alexander Crummell. It also begins the shift in my discussion from *The Souls of Black Folk* as a *general* work of philosophy rooted, at least in part, in classical philosophical traditions, to one that reveals parallels to Hegel's *Phenomenology*. This chapter views Du Bois' discussion of Crummell as much more than a personal tribute to his mentor, but as both a theological and a philosophical comment on Crummell's life. Du Bois' theological representation of Crummell is allegorical: Crummell is a prophet in the tradition of other great religious leaders. But in the philosophical statement that the chapter provides, Crummell also appears to have gone through all of Hegel's "shapes" (or "forms") of Consciousness—from perception all the way to Reason and Spirit. Given that metaphysics is closely related to the philosophy of religion, Crummell's life (he was an Episcopal priest) provided a more fitting example of soul's journey (spiritual striving) than has been obvious.

Between the Crummell chapter and my fifth chapter on the Sorrow Songs, there is something of a bridge. I have labeled it a "preface" to the fifth chapter. First, this brief description attempts to show that the process Du Bois demonstrated for Crummell (his education from Consciousness to Spirit) is also evident within the group—not just for a few scattered exceptional souls, but the souls of black folk. And so this "bridge" helps to illustrate the *collective* process, which is important in the Hegelian construct. Second, while briefly sketching out Hegel's "shapes" of consciousness as they unfold in *Phenomenology*, this preface reveals parallels in the content and structure of the whole of *The Souls of Black Folk* and Hegel's *Phenomenology*. Third, this discussion introduces and situates Du Bois' discussion of art ("The Sorrow Songs") and religion ("Of the Faith of the Fathers") inside the Hegelian tradition of movement to collective consciousness and toward Absolute Knowledge. And, finally, this preface reveals further (beyond my first two chapters) how uniquely important the final four chapters of *The Souls of Black Folk* are.

Chapter 5 begins with a discussion of religion in *Souls* that shows how important black folk religion was *to* Du Bois and *for* the souls of black folk. It then moves to a detailed and very different discussion of the Sorrow Songs. To this point, their significance seems limited to their representing black American culture. When combined with Du Bois' chapter on religion, however, the chapter on the songs completes the Hegelian model, which ends with a focus on the art and religion of the folk. In this chapter I show not only that Du Bois' chapters on religion and songs parallel Hegel's discussion of the art and religion of the folk in the creation of *collective* consciousness, but that Du Bois' discussion of art—his chapter on the songs—surpasses Hegel's study in an extraordinary way. Although Hegel's study challenged Kant's *Critique of Pure Reason* in many ways, including by allowing for the possibility of Absolute Knowledge among humans, Hegel provided no example of it. Here, I attempt to show that Du Bois' Sorrow Songs provide evidence of that knowledge.

My chapter on the songs is, in one way, different from most of the other chapters, which stay, as much as possible, focused on the texts of *Souls*, the two Talented Tenth essays, and/or *Phenomenology*. In this chapter it was important to go significantly beyond the primary texts and to discuss some of the science of these songs in order to make sense of the contemporary perceptions of the songs and the contexts in which people heard them and to reveal their representation as Absolute Knowledge. Inverting the typical focus of studies of Du Bois' Sorrow Songs, which usually concentrate on the lyrics—language—this chapter ultimately pays especial attention to the music. It uses elementary aspects of physics and metaphysics to show how Du Bois could legitimately conclude that the Sorrow Songs were both the "articulate message of the slave to the world" (*phenomena*) and "the singular spiritual heritage of the nation" (*noumena*).

Du Bois' claim was bold but totally consistent with his larger discussion, which was both phenomenological and metaphysical. "Spiritual" things (his Sorrow Songs) are presumed to have "characteristics other than those possessed by a natural object." Such claims for certain music are almost as old as music itself, but efforts to explain what the special characteristics of nineteenth-century black spiritual music were have not been totally successful. The best that nineteenth-century transcribers could do was to try to record the notes on a western (five-line) staff that simply did not have enough space. They also tried to describe the sounds they heard and to explain how the songs made them feel. Recent theorists and critics, in targeting those (and subsequent) descriptions, have, unfortunately, left "the nature of the thing" in this music unidentified. My fifth chapter accepts the nineteenth-century listeners' words as important description/detail and attempts an interpretation of just what that "spiritual heritage" ("the nature of the thing") to which Du Bois referred actually was.[23]

Nine of the fourteen chapters in *The Souls of Black Folk* began as individual essays published in other places. Some scholars have described *Souls* as though some of the chapters have little to do with the others.[24]

Throughout this volume, I have tried to interpret *The Souls of Black Folk* as one whole, coherent study (to which revisions of the previously published pieces contributed much). Indeed, in my chapter on the songs (and its preface), I offer yet another way of thinking about *Souls* as a whole. As already noted, most analysts agree that the first part of *Souls* is driven by the discipline of history, the middle part by sociology, and the last part by discussions of spirituality. I propose in my first chapter that the first part is also about work, the middle part also about culture, and the last part also about liberty. But in chapter 5 and its preface I offer another possible construct, not to confuse but to show again just how profoundly Hegelian *The Souls of Black Folk* is and how complex Du Bois' thought was. If we divide Du Bois' volume differently, as, in fact, he divided it in his "Forethought," the sections would easily correspond to Hegel's stages of Consciousness, Self-Consciousness, Reason, and Spirit. My conclusion shows that the structure of Du Bois' volume was even more Hegel-like than that.

Composed at a time when the world seemed to be moving backward rather than forward, that is, away from freedom and liberty, wholeness and harmony, *Souls* was, in some ways, a deeply melancholy lament. It illustrated the revolutionary potential that the Union victory in the Civil War created and that the abandonment of Reconstruction squandered. The loss put America on a tragic course that could and should have been averted. As Du Bois reminded readers early on in his study, "no secure civilization can be built" on a foundation of greed and oppression and the resulting poverty and despair. It is especially important to relate this idea to the powerful and evocative opening lines of Du Bois' iconic book: the stunning announcement, *in 1903*, that "the problem of the Twentieth Century is the problem of the color-line." In this instance, Du Bois was not talking about a black problem (the so-called "Negro problem") or even a uniquely American problem. In the context of Hegel's study of world-historical individuals, events, and peoples, "the problem of the color-line" about which Du Bois prognosticated was the *world-historical* problem of the century just dawning.[25] Given the course of colonialism, imperialism, and extreme forms of nationalism then and subsequently, Du Bois' statement seems prophetic, in the tradition of the predictions of "seers," clairvoyants, or even individuals born with a veil.[26] But in the tradition of Hegelian phenomenology and metaphysics, Du Bois' announcement was simply the rational that was real.

Few people have had as many labels placed on them as W. E. B. Du Bois. He has been called an Afrocentrist and a Eurocentrist; a nationalist, a pan-Africanist, and a multiculturalist; an elitist and a champion of the folk; a social democrat and a communist; an integrationist and a segregationist; among many other labels. While at different times Du Bois' writings surely reflected one or another of these characteristics and sometimes more than one, it is also the case that at all times he was also a philosopher. Probably no work illustrates this more profoundly than *The Souls of Black Folk*.[27]

Analyses of *The Souls of Black Folk* have generally reflected the time and place in which they were produced. As important as it is to consider the relevance of any historical work to subsequent historical moments, much of the confusion about *Souls* would dissipate if we were to consider more carefully the intellectual environment *during which Du Bois wrote*. Du Bois was an intellectual, par excellence. And not only did his arrival at Friedrich Wilhelms Universität in 1892 coincide with a European/German revival in interest in Hegel (with one of Hegel's most devoted followers, whose lectures Du Bois attended, teaching at this university where Hegel himself spent a significant portion of his professional career), but there was an equally important and comparable movement in America that was already generations old, as evinced by the founding of the St. Louis Hegelians in the 1850s, the Harvard/Cambridge based Metaphysical Club (and all its offshoots) beginning in the 1870s, and the Hegel Club in the 1880s, whose membership included some of Du Bois' Harvard teachers. Du Bois was himself a participant in the Philosophical Club, where primarily Harvard scholars (including a variety of types of Idealists) discussed and debated various philosophical issues/ideas. Adolph Reed has cautioned us that "[s]hoehorning blacks into a chronology of exemplary thinkers is a subspecies of the vindicationist desire to establish the racial presence vis-à-vis a larger intellectual tradition." It is a fair warning. But, intellectually, Du Bois was no "marginal man," as E. Franklin Frazier later labeled him. Du Bois (and *Souls*) was, and should be seen as, at the very center of the intellectual discussions of his day.[28]

As intellectual historian Stephen G. Hall recently demonstrated for black historians generally, black writers and thinkers at the turn of the century deeply engaged the diverse intellectual discussions of their day, even and especially *before* they were *called* historians.[29] There is no better exemplar of that intellectual commitment than W. E. B. Du Bois. In *The Souls of Black Folk*, Du Bois not only engaged the traditional academic disciplines of philosophy, history, and literature, he also engaged the emerging disciplines of his day, including sociology, psychology, and political economy (versions of which all had previously been aspects of philosophy). He also, less obviously, took on, headfirst, some of the most challenging ideas that were then under debate, including Hegelian idealism. The result, *The Souls of Black Folk*, was more than a work of history, social science, or literature. The result was also a work of art.[30] It is no coincidence that philosophers (Hegel, to be sure) considered art to be among the best and clearest illustrations of the political concerns of a people.

A Brief Biographical Sketch[31]

W. E. B. Du Bois was born in 1868 in Great Barrington, Massachusetts, to Mary Silvina Burghardt and Alfred Du Bois. Although Alfred apparently abandoned the family while Du Bois was a toddler, his mother supported her family, sometimes by working as a domestic. Du Bois attended public schools in Great Barrington, and his ambition was to attend Harvard University after graduating in 1884. After a year of working and the death of his mother in 1885, and with financial help from local people and church groups, he entered Fisk University (1885–88) as a sophomore, pursuing a degree in philosophy. He went from Fisk to Harvard, where he was required to complete a second bachelor's degree (enrolling as a junior) before beginning graduate work. There, too, he pursued philosophy (B.A., 1890). He received his M.A. degree in 1891 in history and began his Ph.D. work. In 1892, he went to Friedrich Wilhelms Universität (formerly University of Berlin), where he studied until 1894. Unable to secure funding to complete his third year and his doctorate in Germany, he returned to the United States, taught Latin, Greek, German, and English at Wilberforce University (1894–96), completing his Ph.D. from Harvard in 1895. At Wilberforce, he met Nina Gomer (ca. 1871–1950) whom he married in 1896 and with whom he had two children, Burghardt (1897–99) and Yolande (1900–1961).

Du Bois' postgraduate career was filled with important political, intellectual, and cultural accomplishments. He moved from Wilberforce to Philadelphia to undertake a study of black life in the city, commissioned by the University of Pennsylvania. Upon its completion, he accepted a position at Atlanta University, where he developed the country's first social science research center, producing sixteen *Atlanta University Studies*. He served as professor of economics and history there from 1897 to 1910, and during a second stint at Atlanta University (1934–44) he was the founding chair of the Department of Sociology and started the scholarly journal *Phylon: The Atlanta University Review of Race and Culture*. Du Bois was a founding member of the American Negro Academy (1897), the Niagara Conference (1905) and its offspring, the National Association for the Advancement of Colored People (NAACP, 1909), and he played a leading role in organizing the 1918 Paris meeting of the Pan-African Congress. He founded and edited two more journals, *Moon Illustrated Weekly* (1905–6) and *Horizon: A Journal of the Color Line* (1907–10), both organs of the Niagara Movement, and he created the NAACP's short-lived children's magazine, *The Brownie's Book* (1920–21). But, among his editorial work, Du Bois is best known as the founding editor of the NAACP's magazine, *The Crisis*, which he edited from 1910 until 1934.

It is not possible to separate Du Bois' political life from his intellectual life, and his early editorial role made it possible to disseminate his views widely. His famous "Close Ranks" statement (1918), urging black Americans to support the war effort, angered some of his closest friends. His subsequent, more pessimistic positions on the likelihood of real racial equality in America cost him his editorship of *The Crisis* in 1934. By 1950, however, Du Bois' international associations and travels resulted in the State Department's charging him with being an agent of a foreign government. The trial that began in 1951 was practically over before it began. The sitting judge quickly dismissed the case certainly because of a lack of evidence but perhaps also to prevent the scheduled appearance of Albert Einstein as a character witness. Still, the State Department refused to validate and return Du Bois' passport nearly every year between 1952 and 1957. A Supreme Court ruling in 1958 forced its return, whereupon Du Bois embarked on a world tour, spending time in Europe, Asia, and Africa.

In 1961, Du Bois accepted an invitation from President Kwame Nkrumah to come to Ghana to work on his (Du Bois') lifelong dream project, the *Encyclopedia Africana*, and he and his second wife, Shirley Graham (1896–1977), whom he married in 1951, departed for Ghana. When, while there, the U.S. embassy refused to renew his passport, Du Bois became a citizen of Ghana. Six months later Du Bois died, in August 1963, the night before the historic March on Washington for Jobs and Freedom.

STRIVING

Work, Culture, and Liberty

John Jones to himself (quoting Esther 4:16), on his way to Altamaha to seek a teaching job from Judge Henderson: "I will go unto the king, which is not according to the law; and if I perish, I perish."

Judge Henderson to John Jones upon their meeting about the job: "I knew your father, John, he belonged to my brother, and he was a good Nigger." —W. E. B. Du Bois[1]

"HEREIN lie buried many things which if read with patience may show the strange meaning of being black here at the dawning of the Twentieth Century. This meaning is not without interest to you, Gentle Reader; for the problem of the Twentieth Century is the problem of the color-line." Du Bois opened his classic volume, *The Souls of Black Folk*, with these two sentences. They are attention getting; the second sentence is adamant. Du Bois did not *speculate* on the future's problems, which most of us, more modest, would have done; he announced, *in 1903*, that the color line is the problem of the twentieth century. David Levering Lewis, in his prizewinning biography of Du Bois, concludes, "This problem [of the color line] is the leitmotif of the book, a problem Du Bois examined from the perspective of institutions and ideals, and from that of the educated, the ignorant, the rural hard-pressed, and the urban beleaguered."[2]

But in lines as famous (and as often quoted) as the reference to the color line, Du Bois also wrote:

[T]he Negro is a sort of seventh son, born with a veil, and gifted with second-sight in this American world,—a world which yields him no true self-consciousness, but only lets him see himself through the revelation of the other world. It is a peculiar sensation, this double-consciousness, this sense of always looking at one's self through the eyes of others, of measuring one's soul by the tape of a world that looks on in amused contempt and pity. One ever feels his twoness,— an American, a Negro; two souls, two thoughts, two unreconciled strivings; two warring ideals in one dark body, whose dogged strength alone keeps it from being torn asunder.

Arnold Rampersad's literary biography of Du Bois describes "the Veil" as "the central metaphor both of black existence and of the book." And literary theorist and critic Eric Sundquist concludes that the description of double consciousness is "the most famous idea advanced by Du Bois, perhaps the most famous advanced by any African American." Political scientist and theorist Adolph Reed Jr. describes double consciousness as "a distinctly attractive template for the articulation of both interpretive and substantive, academic and hortatory arguments concerning the race's status."[3]

Du Bois' remarks about the veil, the color line, and double consciousness captured, and for more than one hundred years have continued to hold, scholarly and popular attention.[4] The attention is not unwarranted. To have written with such insight and passion about the color line, practically at the point of its (post–Civil War) institutionalization, was a major accomplishment; the veil was both a powerful metaphor and an important symbol in African American culture; and the concept of double consciousness seemed to capture the way black people lived their lives.[5] Nevertheless, by putting them back into the context of the whole book, this chapter shifts the focus from double consciousness, the veil, and the color line to other, perhaps more important but grossly under analyzed, aspects of the book.[6]

Just a few lines after that "gentle" but dramatic statement about the color line in the forethought to *The Souls of Black Folk*, Du Bois stated his purpose: "I have sought here to sketch, in vague, uncertain outline, the spiritual world in which ten thousand thousand Americans live and strive."[7] Since Du Bois was as much a philosopher as a historian, political economist, and sociologist, his wording should alert us that his description of the material world (the color line), despite its vividness, was merely a vehicle for illustrating a larger point. The phrase "spiritual world" suggests an interest in the incorporeal, however closely related it might be to the physical world. Du Bois was, after all, writing about *"the striving* in the *souls* of black folk" (emphasis added). The veil was undoubtedly central to the discussion, but Du Bois was a careful writer, and his reference to a "veil" obligates our looking through it, rather than at it, for the larger significance of this book.

The "veil" that is internal to the black community served as an allusion to, and/or a metaphor for, what people in a community had the ambition, the potential, indeed the ability, to achieve. In the African American folk tradition, one who is born with a veil is alleged to have the ability to see, feel, and understand things that ordinary people cannot. And many who report having been born with a veil note the predictive/prophetic quality of their dreams. Thus, people born with a veil have greater potential than others.[8]

But beyond that veil ("in this American world") existed a formidable barrier to the fulfillment of that ambition and ability—the color line. The color line did more than separate the two "races," keeping each to its own side. It had the effect of reaching within the veil, into the souls of black folk. At the end of the first chapter, which is called, significantly, "Of Our Spiritual Strivings," Du Bois outlined the book, and he identified the primary objectives of African American striving when he wrote, "Work, culture, liberty,—all these we need, not singly but together, not successively but together, each growing and aiding each, and all striving toward that vaster ideal that swims before the Negro people." Historian Thomas C. Holt has written that Du Bois recognized "work, culture, liberty," as the basis of all people's "effort to live a morally satisfying and useful life."[9] But more than that, to understand African Americans' striving for work, culture, and liberty is to see their souls—to see through the veil. To deny the striving, to stunt the ability, potential, and ambition that resided in the souls of black folk, would be devastating both for those who were striving and those who tried to suppress it.

Despite the enduring importance of *The Souls of Black Folk*, and the extensive appropriation of concepts it incorporated, it is still not possible to take for granted the meaning of expressions it popularized. In Stanley Brodwin's pioneering and compelling interpretation of the book, he wrote: "Du Bois presents an intensely personal vision of how one man confronted and transcended the complex tragic life generated in living *behind the veil of the color line*" (emphasis added).[10] To be sure, Du Bois lived much of his life behind both the veil and the color line. But the veil was more than the color line. Wilson Moses has written that the veil was a metaphor for black skin, and Du Bois, indeed, used "the veil" as a synonym for race.[11] But it was not in that sense that he invoked the metaphor. To find the metaphor, we should think about the veil that is, literally, a caul—the membrane (a "skin") that encloses a fetus in the womb, part of which still covers the head of some babies at birth—and apply the traditional understanding of its significance: people born with a veil are said to possess special gifts—of prophecy, of "second sight," of clairvoyance. The metaphor occurs, then, in the application of the veil as a symbol of black ability or potential.[12]

Where Du Bois' veil was a synonym for the term "race," he could allow us to peer "behind the veil" (behind the facade of skin), where we would see black people's souls. He, and others, could "dwell above the veil" (the color line) in a space where color was irrelevant, perhaps even nonexistent, where only ability mattered. And he could even show us the impact of the "*shadow* of the veil" (emphasis added), which was not the veil at all, but the color line that seemed to follow black folk everywhere they went, even to the grave.[13] And so it is *within* the literal veil, behind black skin, that we must look to see what is most important in this volume. Within (or behind) the most obvious indication of "race," and simultaneously in the realm of the metaphor, lay the source of African American striving—the soul—and black potential. The color line, which Du Bois sometimes called "color prejudice," was the external, artificial construction that obstructed black folks' striving so thoroughly and consistently that it had the ability to damage their souls by destroying that potential.

If one holds to these simple, and perhaps obvious, distinctions between the color line and the veil, Du Bois' writing becomes less ambiguous, eliminating the need for rewriting and/or extrapolation, which occurred in Robert Gooding-Williams's insightful interpretation of *The Souls of Black Folk* as an example of philosophy of history. Gooding-Williams chose to read Du Bois' powerful statement about black "second-sight in this American world" as "second-sight *into* this American world." In this context, second sight became the source of a problem. It caused black folk to "see things as the white world sees them, but only at the price of self-estrangement." Black people became "other" to themselves, and, consequently, according to Gooding-Williams, "Du Bois argues that the Negro internalizes the opposition between a white world and a Negro world."[14] Second sight, the internal condition, was not the problem; second sight was, in fact, empowering. The "American world," with its color line, was the source of the problem. Black skin represented a barrier only if one refused (or was unable) to see behind it (behind it, if looking *at* black people, as many white people did). But even under those circumstances, the veil (whether speaking of color *or* "second sight") was not the source of chaos or confusion, which, according to many, is the nature of double consciousness. Rather, strife arose out of the impact of the artificial external barrier that was the color line, because it regularly impeded black efforts for individual and group development. The material consequence of being unable to vote, go to school, own land, and/or earn a living wage was, obviously, poverty. But the most deadly consequence of the color line was spiritual; it could cause black folk to cease striving.[15] Du Bois clearly understood that, unimpeded, some folks' striving would result in success; for others it might not; and some would not strive at all. But in any case, "striving" (not its outcome) was what mattered to Du Bois.[16] At the very least, striving suggested a soul that was intact. Du Bois argued for the preservation (the "conservation") of that soul in its striving for work, culture, and liberty.

———————

Academics usually divide *The Souls of Black Folk* into three sections. In this division, they say chapters 1 through 3 provide historical background and context. Chapters 4 through 9 provide sociological analyses. And chapters 10 through 14, focus on spirituality.[17] But using that same outline, one can just as easily argue that the first section provides a focus on work, the middle section focuses on culture, and the last section focuses on liberty. What follows are detailed discussions about both frameworks. The goal here is to provide an overview of Du Bois' seminal work while also illustrating the usefulness of viewing its parts differently from how we are accustomed to seeing them. Ultimately, this different emphasis reveals more clearly the objectives of the striving in the souls of black folk.

"Of Our Spiritual Strivings," the first chapter of the book, introduces readers to the veil, the color line, double consciousness, and to each of the chapters that follow it. It provides a clear introduction to the struggle for work, culture, and liberty as well, and an introduction to some of the difficulties, all related to the color line, in attaining or enhancing those conditions. Although it is most common to see the examples Du Bois presented as evidence of "double aims" or as evidence of his interest in culture, his examples also describe stunted aspirations in different areas of work. Artisans, the first example he provides, were caught between the contradictory aims of black and white America and, consequently, were unable to improve their skills. The examples of the artist and the intellectual ("the would-be black savant") make an additional comment about culture, but they, like the artisans and professionals (ministers and physicians), were also stifled in the execution of their vocations.[18] Du Bois went into much more detail in this introductory chapter when he talked about "liberty," which he described as "the single refrain of the bondspeople throughout their enslavement." Yet, he added, forty years after emancipation, "the swarthy spectre sits in its accustomed seat at the Nation's feast." Freedpeople had sought their freedom through the vote—the Fifteenth Amendment—but, Du Bois concluded, it only "partially endowed" them. They also sought "book learning," but education left the goal unrealized as well. And when African Americans began to doubt their own worthiness, white America reinforced the doubt about black striving for work, culture, and liberty, saying:

> Be content to be servants, and nothing more; what need of higher culture for half-men? Away with the Black man's ballot, by force or fraud.

Du Bois insisted, however, that black efforts had not been wrong. Instead, he said,

> each alone was over-simple and incomplete. . . . To be really true, all these ideals must be melted and welded into one. The training of the schools we need to-day more than ever,—the training of deft hands, quick eyes and ears, and above all the broader, deeper, higher culture of gifted minds and pure hearts. The power of the ballot we need in sheer self-defence,—else what shall save us from a second slavery? Freedom, too, the long-sought, we still seek,—the freedom of life and limb, the freedom to work and think, the freedom to love and aspire. Work, culture, liberty,—all these we need, not singly but together, not successively but together, each growing and aiding each, and all striving toward that vaster ideal that swims before the Negro people.

To Du Bois, "that vaster ideal" concerned "human brotherhood." He predicted that "the Negro Problem" would be the "concrete test of the underlying principles of the great republic." Then he moved on, "with loving emphasis and deeper detail, that men may listen to the striving in the souls of black folk."

As most scholars have concluded, chapters 2 ("Of the Dawn of Freedom") and 3 ("Of Mr. Booker T. Washington and Others") form the core of the historical chapters. In them, we learn about the war years, the early postwar years, and the first postemancipation generation. Du Bois documented slaves' pre-proclamation movements toward Union lines and thus toward freeing themselves, the process of creating the Freedmen's Bureau to organize and enhance emancipation efforts, and the passage of constitutional amendments designed to establish citizenship more emphatically and to protect it. Through military policy, legislative enactments, *and* new government agencies, the federal government made freedpeople "the ward of the nation." But in the end, federal officials dismantled the Freedmen's Bureau and withdrew the federal troops from the South, and, ultimately, black people not only remained unfree but also unprotected. Black men lost the vote; black people lost legal and civil status and lost support for their schools. In that context, Booker T. Washington's proposals for vocational education and the acceptance of political and social subordination won such support that "it silenced if it did not convert the Negroes themselves." Often read and interpreted solely as an attack on Washington and the influence he had by the turn of the century, or as a critique of black leadership generally, Du Bois' third chapter also neatly continues/concludes the larger historical discussion of winning, and then losing, freedom.[19]

Du Bois' critique of Washington's ideas first appeared in print in a 1901 review of *Up from Slavery*, before the disagreement between the two men was clearly established. "Of Mr. Booker T. Washington and Others," the third chapter of *The Souls of Black Folk*, however, came to symbolize the apex of that debate. Because of the timing of the publication of the original essay, that is because of its *historical* context, we have failed to see its subsequent *literary* context—the relationship between the discussion of Washington and the rest of the book in which it later appeared. In this literary context, the chapter does not deserve so prominent a role (over all the other chapters), but an equal one for its contribution to the entire narrative.[20] The chapter on Washington is an important part of the history of the black American experience after the Civil War.

The history in chapters 2 and 3 seems broad and general. And it is, undoubtedly, a history of emancipation and its demise. But within this discussion of the development and abandonment of the emancipation and Reconstruction projects is an equally detailed and very important discussion of the first fifty years of free black labor. In fact, one can only view Du Bois' *Black Reconstruction* as his *real* contribution to the analysis of black labor if one ignores that *Souls*, in its entirety and especially in the first chapters, was the first systematic examination of postemancipation black labor.

Du Bois first established that emancipation resulted in "a labor problem of vast dimensions." He followed slaves and ex-slaves from their crossing Union lines and being labeled contraband to their being put to work as "military resources." He explored freedpeople's participation in experimental labor arrangements such as those in Maryland, Louisiana, and most notably at Port Royal, designed to make "free working men out of slaves." He looked at the creation of the Freedmen's Bureau, which grew out of an interest in transforming the "'emancipated and yet to be emancipated blacks from the old condition of forced labor to their new state of voluntary industry.'" Bureau agents moved tens of thousands of freedpeople from the towns to the country—"back to the critical trial of a new way of working." Du Bois believed that the ultimate success of the bureau "lay in the fact that the majority of the freedmen were willing, even eager, to work." They understood, as he noted, that their labor was their capital. And so while Freedmen's Bureau commissioners established schools and hospitals and solemnized marriages, they also drew up labor contracts and mediated labor disputes. So much of the bureau's work involved the protection of freedpeople's right "to choose their employers," to negotiate their wages, and to be free from "peonage or forced labor" that Du Bois could easily conclude that the agency, "[i]n truth, . . . became a vast labor bureau." And when it died, rural black folk became peons, "bound by law and custom to an economic slavery, from which the only escape is death and the penitentiary," and black urban dwellers became "a segregated servile caste." Because, as Du Bois had just noted, "not a single southern legislature believed free Negro labor was possible without a system of restrictions that took all its freedom away," freedpeople now had no place to turn.

Although Du Bois' third chapter on Booker T. Washington might very well be, as David L. Lewis wrote, "the manifesto of the Talented Tenth," Du Bois' turn to Washington and the early twentieth century also, importantly, completed the discussion of the first fifty years of "free" black labor. In this careful but pointed critique of Washington's program, Du Bois charged Washington with creating "a Gospel of Work and Money." Du Bois insisted that black people should have the same rights as whites to choose their line of work and to acquire the necessary education to perform that work, and they were entitled to the legal/political means to protect their work. Finally, he charged that Washington's program prepared black people for a lifetime of "industrial slavery and civic death" and a permanent "position of inferiority"[21] Freedpeople were losing their struggle for land and public schools, their civil and political rights, and much of their ability to work as truly free laborers *before* white America designated Booker T. Washington a leader. Du Bois, however, noted that this anointing changed "a by-path"— the relinquishing of civil and political rights, which Du Bois did not at first oppose as a temporary (and selective) measure—"into a veritable way of life," which he did oppose. Perhaps also, Du Bois remembered from his undergraduate, classical education that in ancient Greece, free men pursued the liberal arts, and slaves pursued the mechanical arts.

The chapters of the middle section, typically described as the sociological analysis, illustrate the way of life that troubled Du Bois so much. "Of the Meaning of Progress," for example, relays the extraordinary obstacles that ordinary people with "an ambition to live 'like folks'" faced in their effort to do so. They struggled for schooling, for wages, for land, and for what, ultimately, ought already to have been theirs—opportunity. But their lives were characterized by roughhewn houses, small farms that "the 'white folks would [eventually] get,'" children with the responsibilities of adults, and schools unable to offer them enough. The urban middle class, though materially better off, did not give Du Bois more hope. Rather than reinforce the then-current tendency to analogize the city of Atlanta and the legendary Phoenix, "Of the Wings of Atalanta" offered a chilling warning to the city of Atlanta (and the nation) in the example of Atalanta's fate. In the postwar period, Atlanta did rise from the ashes, in a manner of speaking, but in the process, the merchant "dethroned the planter," and "work and wealth" became "the mighty levers to lift this old new land." Such dreams, of material prosperity alone, led to the creation of "vulgar money-getters" and lives of "pretence and ostentation." Du Bois warned readers that "Atlanta must not lead the South to dream of material prosperity as the touchstone of all success," for at risk was the lesson in the tale of Atalanta, which unlike the tale of the Phoenix, was tragic rather than triumphant. Atalanta lost her legendary race because of her desire for golden apples.[22]

This chapter on Atlanta is, undoubtedly, a lament. Du Bois wrote, "the old leaders of Negro opinion, in the little groups where there is a Negro social consciousness, are being replaced by new; neither the black preacher nor the black teacher leads as he did two decades ago. Into their places are pushing . . . all those with property and money." Du Bois was not merely whining, as others have argued, because black people of his class were losing or had lost their status. Instead, the discussion reflected concern that their loss of status symbolized the loss of old and, to Du Bois, valuable ideals. Here, the preacher and the teacher were much more than displaced members of the "Talented Tenth."[23] They represented spirituality and knowledge. Preachers and teachers, churches and schools, religion and education, had historically served as significant participants in, examples and objectives of, African American striving. Thus Du Bois undoubtedly feared he was witnessing a shift in cultural values "from a strife of righteousness, from a love of knowing, to regard dollars as the be-all and end-all of life." The striving "to live 'like folks'" that he so lovingly detailed for Josie and her family in chapter 4 as an elegant, even if unfulfilled (and often futile), effort, was being replaced by a quest for "golden apples." And as was the case for Atalanta, such would be the demise of Atlanta and of black folk.

Du Bois complained that with the rise of industrial capitalism in the New South, people came to assume that it was right and normal to aim simply to be rich. He worried that black people (of the "middle class" in particular) were succumbing to this culture of acquisition, and so he suggested how education could arrest this development. Du Bois hoped that the black university would resist the emphasis on "bread-winning" and instead "be the organ of that fine adjustment between real life and the growing knowledge of life, an adjustment which forms the secret of civilization." The schools should "teach the workers to work and the think-ers to think. . . . And the final product of [their] training must be neither a psychologist nor a brickmason, but a man." The South would have to do better in educating both black and white folk if it aimed to "catch up with civilization." But Josie and her family, in the chapter that begins the middle section of the book, symbolized the struggle black folk faced in the meantime. They had no real chance to live "like folks" despite their striving, because children had to work rather than go to school since their parents could rarely earn enough to support the family. And working (even hard work) did not ensure advancement. Josie's brothers were among many who had their wages stolen by crooked white employers and a complicit and corrupt legal system. Even when people worked their own land, they were always aware of the possibility that "'white folks would get it all.'" Virtually all interracial contact had become negative, and young people in particular seemed set up for a lifetime of "crime and listlessness." It was a pervasive, destructive culture in which even Josie, who merely longed to learn, ulti-mately worked (and grieved) herself to death.

These middle chapters, on work, family, class, schooling, and interra-cial relations, are undoubtedly sociological in their subjects and in their method of looking at the conditions black southerners faced after the abandonment of Reconstruction. But it is the substance of the chapters, an extended discussion of the culture of the New South, that is the glue. In the middle of *Souls*, Du Bois carefully illustrated not only how people lived (the social institutions and thus the sociology of the South) but what they learned through living—the broad, anthropological conceptualization of culture.[24] If one looks at what he described in these chapters with this idea in mind, his concerns about the culture of the New South and the souls of black folk are easy to comprehend. The "reconstructed" white South ruth-lessly (and thoughtlessly) exploited both human and natural resources. Consequently, the Black Belt, where most black workers lived, had become a land of "rack-rented tenant[s]," and the White Belt, Du Bois' metaphor for where most of the cotton now grew, had taken on the appearance of what would later be characterized as a postindustrial town—its factories and farms abandoned, fields and lawns overgrown. Government refusal to fund education equitably sent a powerful negative message about the importance of schooling for black people. And if voting had ever been a way to change things, in this context the only vote that seemed to count was one that was bought. Black folk were regularly incarcerated not for crimes but to create an unwaged labor force.[25] Black striving regularly led to debt; land ownership was nearly impossible; and, often, black people, young and old alike, could choose only between crime and poverty.[26] Ultimately, in the cities, where only money seemed to matter, people learned that wealth, rather than character, led to influence. And in the country, where work rarely improved one's circumstances, people became "careless because they have not found that it pays to be careful; . . . improvident because the improvident ones of their acquaintances get on about as well as the provident." The South did not ask much of its black brethren, and upon receiving little, responded with ridicule. Du Bois worried about the confusion that could easily result from this paradox. He worried about the souls of black folk.

Scholars have devoted considerable energy to contextualizing Du Bois' use of the term "folk" at the expense, I think, of accounting for his use of "soul."[27] If the "veil," as an allusion both to "race" and to the great potential of the folk, resonated with Du Bois' black readers, the idea of "souls" must have had equal power considering its religious connotations. After all, in religious contexts, all souls are equal. But it is the philosophical meaning that matters here, and, importantly, it reinforces the symbolism of the veil. A turn-of-the-century philosopher would have understood that "[t]o speak of soul is to speak of a capacity or propensity to function in a certain way . . . or it is to speak of the actual exercise of such a capacity." And if "soul" represented "spirit in potentia" to a philosopher, "spirit" represented "the developed energy of the soul"—the actualization of potential. Thus, as already noted, Du Bois' calling his first chapter "Of Our Spiritual Strivings" spoke directly and substantially to his philosophical concerns about the souls of black folk. In fact, although Du Bois had moved from philosophy as a formal area of study as a Fisk University and Harvard University undergraduate more squarely into the disciplines of history, political economy, sociology, and psychology at Harvard and in Berlin, he had good reason to hold on to some of some of the foundational philosophical ideas of Aristotle (and Plato and Socrates, for that matter) because they all held that "soul is virtually the principle of all life." Socrates insisted, therefore, that the soul required great care. It was the soul, according to Plato, that enabled "'forms' to enter the world of becoming." Aristotle reiterated that "the body is the instrument . . . of the soul."[28]

The final section of the book provides several detailed, if sometimes metaphorical, examinations of Soul. It begins with a study of the evolution of black religion and ends with a discussion of spirituals. As these two chapters, and the ones between them, are about religion, faith, fierce personal struggles, death, and dying, it is not surprising that most scholars see them, collectively, as being about spirituality, which they are. But here we should look at these chapters as examples of "spiritual striving" (Soul's effort to fulfill itself; these individuals' efforts to become what they have the ambition and potential to become) and consider what they say about liberty.

"Of the Faith of the Fathers" describes how slaves, who faced discouragement and disrespect for their religious traditions, assumed a persona other than their own, becoming, outwardly, at least, Christians. That chapter should not be read so narrowly, however, for Du Bois used this "deception" to illustrate much more than religion. In life in general, he argued,

> the young Negro of the South who would succeed cannot be frank and outspoken, honest and self-assertive, but rather he is daily tempted to be silent and wary, politic and sly; he must flatter and be pleasant, endure petty insults with a smile, shut his eyes to wrong; in too many cases he sees positive personal advantage in deception and lying. His real thoughts, his real aspirations, must be guarded in whispers; he must not criticise, he must not complain. Patience, humility, and adroitness must, in these growing black youth, replace impulse, manliness, and courage.

Du Bois had suggested in earlier chapters that it was only through deception that black people gained the "right to share modern culture." Consequently, and in conclusion, he wrote, "The price of culture is a Lie."

And so, this conclusion to the middle section ("Of the Faith of the Fathers") continues the discussion of how the southern way of life could cost black folk more than votes, land, crops, houses, schools, and wages. It could cost their identity—their self-consciousness—their soul, their humanity.[29] While forcefully reinforcing the implications of the earlier chapters in the middle section, the chapter on religion nevertheless provides a hint of hope. Du Bois believed that the (sometimes-disinterested) congregants in some of the churches he described still harbored "the deep religious feeling of the real Negro heart, the stirring, unguided might of powerful human souls who have lost the guiding star of the past and seek in the great night a new religious ideal." Chapters 11 through 14 suggest the different directions that "ideal" might take. In some ways, they represent "case studies" on the prospects for liberty.

"Of the Passing of the First Born" is particularly pessimistic. Du Bois evinced anguish over the loss of this young life, his son. Yet he writes: "Fool that I was to think or wish that this little soul should grow choked and deformed within the Veil!" Du Bois understood the constraints that his son would have faced and was ultimately unable to see his being free except in death. Still, Du Bois expected (again alluding to work, culture, and liberty) that "some mighty morning" would "lift the Veil and set the prisoned free," that on that morning men would "ask of the workman, not 'Is he white?' but 'Can he work?' [And] . . . ask artists, not 'Are they black?' but 'Do they know?'" Clearly, that day had not yet arrived, but the next chapter, on Alexander Crummell, indicates that some might nevertheless manage to prevail.

Chapter 11 is undoubtedly a celebration of Crummell's life and accomplishments, but, more important, it is a forceful example of the potential of the color line to destroy human striving. Despite Crummell's tremendous abilities, his life was characterized by a series of "temptations" that not only threatened his ability to develop himself fully and use his gifts to improve the world, they also threatened to destroy his soul. As was the case in the example of John Jones, Crummell's sense of wholeness was based on the ability to carry out his commitment to striving. Crummell first faced racism as he was growing up during the slavery era. As he grew up and outgrew the schools that were available to black youths locally, he had to travel great distances to continue his education. Local residents tore down one of the schools he entered because of their objection to integrated education. Later, an Episcopal seminary refused to admit him because he was black. After receiving training elsewhere, he turned down an assignment to a Philadelphia church upon learning that neither he nor his congregants could attend the church conventions. After preaching for a time in New York, Crummell left for England in despair. Hanging on to his soul's striving, Crummell completed his studies at Queens' College (Cambridge), went to Africa, where he worked for most of the next twenty years, returned to America, and, over the course of his life, made a tremendous contribution to the world. Even though he died a stranger in his own land (which Du Bois saw as a tragedy), Crummell ultimately won what is now famously viewed as the war of the two unreconciled strivings.

The main subject of chapter 13 seems, on the surface, not to have fared so well. In "Of the Coming of John," there are two Johns—childhood playmates—one white, one black. In an allusion to ideas introduced in chapter 6 ("Of the Training of Black Men"), John Henderson's father, a judge, saw a bright future for his son, a Princeton graduate, but for John

Jones, who graduated from Wells Institute, the judge only saw the ruin of a good boy. Neither graduate wanted to return to Altamaha after his schooling, but Jones returned home after a racist encounter at a New York opera production, which, prophetically, involved his former playmate. Although Jones became one of those "brooding" black men that Du Bois had foreshadowed, after a period of readjustment, Jones threw himself into his teaching and began to see some results. For his hard work, the judge fired him. As he left the school, John Jones came upon his former playmate (Henderson) in the process of assaulting his (Jones's) sister, Jennie.[30] Instinctively, Jones hit Henderson with a tree limb, killing him. After saying goodbye to his mother, John returned to the site of the assaults and waited for the lynch mob, led by the judge. The depravity that enabled (even encouraged) Henderson's assault on Jennie simultaneously fueled John Jones's contempt, and the two deaths proved that the color line designed by whites to restrain or destroy black people's striving could ultimately destroy them, too.[31]

An adequate interpretation of the four final chapters of *The Souls of Black Folk* has eluded some of the best students of Du Bois' work. Like most scholars who conclude that the chapters focus on spirituality, Shamoon Zamir sees them as "concerned primarily with religious culture." Eric Sundquist, who accepted Du Bois' understated characterization of them as discussions of "life within the veil," concluded that Du Bois' including them "was not so provocative a cultural act as was the featuring of the spirituals at the head of each chapter."[32] But in fact, the final chapters—they were new—reflect Du Bois' thinking on liberty, the potential for black folks' achieving it, and potential consequences should they not. And as such they are tremendously provocative.

Du Bois' concern with liberty is evident from the introductory chapter ("Of Our Spiritual Strivings") of the book, where he wrote:

[F]ew men ever worshipped Freedom with half such unquestioning faith as did the American Negro. . . . To him, so far as he thought and dreamed, slavery was indeed the sum of all villainies, the cause of all sorrow, the root of all prejudice; Emancipation was the key to a promised land of sweeter beauty than ever stretched before the eyes of wearied Israelites. In song and exhortation swelled one refrain— Liberty; in his tears and curses the God he implored had Freedom in his right hand. At last it came,—suddenly, fearfully, like a dream. With one wild carnival of blood and passion came the message in his own plaintive cadences:—

"Shout, O Children!
Shout, you're free!
For God has bought your liberty!"

Du Bois went on to describe the first postemancipation decade as an extended, and ultimately only partly successful, search for freedom. The Thirteenth Amendment abolished slavery, but, Du Bois acknowledged, "the ideal of liberty demanded for its attainment powerful means." He believed the Fifteenth Amendment provided those means. And in an important sentence about the freedpeople, one that also clearly differentiated between freedom and liberty, Du Bois wrote, "The ballot, which before he had looked upon as a visible sign of *freedom*, he now regarded as the chief means of gaining and perfecting the *liberty* with which war had partially endowed him" (emphases added). There is no way to know exactly what Du Bois meant in his use of these two terms, "freedom" and "liberty." To be sure, we could consider them in the context of the Constitution and the politics of the Civil War and Reconstruction, to which Du Bois would eventually devote a major book. But here there is good reason to consider them in the context of the American Revolutionary rhetoric.

Du Bois ended each of the first three "history" chapters with direct references to the Revolutionary Era. Near the end of the first chapter, "Of Our Spiritual Strivings," he pointed out that, "there are to-day no truer exponents of the pure human spirit of the Declaration of Independence than the American Negroes." Then he closed the chapter saying:

Merely a concrete test of the underlying principles of the great republic is the Negro Problem, and the spiritual striving of the freedmen's sons is the travail of souls whose burden is almost beyond the measure of their strength, but who bear it in the name of an historic race, in the name of this the land of their fathers' fathers, and in the name of human opportunity.

Chapter 2, "Of the Dawn of Freedom," focusing on the history of the Freedmen's Bureau, concludes:

For this much all men know: despite compromise, war, and struggle, the Negro is not free. In the backwoods of the Gulf States, for miles and miles, he may not leave the plantation of his birth; in well-nigh the whole rural South the black farmers are peons, bound by law and custom to an economic slavery, from which the only escape is death or the penitentiary. In the most cultured sections and cities of the South, the Negroes are a segregated servile caste, with restricted rights and privileges. Before the courts, both in law and custom, they stand on a different and peculiar basis. Taxation without representation is the rule of their political life.

The third chapter, "Of Mr. Booker T. Washington and Others," concludes even more pointedly.

By every civilized and peaceful method we must strive for the rights which the world accords to men, clinging unwaveringly to those great words which the sons of the Fathers would fain forget: "We hold these truths to be self-evident: That all men are created equal; that they are endowed by their Creator with certain unalienable rights; that among these are life, liberty, and the pursuit of happiness."

Du Bois could not have linked his discussion of the plight of black Americans in the post–Civil War period to a more important discourse than the one that underpinned America's founding. The Declaration of Independence spoke of "rights" and was, as Jacob Needleman recently demonstrated, more than a "political statement" but a "metaphysical claim" related to "the nature of the human self and our place in the universal world."[33] By linking his discussion not only to the Revolutionary Era, generally, but to the Declaration of Independence, specifically, Du Bois was able to develop and sustain a complex discussion of freedom *and* liberty.

Freedom, as Du Bois described it, certainly involved the absence of bondage. And the Thirteenth Amendment abolished slavery throughout the United States and established constitutional freedom for all the nearly 4 million former slaves.[34] But since the Revolutionary leaders were already, technically, free men at the time of their revolt, that is to say, not literal slaves, they must have meant something more in their discussions of freedom, they included civil and political rights—citizenship. "Slavery" for these already-free men related to their status as subjects of the British Crown. And voting was the necessary but missing mechanism for their consenting to the acts of government.[35] Thus, the ballot (the Fifteenth Amendment) served as an important symbol or "visible sign of freedom" for Du Bois because voting was an indication of citizenship, and it prevented the imposition of the arbitrary will of others imposed through the government. Free (self-determining) men had to be able to vote. And voting did more than demonstrate the absence of slavery, it established a *political relationship* between men and their government.

But the Revolutionary and Civil War eras were necessarily and dramatically different. The colonists had sought to and had succeeded in abolishing their relationship with an existing government and creating a new one whose powers, experience taught, they should actively seek to limit. They did so not only by putting power in the hands of voters, but, perhaps even more important, they used the new Constitution to invest a substantial amount of power in *state* governments at the expense of the new *national* government. By contrast, freedpeople relished their new post–Civil War political relationship with the national government. Despite the fact that the new (post-Revolutionary) national government had protected slavery, allowed the continuance of the international slave trade (for twenty more years), and gave the South an inordinate amount of political power in this new national government by counting three-fifths of its slaves in apportioning representation, in the 1860s, it was this central power that emancipated and enfranchised black Americans. Moreover, it was *state* governments and officials who, after the collapse of Reconstruction, disfranchised the overwhelming majority of these black men, destroying the political relationship that the Union victory in the war had created.

The creation of the Freedmen's Bureau had, however, initiated an important new political relationship. And when, in 1866, over two presidential vetoes, Congress granted the Freedmen's Bureau two additional years of life, according to Du Bois,

> [t]he government of the unreconstructed South was thus put very largely in the hands of the Freedmen's Bureau. . . . It was thus that the Freedmen's Bureau became a full-fledged government of men. It made laws, executed them and interpreted them; it laid and collected taxes, defined and punished crime, maintained and used military force, and dictated such measures as it thought necessary and proper for the accomplishment of its varied ends.

He described the bureau as a government, "for a government it really was." As long as it lived, the Freedmen's Bureau—the body designated to maintain and protect black freedom—represented the institutionalized relationship between freedpeople and their government.

But the federal government allowed the Freedmen's Bureau to die. And by the time *The Souls of Black Folk* appeared in print southern black men had lost the vote, and the Supreme Court had approved, twice, the elimination of the access that the Constitution supposedly guaranteed to black Americans.[36] Thus, the potential for an important, positive, political relationship with *any* government was gone. These men and women were, however, still technically free, and so a more compelling case about the perverse and abusive relationship then existing between black citizens and their (local/state/national) governments could not have been made than the one provided by Du Bois' extensive appropriation of the Declaration of Independence.[37] Moreover, the Declaration of Independence made the case for an already-free citizenry's ability to pursue life, liberty, and happiness.

Du Bois' discussion of freedom and liberty in the context of the Declaration of Independence is sometimes hidden in plain view. When he complained about the post-Reconstruction conditions, for example, he noted:

> Here was a defenceless people suddenly made free. How were they to be protected from those who did not believe in their freedom and were determined to thwart it? Not by force, said the North; not by government guardianship, said the South; then by the ballot, the sole and legitimate defence of a free people, said the Common Sense of the nation.

It was no coincidence that Du Bois used the expression "Common Sense," or that he capitalized it. Thomas Paine's 1776 pamphlet of the same name held that "Common sense will tell us that the power which hath endeavored to subdue us is, of all others, the most improper to defend us."[38] Paine's 1776 pamphlet, an especially antimonarchy polemic, was, however, also a powerful defense of individual freedom.[39]

In Revolutionary America, "liberty" was, however, a rather imprecise term with both materialistic and philosophical implications. In the most materialistic sense, its connection to individual civil and property rights was paramount, and this was not lost on Du Bois. He devoted a substantial portion of *Souls* to discussing black people's struggle for and loss of these rights. But perhaps even more important, a philosopher pondering the idea of republicanism, as Du Bois did from the very beginning of this book, would have found it difficult not to see liberty at its heart. And for such a person, perhaps for any classicist, liberty not only depended upon civic participation, which presumably accompanies freedom, but demanded the protection of the group in their efforts to realize *collective* ambitions. Scholars have recently described republican liberty in terms of "civic humanism" and characterized it, in part, as a society's respect for the values, abilities, and accomplishments of its members. Liberty related to a "social order" that supported a person's ability "to be what he is." And in this context, "property" was not real estate, but "what . . . comes into being when man functions in the world." Thus, if freedom signified the relationship between men and their government, liberty concerned the relationships *between and among men*.[40]

Du Bois illustrated the lack of productive interaction between black and white men in great detail in the middle section of the book, as indicated above. "Of the Sons of Master and Man," which began with a statement about the then-current rage of imperialism, and the "war, murder, slavery, extermination, and debauchery" that resulted from "carrying civilization and the blessed gospel" around the world, also made it clear that one did not need to travel so far to see these results. As Du Bois put it, "we have in the South as fine a field for such a study as the world affords." His commentary in that chapter focused on what he saw as the main areas of intimate social contact: residency, economics, politics, intellect, everyday life, and religion. Du Bois saw these as the "principle ways in which men living in the same communities are brought into contact with each other," the diverse ways in which "the black race in the South meet and mingle with the whites." Unfortunately, he found no support for or encouragement and protection of black people's aspirations in any of these areas of life. Where a people could not live as free people should have been able to live, one can hardly say they experienced liberty. But, as Kwaku Korang has written about the historical *and* sociological chapters in *Souls*, "'American Civilization' [was] on trial" with Lady "Liberty" serving as the presiding judge. Carrying the metaphor to its logical end, "the plaintiff is the Negro," and all of America, "We the people," serve as jury.[41]

In going beyond freedom—to liberty—in his discussion, Du Bois recognized the importance of political *and* social objectives, civil rights *and* social relations, individual *and* collective potential. In focusing on the Declaration of Independence rather than the Constitution, he also highlighted an important philosophical discussion simultaneously taking place in the book, one that distinguished between the individualistic, positive law of the Constitution and the collective, natural law of the Declaration.[42] And in this light, the final chapters of his book turn out to be perhaps *the most* provocative chapters of the book as they transform civic humanism's ideal of liberty from the abstract (of the middle, sociological, chapters) to the real or concrete.

It was, in Du Bois' view, the absence of civic humanist liberty that led to the death of his child in "Of the Passing of the First Born." It was the prospect of the same lack of liberty for the child that led Du Bois sadly to celebrate the death. The chapter suggests resignation to the prevailing conditions. But in the next chapter, we see that Alexander Crummell, a quasi-expatriate, lived his life fully, succumbing neither to the double consciousness described in Du Bois' first chapter nor to living "the Lie" described in his tenth. Crummell successfully resisted the corrupting culture and limitations that white America placed on his capabilities. He held fast to his ambitions. John Jones, on the other hand, represented the worst possible outcome (if read in a traditional way) for those who remained in the American South and aspired to similar heights without any real possibility for achieving them. Equally important, thwarting Jones's ambitions also created the worst possible outcome for those responsible for frustrating the fulfillment of his potential.

There was, however, one more possible outcome. It existed in the example of the Sorrow Songs. This final chapter of the book is most obviously an analysis of the spirituals, and, therefore, it is an example of (religion-related) spirituality. But the chapter on the songs serves, equally, as a compelling conclusion to the "case studies" on liberty. In his chapter on the songs, and especially in one particular passage, Du Bois drew the three preceding chapters (the "case studies") together. He wrote:

> Through all the sorrow of the Sorrow Songs there breathes a hope—a faith in the ultimate justice of things. . . . Sometimes it is faith in life [Crummell?], sometimes a faith in death [the first born?], sometimes assurance of boundless justice in some fair world beyond [John Jones?]. But whichever it is, the meaning is always clear: that sometime, somewhere, men will judge men by their souls [their striving] and not by their skins [the veil].

As far removed as the Sorrow Songs might seem from notions of liberty, here, Du Bois brought his readers to the full classical understanding of its form, treating social interaction as a hallmark of liberty. He argued that African notions of spirituality and musicality mixed with European notions of Christianity and African American experiences of bondage and oppression and resulted in "the sole American music . . . the singular spiritual heritage of the nation." Du Bois saw the Sorrow Songs as American music because they evolved from black and white social interaction, give and take, respect and sometimes admiration.[43] Thus, this art form, the Sorrow Songs, and the creativity they reflect, served as a symbol of what was possible where the liberty of civic humanism prevailed.

It turns out that "Of the Sorrow Songs" is more than a discussion of spirituals, religion, African survivals, and the African American contribution to American culture—the usual interpretations of the chapter. Equally important, it is more than a conclusion to a detailed discussion about liberty, although it is clearly that as well. It is as much a conclusion to the book as "Of Our Spiritual Strivings" is the book's real introduction. At the beginning of the chapter on the spirituals, Du Bois described the songs as "the greatest gift of the Negro people." But at the end of the chapter, he noted that there were *three* gifts: "the gift of sweat and brawn"; "a gift of story and song"; and "a gift of the Spirit." He explored aspects of all three gifts in the preceding chapters. The "gift of sweat and brawn" was obviously the gift of work. The "gift of story and song" was the gift of culture. And in the chapter on the songs and in all the others, the "gift of the Spirit" was the example of never-ending striving not just for (individual) freedom but for (collective) liberty.

———

Many who have studied *The Souls of Black Folk* point out the centrality of Du Bois' general commentary on the nature of American culture. Eric Sundquist stated it most clearly when he wrote, "Despite the book's exceptional interpretive demands, . . . nothing can cloud Du Bois's cogent arguments that white American culture simply cannot be imagined apart from Black American culture."[44] But beyond this, Du Bois composed a complex, coherent, and consistent discussion about work, culture, and liberty. He demonstrated that the spiritual world in which those "ten thousand thousand [black] Americans live and strive" was full of ambition and potential. The material world in which they resided, however, was both corrupt and destructive. Most scholars have pointed to the color line as a symbol of that depravity, and the death of the fictional John Jones vividly illustrated its potential to waste human life. But some people (like Du Bois) *could*, temporarily at least, escape the boundary and "dwell above the veil." As he so eloquently wrote in one of the most powerful passages of the book, ironically describing his ride in a Jim Crow railroad car:

I sit with Shakespeare and he winces not. Across the color line I move arm in arm with Balzac and Dumas, where smiling men and welcoming women glide in gilded halls. From out of the caves of evening that swing between the strong-limbed earth and the tracery of the stars, I summon Aristotle and Aurelius and what soul I will, and they come all graciously with no scorn or condescension. So, wed with Truth, I dwell above the Veil.[45]

Some individuals, like Crummell, could subvert and/or overcome the debilitating consequences that could result from being both an American and a Negro. Indeed, most people, including those mired in the debt and poverty of "the Black Belt," regularly sought to integrate their own needs and values and those that existed beyond the veil. And as Du Bois concluded, "This, then, is the end of his striving: to be a co-worker in the kingdom of culture, to escape both death and isolation, to husband and use his best powers and his latent genius."

The real problem was that having decided to be a "co-worker in the kingdom of culture," most black people had little opportunity to realize their ambition. Contributing effectively to "the kingdom of culture," an objective of the striving of the souls of black folk, required the opportunity to realize their aspirations and potential for work, culture, and liberty regardless of the side of the color line on which they sought to fulfill their ambition. The destruction of John Jones ultimately lay in the fact that he could not fully "live and strive" on *either* side.[46]

The lack of opportunity might destroy the souls of black folk; it could easily result in hate, doubt, and despair, in Du Bois' own words characterizing the odyssey of the tremendously able Crummell. But just as surely as the culture that worked to stunt black striving had destroyed the Black Belt, John Jones, and probably Josie, it also destroyed the White Belt, the Cotton Kingdom, and John Henderson. Du Bois understood that "no secure civilization can be built" where so significant a segment of the population lacked the opportunity to fulfill its striving for work, culture, and liberty. He used *The Souls of Black Folk* to reconstruct that striving, explore its meaning, and provide a warning should it fail.

THE SOVEREIGNTY OF SOUL

Since it is the supreme law of Nature that each individual thing endeavours, to the full extent of its power, to preserve itself as it is without regard to anything but itself, it follows that each individual thing has this sovereign right, namely, to exist and act just as it is determined by Nature. —Spinoza[1]

"With the best will the factual outline of a life misses the essence of its spirit. Thus in my life the chief fact has been race—not so much scientific race, as that deep conviction of myriads of men that congenital differences among the main masses of human beings absolutely condition the individual destiny of every member of a group. Into the spiritual provincialism of this belief I have been born and this fact has guided, embittered, illuminated and enshrouded my life. Yet, how shall I explain and clarify its meaning for a soul? Description fails—I have tried that."[2]

The above quotation, taken from Du Bois' 1940 reflection on his life, ends with a thinly veiled allusion to *The Philadelphia Negro*. This pioneering social scientific study of turn-of-the-century black Philadelphia offered the empirical "proof" that the poverty, crime, and disease so evident in the urban center did not cause, but resulted from, discrimination, "color prejudice," or the color line.[3] Du Bois had hoped that the data presented in his study would become the basis for new social policy, but the larger public failed to respond to, and even seemed disappointed by, his conclusions.[4] At the very least, the study did not result in any changes in the view that white America generally held of African Americans or any significant efforts to address the problems it detailed. And so, Du Bois aptly repeated some of the Philadelphia conclusions in *Souls*. He purposefully wrote: "[T]hey [black folk] know that the low social level of the mass of the race is responsible for much discrimination against it, but they also know, and the nation knows, that relentless color-prejudice is more often a cause than a result of the Negro's degradation." Having realized, as he later put it, that description (detail) alone was not enough, Du Bois' remarks in *Souls* were not simple repetition. In his subsequent commentary on the souls of black folk, Du Bois went beyond the detail that the new sciences allowed and *The Philadelphia Negro* provided: he *literally* and purposefully brought philosophy back to the study of the new sciences. If America could not or would not respond to the obvious quantifiable/scientific evidence and the material/physical consequence of the color line (so evident in *The Philadelphia Negro*), perhaps a careful depiction including a spiritual/metaphysical perspective, focusing on Soul, would have the desired effect.[5]

Du Bois elaborated on the importance of such an approach in his exquisite 1905 essay "Sociology Hesitant," which, among other things, derided nineteenth-century philosopher-sociologists for their focus on "an abstraction" in their studies of "Society." They focused, Du Bois wrote, on "the Group, the Change, and the Thought and call this new created Thing Society." What they *should* have done, according to Du Bois, was "a minute study of men grouping, changing, and thinking." *Souls* was such a study. It went significantly beyond what Du Bois labeled in "Sociology Hesitant" as *"philosophy of history with modest and mundane ends"* (emphasis added). In other words, *Souls* included what was normally missing in sociological studies—"eternal, teleological purpose." *Souls* surpassed "the metaphysical wanderings" that Du Bois saw as marring the new "Descriptive Sociology."[6]

Unfortunately, Du Bois believed that even *Souls* fell short. As he noted in a reflective moment, his meaning remained vague and allusive for many readers.[7] This was not, however, a result of his not having accomplished precisely what he set out to achieve. It was, instead, that because the book accomplished so much more, readers regularly focused on the proverbial trees (the veils, the color line, double consciousness), rather than the forest (the soul).[8] Although it is impossible to miss the point that Du Bois' volume is about *the souls* of black folk—that is, after all, the title of the book—it is important to examine precisely how, and how prominently, *soul* figures throughout Du Bois' text.

Soul, in ancient philosophy, related to, and depending on whom one reads, was responsible for, all human function—higher and lower, good and bad. But prefiguring Hegel's dialectic, Aristotle, particularly in *De Anima*, maintained that Soul possessed three characteristics or levels of thought: appetite or desire, reason, and spirit. *The Souls of Black Folk* provided a detailed discussion of the historical development and condition of the souls of black folk, within which Aristotle's three characterizations figured prominently. Regardless of the specific topic Du Bois addressed in the volume, he used the three characteristics to insist upon the inviolability or the sovereignty of the souls of black folk.

Du Bois' effort, at the start of the twentieth century, was particularly timely. What is most obvious to us in retrospect is how completely the promise of emancipation and Reconstruction, freedom and liberty, had been obliterated over the thirty-plus years preceding the publication of *Souls*. The obviousness of the fact makes it difficult to see a significance of the book beyond its compelling depiction of the institutionalization of the color line and the havoc it wreaked. But, as already suggested, *Souls* was published at a moment in time that was witnessing the emergence of several of the social and behavioral sciences as full-fledged (independent) fields of scholarly study, correspondingly fracturing the field of philosophy. Philip J. Swoboda's discussion of Russian philosopher S. L. Frank's *Man's Soul* provides yet another way of thinking about the significance of Du Bois' book in that context. Swoboda notes that toward the end of the nineteenth century, "the philosophical study of the human soul languished" as the term "psychology" began to characterize "the investigation of man's mental life." The "modern scientific methodology applicable to the study of psychic phenomena [often called experimental or empirical psychology] had rendered 'philosophical' psychology forever obsolete." And Frank's volume, *Man's Soul*, represented a direct challenge to this new trend. Frank believed that "[t]he practitioners of 'scientific' psychology . . . are neither interested in shedding light on the questions with which 'psychology' had traditionally dealt, nor capable of doing so with the techniques they employed." Frank viewed the practitioners' interests as "narrow" and concerned with "peripheral psychic phenomena which happen to be susceptible of quantitative measurement." Altogether, Frank charged that "the 'science' of psychology" had become "an attempt to understand the soul while ignoring the modes of inner experience which are its essential manifestations."[9] In *Dusk of Dawn*, Du Bois noted some of the turn-of-the-century changes that Frank described, but in slightly different terms: "science was becoming religion; psychology was reducing metaphysics to experiment and a sociology of human action was planned."[10]

In *Souls*, a decade and a half before the appearance of Frank's volume, Du Bois was explicitly critical of the "scientific" studies of his day that claimed to offer some insight into the "Negro problem" without having considered, enough or at all, the inner life of the Negro him- or herself. In the very first chapter of *Souls*, Du Bois not so subtly reminded readers that there were aspects of black life that scientific, or objective, methods simply could not, or regularly did not, convey. He noted, for example, that "[t]he cold statistician wrote down the inches of progress here and there, noted also where here and there a foot had slipped or someone had fallen," while ignoring how far "the child of Emancipation" had come. He complained that "while sociologists gleefully count his bastards and prostitutes, the very soul of the toiling, sweating, black man is darkened by the shadow of a vast despair." And, eventually, in his detailed examination of the cotton kingdom, he urged readers to consider what lay beyond the view of the new scientific methods and conclusions.

> It is easy for us to lose ourselves in details in endeavoring to grasp and comprehend the real condition of a mass of human beings. *We often forget that each unit in the mass is a throbbing human soul.* Ignorant it may be, and poverty stricken, black and curious in limb and ways and thought; and yet it loves and hates, it toils and tires, it laughs and weeps its bitter tears, and looks in vague and awful longing at the grim horizon of its life. (emphasis added)

Before concluding the chapter on the cotton kingdom, Du Bois chided "the car-window sociologists" who sought to unravel "the snarl of centuries" after a "few leisure hours of a holiday trip."[11]

Thus, *Souls* should not be characterized as the rant of a man (an elite man, no less) overlooked (to Booker T. Washington's advantage) in the choosing of America's black leader. Nor did the publication of *Souls* represent devolution from science to emotion and politics, as other critics have concluded. It was, rather, Du Bois' return to his solidly nineteenth-century intellectual roots in *mental* and *moral* philosophy and their central concern for the condition and development of the soul. To be sure, "double consciousness," as the expression was used at the turn of the century, suggested, at least, the possible fragmentation of individual personality. And the threat for black folk was ever present. But Du Bois' discussion of Soul, the inner life, in fact revealed a history of just the opposite. Despite the presence of and struggle against the constricting color line, the striving in the souls of black folk existed quite apart from, and indeed existed independently of, that artificial construction. The color line complicated, stunted, and had the ability to (and sometimes did) destroy the striving; but the color line did not generate it. Striving—the hallmark of a functioning consciousness—originated in the sovereign souls of black folk.

————

The two paragraphs of *The Souls of Black Folk* that have historically attracted the most scholarly attention deserve another look in this context—in a chapter on *spiritual* striving in a book about the *souls* of black folk. The successive paragraphs read:

> After the Egyptian and Indian, the Greek and Roman, the Teuton and Mongolian, the Negro is a sort of seventh son, born with a veil,

and gifted with second-sight in this American world,—a world which yields him no true self-consciousness, but only lets him see himself through the revelation of the other world. It is a peculiar sensation, this double-consciousness, this sense of always looking at one's self through the eyes of others, of measuring one's soul by the tape of a world that looks on in amused contempt and pity. One ever feels his twoness,—an American, a Negro; two souls, two thoughts, two unreconciled strivings; two warring ideals in one dark body, whose dogged strength alone keeps it from being torn asunder.

The history of the American Negro is the history of this strife,— this longing to attain self-conscious manhood, to merge his double self into a better and truer self. In this merging he wishes neither of the older selves to be lost. He would not Africanize America, for America has too much to teach the world and Africa. He would not bleach his Negro soul in a flood of white Americanism, for he knows that Negro blood has a message for the world. He simply wishes to make it possible for a man to be both a Negro and an American, without being cursed and spit upon by his fellows, without having the doors of Opportunity closed roughly in his face.

The two paragraphs obviously make a compelling case about the importance of the idea of double consciousness.[12] And a negative reading of the paragraphs is easy to accomplish. Wilson Jeremiah Moses notes that Joseph Ephraim Casely Hayford, a pan-Africanist whom Du Bois admired, found some of Du Bois' ideas "pathetic" and "absurd." A few years after the publication of *Souls*, Hayford sarcastically wrote: "'Now fancy Candace, Queen of Ethiopia, or Chephron, the Master of Egypt, being troubled with double consciousness.'"[13] Subsequent scholars, who have not judged the idea quite as harshly, have nevertheless viewed double consciousness as psychologically debilitating.[14] But the two paragraphs offer much more hope than these now-traditional readings suggest. First, the paragraphs make it clear that the struggle was not new to the turn of the century, by which time the color line was already entrenched, or even to the earlier postemancipation period. Rather, the struggle was "the *history* of the American Negro." *Souls* demonstrates, albeit briefly, that this struggle was already evident at the start of the enslavement of Africans in America. And second, and equally important, the concluding paragraph suggests that we should *not* view this struggle at the turn of the century as one in which these souls were striving, literally, to be American or African, or even the hybrid Negro, but to be what Spinoza (in the epigraph) described as what they had a "sovereign right" to be—whatever they had the interest in and ability to become.[15] Du Bois had described it simply and profoundly as "self-conscious manhood."

Before Du Bois ended this powerful introductory chapter, he, in fact, noted that the "reflection and self evaluation" in which the former bond-people engaged after emancipation, aided by a limited amount of formal education, changed them from "the child of Emancipation to the youth with dawning self-consciousness, self-realizations, self-respect."[16] Especially important, he concluded:

> In those somber forests of his striving his own soul rose before him, and he saw himself,—darkly as through a veil; and yet he saw in himself some faint revelation of his power, of his mission. He began to have a dim feeling that, to attain his place in the world, he must be himself, and not another.

Joe Sachs, a scholar of ancient thought, has pointed out that in *On the Soul (De Anima)*, Aristotle characterized "soul" as *entelechia*, which suggests "being-at-work-staying-itself."[17] In that light, Du Bois' two extensively quoted paragraphs say as much about a still-functioning being attempting, in spite of everything, to follow the higher dictates of its soul as they say about a psychological disorder characterized by multiple personalities.[18]

Because Du Bois was as good a historian and sociologist as a philosopher, the history and sociology of the study sometimes overwhelm the more subtle philosophical discussion. To recover it quickly, one only has to note that even in the first chapter, the thwarted striving, the lack of possibilities for self-realization, did not lead, at that point, to poverty, crime, or other unfortunate physical/material conditions. Instead, in that chapter, the lack of support for this striving and self-realization led to anger, hatred, and deceptiveness. After, for example, the "tall newcomer" girl snubbed Du Bois' gesture of friendship by refusing to accept his calling card, he focused on the pleasure he got when he "could beat [his] mates at examination-time, or beat them at a foot-race, or even beat their stringy heads." While, for Du Bois, "all this fine contempt [eventually] began to fade," his black classmates, by contrast, shrank "into tasteless sycophancy, or into silent hatred of the pale world about them and mocking distrust of everything white." These souls were only seeking "to be . . . co-worker[s] in the kingdom of culture, to escape both death and isolation, to husband and use [their] best powers and [their] latent genius." Historically, their physical and intellectual "powers" had "been strangely wasted, dispersed, or forgotten." They flashed "here and there like falling stars." And sometimes they died, "before the world rightly gauged their brightness."

But black folk had always, and continued to, strive. As already noted, they at first believed that emancipation (freedom) would enable them to become self-determining beings. That having failed, perhaps they could "vote themselves into the kingdom." Unfortunately, the overthrow of Reconstruction ended whatever potential suffrage held. And so they turned to education and, for the moment, overlooked the material conditions of their lives with their eye on the return their schooling would presumably yield—knowledge, realization (self-development), and self-determination. Education became "the mountain path to Canaan; longer than the highway of Emancipation and law, steep and rugged, but straight, leading to heights high enough to overlook life." Du Bois' conclusion of the chapter was this: "the spiritual striving of the freedmen's sons is the travail of souls whose burden is almost beyond the measure of their strength, but who bear it in the name of an historic race, in the name of this the land of their fathers' fathers, and in the name of human opportunity." Thus he ended the chapter with a most direct commentary that linked black striving and the historic and necessary work of the soul.

Du Bois' narrative on the necessary work of the soul unfolds like a song or a poem, with distinct (different) verses but one consistent refrain. The "tall newcomer" girl's snub first led to contempt—a loathing or disdain of his white classmates—and a determination to prove himself superior to them. But Du Bois also realized that "the world" he was then longing for, "and all their dazzling opportunities, were *theirs*, not [his]." And so he began to think seriously about how he would live *his* life. As a youngster, he could not yet be sure of what occupation he would pursue. All he knew was that he would find "some way" to make "some, all" of "their dazzling opportunities" his own. Du Bois' youthful and negative encounter with the color line did not immobilize *him*, but the chapter indicates that there were several possible responses/outcomes. The first, characterized initially as contempt, anger, hate, and distrust, and later described in other contexts as a spirit of "revolt and revenge," was but one. There was also resignation/acceptance, characterized here as dishonesty or sycophancy, which as the book developed would also take the label of assimilation (and, possibly, "living a lie"). And last, there was transcendence—a kind of self-determination and knowledge that would allow one, as Du Bois would later frame it, to "dwell above the veil." Although the three characterizations would vary slightly as the book unfolded, the three possibilities ultimately constituted a refrain that figured prominently until the end of the book, providing a unified commentary on the Soul.[19]

The next most notable example occurs in the chapter on Booker T. Washington and black leadership, where Du Bois cast the three possibilities as in a contest over the souls of black folk. He described it as a contest between higher and lower moral imperatives. These moral imperatives were not exclusively, as they have been characterized by others, evidence of Du Bois' elitism or contemporary notions of "respectable" or socially acceptable behavior. Rather, moral imperatives relate to conditions, or characteristics, of the soul. In Socratic philosophy, a moral life is one in which one, above all else, cares for the soul. Du Bois noted that up to the mid-eighteenth century, the response of the slaves to the obstructions to their souls' striving was one "of revolt and revenge." His examples included the formation of maroon communities, the rebellions and conspiracies of New York slaves (which we may infer from the phrase "the Danish blacks"), and the Stono rebellion. Du Bois implied that the American quest for liberty (which culminated in the writing of the Declaration of Independence, the Revolutionary War, and, ultimately, the creation of a new nation) caused conditions to improve for slaves (many did gain their freedom, and legislation mandated specific time limits to the bondage of many others), and the "kindlier relations between black and white" allowed the emergence of the poet Phillis Wheatley, revolutionary heroes such as Crispus Attucks, intellectuals including Benjamin Banneker, and political leaders such as Paul Cuffe—people whose lives reflected a kind of assimilation in that they presumably aligned their efforts with larger American (revolutionary) ideals. But the economic crisis of the early nineteenth century ended the movement toward "kindlier relations" between black and white, and slavery became more rigid where it remained. With stories of the Haitian Revolution floating about, the increase in American oppression bred slave rebels Gabriel Prosser, Denmark Vesey, and Nat Turner in the South. In the North, an independent black church movement and an organized antislavery movement developed. In both cases, the ultimate goal was independence and self-determination. The three characterizations parallel Aristotle's delineation of desire/appetite, thought/reason, and spirit as elements of Soul; the first, revolt and revenge, signified the lower level (desire); the second, assimilation and/or cooperation, occupied a middle ground (thought); and the last, self-determination/-realization, reflected the highest (spirit).

The people Du Bois put in the last category were less (or only incidentally) models of Victorian elitism or bourgeois respectability than models of men and women of spirit following the higher dictates of their souls. Even though their turn to abolitionism was spurred by the fact that white America still "refused them recognition save in individual and exceptional cases" (that is, refused to support *the race's* striving), and by the loss of rights that they, as individuals, once enjoyed, "a new period of self-assertion and self-development dawned," symbolized, Du Bois concluded, by Frederick Douglass's position of self-determination and "ultimate assimilation *through* self-assertion, and on no other terms."[20]

But after Douglass's death, Booker T. Washington emerged "the leader," and thus began an intense struggle. To be sure, the struggle related to the opposing social, economic, and political philosophies espoused by Washington and Du Bois, but it was also related to one form of soul (or state of consciousness) or another. Du Bois wrote, "This is an age of unusual economic development, and Mr. Washington's programme naturally takes an economic cast, becoming a gospel of Work and Money to such an extent as apparently almost completely to overshadow *the higher aims of life*" (emphasis added). Although Du Bois clearly subordinated (Washingtonian) material objectives to his own spiritual ones, the sentence (and the rest of that chapter) represents much more than evidence of the proverbial battle line's being drawn in the sand between him and Washington as individuals.[21] Du Bois' criticism was even substantially larger and far more important than that Washington exchanged black rights for a promise of money. Its importance was, significantly, that the exchange represented the acceptance of a less-developed consciousness (or soul)—desire (or the lure of money)—in the place of a higher order—spirit (whose motive was self-determination). Desire, which Aristotle characterized as appetite and/or greed, represented something that one has to transcend. (Du Bois' depiction of Atalanta's weakness as a warning to Atlanta and America was not coincidental.) And so the problem was not only that Washington's exchange was likely to cause black folk to remain politically powerless and trapped in the material poverty of the postemancipation period, a traditional interpretation of Du Bois' criticism of Washington, but that it would also result in spiritual impoverishment and stunt the further development and growth of the souls of black folk.[22]

The issue for Du Bois was at least as much philosophical as economic or political; the moral imperatives ("the higher aims of life") related to spiritual striving and Soul as much as class and Victorian ideals, personal or individual power. But Du Bois put it best: "manly self-respect is worth more than lands and houses," and "a people who voluntarily surrender such respect, or cease striving for it, are not worth civilizing." That is to say that without the continual development toward the demands of spirit, the soul could not grow or develop, and, under such circumstances, the body it inhabited was practically worthless. Possessing "lands and houses," traditional turn-of-the-century markers of bourgeois respectability and the centerpiece of Washington's strategy, was not nearly as important as self-possession.

Our failure to remember Du Bois' philosophical training easily (mis) leads us into reading the chapter on "Washington and others" almost exclusively as evidence of a power struggle between the two men. But if it is yet not believable that Du Bois' critique of Washington's program was more related to the growth and development of the soul than to his own place in the hierarchy of black American leadership, one only has to read a few pages further. Explicitly repeating two of the three characterizations of the conditions of the soul, and alluding to the third, Du Bois described two groups of people leveling criticism against Washington.

One class is spiritually descended from Toussaint the Savior, through Gabriel, Vesey, and Turner, and they represent the attitude of *revolt and revenge*; they *hate* the white South blindly and *distrust* the white race generally, and so far as they agree on definite action, think that the Negro's only hope lies in emigration beyond the borders of the United States. . . . [23]

The other class of Negroes who cannot agree with Mr. Washington has hitherto said little aloud. They deprecate the sight of scattered counsels, of internal disagreement; and especially they dislike making their just criticism of a useful and earnest man an excuse for a general discharge of venom from small minded opponents. . . .

But, nevertheless, they insist that the way to truth and right lies in straightforward honesty, not in *indiscriminate flattery*; in praising those of the South who do well and criticizing uncompromisingly those who do ill; in taking advantage of the opportunities at hand and urging their fellows to do the same, but at the same time in remembering that only *a firm adherence to their higher ideals and aspirations* will ever keep those ideals within the realm of possibility. (emphasis added)

The paragraphs raise several points worth noting. First, despite the almost-exclusive focus scholars have since placed on the rift between the two men, Du Bois' characterization of Washington as a "useful and earnest man" and the caution against turning "just criticism" into "venom" represent an effort *not* to personalize the disagreement. Second, the paragraphs ultimately repeat *all three* characterizations of the soul. The unnamed Washington supporters being criticized (sycophants who, in this case, aimed their flattery at Washington) represent the middle group in that they are assimilationists, people who took certain positions in order to get along with whites (and with Washington). The critics of Washington's program and supporters are undoubtedly the spiritually "higher" group because of their efforts to assert themselves and because of their insistence on self-determination and the highest possible development of the race. The emigrationists, people we generally celebrate for their militant ("nationalist") race loyalty, actually represent the lower (or less developed) order of "revolt and revenge."[24] And finally, the paragraphs also reveal, again, that Du Bois' use of "higher ideals and aspirations" was more than a class-based value judgment from a member of the so-called Talented Tenth. These "ideals and aspirations" allude to the pursuit of self-development and the importance of self-determination, and they reflected values, philosophers call them *ideals*, which every ensouled person possessed. One need only look at the chapter "On the Meaning of Progress" to see this.

"On the Meaning of Progress" is best known for Du Bois' loving depiction of Josie and her family. "The father was a quiet, simple soul, calmly ignorant, with no touch of vulgarity. The mother was different,—strong, bustling, and energetic, with a quick, restless tongue, and an ambition to live 'like folks.'" These parents were good people, strivers, but Josie, the young, central character of this chapter, was the epitome of soulfulness. "She had about her a certain fineness, the shadow of an unconscious moral heroism that would willingly give all of life to make life broader, deeper, and fuller for her and hers."[25] Had this story about Josie been written during the Heroic Age—Du Bois' description of her in terms of "moral heroism" was not accidental—she might indeed have been immortalized. But, then again, perhaps she was, even if she was never formally named a saint. In any case, Du Bois loved this family for its striving, "for their honest efforts to be decent and comfortable, and for their knowledge of their own ignorance."

It is likely that no scholar before or since Du Bois has written so sensitively and tenderly about ordinary, poor, rural, black folks.[26] He did not criticize their apparent social or economic deficiencies, nor did he turn them into caricatures; he admired and celebrated their efforts to realize *their own* ambitions and honored them for recognizing what they did not know. That would not surprise us if we recalled that Socrates, who was recognized as a wise man, understood that some portion of his wisdom derived from his knowledge of, and acknowledgement of, his ignorance. It *should* not surprise us given that Du Bois was first, and perhaps foremost, a philosopher who understood that self-development began with self-knowledge.[27]

Before the chapter ended, Du Bois gave us the three conditions of the soul again, based this time on the black residents of this rural Tennessee community. He saw among them those who had witnessed the war, those who had vague memories of it, and those for whom "War, Hell, and Slavery were but childhood tales." Members of the first group had become fatalistic; the second group conformed and did what they were asked, were never recognized for it, and "sank into listless indifference, or shiftlessness, or reckless bravado." But the last group—including Josie, Jim, and Ben—had tasted knowledge, that which soul seeks. "Ill could they be content. . . . And their weak wings beat against the barriers,—barriers of caste, of youth, of life; at last, in dangerous moments, against everything that opposed even a whim." They sought to live as free people should have been able to live, and thus, only in their material circumstances did Du Bois substantially distinguish Josie and her family, people who "longed to know" and sought "to live 'like folks,'" from his characterization of those strivers who were already well informed and had lived at least part of their lives, materially and spiritually, well—elites including Frederick Douglass, Alexander Crummell, or Daniel Payne. If we could set aside the material conditions that characterized the circumstances of Josie's family and think about Du Bois' spiritual characterization of them—their aspirations, values, or ideals— the two groups of folks would be virtually indistinguishable.

Du Bois' meditation at the end of this chapter on "progress" perfectly set up his discussion of Atlanta in the next:

> "My journey was done, and behind me lay hill and dale, and Life and Death. How shall man measure Progress there where the dark-faced Josie lies? How many heartfuls of sorrow shall balance a bushel of wheat? How hard a thing is life to the lowly, and yet how human and real! And all this life and love and strife and failure,—is it the twilight of nightfall or the flush of some faint-dawning day?"

If one could not be certain whether day was dawning or night was falling in rural Wilson County, Tennessee, where children *and* adults struggled for basic education and survival, one should think the answer would be clearer in Atlanta, where a major black institution of higher education provided hope for the souls of black folk, given that knowledge is what souls seek. But even there, the highest mission of the university from a philosopher's perspective—the growth and development of souls, self-expression, the fulfillment of spirit—was threatened by those whose primary goal was simply to make Atlanta a center of wealth. The contradiction between the two aims did not bode well for Atlanta's future. She might indeed win the race for riches, but Du Bois insisted that Atlanta would ultimately be the loser just as surely as was Bœotia's daughter Atalanta if Atlanta's (and black folks') successes came at the expense of the quest for "Truth, Beauty, and Goodness."

The idea of a quest for "Truth, Beauty, and Goodness" no longer resonates as it once did, but such a quest was once a serious life choice for a philosopher, for any wise person, or for one serious about the development of Soul. Irwin Edman, in an analysis of Plato's works, described such ideas (of truth, beauty, and goodness, especially as Plato used them in the *Phaedrus* and the *Symposium*) as "esthetic objects and moral objectives and ideals." He went on to characterize them (again, as ideas) as "eternal," "absolute," and "transcendent to human knowledge or earthly [physical/material] existence."[28] In his chapter that focused on higher education, Du Bois discussed the obligation of universities to encourage the pursuit of these ("eternal") esthetics and ideals. "Nothing new," he wrote; "no time-saving devices,—simply old time-glorified methods of delving for Truth, and searching out the hidden beauties of life, and learning the good of living." The curriculum he thought best for achieving those ends was older than most of us might automatically conclude but hardly antiquated to one who was a philosopher. As Du Bois put it:

> The riddle of existence is the college curriculum that was laid before the Pharaohs, that was taught in the groves by Plato, that formed the *trivium* and *quadrivium*, and is to-day laid before the freedmen's sons by Atlanta University. And . . . the true college will ever have one goal,—not to earn meat, but to know the end and aim of that life which meat nourishes.[29]

The discussion of higher education in *Souls* is important for much more than the possibility of its leading to the creation of a "Talented Tenth," which Du Bois clearly hoped, and expected, would emerge. A good education had the potential for leading people through the Aristotelian stage of desire, which, in African American history, was often reflected in futile "revolt and revenge," past the dishonest state of sycophancy, sometimes reflected in simple assimilation, and to the highest development of soul, or spirit. The mandate would not be easy to fulfill in a land where,

> For every social ill the panacea of Wealth has been urged,—wealth to overthrow the remains of the slave feudalism; wealth to raise the

'cracker' Third Estate; wealth to employ the black serfs, and the prospect of wealth to keep them working; wealth as the end and aim of
politics, and as the legal tender for law and order; and, finally, instead of Truth, Beauty, and Goodness, wealth as the ideal of the Public School.

Still, the southern universities were, in Du Bois' mind, both the literal and
figurative wings of Atlanta, and they could "guide her over and beyond" the
"golden apples" that had forever doomed Atalanta because of her spiritual
weakness—desire/greed. Ultimately, the warning raised by "Of the Wings
of Atalanta" was no different from the point of the chapter "Of Mr. Booker
T. Washington and Others." That is to say, the universities must lead scholars to succeed in the ultimate goal of life, which, in Du Bois' own words
was, at its base, *"the conservation of soul"* (emphasis added).[30]

From Du Bois' perspective, the conservation of soul required college-
trained teachers who could reach people "whose ignorance was not simply of letters, but of life itself." And as vague as his various incantations of
"Knowledge of life itself" may be, it was an important enough idea that Du
Bois repeated it, in numerous ways, throughout the text. In some places in
the volume, the goal of education was to prepare people "not to earn meat,
but to know the end and aim of that life which meat nourishes." In other
instances, Du Bois posed it as a question: "Is not life more than meat, and
the body more than raiment?" And where he became more descriptive,
Du Bois still left us with ambiguity: "The function of the university is not
simply to teach bread-winning, or to furnish teachers for the public schools
or to be a centre of polite society; it is above all, to be the organ of that fine
adjustment between real life and the growing knowledge of life, an adjustment which forms the secret of civilization." "Real life" only superficially
related to physical/material circumstances. "The growing knowledge of
life" concerned the development of consciousness, the growth of soul, and
the achievement of spirit.

Obviously, black colleges had to provide basic education; they had to,
in nineteenth-century parlance, "uplift the race"; and they had to facilitate productive interracial relations. But as important as these things were,
much more was necessary. About this additional requirement, Du Bois was
explicit:

Above our modern socialism, and out of the worship of the mass,
must persist and evolve that higher individualism which the centres
of culture protect; *there must come a loftier respect for the sovereign*

human soul that seeks to know itself and the world about it; that seeks a freedom for expansion and self-development; that will love and hate and labor in its own way, untrammeled alike by old and new. (emphasis added)

His conclusion of the comment revealed what was at stake not just for black folk or America, but the world.

Such souls aforetime have inspired and guided worlds, and if we be not wholly bewitched by our Rhinegold, they shall again. Herein the longing of black men must have respect: the rich and bitter depth of their experience, the unknown treasures of their inner life, the strange rendings of nature they have seen, may give the world new points of view and make their loving, living, and doing precious to all human hearts.[31]

Thus, education had to value all experience, cultivate individual growth and development, facilitate introspection, and, ultimately, encourage and support self-determination. In short, education had to help develop, grow, and protect human souls.

In Socratic philosophy, "if any one is to care rightly for himself, he must first of all know what he is; it is then proved that each of us is soul, and therefore that to care for ourselves is to care for our souls."[32] Other words, attributed directly to Socrates, perfectly link Du Bois' chapters on Atlanta, education, and Booker T. Washington. During the trial that would determine Socrates' fate (and result in his receiving a death sentence), Socrates defended his condemnation, insisting that even if he received leniency he would continue doing precisely what caused his arrest and conviction. He added that should he meet "a citizen of the great and mighty and wise city of Athens," perhaps with a bit of sarcasm in that characterization, he would ask,

"[A]re you not ashamed of heaping up the greatest amount of money and honour and reputation, and caring so little about wisdom and truth and the greatest improvement of the soul, which you never regard or heed at all? . . . I do nothing but go about persuading you all, old and young alike, not to take thought for your persons or your properties, but first and chiefly to care about the greatest improvement of the soul. I tell you that virtue is not given by money, but that from virtue comes money and every other good of man, public as well as private."[33]

If young black scholars in Atlanta or elsewhere were properly educated, more than being able to provide for person and property, in Socrates' words, or meat and raiment in Du Bois' (which ultimately did, whether deliberately or not, have the effect of mocking Booker T. Washington), they would, as were the scholars in Socrates' groves (or Plato's Academy), be prepared for life.

Although the next several chapters of *Souls* clearly illustrate some of the material consequences of not preparing men for life, Du Bois used the devastating material and/or physical characterizations, something to which all readers could relate, to make an equally important point about the easier-to-overlook spiritual condition, or Soul. Dougherty County, in "Of the Black Belt," provided a dramatic and haunting example: in this obviously impoverished county he found people "hopelessly in debt, disappointed, and embittered." Although Du Bois made it clear that the physical or material impoverishment was a direct result of racism and greed, in the tradition of Socratic thought, both resulted from *spiritual* impoverishment. One cannot help but feel the (material *and* spiritual) emptiness of the place in the first half of the chapter: there was a "half-desolate spirit of neglect." Indeed, one rarely directly encounters people in "Of the Black Belt," except on Saturday, when they all seemed to converge on Albany, where they talked and laughed and drank and shopped. And then they went home, Du Bois recalled, "not exactly happy, but much happier than as though they had not come." Young people had not learned of their "individual worth and possibilities" in this poor, mostly rural county, but they worked—"to-morrow morning they'll be up with the sun"—hard and willingly. Unfortunately, they had no real "incentive beyond the mere pleasure of physical exertion." Work, like knowledge, should have enhanced their ability to live. In lieu of living, on Saturdays they went to town.

Du Bois understood that one important key to changing conditions for black folk in a manner that would allow their "souls to soar . . . above the smoke" lay in the nature of interracial relations, or the elimination of the color line (or what I have characterized as the relationships between and among men). In "Of the Sons of Master and Man" he wrote, "It is, then, the strife of all honorable men of the twentieth century to see that in the future competition of races the survival of the fittest shall mean the triumph of the good, the beautiful, and the true; that we may be able to preserve for future civilization all that is really fine and noble and strong, and not continue to put a premium on greed and impudence and cruelty." This chapter, in which Du Bois argued most directly against the color line, was romanticized (or over generalized). But more important than his overly

stereotyped characterization of the fine relationship that once existed between former house slaves and their owners was the fact that interracial
relations had become limited to "the saloon, the gambling-hell, and the
brothel" rather than the school, theater, concert hall, lyceum, library, or
even private homes. As a consequence, Du Bois wrote, "there has been
going on for a generation as deep a storm and stress of human souls, as intense a ferment of feeling, as intricate a writhing of spirit, as ever a people
experienced." Du Bois' last section of the book provided the most poignant
illustrations of that "writhing of spirit" and reiterations of this goal.

Where he presented a history of the black church, he drew together a
number of the ideas that had become tropes in the book by this time. First
was the evidence of still-striving spirit in the souls of black folk. Second was
his unfailing respect for "the folk."[34] And third was what I have called the
three characterizations of Soul (and levels of thought). Although the chapter is clearly about religion, here is where Du Bois also began to use music
in a direct and explicit way to provide additional commentary on the soul.

In his characterization of the church and its music, it was not status
(traditionally defined), education, or Victorian manners that proved the
presence of spirit or the character of soul. In fact, the church that Du Bois
celebrated in this chapter was as it existed *before* "civilization" reformed
(or refined) it. And although most scholars, then and today, generally
and rightly conclude that slavery and slaveholders had worked to debase
slaves and crush their humanity, or destroy their spirit and soul, Du Bois
witnessed in sermons and especially in songs a spirit in the church that
had *not* been destroyed (nor was it suffering from double consciousness).
It sprang "from the African forests, where its counterpart can still be
heard, . . . was adapted, changed, and intensified by the tragic soul-life
of the slave, until, under the stress of law and whip, it became the one
true expression of a people's sorrow, despair, and hope." Du Bois was not
embarrassed by "the stamping, shrieking, and shouting, the rushing to
and fro and wild waving of arms" that took place in those churches. He
seems to have been convinced that it was a "visible manifestation of the
God" (Spirit). Indeed, Du Bois reserved his real criticism for the imita-
tors, largely in the white church, whose congregants, he said, "caught the
jingle but not the music, the body but not the soul." *These* black churches
in *Souls* became Socrates' groves—a place where, through sermons and
songs, "the inner ethical life of a people"—their soul—developed and was
conserved.[35]

In this chapter on religion and church, Du Bois again characterized
the soul in three ways. He reminded us that enslavement had nurtured "a

spirit of revolt and revenge" in the slave. After generations of slavery, and its attack on (and weakening of) the spirit of those folk, they were "ripe" for the "new philosophy of life" that Christianity (a level of assimilation) represented. Spirit moved, understandably, in different directions in the North and the South. While in the North, the abolitionists moved toward "ideals remote, whimsical, perhaps impossible" to realize, slaves seized on "the avenging Spirit of the Lord," certain that eventually (perhaps in the next life, if not before) their dreams of freedom *and* liberty would be fulfilled. Du Bois certainly understood why some people later turned to flattery, becoming masters of deception; they were determined to survive. But this "hypocritical compromise" threatened (could, perhaps, cost them) their soul. Nor did it surprise Du Bois that some became radicals. Freedom for them, enhanced by schools and learning, awakened a "long pent up and dwarfed" soul (much the same as it did for Josie and her siblings earlier in the volume and would for John Jones later). But in addition to these two groups were folks who still possessed "the deep religious feeling of the real Negro heart, the stirring, unguided might of powerful human souls," seeking "a new religious ideal." Du Bois looked forward to the day "when the pent-up vigor of ten million souls shall sweep irresistibly toward the Goal, . . . where all that makes life worth living—Liberty, Justice, and Right," was not marked "For White People Only." If Du Bois could not argue conclusively that the church could do what schools to that point had not, he was at least certain that in these rural, southern black churches, there was much evidence of the still-striving spirit, and there one could gain some insight as to what its soul was seeking.

It would have been nearly impossible for Du Bois' discussion of religion and the black church to ignore the power and the meaning of its music. And so, music figured prominently in "Of the Faith of the Fathers." But quoting the poet Tennyson, Du Bois deployed an important music metaphor just before the chapter on religion began, as he ended the chapter on interracial relations, where he wrote:

> That mind and soul according well,
> May make one music as before,
> But vaster.

Here, Tennyson's joining intellect (reason) to soul (potential) to create an implied harmony anticipated Du Bois' use of music in the chapter on religion while pointing to what the souls of black folk sought. Under slavery, "his bards sang,

Children, we all shall be free
When the Lord shall appear!

Upon emancipation, no longer other/outward oriented but full of aspirations and potential self-determination, "The black bards caught new notes, and sometimes even dared to sing,—

O Freedom, O Freedom, O Freedom over me!
Before I'll Be a slave
I'll be buried in my grave,
And go home to my Lord
And be free.

Even in the chapter on John Jones, Du Bois used music not only to foreshadow the ultimate discussion of the Sorrow Songs but to talk, then and there, about soul and spirit. It is necessary, however, to consider Jones's whole story in order to make sense of the music in this place and its message about the soul. During his early days at Wells Institute, Jones was inattentive, clownish, disorganized, loud, and, most important, not very serious about life. When Du Bois described Jones as "clay [that] seemed unfit for any sort of moulding," it was the suggestion of a poorly developed soul, Jones's lack of seriousness about life, rather than his uncouth behavior, too easily read as an indication of (and a judgment about) his class background, that was most troubling to Du Bois. In fact, rather than revealing class implications, Du Bois' characterization of Jones as clay instead suggests that he was not yet fully human (or, better put, had not fully realized his humanness) when he arrived at Wells. Such an interpretation is not intended to place Jones in the *tertium quid* category, which Du Bois in fact despised.[36] Rather, in this instance, it is an allusion to the fact that it is the condition of one's soul that establishes one's humanity or humanness.

If Jones were properly educated, that problem would be resolved. But Jones had arrived at Wells undeveloped, intellectually and spiritually. His being expelled (or suspended) from school caused him to reflect on his life and on the opportunity he was squandering, and he resolved to return, work hard, and master the course that had been laid out. The introspection that his expulsion allowed and even demanded, and Jones's subsequent hard work, created the circumstances under which "he grew in body and soul."

His growth and development awakened him to the injustices around him, and he grew angry and resentful of the expectations imposed on him.

But upon graduating, Jones set out to do what other (white?) people were doing. It would not last for long. In the brief moments of this "escape" from bitterness, and in his first real move toward assimilation into the larger world, he sat enraptured by "the music of Lohengrin's swan" and began to ponder "some master-work, some life-service." He wanted it to come "without the cringing and sickening servility, without the cruel hurt that hardened his heart and soul." But John's deeply contemplative moment was abruptly interrupted, and in that moment of racist hate he decided that he would return to Altamaha. He would teach other young (black) scholars.

It is clear that in his first public presentation after his return to Altamaha, the new college graduate offended (or at least confused) the preacher, the congregation, his friends, and his family members. But the most important story embedded in Jones's biography has heretofore remained invisible. He had successfully moved through Du Bois' (Aristotle's) three levels of soul. Jones's growth and development had taken him from a state of soullessness (clay), to the state of revolt and revenge (desire), to and through an effort at assimilation (reason/thought), and finally to the meaning of *his own life* (spirit).[37] Upon his return to Altamaha, he began to teach his young scholars what he thought they should (needed to) know, and because of it his teaching career was a short one. The ending of his life's work (his spiritual calling) signaled the end of his life, figuratively and literally. Still, as he was about to be lynched, he heard "the faint sweet music of the swan," smiled, hummed, and pitied those who were about to murder him.[38]

One ought to wonder why John Jones heard the "sweet music of the swan" as he died. Was he hallucinating, as even he thought might be the case? One ought to wonder why the melody he heard as he was about to die was the same one he was listening to at the moment that he came to understand and accept his life's work. Without a sufficient explanation of the music throughout the text, John Jones's melody cannot fully make sense. Eric Sundquist's conclusion about the use of the spirituals throughout the book is that they relate to Du Bois' interest in premiering this important and ancient aspect of African American culture.[39] But Jones was listening to Wagner(!) at the moment of his epiphany. Consequently, it would even be logical to opine that Jones's hearing Lohengrin's swan was an allusion to the success (in a traditional/materialist way) of his education—which had introduced him to "high culture." The classical music perhaps identified him as a new member of the educated elite, the Talented Tenth. In a very complex interpretation of Du Bois' appropriation of Wagner, Russell Berman even raises the possibility of the swan's representing Du Bois, a species (of animal) that can never actually possess Dora Marbach, the young white woman with whom Du Bois had a romantic relationship while he studied in Berlin and who is symbolized by Elsa in the opera.[40]

But there is another likely reason for the presence of this particular music in this particular place. Theologian Jonathan Brierly, writing about the same time that Du Bois published *The Souls of Black Folk*, included a chapter titled "The Soul's Music" in his book, *Studies on the Soul*. In it, Brierley concluded that music revealed "principles which man's feebler intelligence [only?] spells out bit by bit." He described music as "an intense esthetic feeling" and noted that "one of the first [facts] is that the soul finds in musical sounds, arranged . . . by a mathematical mind, a mysterious language addressed to itself, which it intuitively understands and to which it immediately responds."[41]

Whether or not Du Bois read Brierley's words (and it *is* possible that he read them because the book had quickly gone through five printings by the time *Souls* was published), it is unlikely that he would have disagreed with them, for, as a philosopher, Du Bois understood the significance and power of music.[42] He started each chapter of *The Souls of Black Folk* with music; he premiered music in the chapter on churches/religion; he concluded the book with a chapter on songs; and he closed the book with a song—the words and music to "Cheer the Weary Traveller."

Equally noteworthy, Du Bois was adamant in his insistence that "[t]he Music of Negro religion . . . despite caricature and defilement, still remains the most original and beautiful expression of human life and longing [spiritual striving] yet born on American soil." He imagined that on the day Crummell died, "the morning stars sat singing." And John Jones was in a veritable state of rapture, listening to the performance of Wagner, when he seriously began to contemplate his life's work. When the movement changed to a "soft sorrow" of violins, Jones appropriately remembered Altamaha. Music spoke to the soul. And it was through music that the soul spoke. Throughout this volume, music spoke of and to black people's spiritual striving—their dreams, their aspirations, and their accomplishments. If white America could not recognize the striving of the souls of black folk in their everyday "loving, living, and doing," perhaps it would be easier to comprehend in the form of their "plaintive songs."

But the matter of John Jones's melody is not yet resolved. If the music throughout Du Bois' volume aimed, generally, to cause us not only to see some of the evidence of black culture, as most scholars have noted; to see the spirituals as an important contribution to American culture, as Sundquist insists; to understand the statement the spirituals (black people) made *about* American culture; and if it was designed, specifically, to cause us to listen to, respect, and honor the striving in the souls of black folk, then the music that John Jones heard was probably a commentary on *his* soul.[43]

Most people who have read *Souls* have questioned, and come to their own conclusions about, Du Bois' placement of this fictional piece in a volume full of history, sociology, political science, psychology, economics, and the like—scholarship.[44] On the surface, the inclusion is, indeed, anomalous. But, in fact, there is no inconsistency here, and explaining why simultaneously reveals the relevance of Jones's melody. "Of the Coming of John" was, itself, an important scholarly exercise, representing Du Bois' rendering of a *specific* genre of literature. The story of John Jones is a fable, and *all* fables are fiction, even though they are designed to teach important moral lessons about life. Du Bois' use of this particular opera in *his* fable allowed him to provide us two (probably three) powerful metaphors in the story of John Jones's life and death, both (all) more compelling than the now famous metaphor of the veil.

It is particularly common at the end of ancient fables for the dying swan to sing sweet music. From that literary tradition comes our notion of the swansong. And in this single instance Du Bois stacked the metaphors to a level that was uncommon even for him (or perhaps any philosopher). First, rather than thinking of the murderous episode in terms of Jones's hearing Lohengrin's swan, we should think of the melody in this place as Jones's *own* swansong—a dying declaration—or in this case, confirmation, of his humanity, his soul. Second is the transubstantiation that takes place in this story (and in other fables), which simultaneously illustrates more of what Jones's death and declaration announced. Lohengrin's swan, by the end of the opera, is transformed into a fully human being. As John Jones, upon first hearing the music in the New York opera house, discovered his life's work, so was he transformed. Discovering the meaning of one's life was critical (imperative) to the process of becoming a fully human, ensouled, being. And, finally, further connecting the music to the story, and John Jones's life choices to his soul, in Jones's *not* going "North," as his mother believed he had decided to do when he said goodbye and told her that he was going to be free, but instead returning to the site of his impending death to await the arrival of the lynch mob led by the judge, Jones also became Du Bois' symbolic Socrates, the philosopher/teacher who refused to give up his life's work and delivered himself to the Athens judges and, thus, to a death sentence. Indeed, Plato's *Crito* informs us that Socrates refused to escape even though his friends were ready to assist and the judges in the case were equally sympathetic.[45] Likewise, in the righteous tradition of slaves and many subsequently freed people who were trapped in the ruin of tenant farming and sharecropping, Jones could have run away after telling his mother, "I'm going away—I'm going to be free." But he, like Socrates, chose to free his soul rather than surrender it by denying his life's work. For both "beings at work staying themselves" to have given up their life's work would have been tantamount to ignoring their soul's (spiritual) striving. To have done so might have left them alive, but (as was the case for many of the citizens of Dougherty County) it would not have left a "life" at all.

Ultimately, if "Of the Coming of John" was not intended to mirror aspects of the life of Socrates; even if it is not properly a fable, the story of John Jones's life and death was, at least, the flawless execution of a series of metaphors, each more important than the ones we normally discuss from the book, and all of which aimed to teach important lessons about the development, the conservation, and the sovereignty of Soul.

There is, however, (at least) one more parallel in Jones's and Socrates' deaths. Just before Socrates fulfilled his death sentence by drinking the poison that his executioner presented to him, his friend Crito turned to what he believed was important final business: he inquired as to how they (Socrates' friends) should bury him. Socrates teased in his response: "In any way that you like; but you must get hold of me, and take care that I do not run away from you." Socrates' colleagues were puzzled, and so he explained. They could hardly catch and/or bury his real (true) self, his soul: they could *only* bury his body.[46] Both Du Bois' John Jones and Plato's Socrates had already abandoned the physical/material concerns of the body when they recognized the meaning of their life and accepted the pursuit of their spiritual calling. Thus, the swan's song, or the swansong, whether one thinks of Jones's hearing Wagner's movement ("Song of the Bride") as he died or imagines the (usually) concluding melody of an ancient fable, is always a sweet, rather than sad, song because the point of the swan's (physical/material) life had always been to relinquish it (which Jones did when he decided to return to Altamaha) and, thereby, to experience the complete development of the soul.[47] Although it is nearly impossible for us today to see the death of either man as anything other than tragic, like Socrates, John Jones's *choosing* to surrender his body for the sake of his imperishable soul was an especially emphatic declaration of its sovereignty.

If Du Bois actually missed the mark in *The Philadelphia Negro*, as he later suggested, it was we who (at least partially) missed it in *The Souls of Black Folk*, which unambiguously focused on "the essence" of life, Soul—its development, its growth, and its sovereignty. For those of us who grew to maturity at a time when a "good" education was more "liberal" than "classical," the oversight is easy to explain. Moreover, Du Bois' engaging the new social and behavioral sciences also directed some of our attention away from the philosophical streams of the study. Still, whether or not people noticed it, *before* Du Bois penned "Sociology Hesitant" (1905) and even before the major meeting that apparently inspired it, he had significantly surpassed any tendency to produce "philosophy of history with modest and mundane ends." In *The Souls of Black Folk* he put philosophy back into history and sociology and constructed a moving and powerful study of the spiritual striving of the souls of black folk in nineteenth-century America.

The story took on a familiar philosophical pattern—one that paralleled Aristotle's construction of the three levels of thought that characterized soul's development. Spiritual striving did not develop in response to white racism; nor was it imposed upon black folk from some other "outsider." It came from within and reflected the essence of humanity—Soul. By embedding his discussion of soul and spiritual striving in the history, sociology, and political economy of "the New South," Du Bois could raise important questions about its future: "How shall man measure Progress there where the dark-faced Josie lies?" The material "progress" that the New South exhibited to that point had been achieved in part by the neglect, abuse, and exploitation of the souls of black folk. If history was any indication, ignoring the sovereignty of the souls of black folk would not only stunt black folk, it would cripple the rest of the South, the nation, and, as later chapters will show, World Soul, too.

"THE TALENTED TENTH"
REVISITED

The age in which we live, inferior to many in some departments of human achievement, is yet an original one. It has its own character, its own genius, its own work, its own destiny, and being indeed the product of all time, inheriting the blessings and the banes of past ages, there is necessity that the men and the women of the present generation be acute and trained to disentangle the two elements, so as to accept the one and reject the other. —Rev. W. V. Tunnell[1]

In an essay published in 1903, Du Bois introduced a theory of group leadership that is popularly known as the theory of "the Talented Tenth."[2] The essay was, most of all, a plea for the support of higher education for black Americans, from among whom a "Talented Tenth," 10 percent of the black population, would emerge as leaders of the race. The publication of *The Souls of Black Folk*, also in 1903, contributed to the popularization of the idea, no doubt in part because of its direct challenge to Booker T. Washington's support of vocational and industrial education for black Americans and the extensive support that Washington's programs attracted.

Du Bois' idea was, however, much more than a reaction to Booker T. Washington. It was a philosophical ideal and a commitment so deep that in 1948, more than thirty years after Washington's death and forty-five years after Du Bois published the first essay on the Talented Tenth, he revisited the idea in a major lecture. He spoke at Wilberforce University, the oldest black university in America, before the Nineteenth Grand Boulé Conclave of Sigma Pi Phi, indisputably the most elite organization of black Americans at the time. Although he also titled this later presentation "The Talented Tenth," in it Du Bois revised his proportion, advocating this time for what he called "the 'Guiding Hundredth.'"[3]

Scholars have regularly held up Du Bois' Talented Tenth ideal as conservative and as evidence of his elitism. Political scientist and theorist Adolph Reed, who sees Du Bois as an elitist but not exclusively because of the Talented Tenth proposal, succinctly noted that "scholars have tended to collapse that elitism into . . . the famous 'Talented Tenth' concept." Reed also noted that even those scholars who are among Du Bois' greatest admirers see the Talented Tenth proposal as elitist but forgive him for it because, they say, he later changed his views and stopped advocating it.[4] With few exceptions, the general conclusion is that the theory was designed to protect (or certainly would have the effect of protecting) the status and privileges of elites.[5]

If, however, we explore the probable origins of Du Bois' theory and look more closely at what he wrote about the Talented Tenth in that context, it will be possible to come to very different conclusions. In particular, if we consider his foundational study in and commitments to philosophical ideals, his ideal of the Talented Tenth does not look so much like a conservative, elitist theory designed to protect the privileges of a precious few and instead reflects genuine concerns about how to create a better society, perhaps "the good society," in which the needs, interests, and abilities of all gained respect and support.

Because so much of Du Bois' postgraduate work is easily identified as history, political economy, and sociology, it has been easy to forget that his academic foundation was in philosophy. But he reminded us in one of his autobiographies that in high school and at Fisk he studied "Latin and Greek, philosophy and some history."[6] Both of his undergraduate degrees (Fisk, 1888; Harvard, 1890) were in philosophy. When he began his graduate studies at Harvard, he turned to "United States history and social problems" not because of a personal desire to abandon philosophy but because his academic adviser, William James, said to him: "'If you must study philosophy you will; but if you can turn aside into something else, do so. It is hard to earn a living with philosophy.'" And so, Du Bois said, "I turned toward history and social science." But while at Harvard, Du Bois studied with philosophers including George Herbert Palmer, Josiah Royce, George Santayana, and William James. He also joined, and was an active member of, the Philosophical Club.[7] It is likely that no idea promoted by Du Bois is better known than his doctrine of the Talented Tenth. It is equally likely that there is no other idea so clearly linked to his intellectual foundation in philosophy.

Du Bois' Talented Tenth proposal bears a striking similarity to aspects of Plato's *Republic*, which addresses, in part, the structure of an ideal society, including the place of elites in it.[8] Plato's ideal Republic was clearly characterized by a social hierarchy, at the top of which was a highly educated, elite cadre of men whose charge it was to organize society, lead the masses, and do the things we generally think of as in the purview of "the government." They were the leaders—the Philosopher Kings or Rulers. And because these Rulers would comprise such a small segment of society, it might be difficult to see beyond their exclusiveness. But if we consider how they were to arrive at their positions, the group might not seem quite so exclusive.

The process began in a state-financed educational system. Up to about the age of ten, students pursued a course of study that focused on reading and writing and also included music and gymnastics. For the next several years, the focus was literary and included literature, poetry, and music, along with physical education and probably some mathematics. Music and mathematics were the focus of the next five or so years, after which all students (now about eighteen years old) completed a mandatory two-year gymnastics course designed to prepare them for the military. From there, some students moved on to the higher educational process, lasting about fifteen years and focused on mathematics, science, and dialectics. Mathematics provided the skills necessary for determining the unity behind the other disciplines, and dialectics provided the foundation "for reducing math to logic." Mastery of math and dialectics enabled students to transcend the limitations of knowledge that were based on experience (senses). Thus, successful students would be able to find the truth themselves. Those who completed this extensive educational program comprised the class of Guardians from which the Rulers (or philosophers) and their Auxiliaries would eventually come. But until that time, people went on with their lives, pursuing fields and interests according to their calling or capacity. After fifteen years or so, those highly educated men, approaching the age of about fifty, presumably would have gained the experience, vision, patience, courage, wisdom—the character—necessary to be among those from whom the Philosopher Rulers, or the leaders, would come. Even though those who would become rulers or leaders would automatically become members of an elite class (and often, in fact, descended from elites), because all free men, theoretically, would have had access to the process that created the pool of people from which those elites eventually came, it would probably be a mistake to view it as a totally closed society. Indeed, Plato warned against pushing people into this leadership group simply because they were well born, and excluding people merely because they were not. Those who would ultimately be selected as rulers would have to be chosen purely on the basis of their ability and their commitments. The potential and actual members of this class simply had to be properly educated, to be talented, to manifest certain abilities and disposition or character, and to be committed to goodness and justice.[9]

Plato's "Foundation Myth" provides the most detailed caution against limiting the Rulers to members of elite families. The creation story in *The Republic* reminds the community:

You are, all of you in this community, brothers. But when god fashioned you, he added gold in the composition of those of you who are qualified to be Rulers; . . . he put silver in the Auxiliaries, and iron and bronze in the farmers and other workers. Now since you are all of the same stock, though your children will commonly resemble their parents, occasionally a silver child will be born of a golden parent, or a golden child of a silver parent, and so on. Therefore the first and most important of god's commandments to the Rulers is that in the exercise of their function as Guardians their principal care must be to watch the mixture of metals in the characters of their children. If one of their own children has traces of bronze or iron in its make-up, they must harden their hearts, assign it its proper value, and degrade it to the ranks of the industrial and agricultural class where it properly belongs: similarly, if a child of this class is born with gold or silver in its nature, they will promote it appropriately to be a Guardian or an Auxiliary. And this they must do because there is a prophecy that the State will be ruined when it has Guardians of silver or bronze. (*PR*, §415a–b)

The legacy of hundreds of years of enslavement and a generation of postemancipation segregation and discrimination undoubtedly made it impossible for Du Bois to talk, literally, about "natural abilities," which the Jim Crow system had deliberately stunted in millions of individuals. Moreover, by the turn of the twentieth century, a variety of misapplications of science to society, particularly Darwinist theories, seemed to substantiate conclusions about black (and immigrant) inferiority in America while justifying the colonization of Africa, Asia, and the Caribbean. And so when, in *The Souls of Black Folk*, Du Bois addressed the critical question about whether to provide vocational or classical education for black Americans, he used language that was slightly different from that which Plato used. Du Bois wrote:

Teach workers to work—a wise saying; wise when applied to German boys and American girls; wiser when said of Negro boys, for they have less knowledge of working and none to teach them. Teach thinkers to think,—a needed knowledge in a day of loose and careless logic; and they whose lot is gravest must have the carefulest training to think aright. If these things are so, how foolish to ask what is the best education for one or seven or sixty million souls! shall we teach them trades, or train them in liberal arts? Neither and both: teach the workers to work and the thinkers to think; make carpenters of carpenters, and philosophers of philosophers, and fops of fools.

Du Bois' characterization of carpenters, philosophers, and fools appears to reinforce rigid, hierarchical class structures, but he provided us good reason not to view it that way. He continued: "Nor can we pause here. We are training not isolated men but a living group of men,—nay, a group within a group. And the final product of our training must be neither a psychologist nor a brickmason, but a man."[10]

Despite his not using Plato's characterization of people of gold, silver, bronze, and iron, Du Bois clearly recognized that people had different interests *and* abilities, that those conditions should help to determine aspects of their future, that people should be supported whichever direction they pursued, and, most important, that the goal of the training related to more than the job the man was being prepared to do but the man being prepared for the job. "And to make men," Du Bois added,

we must have ideals, broad, pure, and inspiring ends of living,—not sordid money-getting, not apples of gold. The worker must work for the glory of his handiwork, not simply for pay; the thinker must think for truth, not for fame. And all this is gained only by human strife and longing; by ceaseless training and education; by founding Right on righteousness and Truth on the unhampered search for Truth; by founding the common school on the university, and the industrial school on the common school; and weaving thus a system, not a distortion.

Clearly, as many scholars have noted, Du Bois did not believe that everyone would or should go to college. He wrote: "All men cannot go to college but some men must." And he did not oppose vocational education. Thus, he noted, "I am an earnest advocate of manual training and trade teaching for black boys, and for white boys, too." It was also as important to him as to Washington that people learn to work "steadily and skillfully." But Du Bois also insisted that the success even of schools such as Hampton and Tuskegee (normal, industrial, and vocational schools) would be in proportion to their employment of college graduates.[11]

Indeed, what has regularly been lost in discussions of Du Bois' Talented Tenth is that its most pointed argument for higher education was for teachers—the people whose work was so critical to the *creation* of a Talented Tenth. He characterized teachers as "the group-leaders of the Negro people—the physicians and clergymen, the trained fathers and mothers, the influential and forceful men about him of all kinds." The teachers were responsible for disseminating "the culture of the surrounding world" to and through "the graduates of the higher schools." The college-educated teachers were potential revolutionaries whose primary obligation was to teach "what life means." Their second obligation was to provide the student with "sufficient intelligence and technical skill to make him an efficient workman."[12] Du Bois predicted that if "the leaders of thought among Negroes are not trained and educated thinkers," people would simply become the prey of "a hundred half-trained demagogues . . . and hundreds of vociferous busy-bodies." And he issued the warning that "either you must help furnish this race from within its own ranks with thoughtful men of trained leadership, or you must suffer the evil consequences of a headless misguided rabble." If the teachers were properly prepared, their former students would become "useful" and helpful to the larger group. The leaders among them, presumably members of the Talented Tenth, would rise and pull the rest up with them. Du Bois added, "this is the history of human progress." The idea that this hypothetical 10 percent of the population would "uplift" the rest was an extremely lofty idea. But philosophers are, often, idealists. And Du Bois' proposal of a Talented Tenth was an ideal, not unlike the one proposed in Plato's *Republic*.[13]

In *The Republic*, those fifteen or so years after the completion of formal schooling were critical to identifying those who might become Rulers or leaders. One can easily conclude from Plato's discussion that a person who lived life totally for himself would simply never be chosen as a leader. And a person's desire to become a ruler/leader could eliminate him from the potential candidates. That is, people who wanted to be "in charge" probably lusted after power and might attend only to their personal interests once they had it. People could be eliminated because of their relationship to money. In fact, a person who aspired to being rich would not be chosen. And those who were chosen could not accept pay for the work. Money could spoil their vision, make them self-interested, and render them too vulnerable to special interests to be involved in politics. Because it was important for *all* citizens to live full, meaningful lives, Rulers had to be willing to work to prevent the development of extremes of wealth *and* poverty among individuals. The primary concern of those who would be Rulers was the creation of a good society, the foundation of which was justice.[14]

Du Bois' discussion of the black leadership class was not dramatically different from Plato's. While Du Bois certainly believed, as he wrote, that "[t]he Negro race, like all other races, is going to be saved by its exceptional men," being a college graduate did not automatically put a person in that category. The exceptionally well-educated professionals Du Bois *named* in his essay, presumably representatives of the Talented Tenth, were known more for the ways they served the public than for the education they had achieved and the occupations they held. But the first individuals he characterized as leaders—the exceptional men and women—were abolitionists, and among them were David Walker, Sojourner Truth, and Frederick Douglass, individuals who had very little or no formal schooling. They were leaders, Talented Tenth examples, because of the way they led their lives— working to save others from slavery, to force the country to live up to its creed that all men were created equal, and, in general, to improve life for all black people. Their status in America during the eighteenth and nineteenth centuries precluded their becoming very highly, formally educated. Still, the way they lived their adult lives did not preclude their serving the public good or their being examples of the Talented Tenth.[15]

When Du Bois returned to the topic in his 1948 address, he attempted to clarify his original proposal, revise it based on mid-twentieth-century circumstances, and restate the importance of the idea. The first thing Du Bois did, however, was to acknowledge the criticism his original proposal had attracted. "It has been said that I had in mind the building of an aristocracy with neglect of the masses," he wrote. He believed that the popularization of Marxist theories contributed to this criticism, and, given that, he decided, he said, "to re-examine and restate the thesis of the Talented Tenth which I laid down many years ago." Although scholars view his incorporation of socialist ideas as an indication of his radicalization and his moving away from the Talented Tenth ideal, he was especially emphatic in his support in this second iteration of it (perhaps more than in the original proposal).[16]

In the 1948 presentation, Du Bois understandably emphasized the changes that had taken place in the world political economy and the emergence of new knowledge, especially in the sciences, since the turn of the century, and, for that reason, he continued to emphasize education. He emphasized, even more than before, the responsibility of the small group of leaders to the larger group. But most important of all, he made especially (perhaps painfully) clear that traditional markers of elite status did not automatically qualify one for membership in the Talented Tenth.

In 1948, Du Bois was contrite about his naiveté in 1903. He pointed out the particulars of "the Negro Problem" (lynching, segregation, disfranchisement) in that earlier moment and said he "saw salvation through intelligent leadership . . . through a Talented Tenth" as the possible solution. He added, "Willingness to work and make personal sacrifice for solving these problems was, of course, the first prerequisite and *Sine Qua Non*. I did not stress this, I assumed it." He "assumed that with knowledge, sacrifice would automatically follow," but he conceded that his youthful idealism had prevented his seeing that "selfishness is even more natural than sacrifice." He had taken for granted people's willingness to sacrifice for the greater good because of his training at Fisk, where it was an expectation. By 1948, however, he realized that his original Talented Tenth proposal *could* "put in control and power a group of selfish self-indulgent, well-to-do men, whose basic interest in solving the Negro problem was personal; [and whose interests were instead in] personal freedom and unhampered enjoyment and use of the world, without any real care or certainly no arousing care as to what became of the mass of American Negroes, or of the mass of any people." By 1948, Du Bois could see how his original proposal "might result in a sort of interracial free-for-all, with the devil taking the hindmost and the foremost taking anything they could lay hands on." He added, "This, historically, has always been the danger of aristocracy." While Plato had warned about the inherent danger of tolerating the development of extremes of wealth and poverty in a society, Du Bois insisted in his 1948 presentation "that the poor need not always be with us, and that all men could and should be free from poverty." And probably reflecting the changes in the world since 1903 as much as what he actually thought *in* 1903, Du Bois noted in 1948: "My Talented Tenth must be more than talented and work not simply as individuals. Its passport to leadership was not alone learning but expert knowledge of modern economics as it affected American Negroes; and in addition to this and fundamental would be its willingness to sacrifice and plan for such economic revolution in industry and just distribution of wealth as would make the rise of our group possible." Du Bois' (much more detailed) analysis of the changes in the world political economy during the first half of the twentieth century ended on the role of the Talented Tenth in making a difference.

Here comes a new idea of a Talented Tenth: The concept of a group-leadership not simply educated and self-sacrificing but with clear vision of present world conditions and dangers and conducting American Negroes to alliance with culture groups in Europe, America, Asia, and Africa, and looking toward a new world culture. We can do it. We have the ability. The only question is, have we the will?[17]

Du Bois' proposal in 1948 included a leadership group of "[o]ne one-hundredth, or thirty thousand persons" in a organization with a paid staff. When he looked around for "an already existing body [that] could be adapted to this work," the college fraternities (presumably because of their connection to higher learning, their large membership, and their national dispersion) held some potential. But their members were too young (spirited, impulsive) and too preoccupied with making a living to place in this important position. And so he turned to the Boulé, his host, which held both limitations and potential.[18]

Some of the most significant limitations of the Boulé related to its composition. First, it was so small. Du Bois noted that there were only 440 families represented in the Boulé (not including the Baltimore membership, which had not responded to prior communications), and he calculated this membership as one ten-thousandth of the 3 million black families in America at the time. Second, the Boulé families were so small (more than half had only one child or no children) that Du Bois saw the organization as headed for extinction. The average age of the membership did not help matters, either. "[W]e are old men," he noted. There was only one member under thirty years old. Three-fourths were between thirty and sixty; most, he believed, nearer to sixty. A quarter of the members were *over* sixty. To these conditions Du Bois added the lack of diversity among occupations of the members, feelings of helplessness, a live-for-today philosophy, and a lack of belief among them in black ability.[19]

The expansion of the Boulé membership in age, occupation, and number would not be so difficult to accomplish. Du Bois urged direct recruiting: "Nothing but congenital laziness should keep us from a membership of 3,000 by the next biennium . . . and a membership of 30,000 by 1960." This number represented one one-hundredth of the black population. As did Plato, Du Bois sought "active virile men of middle age and settled opinions who have finished their education and begun their life work." He especially wanted these members to realize that their positions derived as much from opportunity as from ability and that, therefore, paramount among their responsibilities was extending these opportunities to others.[20]

Probably the most important and most neglected aspect of Du Bois' call for growing a Talented Tenth, now a "Guiding Hundredth," was his concern that this not become a closed society of any sort. He wrote: "This new membership must not simply be successful in the American sense of being rich: they must not all be physicians and lawyers. The technicians, business men, teachers and social workers admitted must be those who realize the economic revolution now sweeping the world and do not think that private profit is the measure of public welfare." He especially emphasized "honest men" and "self-sacrificing leadership." About the latter, he demurred, "this is primarily a question of character which I failed to emphasize in my first proposal of a Talented Tenth."[21]

Despite persistent scholarly conclusions that Du Bois' efforts celebrated and almost blindly advocated for the elite at the expense of the masses, the 1948 speech, in fact, represents Du Bois' most direct challenge to some who might have seen themselves as the leaders of race. After he explained why the college fraternity members were unsuitable for this work, he said, "I turn then to this fraternity [the Boulé] but *with some misgiving*" (emphasis added). He explained: "What the guiding idea of Sigma Pi Phi was, I have never been able to learn. I believe it was rooted in a certain exclusiveness and snobbery for which we all have a yearning even if unconfessed." He went on to describe the Boulé (of which he was a member) as "an old, timid, conservative group" characterized by the "unconscious and dangerous dichotomy" of possessing an "identity with the poor" while "act[ing] and sympathiz[ing] with the rich." After explaining all his other misgivings about the Boulé, some of which are noted above, he went on to describe the work they had to undertake. He ended his commentary with a profoundly pessimistic prediction that simultaneously reflected badly on the character of the Boulé members:

> Naturally, I do not dream that a word of mine will transform, to any essential degree, the form and trends of this fraternity, but I am certain the idea called for expression and that the seed must be dropped whether in this or other soil today or tomorrow.[22]

It is no wonder that Du Bois sat alone on a bench on the college campus after his speech; it must have deeply offended his hosts, many of whom undoubtedly (mistakenly) saw themselves as true representatives of the Talented Tenth.[23]

Not only did Du Bois' presentation before the Boulé not assume that the people we might readily identify as elites were (or should be) the leaders of the race, it made profoundly clear that he did not see traditional elites and the Talented Tenth as analogous.[24] Indeed, what is so remarkable about the speech is that it clearly *slurred* the Boulé members as *mere* elites and, potentially worse, as people protecting their exclusive little club and the lifestyle enclaves that their occupations, incomes, and social networks helped to create.[25] Although Du Bois' "new idea of a Talented Tenth" included people who were well educated and self-sacrificing but with more awareness of and interest in world affairs, he seemed pretty certain that even in the meeting of the Boulé, composed presumably of America's true black elite, he was planting that seed in fallow ground.

That Du Bois would have made the negative remarks he made is phenomenal, and that Du Bois scholars since then have not recognized their significance is even more remarkable. But also lost to many of us until now is the *extreme* irony in the fact that the Boulé in ancient Greece *was* the leadership class, the advisory body during the transition of city-states (Athens, Corinth, Argos, etc.) from government by aristocracy to more democratic-like structures. Du Bois certainly knew this: he referred to the leaders of his hypothetical Guiding Hundredth as "a directing council." Moreover, the (Sigma Pi Phi) Boulé administrative structure incorporated official titles of the ancient society. Some of the Boulé members were labeled "the Archons," the actual title of a handful of civil officers who administered and enforced the law in ancient Athens. But finally, despite the obvious shortcomings in, and Du Bois' misgivings about, the Boulé, he remained convinced that "[t]here is no reason why the sort of thought and teaching which 2,000 years ago made the groves of Athens the center of the world's salvation, could not live again in ten thousand Negro homes in America today."[26]

The characterization of the Talented Tenth theory as elitist and conservative is a consequence of our own narrow assumptions that put people in this group simply because they were well educated, had a "good" job, and/or came from a "good" family. Du Bois' remarks before and about the Boulé made it clear that its members were not *necessarily* representatives of the Talented Tenth, and, again, one would not likely find a more elite black collective in America at the time. It is precisely because Du Bois *did not* conflate leadership with a good education, a lucrative job, and/or a fine pedigree that his proposals were so much more radical than we have recognized. And, further, we should remember that both his 1903 and 1948 presentations sought to lay out a *program* for *developing* leadership and, especially in 1948, a *plan of work* for that leadership class. Leadership would not be an indication of privilege, but evidence of sacrifice ("self-sacrificing leadership"). It would be the responsibility of the leaders to "*find* desert, ability, and character among young Negroes and get for them education and opportunity." If the entire program succeeded, "the American Negro . . . will be *able to* lead the world and will *want to* do so" (emphasis added).[27]

Du Bois' original discussion of the ideal of the Talented Tenth appeared at a time when many people were seeking alternatives to the so-called "Gospel of Wealth," whose effects Du Bois brilliantly illustrated in *The Souls of Black Folk*. That gospel had fostered massive capital accumulations, a grossly uneven distribution of wealth, and unhealthy living and working conditions for many, if not most, of the masses. In the late 1870s, Henry George offered one possible alternative in *Progress and Poverty*, in which he proposed his potentially revolutionary "single tax" on what he considered to be the source (private property) of most of the unearned wealth accumulating in private hands at the time. Ten years later, Edward Bellamy's utopian novel *Looking Backward* looked all the way (forward) to the year 2000 in order to suggest what the ideal society, which seemed unobtainable in the 1880s, might ultimately resemble. It was not only a socialist society but one in which the governing structure was another version of the dispassionate talented elite. Equally significant, the nineteenth century saw dozens of utopian communities, especially in the northeastern and midwestern regions of the United States, start up and mostly fizzle out soon thereafter.[28]

Du Bois' 1948 speech alluded to some of these proposals. After briefly discussing the new economic organization of the world, he encouraged the division of resources based on "need and not . . . chance, or privilege, or . . . power." He said that "industry should be controlled by the state, and planned by science and . . . all goods should be owned and distributed in such ways as result in the greatest good to all." He pointed out that such organization "is called by many names: Socialism, Communism, Liberalism, Consumers-Cooperation, The New Deal, or Progressivism, taking its name according to place and time and emphasis."[29] Viewed alongside these well-known programs and philosophies, even the original Talented Tenth proposal, rather than seeming conservative or elitist, can more easily be seen as one of the most radical of the many proposals for social, political, and/or economic reorganization to have appeared in America by the turn of the twentieth century.

The 1948 speech *seemed* more radical than the original presentation because of its socialist propositions. But the ideal was radical from its inception. As Thomas Holt writes, examining a larger body of work than under examination here, Du Bois' "program was not defensive and reactionary, but forward looking and militant"; it was "not a retreat to nationalism, but a recognition of the international dimensions of the racial conflict." By Du Bois' formulations, black Americans "could be the vanguard of an international assault on class privilege." And as Fiona Spiers rightly notes, rather than suggesting "a closed caste," this Talented Tenth proposal represented "the pinnacle of a meritocracy." Given how consistently black people were excluded at every turn, a true meritocracy would have been radical indeed.[30]

Conclusions that Du Bois' Talented Tenth proposal was a conservative idea are, nevertheless, easy to defend. Again, the original version *seems* conservative or elitist precisely because of Du Bois' subsequent, clear socialist references. It also seems conservative and elitist because when Du Bois originally proposed it, the people who *appeared* to be members—the college educated—comprised such a small and exclusive group. Not even a tenth of 1 percent of the black population at the time had graduated from college.[31] The Talented Tenth idea certainly seems conservative because it has become almost impossible to separate it from turn-of-the-century "uplift" rhetoric, which often carried a big, paternalistic footprint, if not outright condescension. Du Bois' own words in the 1903 paper presented the two ideas in tandem. Again, he wrote, "The Talented Tenth rises and pulls all that are worth the saving up to their vantage ground. This is the history of human progress."[32] We can also point to Du Bois' early emphasis on higher education as the most important site of production for the Talented Tenth as evidence of his elitism. But, in *this* examination, the most compelling reason for possibly seeing this theory as conservative rather than radical is that ancient Athens, the home of the hypothetical Philosopher Rulers whom I have proposed as a possible model for Du Bois' leadership class, was itself a highly hierarchical society—with slaves; and Plato, himself, did not think very much of democratic forms of government. He pretty soundly rejected them.[33]

If, however, one considers that it was not until *1984* that at least 10 percent of black Americans over the age of twenty-five had completed at least four years of college, the turn-of-the-century proposal for a Talented Tenth can take on more meaning.[34] What if at least 10 percent of black Americans had been college trained three generations earlier, around 1900, when Du Bois first proposed the Talented Tenth, and a significant enough portion of that small percentage had been trained for, and was committed to the specific purpose of, working to create a good—just—society? Would it have taken two whole generations more for the eruption of the modern civil rights movement? Would such a movement even have been necessary? These questions are of a sort that historians should never ask, of course, because we cannot answer them. But such questions nevertheless might help us to see the idea of the Talented Tenth differently from the way we are accustomed to seeing it.

If it were possible to see Du Bois' proposal of a Talented Tenth beyond the contexts in which we normally see it embedded, and particularly as something other than (something bigger and fundamentally more important than) a reaction to Booker T. Washington's best-selling industrial-education proposals, then Du Bois' idea of the Talented Tenth might better resemble the kind of radical idea that it actually was. And Du Bois' move toward Marxism might then reflect his expanding, internationalizing, or in today's parlance, globalizing, rather than retreating from, his original proposal.[35]

Du Bois did not back away from any of his 1903 positions in the 1948 presentation. He continued to insist that "[a]ll persons should be educated according to ability and labor according to efficiency," that people should "work according to gift and training" and receive a decent wage for that work, and that the society would work best when everyone did what they were best suited to and best trained to do.[36] As conservative as this all seems in isolation, it was probably more an argument *against* limiting black folk as a group to menial occupations than an argument *for* solidifying the higher status of a smaller group among them. But, finally, even if the Talented Tenth/Guiding Hundredth should *not* be related to Plato's Philosopher Rulers, we should remember Du Bois' lifelong insistence on state-financed public education, equal access to it, the best possible training for all individuals, and the availability of a college curriculum to any who had the capacity to and interest in pursuing it. Had that vision been fulfilled, the so-called Talented Tenth/Guiding Hundredth would still have been an elite group, but its origins would have been incredibly broad based. Had the *total* vision been fulfilled, it would have been the work of the members, rather than their occupations and degrees, which defined them. And, most important, if the theory worked as Du Bois proposed it, not only would black Americans be *prepared to*, they would *want to* lead not only the race but the world to that good society about which the philosopher always dreamed. Whether we consider the 1903 or the 1948 proposal, it is difficult to imagine an idea(l) more radical than that.

SPIRIT

Alexander Crummell, Prophets, and Destiny

This planet was built for the growth of manhood. Everything on earth and in the sea, above, beneath, like the geist in Goethe's Faust, plies at the whizzing loom of time to weave for humanity the garments of nobler manhood. No man can degrade the manhood of another without doing violence to his Maker. No man can surrender his manhood to another without dishonoring God. To know this is to know the meaning of life and of the world. —Reverdy C. Ransom[1]

Scholars who have written on *The Souls of Black Folk* regularly take special note of Du Bois' chapter on Alexander Crummell. Some of the most useful discussions explore the intellectual links between the two men, recognizing Crummell as a mentor, a role model, even a father figure to Du Bois. Other interpreters read political motives into the chapter, one concluding that through it Du Bois castigated Booker T. Washington perhaps even more than through the earlier chapter that focused on him. And, in one instance, the ascribed motives behind the chapter appear more self serving and designed by Du Bois to situate himself in a lineage of great black men, of which Crummell was the patriarch.[2]

Certainly, Du Bois' veneration of Crummell is obvious in *Souls*, and all of the above conclusions provide insight into the chapter on him. But as clear as Du Bois' admiration, even adoration, of Crummell is in *Souls*, as much as Du Bois feared the potential consequences of Washington's program (and his power to implement it beyond Tuskegee), and as highly as Du Bois might have thought of himself, none of these conclusions fully explains the chapter on Crummell. What remains missing from these careful and useful analyses is a discussion that focuses on the chapter as an intellectual exercise, a literary accomplishment, and a philosophical statement. If we are able to see the story of John Jones as Du Bois' rendition of a fable and his Talented Tenth as analogous to Plato's Philosopher Rulers, then the life of Alexander Crummell, as Du Bois presented it, might similarly speak to us allegorically *and* philosophically and as another intellectual exercise, in this case, about destiny and spirit in the case of truly special people.

Consider, first of all, the manner in which Du Bois wrote of his and Crummell's meeting.

> I spoke to him politely, then curiously, then eagerly, as I began to feel the fineness of his character,—his calm courtesy, the sweetness of his strength, and his fair blending of the hope and truth of life. Instinctively I bowed before this man, as one bows before the prophets of the world.

In that passage alone, Du Bois provided a powerful image, that of a prophet. The passages that precede it, beginning with the first sentence of the chapter, make the significance of the above sentences even more poignant.

> This is the story of a human heart,—the tale of a black boy who many long years ago began to struggle with life that he might know the world and know himself. Three temptations he met on those dark dunes that lay gray and dismal before the wonder-eyes of the child: the temptation of Hate, that stood out against the red dawn; the temptation of Despair, that darkened noonday; and the temptation of Doubt, that ever steals along the twilight. Above all, you must hear of the vales he crossed,—the Valley of Humiliation and the Valley of the Shadow of Death.

Henry Louis Gates Jr. and Terri Hume Oliver relate Du Bois' "geographical language" in these sentences to "the spiritual struggle" embodied in "John Bunyan's classical allegory *The Pilgrim's Progress*."[3] Du Bois was, without a doubt, outlining Crummell's spiritual struggle for the reader, and Bunyan's classic work would have been a good model. But not only did the language embedded in the opening paragraph of the chapter reflect traditions that were much older and deeper than Bunyan's seventeenth-century work, it simultaneously reflected intellectual traditions that were much more recent.

David L. Lewis, more than anyone else, has articulated both the literary and intellectual traditions Du Bois deployed in the chapter on Crummell. Lewis wrote:

> In "Alexander Crummell" Du Bois offers a secular parable that mimics the Calvary—a moral and racial instruction in which the anointed

messenger is tested, forsaken, rebuked, and allegorically sacrificed in order to redeem a people. However, the unmistakable New Testament imagery no longer represented deeply held religious convictions. By the time he reached Wilberforce, Du Bois's religious views were wholly decoupled from orthodox Christianity and from any notion of a personal deity. At best, he recognized a vague presence manifesting itself in laws slowly revealed through science—a force best expressed in Hegelianisms such as *Weltgeist* (world spirit) or *Dasein* (presence) and above all in private and without emotion. But although he had relinquished the Bible's theology, Du Bois would hold in reserve the language of the King James Version whenever, as with the import of Crummell, he strove to give an idea maximum emotional force.[4]

As clearly and aptly as Lewis articulates Du Bois' literary (theological/allegorical) and intellectual (philosophical) reference points, it is possible to "unpack" the rich meaning of Du Bois' words in even more detail.

Much of the unpacking of the literary contribution revolves around the image of a prophet.[5] Because Du Bois was reared in a Christian environment (if not in a strictly orthodox Christian tradition), attended Christian schools (and churches), and associated with and even adored at least one Christian minister (Crummell), the Christian tradition provides one window through which to view Du Bois' chapter. But despite his deploying "wilderness" motifs and describing various "temptations," which we might correctly associate with Jesus, the New Testament (Matthew 4), and Christianity, the rendering of Crummell as a prophet makes it equally useful to view the image of him that Du Bois constructed in the context of the Old Testament and especially its stories about Moses. After all, *all* seventeen major *and* minor prophets of the Bible are Old Testament prophets; the highest standard among the men accepted as prophets was a Hebrew; and many of the images presented in the chapter on Crummell, including the now almost- cliché "Valley of the Shadow of Death" remark, are Old Testament rather than New (Psalms 23:4).

And so, our effort to comprehend more fully the import of Du Bois' characterization of Crummell as a prophet should begin, at least, by accepting Du Bois at his word, not assuming that he used his genius simply to beguile us. Because he told us that he saluted Crummell as one might a "prophet of the world," we should, even if only as an intellectual exercise, consider the Crummell chapter in that light. Then, given that the biblical prophets were (overwhelmingly) Old Testament prophets, we must acknowledge that perhaps Du Bois' inclinations were, as Lewis suggests, *not* particularly

Christian. Even though Du Bois was paying tribute to a high-church Episcopal priest, the Old Testament *is*, largely, a collection of writing about a pre-Christian era. And then we should consider who the "prophets of the world" might have been to a turn-of-the-century intellectual. The point is not to establish Crummell as a true prophet, the equal of Moses or Jesus or Mohammad.[6] The intention here is simply to see, in detail, the particular literary contribution present in Du Bois' construction of Crummell's life in the prophetic tradition.[7] And, in such a context, rather than seeing Du Bois as having abandoned (or accepted) "orthodox Christianity," we might see the depiction of Crummell as a literary example that *transcended* orthodox Christianity to reflect a very important aspect of *all* the major religions of the world. That is to say that *all* the best-known "prophets of the world" were, to borrow Lewis's words, "tested, forsaken, rebuked, and allegorically sacrificed in order to redeem a people."[8]

The literary form of the Crummell chapter—allegory—is thus especially clear. The chapter is an "extended metaphor, in which objects, persons, and actions in a narrative, are equated with the meanings that lie outside the narrative itself. The underlying meaning has moral, social, religious, or political significance, and characters are often personifications of abstract ideas. . . . Thus an allegory is a story with two meanings, a literal meaning and a symbolic meaning."[9] The literal story here is obviously the reconstruction of Crummell's life—a biography. The symbolic representation is that of Crummell as a prophet. This study maintains that the abstract idea, which heretofore has remained largely hidden, is the use of Crummell's life to talk about Spirit in the tradition of nineteenth-century philosophical discussions.[10] The philosophical principle of Spirit is, however, not abstract at all. Indeed, reading the chapter as a philosophical discourse makes the details of Crummell's life more real.

Because of Du Bois' philosophical training, he did not need to be a traditionally religious man to write the essay he wrote. Nor was it necessary for him to believe, literally, the religious stories that gave the Crummell essay its form. Nineteenth-century training in philosophy began with the study of the Bible, and religion was always central to the study of philosophy. Not only were the two areas not clearly separate until the seventeenth century, but even Bible scholars recognize that "[t]he appreciation of the relationship between Christ, who is fully the Way, the Truth, and the Life, and *other noble ways, truths, and lives*, is a vital part of the theologian's task, and the Bible itself . . . does not so much forbid this wider theological exploration as emphatically demand it. To repudiate philosophy and the comparative study of religion is not truly biblical, but narrowly Biblicist" (emphasis added).[11] Du Bois' knowledge of the Bible easily enabled him to use well-known religious images to make a statement about Spirit and destiny that simultaneously supported his philosophical interests in Soul.[12] Indeed, given the relationship between traditional religious and philosophical concerns, an analysis of Du Bois' use of both, together, will reveal more about his intellectual accomplishment than efforts to define either orientation alone can.

The different views of philosophers and theologians are nevertheless important to note. Modern discussions range from a complaint among theologians that there is not enough religion in philosophy and from philosophers that there is not enough science in religion to the more explicit charge from theologians that there is not enough faith in philosophy and the countercharge from philosophers that there is not enough reason (thought/intelligence) in religion.[13]

What might be more important is that serious thinkers in religion *and* philosophy are very much concerned with spirit. And both groups of scholars are ultimately concerned with what a being has to do to fulfill his/her being—destiny. Because Du Bois viewed Crummell as a person of Spirit, evidence of the most complete development of the soul, there was no better way to evoke this special character than to cast Crummell as a prophet. And casting Crummell's spiritual journey in allegorical form made the story especially accessible for any reader who possessed the most basic knowledge of religious history, regardless of the orthodoxy. But readers who had a general knowledge of the history of philosophy undoubtedly gained a much deeper understanding of Du Bois' tribute to Crummell.

When Du Bois introduced Crummell to us, through his report of their meeting, he provided as many explicit pointers to his philosophical interests as he provided to his theological effort. First, he recognized in Crummell "the fair blending of the hope and *truth of life*" (emphasis added). The wording suggests the primary interest and scholarly concern of any philosopher. Second, Du Bois' characterization of Crummell as "a human heart" was an allusion to his humanity, Soul. And third, when Du Bois noted Crummell's mighty struggle to "*know the world* and *know himself*" (emphasis added), Du Bois not only framed concerns with both the material and spiritual worlds, he did so in a way that also reflected the dual perspectives of Hegel's *Phenomenology of Spirit*. To "know the world" suggests Hegel's experience of consciousness, which situates the development of consciousness (soul) in the context of the phenomenal/the world. And the words "know himself" evoke Hegel's philosophy of spirit in which conscious's objective is to know itself (as spirit).[14]

The remainder of this chapter is written in two substantial parts. In order to demonstrate as fully as possible the allegorical nature of Du Bois' construction of Crummell's biography, the first part pays particular attention to aspects of the lives, journeys, temptations, and failures of the great prophets of various "world religions" juxtaposed with Du Bois' rendering of Crummell's life. Part II focuses on Du Bois' chapter as a philosophical exposition. This section moves from Du Bois' general use of classical philosophy (in my first three chapters) to his more explicit use of modern (nineteenth-century) philosophy as it draws out the parallels between Du Bois' characterization of Crummell's life and Hegel's "shapes" (or "forms") of consciousness in the philosophic journey of individual consciousness toward spirit. The conclusion to this chapter attempts to bring together Du Bois' framing of Crummell's life through *both* a theological and philosophical commentary on spirit—the *"developed energy of the soul"* (emphasis added)—the actualization of potential, or destiny.

Ultimately, Du Bois' chapter on Crummell is much more than a biographical tribute, a eulogy, and/or a celebration of Crummell's life; more than a snipe at Booker T. Washington; and more than simple self-aggrandizement. In a rather significant way, in the chapter on Crummell Du Bois provided two distinct but equally important discussions of Soul—one allegorical, situated in theology in the literary tradition of innumerable religion-based stories, and the other based on philosophy in the Hegelian tradition that pays particular attention to the development of consciousness. In both cases, Du Bois illustrated an *individual's* journey toward spirit—destiny. And, ultimately, whether one reads the spiritual journey represented in Du Bois' chapter as sacred or secular, Du Bois logically cast Crummell as a prophet because *only* a prophet is ever trusted with the destiny of a people.

Part I

As Old Testament literary analyst Dewey M. Beegle put it, "a person of destiny must have . . . a remarkable beginning."[15] And the birth stories of the true prophets are indeed remarkable. Mohammad was born clean and circumcised. His mother never felt the discomfort of being pregnant, and because soon after Mohammad's birth he was (despite his family's poverty) placed in the care of an unlikely nurse who successfully reared him in the desert, he thrived as a child.[16] The story of Moses's infancy and childhood is equally remarkable. After an order from the Pharaoh to drown all male Israelite babies, Moses's mother carefully placed him in a river in a waterproofed basket. He was not only rescued by the daughter of the Pharaoh who had ordered the killings, but this princess called on Moses's natural mother to take care of him (Exod. 1, 2:1–10).[17] Jesus was born of a virgin, in an animal shed, and cribbed in a feed trough. Although Herod sent for the baby with the intention of killing him, the family escaped to Egypt (Matthew 1:18–25, 2; Luke 2:1–7).

There was no reasonable way for Du Bois to write a birth story for Crummell that compared in its drama to those of the true prophets without turning the story into fiction, but he did manage to draw at least the image of a parallel, though very unequal, in the issuance of the various edicts. The Pharaoh ordered the death of all male Jewish babies born in Egypt. Herod commanded the killing of male children under the age of two in Bethlehem. America issued the Missouri Compromise. Despite the compromise's ban on slavery above the 36° 30' north latitude line, and despite the ongoing gradual abolition of slavery in the North, the Missouri Compromise made it clear that American slavery was not going away. The Missouri Compromise was not the Compromise of 1850, however, whose Fugitive Slave Act directly and profoundly imperiled the freedom of all black people, including (perhaps especially) those in the North. But *Souls* is a work of literature, and writers are allowed some license. And so Crummell, if not born in the imminent danger that Du Bois suggested in his "born with the Missouri Compromise" passage, was at least born into inherent difficulty just because he was a black child living in America during the slavery era. And so, Du Bois informed us, Crummell's mother kept a close watch over his whereabouts and constantly fretted over his safety.

Not surprisingly, those who would become prophets manifested special attributes early in their lives. Although Du Bois' description of Crummell's childhood suggests a special character in development, the description is, nevertheless, much more enigmatic than, for example, Jesus's stunning rebuke of his mother when she chastised him for not staying with their caravan after the Feast of the Passover. Jesus informed her that he was attending to his father's business (Luke 2:41–50). Du Bois' characterization of Crummell does not reveal this kind of audaciousness, but there is still evidence of a special character in development. As a child Crummell "paused over his mud and marbles" and "saw puzzling vistas as he looked down the world." "[H]is young mind worked and winced and shaped curiously a vision of Life." And while his father's presence was always evident, so was "a form that fell in vast and shapeless folds." Because much of Du Bois' brief discussion relates to groaning slave ships and "faint cries [that] burdened the Southern breeze," one can easily surmise that, even as a child,

Crummell, partly as a consequence of his father's stories to him but also because of his own special character, possessed some vague understanding of the barbarism of enslavement and the oppression of his people. This construction, an important part of Du Bois' situating Crummell in the prophetic tradition, established Crummell as one who knew, saw, heard, felt, and experienced things that ordinary children did not. Because Du Bois never suggested that Crummell was born with a veil, we should interpret Crummell's visions as the suggestion of the kind of supernatural experience that prophets regularly reported. Du Bois was sensitive (careful) enough *not* to claim explicitly a relationship to God for Crummell like that of the true prophets, but it is still extremely important that early in his life Du Bois' Crummell experienced visions.

The visions of the true prophets were unmistakable, direct communications from God. Moses's most important instructions commanded him to return to Egypt (which he had fled after killing a man) and to bring the children of Israel out (Ex. 2:11–16; 3:1–10). Jesus and Mohammad also experienced mysterious visions: Jesus after being baptized by John the Baptist (Matt.3:16–17), and Mohammad initially while tending his foster family's sheep and, later, while tending his father-in-law's herds.[18] Rather than symbolizing some sort of psychosis, visions in the prophetic tradition suggest that something else very important is on the horizon. It is at this point in the literary construction that Du Bois achieved the most success in planting Crummell's life in the prophetic tradition.

Visions often presaged, or occurred in the middle of, a wilderness experience. Wilderness experiences were periods filled with chaos, confusion, gloom, and a sense of being lost or adrift. The wilderness provides an opportunity for the prophet to discover his true self, and if he is to survive and take up his true mantle (fulfill his destiny), he has no choice. Prophets encounter snares or challenges (temptations) in the wilderness. Overcoming or defeating these temptations is the process of overcoming potential personal weaknesses or deficiencies, which is important in proving one's leadership capacity to oneself and to those whom one is to lead. Because the wilderness experience is brutal, it strips away all the illusions of personal power and status and allows (perhaps forces) the development of humility (especially important for a true leader) and the emergence of the true self, stripped of all the external content that is ultimately a source of self-deception. Thus, the wilderness experience provides an opportunity for purging oneself of doubt, fear, self-loathing, and material trappings, and it forces one, in the religious tradition, to depend on God. The survivor emerges from the wilderness clear about his purpose and better prepared to fulfill his destiny.

Jesus's wilderness experience, accompanied by a fast, lasted forty days. Almost as soon as he emerged from it, he faced three very serious challenges ("temptations").[19] First, Satan tempted Jesus to use his power, since he was the Son of God, to turn stone into bread. Then, in Jerusalem, at the highest point of a temple, Satan goaded Jesus: "If You are the Son of God, throw Yourself down. For it is written: 'He shall give His angels charge concerning you,' and 'In their hands they shall bear you up, Lest you dash your foot against a stone.'" And, finally, Satan offered Jesus control of "all the kingdoms of the world" in exchange for worshipping him instead of God. Jesus rejected all three temptations, and the devil left (Matt. 4:1–11).

Succumbing to any of these temptations could have fulfilled an immediate need or desire. Turning the stone into bread, for example, would have provided Jesus something to eat when he was clearly hungry. Throwing himself from the rooftop could have satisfied his ego, allowing him to prove his special relationship with God. And the offer of a kingdom provided a quick and easy way for Jesus to fulfill his destiny as a leader of people. But during these particularly earthly and human experiences (temptations), he had to make important decisions about priorities and destiny and endure these trials without losing the original commitments. Enduring the kinds of temptations that men regularly face (of the body, mind, and soul), made it possible to begin his ministry, sure of his mission, his faith, and himself.

Du Bois' characterization of Crummell's life has an explicit New Testament–like element in that Crummell also faced three highly personal, and equally human, temptations—Hate, Despair, and Doubt. The first temptation, Hate, developed during Crummell's childhood, in the shadow of slavery. Hate "glid[ed] stealthily into his laughter, fad[ed] into his play, and seiz[ed] his dreams by day and night with rough, rude turbulence." When Crummell went to New Hampshire—Canaan, no less—to pursue his education, townspeople tore down the school rather than allow black children to attend. But after Beriah Green admitted several black boys, including Crummell, to his school in Oneida County, New York, "[t]he shadowy, formless thing—the temptation of Hate, that hovered between him and the world—grew fainter and less sinister."

Crummell's struggle for education and the temptations it elicited were very important biblical allusions. The first one seems somewhat ambiguous:

A vision of life came to the growing boy,—mystic, wonderful. He raised his head, stretched himself, breathed deep of the fresh new air. Yonder, behind the forest, he heard strange sounds; then glinting through the trees he saw, far, far away, the bronzed hosts of a nation calling,—calling faintly, calling loudly. He heard the hateful clank of their chains, he felt them cringe and grovel, and there rose within him a protest and prophecy. And he girded himself to walk down the world.

Crummell's act of girding himself "to walk down the world" (to be distinguished clearly from his earlier act of having "looked down the world") alludes to more than his pursuit of education; it also suggests certain well-known New Testament scriptures. The short book of Ephesians offers the clearest instructions about walking in the spirit in a mean, wicked world. One had to "take up the whole armor of God" for protection. Those who were "girded" with the "waist of truth," the "breastplate of righteousness," shoes prepared with the "gospel of peace," the "shield of faith," the "helmet of salvation," and the "sword of Spirit," would be able to defeat the wicked.[20]

Crummell was in the process of girding himself properly when he experienced another vision, this time accompanied by a calling that also led him to his second temptation.

A voice and vision called him to be a priest,—a seer to lead the uncalled out of the house of bondage. He saw the headless host turn toward him like the whirling of mad waters,—he stretched forth his hands eagerly, and then, even as he stretched them, suddenly there swept across the vision the temptation of Despair.[21]

Crummell's Despair was rooted in the refusal of the men of God, the church bishops, to admit him or any Negro student to the General Theological Seminary of the Episcopal Church. He became so distressed that he was unable to distinguish "the kind hands that stretched themselves toward him" from the not so kind. But Crummell refocused his energy: "He would gather the best of his people into some little Episcopal chapel and there lead, teach, and inspire them, till the leaven spread, till the children grew, till the world hearkened."

The renewed commitment did not forestall Crummell's facing the third temptation. Despite much intensive labor, often at great personal sacrifice, his congregation not only did not grow, it dwindled. And Despair gave way to Doubt—in himself and his people. Du Bois wrote:

Of all the three temptations, this one struck the deepest. Hate? He had outgrown so childish a thing. Despair? He had steeled his right arm against it, and fought it with the vigor of determination. But to doubt the worth of his life-work,—to doubt the destiny and capability of the race his soul loved because it was his; to find listless squalor instead of eager endeavor; to hear his own lips whispering, 'They do not care; they cannot know; they are dumb driven cattle,—why cast your pearls before swine?'—this, this seemed more than man could bear; and he closed the door, and sank upon the steps of the chancel, and cast his robe upon the floor and writhed.

Crummell eventually relocated to Philadelphia, but when Bishop Onderdonk offered him a church without the ability to participate in the church convention, Crummell declined the offer and went to New York, where he worked, mostly in poverty, for several years. Then, "[h]alf in despair, he wandered across the sea, a beggar with outstretched hands." In England, Crummell found some physical and mental recovery. He completed his education at Queens' College (Cambridge), and then he went to Africa, where he worked for most of the next twenty years, at the end of which he returned to America.

Du Bois' depiction of the three temptations Crummell faced is an unmistakable New Testament–like construction. But because Du Bois blended into the story a decades-long wilderness experience filled with fear, doubt, and apparent leadership failure, we have to turn to the equally important Old Testament, Moses-like, elements of his chapter. Old Testament parallels concern the visions and the calling, the wilderness experience, and the outcome of the efforts.

As already noted, Moses was watching his father-in-law's flock when an angel of God spoke to him from a burning bush. Moses was somewhat confused, and then God spoke directly, telling him: "I have surely seen the oppression of My people who are in Egypt, and have heard their cry because of their taskmasters, for I know their sorrows." He then instructed Moses: "Come now, therefore, and I will send you to Pharaoh that you may bring My people, the children of Israel, out of Egypt" (Ex. 3:7, 10). Although there was neither a burning bush nor a recognizable angel in Du Bois' depiction of Crummell's visions, the similarities to those of Moses are too obvious to ignore. "Yonder, behind the forests, he heard strange sounds; then glinting through the trees he saw, far, far away, the bronzed hosts of a nation calling." And then, "[a] voice and a vision called him to be a priest,—a seer to lead the uncalled out of the house of bondage." And so it was a forest rather than a bush, a glinting rather than a flame. But in both instances, there was a calling, an enslaved nation, and a voice directing the called to break the nation's bondage.

The most compelling parallel to the Moses tradition, however, is in the miserable, decades-long wilderness experience, characterized by dissention, fear, and doubt. Once Moses and the Israelites departed Egypt, they endured hunger, thirst, and war. Some people questioned Moses's leadership; some reverted to idolatry; and many concluded that they would have been better off as slaves in Egypt than dying in the wilderness (Ex. 12–18). The strife and near rebellion among Moses's followers was so great that he, too, began to complain to God and, perhaps, to doubt his destiny. "Why have You afflicted Your servant? And why have I not found favor in Your sight, that You have laid the burden of all these people on me?" (Numbers 11:11) Crummell's congregants apparently did not face the threats of starvation, dehydration, or war, but they were, like the Israelites and their view of Moses, unimpressed by Crummell's leadership. Unlike the Israelites, they had the ability to leave, and leave they did. Then Crummell, also questioning God ("'What, in God's name, am I on earth for?'"), understandably moved from Despair to Doubt. Crummell, like Moses, had to overcome these fears and doubts about his people, himself, and his God, if he/they would have any chance of fulfilling his/their destiny.

The Moses-like comparisons pertain until the end of Du Bois' chapter on Crummell. First, when one considers that only two members of the original group that left Egypt entered Canaan, it is easy to argue that Moses failed in his ultimate mission. Before leaving for England, Crummell was similarly never able to inspire his congregants. He had "worked and toiled," but "month by month the congregation dwindled, week by week the hollow walls echoed more sharply, day by day the calls came fewer and fewer." And second, Moses was among those who did not enter Canaan; he died alone and was buried in an unknown grave (Numbers 20:12; Deut. 32:52; 34:5–6). Crummell, of course, did not die alone, nor is his gravesite unknown; the best parallel Du Bois could draw was that he died unknown.[22]

But ultimately Crummell did not fail. During his decades-long wilderness, he faced whatever fears and weaknesses he had, overcame the Hate, Despair, and Doubt that were triggered by various negative external conditions (the people and environment around him) but nevertheless conditions of his own mind, and realized the purpose of his life. And so, as Du Bois put it, although "the Valley of the Shadow of Death" usually swallowed up its victims, "Alexander Crummell it gave back. Out of the temptation of Hate, and burned by the fire of Despair, triumphant over Doubt, and steeled by Sacrifice against Humiliation, he turned at last home across the waters, humble and strong, gentle and determined. He bent to all the gibes and prejudices, to all hatred and discrimination, with that rare courtesy which is the armor of pure souls."

Crummell, clearly preserved by his "armor," was very different upon his return to America compared to his leaving. His having to fight "among his own, the low, the grasping, and the wicked," evokes the traditional reaction even among the closest associates of the true prophets.[23] Among Jesus's closest followers was a famous "doubter" and an impossible-to-forget traitor. And Moses grappled constantly with "whisperers" and "murmurers."[24] Crummell, however, faced his trials "with that unbending righteousness which is the sword of the just." And although just before he left America, full of doubt, he wondered, "'What, in God's name, am I on earth for?'" having earlier announced to the bishop, "'I have failed,'" upon his return from Africa, "[H]e never faltered, he seldom complained; he simply worked, inspiring the young, rebuking the old, helping the weak, guiding the strong." We can assume that, finally, Crummell had stopped thinking of himself, focused on his work, and trusted God.

Before closing the chapter, Du Bois cast Crummell, yet again, in the Moses tradition, in a way that went beyond the obvious traditional prophetic framework of suffering and redemption. Du Bois wrote:

> So he grew, and brought within his wide influence all that was best of those who walk within the Veil. They who live without knew not nor dreamed of that full power within, that mighty inspiration which the dull gauze of caste decreed that most men should not know. And now that he is gone, I sweep the Veil away and cry, Lo! the soul to whose dear memory I bring this little tribute.

The most obvious interpretation of this passage relates to race relations. Perhaps the first sentence of the passage, Crummell's having "brought within his wide influence all that was best of those who walk within the Veil," was an allusion to his work in/with the American Negro Academy, which aimed to harness the power of the best black minds to do battle in the cause of black progress. White America ("[t]hey who live without," beyond the veil) needed to be introduced to this important and inspired man. And so Du Bois swept "the veil away" by writing this tribute.[25] In this context, it appears that Du Bois harkened back to his original uses of the veil as a metaphor for color. The second line, however, also suggests other possibilities. It can also be read as an allusion to the folk tradition about the power of the veil that few are blessed to possess, or even the tradition of "second sight" among the biblical prophets.[26] But in that same line, Du Bois' calling the cover "gauze" suggests something different from or in addition to both the folk tradition and the idea of race, although his words evoke both ideas and reinforce biblical traditions. According to legend, after witnessing the burning bush and hearing from God, Moses's face was never again seen directly by anyone but God. His face was, from that point, covered with a veil. Even if Moses's face was covered because it was so bright (with light) after facing God that people could not look directly at him, as some literary analysts suggest,[27] Paul wrote that Moses's face was covered "because of the glory of his countenance, which glory was passing away" (2 Corinthians 3:7, 13). He was approaching death.[28] But perhaps now that Du Bois has provided us his version of Crummell's story, we can see this veil differently—in a more metaphorical way. After Moses witnessed the burning bush and spoke with God, Moses, now clearly identified as a prophet, could simply no longer be looked upon, in life, as an ordinary man.[29] Du Bois' narrative, likewise, would have us see Crummell first as something other than, as more than, a man. Du Bois' Crummell was a prophet. But with his death (and Du Bois' story), we also need to be reminded of and to see his humanness; that he was still just a man. And so Du Bois encouraged us to do just that: "And now that he is gone, I sweep the Veil away and cry, Lo! [Look!]."

Whichever explanation for Moses's being veiled one accepts (and we could add the legend of Moses's having horns after his vision, which he kept covered so as not to frighten people),[30] and whether or not one accepts that Du Bois attempted to write Crummell's biography in the prophetic tradition and to construct Crummell as a prophet, Du Bois further complicated the matter of Moses-as-model in his closing paragraph.

> I wonder where he is to-day? I wonder if in that dim world beyond, as he came gliding in, there rose on some wan throne a King,—a dark and pierced Jew, who knows the writhings of the earthly damned, saying, as he laid those heart-wrung talents down, "Well done!" while round about the morning stars sat singing.

Although it is to the Hebrews that Christianity owes a debt for the prophetic tradition, and the "morning stars" passage is from the Old Testament book of Job (38:7), there is obviously no neat way to link Du Bois' discussion exclusively to the Old Testament traditions. Even Jesus, in despair, asked, "My God, My God, why have You forsaken me?" (Psalms 22:1) And, like Moses, he appeared to have failed in his mission as he was executed like and with criminals. But Du Bois' closing paragraph of the Crummell chapter also reveals the Christian (New Testament) tradition in both clear and subtle ways. The obvious identity of the "dark and pierced Jew" certainly reflects an inclination toward Christian traditions. Less obvious, but equally important, the implied life after death, Crummell's potential appearance before the "throne," suggests the immortality of the soul. Hebrew thought characterized man "as an animated body" rather than "an incarnate 'soul,'" and it was unthinkable in ancient Hebrew traditions that the body and the soul could be treated separately. (The Greeks introduced the idea of the immortal soul, which subsequently became a part of Christian thought.)[31] Thus, it was the Christian (New Testament) tradition that made it possible for Crummell (his soul) to appear after his death before "a King." Still, the fact that Du Bois wondered whether, but was not certain that, Crummell made it into heaven, suggests, as David Lewis and others have indicated, the knowledge of rather than a commitment to Christian tenets, for if Du Bois accepted that such a place existed, the biography he wrote suggests he would not have doubted it as Crummell's ultimate destination.

––––––––––

Wilson Jeremiah Moses has concluded that "Du Bois's internal religious beliefs, like those of most complicated people, remain an unsearchable mystery, and his writings on religion always reflect the complexity of his 'spiritual strivings.'"[32] And Du Bois' religious thought certainly *appears* to be messy. But as Eugene Wolfenstein recently wrote, while Du Bois was not "conventionally religious," he "was born into a world where the Old and New Testaments provided a virtual second language, and he was both proficient and at home in the use of it."[33] Indeed, it is impossible to separate Du Bois' characterization of Crummell from either Old or New Testament traditions and recognizable principles in other religious traditions as well. But if we consider Du Bois' effort as an intellectual exercise as much as a biographical statement or eulogy, the major literary accomplishment of his rendering of Crummell's life as allegory is clear and unmistakable; and the parallels need not be exact. Moreover, regardless of Du Bois' personal beliefs, there was hardly a better way at the time to illustrate the struggles of a great man than through allegory, especially a man presumed to have been born, or subsequently endowed, with a special destiny.

Part II

Early in the Crummell chapter, Du Bois wrote:

The nineteenth was the first century of human sympathy,—the age when half wonderingly we began to descry in others that transfigured spark of divinity which we call Myself; when clodhoppers and peasants, and tramps and thieves, and millionaires and—sometimes—Negroes, became throbbing souls whose warm pulsing life touched us so nearly that we half gasped with surprise, crying, "Thou too! Hast Thou seen Sorrow and the dull waters of Hopelessness? Hast Thou known Life?" And then all helplessly we peered into those Other-worlds, and wailed, "O World of Worlds, how shall man make you one?"

Despite the "Progressive Era" social reforms well under way, especially in the United States and England at the time that *Souls* was published, and their underlying assumptions about the humanity of all people, Du Bois was probably alluding to the early nineteenth-century developments in philosophy centered especially in Germany (but also Britain) and known as Idealism.[34] Fichte, Schelling, and, obviously, Hegel (and before them, Kant) were all concerned, to varying degrees, with the "I" and "thou," or subjectivity; with self-consciousness and its being-for-self (Du Bois' capitalized "Myself"); with the doctrine of Soul, which is implied in Du Bois' capitalized "Life"; and with what Hegel labeled Spirit, which Du Bois characterized as man's making worlds one.[35] Du Bois' whole description of Crummell's life reflects all of these concerns while hearkening back to most of the themes repeatedly called up throughout *The Souls of Black Folk*: striving, soul, finding one's purpose, being one's self, the meaning of a life. He reminded us of them again as he encapsulated Crummell's life near the close of the chapter.

So the man groped for light; all this was not Life,—it was the world-wandering of a soul in search of itself, the striving of one who vainly sought his place in the world, ever haunted by the shadow of a death that is more than death,—the passing of a soul that has missed its duty. Twenty years he wandered,—twenty years and more; and yet the hard rasping question kept gnawing within him, "What, in God's name, am I on earth for?"

Indeed, within the discussions of the theologically rooted New Testament–like "temptations" and Old Testament–like "wilderness" that Crummell experienced was also evidence of the philosophical stages (or "shapes") of consciousness that Hegel described in the process of conscious's development (to Spirit). Perhaps Du Bois did not explicitly inform us of this concurrent meaning of his story of Crummell's life because the conscious itself is not aware of the process it is undergoing. Thus, to have written about Crummell's life explicitly as the journey of individual conscious to Consciousness, Self-Consciousness, Reason, and Spirit (knowledge) would have been a misrepresentation. It is, instead, up to us, the "phenomenological observers" as Hegel put it, to provide this analysis.[36]

The all-too-brief summary of Crummell's life began, as noted above, with Du Bois' informing us that "[t]he black-faced lad that paused over his mud and marbles . . . saw puzzling vistas as he looked down the world." Later, Crummell's "young mind worked and winced and shaped curiously a vision of Life." In addition to the presence of a "bitter father" in his life, there was also "a form that fell in vast and shapeless folds." The real content of these puzzles, shapes, and forms is not evident for a reason. At the level of Consciousness that Hegel characterized as sense-certainty, conscious is capable of recognizing "a thing" but has no way to make anything of it beyond the fact that it is a thing. Hegel called this sensual (perceptual) recognition "immediate knowledge"—the recognition of the thing as a thing. At this point, there is no analysis of what it is "in itself." Consequently, the possibilities of what it is are infinite. This immediate knowledge, because it appears to be universal (the thing simply *is*), seems to be true. But this is, in fact, the most abstract and least true type of knowledge. Du Bois showed us that Crummell *sensed* something; it might even have been important. But there was no way for Crummell to understand it at that point, and no reason, in this light, for Du Bois to interpret it for us. At this point, it is important for us simply to witness/observe Crummell's journey, which at this point was not even clear to him. Du Bois' chapter begins with Crummell's apprehending. Hegel's discussion indicates that for the conscious (Crummell) to develop further, it (he) must comprehend rather than merely apprehend its (his) object.[37]

Upon Crummell's eventually reaching the school at Oneida, Du Bois told us, "there came to those schoolboys a revelation of thought and longing beneath one black skin, of which they had not dreamed before." The "sympathy and inspiration" that Crummell experienced at Oneida not only led to a reduction in the temptation of hate that once had overwhelmed him, but more important in this context, Crummell gained "a vision of life" that included his being called to become a priest. This point resembles the beginnings of Hegel's stages of Self-Consciousness—"being-for-self." In this stage, characterized by ego and desire, consciousness/Crummell begins to recognize contradictions in the object (thing), and because these contradictions are now evident, it is impossible to continue to view the thing simply as a thing. Consciousness at first blames itself for these contradictions but subsequently attributes the contradictions to the thing, whose contradictions are especially apparent in contact with other objects. Such contradictions could easily cause Crummell, or anyone, to ask, "'Why should I strive by special grace when the way of the world is closed to me?'"[38]

Moving from Consciousness fully to Self-Consciousness is, according to Hegel, especially difficult because "the Notion of knowledge" (Crummell's recognition of the contradictions) is often mistaken for real knowledge. Realizing that is it not real knowledge (which Crummell's subsequent "failures" made apparent) can be devastating, but Hegel described it as a necessary "*education* of consciousness." Hegel wrote: "The road [between Consciousness and Self-Consciousness] can therefore be regarded as the pathway of *doubt*, or more precisely as the way of despair," in part because "[t]he skepticism that is directed against the whole range of phenomenal [natural, or the notion of] consciousness . . . renders the Spirit for the first time competent to examine what truth is. For it brings about a state of despair about all the so-called natural ideas, thoughts, and opinions, regardless of whether they are called one's own or someone else's, ideas with which the consciousness that sets about the examination [of truth] *straight away* is still filled and hampered, so that it is, in fact, incapable of carrying out what it wants to undertake" (*PS* §78).

Du Bois' Crummell reached similar dangerous points. He experienced Despair when refused admission to the seminary. Nevertheless, Crummell resumed his work, focusing on the larger black community. But even in this stage that Hegel described as self-consciousness for others, Crummell's churches not only did not grow, they shrank. When he sought a larger church but learned that it would not come with the usual privileges of membership, Crummell, now full of Doubt, reached the real crisis point between consciousness and self-consciousness, on Hegel's pathway of potential devastation. Du Bois noted that we would have noticed Crummell's physical frailty at this point—"the shattered frame and hacking cough; but in that soul lay deeper death than that."

Hegel's detailed illustration of the journey to self-consciousness—partly embedded in a discussion of "Lordship and Bondage" in which master and slave (or serf) both struggle for recognition from the other—provides an important perspective on Crummell's journey. The bishops and priests in Du Bois' chapter suggest Hegel's lords or masters and self-consciousness's independent being-for-self. Crummell in that context appears to be the independent self-consciousness's dependent being-for-*other*, in bondage. To be sure, in the Hegel construct, both of the apparently opposing consciousnesses have to recognize the other, but Du Bois' chapter is also about *Crummell*, and *his own* (internal) struggle. And so we may also think of the struggle as being between his own independent and dependent being (to make consciousness for both self and its *own* other). That is to say that in the Hegelian context, it is *we*, again, as phenomenological observers, who must recognize what Crummell could not at that point: in addition to the immediate struggle Crummell endured against bigotry and indifference, there is also a struggle between his own independent being (for-self) and his fear-filled, dependent being (for-other). Crummell had to reconcile the two as one—a single consciousness both for its self and for its other irrespective of external conditions. If he succeeded at this resolution, Crummell would no longer have had to ask why he should continue to strive given all the apparent obstacles in place; he would have known that the important thing was to continue to strive.[39]

Du Bois' discussion of Crummell evokes all three of Hegel's stages of self-consciousness. Stoicism, in which things become important because consciousness thinks they are, was evident when Crummell decided to become a priest. In making this decision, consciousness seems free because freedom is manifested in thought or self-will. But the stoic consciousness is ignoring the details of life. "[T]he General Theological Seminary of the Episcopal Church cannot admit a Negro." When Crummell fought against this tradition, the priests simply saw "him as foolish, unreasonable, and injudicious, a vain rebel against God's law."

Crummell's eventual ordination as a deacon, creating a reason for optimism, provided the foundation for his movement from stoicism to skeptical consciousness, Hegel's second stage of self-consciousness. As Du Bois told us, Crummell "[s]lowly and more soberly . . . took up again his plan of life." Upon studying the situation, he came to the conclusion that slavery had debased and degraded black people. And so, "[h]e would gather the best of his people into some little Episcopal chapel and there lead, teach, and inspire them, till the leaven spread, till the children grew, till the world hearkened." Just as Hegel's skeptical self-consciousness did, Crummell made his "other," the priests, "vanish," along with "[his] relationship to [them]," particularly after their half-hearted offer of a church. The skeptical self-conscious, "in the simple negativity of its own thinking," simply ignored the world or rose above it. But as Findlay notes, this withdrawal was not evidence of freedom but an indication of "solitary sovereignty." Although the work Crummell continued to do for "The True and Good" was still "uplifting," it could only become tiresome, monotonous, and even life-draining because it was based on what Hegel described as empty scientific abstractions ("pure thought") rather than the real (life) from which consciousness had actually withdrawn (*PS* §200–204).[40]

Not surprisingly, this "skeptical freedom" becomes enmeshed in an internal (self-generated) chaos of personal belief, which Hegel described as "*absolute dialectical unrest.*" At one point consciousness (Crummell) "rise[s] above all the confusion"; at another, it/he "relapse[s] into occupying itself [himself] with what is unessential" (PS §205). In this stage, there is still a division, but it resides in one individual instead of two. Until consciousness overcomes the idea of "self as a dual-natured, merely contradictory being" (Du Bois' "double consciousness") and becomes a real unity, there can only be an unhappy consciousness, bouncing back and forth between one extreme and the other (*PS* §206). This "*unhappy; inwardly disrupted* consciousness" is Hegel's third state of self-consciousness, which he described further as "the gazing of one self-consciousness into another," while "itself *is* both, and the unity of both is also its essential nature" (*PS* §207).

The unhappy consciousness results from viewing the two sides as opposites rather than the same, which forces it to distinguish between "the *essential* [unchangeable] Being" and "the protean [unessential] Changeable." The unhappy consciousness identifies itself with the unreliable, shifting consciousness, the unessential being. Because the unhappy consciousness sees itself as the changeable, and true consciousness is actually unchangeable, the unhappy consciousness is constantly engaged in an internal battle to free itself (unessential changeable) from itself (essential unchangeable), which it has rendered alien. It is, in a way, a struggle to be what it already is (*PS* §§206, 208).[41]

The process of bridging this division and moving unhappy consciousness to Spirit involves work. Hegel described work as "formative activity" that dissolves fear and creates the circumstances that allow consciousness to move to reason (*PS* §§195–96). Thus, through work, the unhappy consciousness unites the pure thinking of stoicism and the fickleness of skepticism so that consciousness can know the one as the other, and in that unity the divided consciousness achieves Reason, "the certainty of consciousness that it is all reality" (*PS* §233). The discipline and service of work allow self-consciousness to rise "above petty finite [personal] interests."[42] The discipline of work, the surrender of any personal concerns about it, and the acceptance of the directions of consciousness, signals a united consciousness and the arrival at Reason.[43]

Having reason, consciousness has "a universal interest in the world" and knows it belongs there. To move from *having* reason to *being* reason, consciousness has to get beyond its self (the "superficial 'mine'" or "pure ego").

In order to do so, consciousness embarks on a quest for truth—observing nature—seeking universal laws.[44] When conscious observation results in an awareness that distinguishes between action and intention, that resists labeling or judging (labeling a thing denies the full range of its characteristics), and that sees the relation between the internal (inner/psychological) and external (outer/social/political) in the object, thus eliminating the contingent in the object (making it both universal and subject), it is possible for self-consciousness to recognize itself in another self-consciousness and to see itself, ethically, as a *part of a social whole*. At this point, consciousness has moved from *having* reason to *being* reason, which is Spirit (*PS* §436).[45]

Because Hegel told us that self-conscious reason can only be actualized "in the life of a people or a nation," it is not difficult to imagine that it was this type of relationship to which Du Bois alluded in his description of Crummell's work over nearly two decades in Africa and especially upon his return to America (*PS* §350). Crummell became a participant in a world that was no longer just an existent object upon which he imposed himself, and that world became a part of him. Crummell's work, from the dictates ("law") of his heart, demonstrated virtue or individual sacrifice rather than reflecting some externalized "duty" (*PS* §359). And, finally, Crummell has come to terms with alienation in which one might become a "beautiful soul" but ultimately an empty soul and in which conscience is a form of vanity or self-worship.[46] Once Crummell resolved the (immediate) "otherness" that is suggested by each of the above intermediate (dichotomous) conditions, Reason's "certainty of being all reality has been raised to truth, and it [Crummell] is conscious of itself [himself] as its [his] own world, and of the world as itself [himself]" and is, thus, Spirit (*PS* §438).[47]

Work provided the means by which self-consciousness discovered *itself* in otherness. Crummell could only doubt and despair so long as he continued to oppose otherness in the context of the thing—the school, the church, the bishops; "the low, the grasping and the wicked." But in working anyway and enduring all sorts of conflicts and deprivation, Crummell/consciousness surrendered to the "middle term" (Hegel's unhappy consciousness) (*PS* §227) that mediated the extremes of the unchangeable (essential) and the unessential (changeable) consciousness. This mediator made it possible for consciousness to relinquish its will and even the pleasure and enjoyment it normally derived from its work, its property, and its things, and simply to work, "divested . . . of its 'I,' and having turned its immediate self-consciousness into a *Thing*, into an *objective* existence" (*PS* §229). No longer being responsible for its work (it now being directed by the mediator rather than the self), consciousness/Crummell also no longer has to suffer the misery of it.

The extended discussions of work in *Souls* (and other Du Bois texts) easily remind us of the oppression and exploitation under which black folk worked. Aspects of the discussion also evoke the turn-of-the-twentieth-century obsessions with industrialization and the transformation of peasant people into clock-oriented, scientifically managed minions, an interpretation at least partly influenced by Karl Marx's successful application of Hegel's discussion of "Lordship and Bondage" to the alienated industrial proletariat. But Du Bois' use of Cambridge-educated Crummell lifts the discussion of work out of the framework of retraining peasant/working-class populations. And if gaining "meat and raiment" was not the objective of work, not even for the poor, rural inhabitants of Dougherty County, what was the point? For Du Bois (and Hegel), one *works* to nurture Soul, to find oneself, to discover (to meet, to know, and to know oneself as) Spirit.

The implication of Du Bois' chapter is that Crummell did in fact achieve the "perfect freedom and independence" that is Spirit.[48] As Du Bois noted, while "the Valley of the Shadow of Death" usually swallowed up "its Pilgrims," it released Alexander Crummell. When he returned to the United States, faced with some of the same adversities that existed before he left, he no longer asked "'What, in God's name, am I on earth for?'" Instead, Du Bois says, Crummell was "humble and strong, gentle and determined." He simply went to work. He sometimes fought against "the low, the grasping, and the wicked," and he endured "the gibes and prejudices, . . . hatred and discrimination." "[H]e worked alone, with so little human sympathy." And he worked "nobly and well." If Hegel's model is an appropriate one for Du Bois' Crummell chapter, we must assume that in working anyway, and enduring all sorts of conflicts and deprivation (in America and in Africa), Crummell/Consciousness moved from *having* to *being* reason, and thus to Spirit (*PS* §196).

Even though sparse, the details Du Bois provided about Crummell's life helped to illustrate the process by which a "protean consciousness," which is at first only able to distinguish "forms" and "shapes," gains an education characterized by movement through a series of stages of consciousnesses. In this process, consciousness is ultimately relieved of the bondage of its reliance on what it learns through the senses. Thus, Crummell's "education of consciousness" liberated him "from the dominance of naturalness," which Werner Marx described as "the given circumstances, situation, habits, customs, religion and so forth" of a place, time, and/or people. Crummell ultimately "grasp[ed] the rationality of objecthood, of objectivity—whether it be that of nature or of the institutions and thought-habits of a people or epoch—and thus [became] aware of [his] identity with this objectivity."[49]

Hegel's *Phenomenology* traced the movement of "the individual mind from its unscientific [natural] standpoint to that of science [knowledge]."[50] Crummell's life as Du Bois constructed it provides a useful example of that individual journey. In deference to Crummell's life choices, Du Bois could hardly have done anything other than invoke the religious metaphors and theological images that we see in his chapter. But given Du Bois' own training and probable inclinations it is equally likely that he could not ignore important philosophical concerns. In Du Bois' rendition, because of the development of Crummell's consciousness, his soul, Crummell was a prophet, whether we see him in the context of the seekers of truth and knowledge in the centuries before the Common Era when such seekers, philosophers, *were* prophets, or, if we prefer, after the likeness of some of the great leaders of world religions. Both pursued a united consciousness, whether one represents that consciousness as God or as Spirit, through a process of *becoming* in and for itself and in and for its other, and, particularly, through engaging, rather than withdrawing from, life.

Du Bois' discussions of work in his presentation on Crummell's life might have reflected a personal investment in ideas that we relate to the Protestant work ethic. As Wilson Moses has written,

> A Calvinistic celebration of work and restraint was in evidence when Du Bois called for "work, continuous and intensive; work, although it be menial and poorly rewarded; work though done in travail of soul and sweat and brow, must be so impressed upon Negro children as the road to salvation that a child would feel it a greater disgrace to be idle than to do the humblest labor."

Moses added, "the work ethic, what Cotton Mather called a Christian's 'calling,' remained central to Du Bois's religious spirit."[51] Although it is possible that "salvation" in the Du Bois quote relates to a religious experience of deliverance, this soul is also saved through the developing education of consciousness, which takes place in the process of working. Work served very different (somewhat opposing) purposes for colonial New England Calvinists and classical philosophers. For the former, work was necessary for controlling one's (natural) darker side—"passions" and impulses, for example. Unlike Calvinists, philosophers assumed that man was not inherently bad but essentially good, and work nurtured that goodness.[52] It is for this reason that work is so central to Du Bois' entire discussion, not just the chapter on Crummell.

Another prayer that Du Bois wrote to deliver at an Atlanta University religious service also highlights his philosophical concerns with work.

> God teach us to work. Herein alone do we approach our Creator when we stretch our arms with toil, and strain with eye and ear and brain to catch the thought and do the deed and create the things that make life worth living. Let us quickly learn in our youth, O Father, that in the very doing, the honest humbled determined striving, lies the realness of things, the great glory of life. Of all things there is fear and fading—beauty pales and hope disappoints; but blessed is the worker—his are the kingdoms of earth—Amen.[53]

Without a doubt, Du Bois' words reflect well-known Calvinist or Protestant notions about work, but they also reflect aspects of the traditional philosophic journey of finding the meaning of one's life, the journey to self-knowledge. Working, which allows one "to catch the thought and do the deed and create the things that make life worth living," is one central component of a good, purposeful life, a philosophic life. It is evidence of striving and the path to the *real* ("essence"), as Du Bois noted in the remark.[54] And most important and ironic, for Du Bois, it also leads to the "kingdoms of earth"(!). Through work, Consciousness becomes, in Hegel's words and as already noted, "conscious of itself as its own world, and of the world as itself" and is, thus, (united) Spirit (*PS* §438).

When Hegel characterized work as a "formative activity" and the foundation and source of life, he was not talking about the kind of mind-wasting, numbing work that most of the black residents of Dougherty County had no choice but to do, or the compromise work that the artists, professionals, and craftspeople described in Du Bois' first chapter settled for. Hegel was referring to the kind of work that allowed one to become "conscious of what he truly is." To be sure, Hegel saw work as controlling impulse or desire, which was later an apparent obsession of people characterized as turn-of-the-century "uplifters." Hegel wrote, "[w]ork . . . is desire held in check, fleetingness staved off." But even more important, Hegel insisted that "work forms and shapes the thing" (*PS* §§195–96).

Throughout *The Souls of Black Folk*, the purpose of work was not merely to develop discipline, and certainly not to accumulate capital or even to eat (the immediate, determinate, and material objectives of labor), but to discover one's self (self-consciousness), to realize the meaning of a life (reason), to arrive at true being (spirit). Du Bois could not have ignored the particular (unique) details of Crummell's life story: it was without a doubt a Christian's journey, and, consequently, the study easily took the literary form of allegory. But Du Bois, the philosopher-intellectual, was, himself, a phenomenological observer who saw Crummell's life not only as a spiritual journey in which a Christian constantly searched for evidence of God's presence, but also as a spiritual journey like that which Hegel characterized as consciousness's seeking its wholeness of being. And in this context, too, Crummell's life story provides a perfect example.

READING *SOULS*

WITH *PHENOMENOLOGY*

A Preface to Chapter 5

Du Bois' rendering of Crummell's life story not only allowed him to pay tribute to someone who was obviously a friend but also provided a useful vehicle for illustrating the journey of an individual soul to spirit. Crummell's life was especially ideal, however, because Hegel's example of the "unhappy consciousness" involved a priest (a religious self-consciousness) engaged in a struggle with God.[1] Although suggestions of such a journey in the lives of other individuals are evident from the start of Du Bois' book, a complete Hegelian example requires that we see the *individual* process in its entirety, which Crummell's life story accomplished. Given, however, that *Phenomenology* is about *groups* and about their relationship to World Soul, even more evidence is necessary for the comparison between *Souls* and *Phenomenology* to hold up.[2]

Although it is widely accepted that some of Du Bois' published work reflects the influence of Hegelian idealism, the debate over the extent to which any of this work was influenced by *Phenomenology* remains unsettled. Most recently, Robert Gooding-Williams wrote: "I do wish emphatically to reject the much stronger thesis that the Hegel-echoing features of Du Bois's concepts and language belong to a narrative that palpably parallels the narrative of a well-defined stretch of the *Phenomenology*."[3]

"Proving" an exclusive relationship is not the purpose of this brief exploration. Even where the similarities between the two texts are strong, intellectual thought at any particular point in time usually derives from a line of thinking and a series of thinkers representing a span of time. That is to say that Hegel's *Phenomenology* bears the influence of Fichte, Schelling, and others, most of whom were partly indebted to Kant. Moreover, philosophers can trace lines of reasoning in all of these works all the way back to the classical philosophers.[4] The goal here, however, is simply to show that *The Souls of Black Folk* has a closer and more complete relationship to *Phenomenology* than has previously been demonstrated. The point is *not* that it is the only influence.

Du Bois was not deterred by the fact that Hegel did not consider the role of black folk in Soul's/Consciousness's journey toward self-determination/freedom and Spirit's quest for knowledge in his philosophy. The relative absence of black people in Hegel's studies likely created a purpose rather than an obstacle for Du Bois. Subsequently published literature—scholarly and popular—that characterized black people as *tertium quid* was not daunting, either. Instead, Du Bois simply went to work. His history of the *striving* of the souls of black folk established their *humanity* and their rightful placement in the narrative of World Soul's journey to freedom and to knowledge.

It is easy to miss the parallels between *Souls* and *Phenomenology* for a number of reasons. First, Du Bois was writing to a very diverse audience; the text had to hold relevance for all of them (or as many as possible). Second, Du Bois was more than a philosopher: he was a historian, sociologist, political economist, and creative writer, at least, and carrying out the methods and objectives of these diverse areas easily obscured some of the philosophical revelations. Third, because Du Bois' chapters are not named for the aspects of consciousness discussed in them as Hegel's chapters are, even the sometimes-striking parallels in content and structure can recede into the background of the more obvious history and sociology. And finally, and perhaps related to all of the above, rather obvious historical reference points (e.g., Du Bois' appropriation of Revolutionary Era rhetoric) scattered throughout the text also have the potential to lead readers astray. Despite all these potential diversions, explicit Hegelian parallels are clear across the book. Looking directly at Du Bois' first nine chapters as Hegelian in structure and content provides a useful introduction to his final four chapters, which have no direct parallel in Hegel's study. Thus, the first nine chapters in *Souls* also give the final four chapters new significance.

The first section of Du Bois' study, in which these black folk who were finally legally free and attempting to make sense of a world that was simultaneously familiar and unfamiliar, replicates important parts of Hegel's first chapter, "Consciousness." Du Bois' first three chapters, in fact, should be compared to the content of Hegel's three subsections of "Consciousness": "Sense-Certainty," "Perception," and "Force and the Understanding."

In the first chapter of *Souls* ("Of Our Spiritual Strivings") Du Bois described "[t]he first decade [after emancipation as] merely a prolongation of the vain search for freedom," which continued to elude the former slaves. They pursued suffrage and education, but "the Canaan was always dim and far away." These first steps toward education did not get the freedpeople to their promised land, but there was "dawning self-consciousness, self-realization, self-respect" and "a dim feeling that, to attain [their] place in the world, [they] must be [themselves] and not another." In "Of Our Spiritual Strivings," the former slaves did not reach consciousness fully—things remained "dim"—there was only sense-certainty, but this was only the beginning of conscious's development to reason. In "Of the Dawn of Freedom," which parallels Hegel's second subsection of consciousness—"Perception: or the Thing and Deception"—in which "the Thing," freedom, was symbolized by the Freedmen's Bureau, and the "Deception" was the bureau's dissolution, the freedpeople sank to a state of peonage and servility, and "a figure veiled and bowed" sat at a metaphorical crossroad ("in the King's Highways"). Du Bois concluded: "Three centuries' thought has been the raising and unveiling of that bowed human heart, and now behold a century new for *the duty* and *the deed*" (emphasis added). Sense-certainty that has developed into perception makes it possible for an "unconditioned universal" to appear. Hegel described it as a "one-sided extreme of *being-for-self*." It appears to be a true consciousness, but, as Hegel noted, "the object has returned into itself from its relation to an other and has thus become Notion *in principle*; but consciousness is not yet *for itself* the Notion, and consequently does not recognize itself in that reflected object" (*PS* §132). Hegel continued, "this reduction of the diversity to a pure *being-for-self*, is nothing other than the medium itself, and this is the *independence* of the different 'matters'" (*PS* §136).

This medium, which reduced the diversity (of opinions, thoughts, and ideas) to a universal being-for-self, is, in Du Bois' text, none other than Booker T. Washington (Du Bois' chapter 3). And because, in this case, consciousness is not yet "True" and is merely apprehending itself (rather than realizing itself; its self is still object), "*we* must step into its place and be the Notion which develops and fills out what is contained in the result" (*PS* §133). Although we may, indeed, become "the Notion," in the chapter "Of Mr. Booker T. Washington and Others," the "we," the phenomenological observer, is Du Bois, who becomes the Understanding which preserves "the two moments" (the difference in thought between Washington and others) that have to be reconciled by "Force" or "movement" to true (self-) consciousness (*PS* §136). In a particularly transparent adaptation of Hegel's discussion of "Force(s)," and probably alluding, again, to Washington, Du Bois observed, perhaps snidely, "[i]t is as though Nature must needs make men narrow in order to give them force."[5] Du Bois' discussion ends as Hegel's ends, by introducing the "*universal difference*" that is "expressed in the *law* [the supersensible world], which is the *stable* image of unstable appearance" and inherent opposition (*PS* §149). Du Bois challenged the appearance of stability that Washington's influence encouraged, urging opposition to any injustice or limitation in rights or opportunities: "By every civilized and peaceful method we must strive for the rights which the world accords to men." Doing anything less would have left the question of black humanity and its place in World Soul's striving unanswered.

The middle chapters of *The Souls of Black Folk* have the unmistakable stamp of the then-new sociological methods (along with new developments in anthropology). Dividing them in a particular way, however, transforms them into representations of Hegel's discussions of "Self-Consciousness," "Reason," and "Spirit." Hegel's discussion of "Self-Consciousness," for example, finds parallels in Du Bois' "Of the Meaning of Progress," where nearly all the personalities who appear are involved in an unmistakable "Lordship and Bondage" type of struggle. And in the details of the lives of nearly all the black folks whose experience he examined, stoicism, skepticism, and unhappy consciousness are impossible to miss.

"Of the Meaning of Progress" is, however, written in two parts of a different sort. The first part details Du Bois' summers as a teacher in western Tennessee while he was an undergraduate at Fisk, and the second part relates to his return fifteen years later. The first part ends with a direct observation of there not yet being a collective consciousness there, only individual consciousnesses.

> I have called my tiny community a world, and so its isolation made it; and yet there was among us but a half-awakened common consciousness, sprung from common joy and grief, at burial, birth, or wedding; from a common hardship in poverty, poor land, and low wages; and, above all, from the sight of the Veil that hung between us and Opportunity. All this caused us to think some thoughts together; but these, when ripe for speech, were spoken in various languages.

These diverse languages—these separate consciousnesses—could eventually be joined into one collective consciousness. But when Du Bois returned to Wilson County fifteen years later, there was mostly debt, anger, and poverty and, correspondingly, stoicism, skepticism, and unhappy consciousness. Some people had died, far too young. Others had left. Most continued to strive, but many among them were still certain that the white folks would, by hook or by crook, eventually get all they had.

As bad as the circumstances were, there were, however, glimmers of hope. Among them were the Burkes. "The Burkes held a hundred acres, but they were still in debt. Indeed, the gaunt father who toiled night and day would scarcely be happy out of debt, being so used to it." In the Hegelian construct, Mr. Burke had accomplished something very important. He (and some of the other individuals in the chapter) symbolized consciousness as a "completely developed single individual, or the single individual that is an *actual* consciousness, as the *negative* of itself, viz. as the *objective* extreme; in other words, it has successfully struggled to divest itself of its being-for-self and has turned into a [mere] being" (*PS* §231). Hegel explained in detail:

> Through these moments of surrender, first of its right to decide for itself, then of its property and enjoyment, and finally through the positive moment of practicing what it does not understand, it truly and completely deprives itself of the consciousness of inner and outer freedom, of the actuality in which consciousness exists *for itself*. It has the certainty of having truly divested itself of its "*I*," and of having turned its immediate self-consciousness into a *Thing*, into an *objective* existence. Only through this *actual* sacrifice could it demonstrate this self-renunciation. For only therein does the *deception* vanish. (*PS* §229)

For Mr. Burke and many others,

> *for itself*, action and its own actual doing remain pitiable, its enjoyment remains pain, and the overcoming of these in a positive sense remains a *beyond*. But in this object, in which it finds that its own action and being, as being that of this *particular* consciousness, are being and action *in themselves*, there has arisen for consciousness the idea of *Reason*, of the certainty that, in its particular individuality, it has being absolutely *in itself*, or is all reality. (*PS* §230)

This "freedom of self-consciousness" suggests a promising answer after all to Du Bois' wondering whether "all this life and love and strife and failure" was "the twilight of nightfall or the flush of some faint-dawning day." The evidence unfolds in his "middle" chapters.

Hegel's "Reason" chapter, "The Certainty and Truth of Reason," is divided into three substantial subsections: "Observing Reason," "The actualization of rational self-consciousness through its own activity," and "Individuality which takes itself to be real in and for itself." These three topics, although in bits and pieces, are also among the subjects of Du Bois' next three chapters, where we find self-consciousness in the world. In "Of the

Meaning of Progress," consciousness (Mr. Burke, Josie and her family, and others) "did not understand the world; it [they] desired it and worked on it, withdrew from it into itself [themselves] and abolished it as an existence on its own account, and its own self *qua* consciousness." In "Reason," however, self-consciousness is very interested in the world, "for the *existence* of the world becomes for self-consciousness its own *truth* and *presence*; it is certain of experiencing only itself therein" (*PS* §232).

Du Bois' "Of the Wings of Atalanta" includes some aspects of Hegel's "Observing Reason" in which consciousness, now in the world, struggles to determine the essence of things (rather than of itself); reduces "observation and experience" to truth, though these observations are mere perceptions; seeks "laws" in very self-interested ways; and reduces organic existence to abstractions and the inorganic environment, which is constantly changing, into something fixed. Self-consciousness has clearly missed the mark here, but the point is that it is still striving. Although Du Bois' Hegelian parallels here are less complete than they are in other chapters, his lament that black folk have adopted the ways of the world (presumably based on experience and observation) and made "the Gospel of Pay" their truth, too, at least suggests the trajectory of Hegel's discussion.

Hegel's "The actualization of rational self-consciousness through its own activity" describes three "universal forms" that appear in the process of actualization. The first is "pleasure and necessity," in which consciousness pursues its own happiness, indulging "to the full the pure individuality in which it appears." This relationship with its other is "a *dead* actuality" (it is defined by "moments" and has no real content) and is thus "the poorest form of self-realizing Spirit." It will remain vacuous until it is more than being-for-itself and being-in-itself and recognizes its relationship to its opposite and unites with it (the *necessity*) by engaging life, or as Hegel put it, by "[taking] hold of life and [possessing] it." The second of the three universal forms is defined by the law of the heart (*PS* §361–67). Consciousness confronts this law in the world, where there is great suffering because of the conflict between "individuality and its truth." Consciousness works to eliminate this other necessity (the law in the world) and to promote "the welfare of mankind" (its pleasure is now "the universal pleasure of all hearts"). Others, however, find this is not "the law of *their* hearts"; it is, rather, little more than conceit or a kind of arrogance. And the "public order" that appears to emerge in this case is rather a "universal state of war, in which each wrests what he can for himself" (*PS* §§370, 373, 379). Ultimately, consciousness sacrifices this individuality and creates a new consciousness, Hegel's third and final form, virtue.[6]

In "Of the Training of Black Men," Du Bois' "three streams of thinking" that "have flowed down to our day" since the first slave ships landed in Virginia are not quite the three "universal forms" that Hegel described, but they bear some similarities. The first for Du Bois was "the multiplying of human wants in culture-lands [that called] for the world-wide coöperation of men in satisfying them" (Hegel's "pleasure and necessity"). Du Bois described this as "a new human unity" that drew men of all colors closer together, but fulfilling *this* "pleasure and necessity" depended on trickery, "force and dominion" (Hegel's "dead actuality"). Du Bois' second stream relays the conflict between the competing laws that Hegel described. The law in the world denied that these (black) beings were human and built an environment around them that made it nearly impossible for them "even [to] think of breaking through." The law of the heart was expressed in the thought that came from those walled-in souls: "'Liberty, Freedom, Opportunity—vouchsafe to us, O boastful World, the chance of living men!'"

In Hegel's third universal form, "The actualization of rational self-consciousness through its own activity," self-consciousness finds "the Thing to be like itself, and itself to be like a Thing, i.e. it is aware that it is *in itself* the objectively real world." With that understanding, self-consciousness becomes a real united "self-consciousness that is recognized and acknowledged," not just an "outer existence" but an "absolute spiritual *unity* of the essence of individuals in their independent *actual existence*." Du Bois understood, as Hegel wrote, that this can only happen "in the life of a people or nation," or collectively. The work (activity) of the "separate independent beings" is to give up their particularity for the "universal Substance as their soul and essence." Those individuals working in this way turn themselves into a thing in the process and in return receive back their "own self." The best examples of these souls (this self-consciousness) in the social world are Du Bois' "Negro college-bred men," whom he maintained had no parallel in their "broader spirit of helpfulness, . . . deeper devotion to their life-work, or . . . consecrated determination to succeed in the face of bitter difficulties." These men, through their work (their own activity), represent virtue. For this self-consciousness, rather than the "resistance from an actual world opposed to it," its "aim and object are only this expressing of itself" (*PS* §§347, 349–51, 359).[7]

Du Bois' final chapter related to Reason is "Of the Black Belt." Based primarily on life in Dougherty County, Georgia, with its "ten thousand Negroes and two thousand whites," Du Bois characterized the region as the "forlorn and forsaken" heart of the former "Cotton Kingdom—the shadow of a marvelous dream." Upon his arrival there, he launched himself on a search for its king, but he only found men, women, and families of workers who rarely managed to earn any money and farmers who had bought and paid for land and lost it through thievery. It is difficult to imagine "Of the Black Belt," as hopeless as it seems, as a possible illustration of Hegel's "Individuality which takes itself to be real in and for itself," but it could be just that.

In Hegel's final section on Reason, "self-consciousness holds fast to the simple unity of [objective] being and the self, a unity ["being for *itself*"] which is its *genus*." In this state, consciousness casts off its opposition, ignores its other, and concerns itself only "with *itself*" (*PS* §§394–396). This consciousness has successfully negotiated "the matter at hand" and resolved the conflicts between, on one hand, its desire, ability, and work, and, on the other hand, the actual circumstances in which it is all embedded. Consciousness now knows that its work produces no value for itself ("the work . . . exists for other individualities"), and so to unite its "doing and being," this consciousness focuses on and makes *work* the end, preserving "its Notion and its certainty as what objectively exists and [enduring] in face of the experience of the *contingency* of action." It "now acquires its significance through self-consciousness and through it alone" (*PS* §§405, 409, 410). Thus, even though the black Dougherty County residents rarely succeeded in a material sense, they know that "something was taken in hand and done" (*PS* §413). Having made *work* "its [their] own affair," they point to what they actually accomplished. Their land and labor were routinely stolen, but what mattered even more for them is that they *worked, bought* a farm, *raised* a crop, and/or *leased* a tract. Their "*own* action and . . . *own* effort" becomes the new "matter in hand," and thus "*this particular* consciousness knows it to be its own individual reality and the reality of all" (*PS* §§417, 418). This consciousness is aware of the laws of reason and what is ethical, but it also knows that challenging the law leads nowhere and only destabilizes "the ethical consciousness." And so this consciousness remains itself "within the ethical substance . . . the *essence* of self-consciousness." And "this pure unity of the *I* and *being*, of being *for itself* and being *in itself*, is determined as the *in-itself* or as *being*, and the consciousness of Reason *finds* itself" (*PS* §§432, 437, 438).

Du Bois provided numerous illustrations to support his points. When he asked one tenant farmer what he paid in rent, the farmer responded that he did not know. When the man asked his colleague, the response was "all we make." Another, when asked whether he owned the land he farmed, replied "only this house." His wife added that they had previously bought and paid for 700 acres of land but were cheated out of it. The husband subsequently worked for the owner of the land for thirty-seven days and got paid "in cardboard checks" that were never honored. Finally, the sheriff seized the couple's work animals, crop, and household goods. When Du Bois reminded the man that "furniture is exempt from seizure by law," the farmer replied, matter of factly, "'Well, he took it just the same.'"

The next three chapters of *Souls* are especially transparent illustrations of Hegel's lengthy discussion of "Spirit." "The Quest of the Golden Fleece" parallels Hegel's "The *true* Spirit: The ethical order." "Of the Sons of Master and Man" represents Hegel's "Self-alienated Spirit: Culture." And "Of the Faith of the Fathers" is Hegel's "Spirit that is certain of itself: Morality," where we see the fulfillment of Hegel's announcement in his chapter on Spirit that "Reason [becomes] Spirit, when its certainty of being all reality has been raised to truth, and it is conscious of itself as its own world, and of the world as itself" (*PS* §438).

"The Quest of the Golden Fleece" provides extensive empirical detail about life for black folk in the cotton belt, but by continuing the examination of life in Dougherty County, the chapter also illustrates what Hegel detailed in "The True Spirit: The Ethical Order." Hegel's chapter is about human and divine law and the discord between them and between individual action and essence/substance. In Hegel's discussion of the ethical world, spirit is the nation, and the citizens of that nation represent consciousness. Consciousness is reflected in the law, which, along with customs, represents universality. As that universality manifests in an "individuality," it is self-certainty, or the government. The general acceptance of these aspects becomes the manifestation of "its truth." It appears to be "a *concrete existence* . . . that has freely issued forth" (*PS* §§447–48). The cotton belt district that Du Bois described was his symbolic "nation" with its laws, its citizens, and its customs, all which seem to crush the life out of its poor black residents. In Hegel's words, "the ethical world [the world of laws] showed its fate and its truth to be the Spirit that had merely passed away in it, the *individual self*" (or the government as a "*legal person*") (*PS* §596). In this world of laws and customs, these black residents became an "absolute unessentiality" and "self-estranged . . . in a world of 'culture.'"[8]

Du Bois explored this isolated spirit (Hegel's "Self-Alienated Spirit: Culture") in "Of the Sons and Master of Man," expanding it out from Dougherty County. In Hegel's chapter, spirit has to navigate "this world," a world of civilization and culture from which it (spirit) is alienated, and the "other-world," which is actually the essential. Du Bois maintained that "[w]hatever we may say of the results of such contact in the past [between the "world of civilization" and the "other world"], it certainly forms a chapter in human action not pleasant to look back upon." He acknowledged that the "[w]ar, murder, slavery, extermination, and debauchery" that resulted from this contact could easily be explained away as strength over weakness, civilization over heathenism, good over bad, and superior over inferior, but none of these was an adequate explanation. In totality, the discussion of the relationship between and among men showed that the development of "civilization" and "culture," as it happened in "this world," was no substitute for the development of mind/soul.[9]

"Of the Faith of the Fathers," which incorporates a discussion of the antislavery movement, the Civil War, and its aftermath, replicates parts of Hegel's "Spirit Certain of Itself: Morality," which developed around the history of the Enlightenment and the French Revolution and "the terror" that followed it. Although my detailed discussion of Du Bois' chapter on religion unfolds below in chapter 5, it is useful to point out here that morality as the negative (some would say the opposite or antithesis) of the ethical world of laws and customs, which both Hegel and Du Bois discussed earlier, holds a significant place in Du Bois' discussion. "Morality" in this context is not the more modern, value-laden judgments of people's perceptions of "right" and "wrong." Rather, morality here is the execution of the "Will" and self-determination. Du Bois' chapter on religion illustrates Hegel's "The moral view of the world," in which the individual consciousness is finally no longer "alienated from its own 'concept' in the worlds of culture [and] faith" but has "achieved unity with its own inherent universality."[10] It was through religion that consciousness achieved this unity or Hegel's "concrete."

Hegel's discussion of morality, however, includes other important detail that will matter in explaining Du Bois' final chapters. It relates to the discussion of "the harmony of morality and nature," which at first eludes consciousness because it is focused on immediate knowledge. Because this consciousness is totally consumed with itself, its otherness, self-consciousness, is left free to focus on itself as well. "The freer self-consciousness becomes, the freer also is the negative object of its consciousness," which becomes "a complete world within itself." In that world, "the absoluteness of morality and the absoluteness of Nature" are completely discordant. Moral consciousness, whose essence is duty, "learns from experience that Nature is not concerned" with their unity, which leaves the moral consciousness with *pure duty* (rather than self-realization) as its object. Because moral consciousness cannot be happy with the mere appearance of self-realization, this actualization becomes something that is "*postulated*" even though it is "a demand of Reason" (*PS* §§599–602).[11]

The prospect that this unity/harmony "cannot be attained, but is to be thought of merely as an *absolute* task, i.e. one which simply remains a task," can only lead to frustration because of the inherent contradictions: there is a task "which is to remain a task and yet ought to be fulfilled," and, equally contradictory, there is the idea "of a morality which is no longer to be [a moral] *consciousness*, i.e. not actual." A "perfected morality" that cannot be fulfilled raises questions about the "essence of morality," and "pure duty" is a poor ("unreal") substitute. And so we are left with two postulates: "the harmony of morality and objective Nature, the final purpose of the *world*" (or "*implicit* being") and "the harmony of morality and the sensuous will, the final purpose of *self-consciousness* as such" (or "*being-for-self*"). Each is "the *other* of the *other*" (*PS* §603, 604).

Du Bois' "Forethought" introduced us to all of his chapters, separating them into two distinct groups. The first eight chapters, comprising the first group, he further subdivided into three smaller sections (which, again, suggest the movement of the souls of black folk from Consciousness to Self-Consciousness to Reason). He characterized the first two chapters as about emancipation; then there was a chapter on leadership (Booker T. Washington) standing alone. He then coupled two chapters focused on "the two worlds within and without the Veil" to two more chapters of "deeper detail" on those worlds. Then Du Bois offered some guidance for our movement from this group of chapters to the second group (the next five chapters): "Leaving, then, the white world, I have stepped within the Veil, raising it that you may view faintly its deeper recesses,—the meaning of its religion, the passion of its human sorrow, and the struggle of its greater souls." Du Bois' division of these chapters in this way is, to say the least, provocative. Situating his characterization of them as white and black worlds within the Hegelian construct provides an important new way of thinking about the three most recognized concepts of Du Bois' book—the veil, the color line, and double consciousness—and it gives greater significance to the final chapters of the book.

In *Phenomenology*, in order for Consciousness to reach Self-Consciousness, two extremes had to be reconciled—the "pure inner world" and "the inner being gazing into this pure inner world." The two are separated by a middle term that Hegel called a "curtain," which he characterized as a form of "appearances" that has to be "drawn away" so that Consciousness can see that it is only gazing at itself in "different moments." Once Consciousness understands that these two worlds coincide, the "middle term" (of appearances) "vanishes," and we see Self-Consciousness (*PS* §165). Du Bois' characterization of his first eight chapters as being about the white world and the next five as about the black world indicates (from the very first pages of the book) that the form of appearances—Hegel's "curtain"—is keeping white America from seeing that when it looks at black America, it is only seeing itself at a different "moment."[12] And so, just as Hegel's "curtain" had to be "drawn away" to reveal what was behind it, Du Bois had to "raise" the veil—the middle term "of appearances"—that stood between *America's* divided (double) consciousness.

When Du Bois raised his veil—of color, race, the color line—to show us what was behind it, there was, literally, a study of black religion ("the meaning of its religion"), a story about the death of a child ("the passion of its human sorrow"), and stories about the growth, development, and demise of John Jones and Alexander Crummell's long but ultimately triumphant wilderness experience ("the struggle of its greater souls"). They are illustrations of consciousness's (soul's) increasing development of self-knowledge or the philosophy of spirit. Recall that in Hegel's construct, as consciousness (Du Bois' white world) remained concerned only with itself, self-consciousness, "the negative object of its consciousness" (Du Bois' black world), became "a complete world within itself." And as its own world, it developed from consciousness (Du Bois' firstborn represents Hegel's perception and sense-certainty or early stages of Consciousness) to self-consciousness and having reason (the story of John Jones) to being reason and thus spirit (the story of Alexander Crummell). At least it certainly seems that Crummell got past "pure duty" to self-realization. We have to assume that, as was the case for Hegel, religion served as the necessary movement or "force" that allowed this accomplishment. In Du Bois' chapter, it also provided the necessary bridge between the material (phenomenal) and the spiritual (noumenal) for the souls of black folk.[13] And Du Bois' placing his religion chapter between these two parts (rather than at the end of the volume as Hegel did) even suggests that religion might also provide the bridge between American consciousness and self-consciousness and, therefore, the white and black worlds.

But finally, after Du Bois introduced and described the two groups of chapters, he brought up the last chapter on the Sorrow Songs: "All this I have ended with a tale twice told but seldom written." Explicitly separating this chapter from the other two parts suggests some special significance. Having placed a few measures of music from a "sorrow song" at the beginning of each chapter did more than introduce us to this important aspect of black culture, it presaged a conclusion that uses the songs in a much more radical way—to take us through to the culmination of the "science of philosophy" (*Wissenschaft*) in Absolute Knowledge.

Music was a logical vehicle for this demonstration. Not only was this medium important in black American culture, but music can keep us anchored to ideas related to the larger discussion of World Soul. For much of human history, nature was the defining force in man's life, and in this natural world there existed "true harmony." Music, a form of speech or a language to some people, not only provided an accessible way to illustrate that harmony metaphorically, but phenomenologically and metaphysically it also represented "the speech of nature and the speech of the spirits." Eventually, the awareness of this harmony and unity was lost as "the reasoning of man asserted its independence, . . . and man became aware of and bound by his individuality." But "the truest form of music, [that which] comes closest to the original [in nature]" is presumed, still, to reflect this "harmony and unity." It is "a precision and order [that is] characteristic of the universe," and I believe that we can demonstrate it in "the mathematical relationships" within the songs of *Souls*.[14]

There was a good reason for Du Bois' not including the Sorrow Songs chapter in his introduction to the two groups of chapters (life beyond and within the veil). I propose that in Du Bois' chapter on the songs, this consciousness (the souls of black folk) accomplished something that Hegel's final chapter did not. In the chapter on the songs, the unity of absolute morality and absolute nature no longer remained "an absolute task"— something "postulated" but "not yet actual." In my final chapter, not only is this harmony actual/real, but it is evidence of Absolute Knowledge. Although the religion and art of the folk provided a route to it for both Hegel and Du Bois, only Du Bois actually arrived there.

THE RELIGION

AND SONGS OF *SOULS*

What kind of knowledge is it that considers what continues
to exist outside and independently of all relations, but which
alone is really essential to the world, the true content of its
phenomena, that which is subject to no change, and is therefore known with equal truth for all time, in a word the Ideas
that are the immediate and adequate objectivity of the thing-
in-itself, of the will? It is art, the work of genius. It represents
the eternal Ideas apprehended through pure contemplation, the essential and abiding element in all the phenomena
of the world. According to the material in which it repeats,
it is sculpture, painting, poetry or music. Its only source is
knowledge of the Ideas; its sole aim is communication of this
knowledge. —Schopenhauer[1]

Hegel's attention to religion created as much debate about
his religiosity as there has been about Du Bois'. Around the mid-nineteenth
century, James Stirling wrote that "the secret of Hegel" was that he was a
Christian. More recently, however, philosopher Robert C. Solomon concluded that Hegel was "not the great abstract thinker of Christianity but
rather the precursor of atheistic humanism in German philosophy." Solomon maintained that "Hegel used religion and religious vocabulary as his
instruments, as if the last logical consequence to be drawn from Christian
doctrine is humanism, and the final meaning to be given to theological
terminology is a meaning which refers strictly and exclusively to man's
conception of himself." Hegel's early writings more than suggest that he
(at least then) held little regard for religious dogma. But, as Solomon concluded, and as Hegel's subsequently toned-down writing on religion certainly suggests, "he recognized its social power." For Hegel, and for Du Bois,
too, it seems, religion generally (as opposed to a particular orthodoxy,) was,
as Solomon continued,

a striving for the infinite . . . the "genuine infinite" of total comprehension and participation in the world. . . . Religion is mankind's impulse to a better life. It is not the lust for "otherworldly" after-life of the Christian Heaven but the "this worldly" aspiration of great artists, philosophers, statesmen, and truly religious people. Anticipating Nietzsche, Hegel tells us that religion is a "Reconciling Yea" to the world, not an escape from it.[2]

Hegel's linking philosophy to experience (life in the world) was undoubtedly important. But in addition to demonstrating that philosophy/knowledge was conditioned by historical and social circumstances, Hegel also posited that beyond perceptual knowledge in and of the world and everyday life in general there existed a higher level of knowing that was "eternal." For one important earlier metaphysician (Leibniz), this eternal was an all-knowing God. In Hegelian idealism, however, even though he provided no illustration of it, "finite creatures" (humans) are capable of realizing/manifesting this eternal (absolute) knowledge.

The discussion of the development of this knowledge ultimately comes to focus on the art and religion of the folk. Hegel's discussion of religion, his penultimate step to Absolute Knowledge, is divided into three parts that Hegel scholars regularly relate to consciousness, self-consciousness, and reason and spirit. They are "Natural Religion," "Religion in the Form of Art," and "The Revealed Religion."[3] A brief examination of them might further illuminate aspects of Du Bois' discussions in "Of the Faith of the Fathers" and "Of the Sorrow Songs."

Hegel's discussion of "natural religion" begins with a focus, literally, on nature—plants, animals, and other "natural" manifestations of spirit/god. But eventually, Spirit "appears as an *artificer* [Hegel's taskmaster] and . . . produces itself as object" (*PS* §691). We would recognize some of these objects as obelisks, pyramids, and statues. While the "in-itself" of the object and the self-consciousness (the "of itself") of the artificer-spirit are both apparent, they are separate. But, as Solomon points out, creating "its sacred images through art instead of simply finding them growing and running around in the woods," makes it easier to realize eventually "that one is oneself sacred, not only as object or object-maker but, more essentially, as subject." Until that happened, Hegel characterized this "as art" (that was not also "in art") as inferior and abstract, merely "an *object* for devotion or appreciation" and nothing more because, as Solomon put it, "[a] statue is always just a statue"; it resembles a person, but "it is not yet 'like himself.'"[4]

Art had always been an intricate part of ancient folk religions, but during the Enlightenment, art and religion separated. The separation caused Spirit to mourn its loss and to strive to recover the relationship. In the striving, Spirit transforms the "misfortune into *pathos* and pathos [becomes] the material for art" (not just its source), beginning a stage of Absolute Art.[5] Hegel described the process:

> The concrete existence of the pure Notion into which Spirit has fled from its body is an individual which Spirit selects to be the vessel of its sorrow. Spirit is present in this individual as his universal and as the power over him from which he suffers violence, as his 'pathos,' by giving himself over to which his self-consciousness loses its freedom. But that positive power of universality is subdued by the pure self of the individual, the negative power. This pure activity, conscious of its inalienable strength, wrestles with the shapeless essence. Becoming its master, it has made the 'pathos' into its material and given itself its content, and this unity emerges as a work, universal Spirit individualized and set before us. (*PS* §704)

Hegel's illustration of the process whereby this art evolves from Absolute Art to Absolute Being, in which consciousness comes to recognize its object as itself and its self as subject, ultimately depends on language (Hegel's "soul existing as soul," which others have translated as spirit meeting spirit).[6] His art forms are the hymn, the epic poem, the tragedy, and the comedy. These art forms not only represent the individual who created them (though the individual creator ultimately becomes unimportant) but "the Cult" (which may be read as the race, nation, or community). And as this art moves from thing-like to self-conscious art, it fulfills both practical work, Hegel's "The Living Work of Art," and transcendent work, or Hegel's "The Spiritual Work of Art."

In the living work, as already noted, art becomes the vessel of essence. Hegel's history of the transformation begins during the ancient period with the hymns. One might witness the overtaking/possession of the individual in the scenes of (what appear to be) "the meaningless stammer of Bacchic frenzy." In these frenzies, "specific character of the divine nature" becomes conscious of its universality as it "roams about as a crowd of frenzied females [and] the untamed revelry of Nature in self-conscious form." The minstrel, who is a member of this "pantheon" and the spirit that produces and is produced by it, actively works to transform the pantheon from a collection of individuals into a single collective entity. As a result of this process, "his 'pathos' is [no longer] the stupefying power of Nature but Mnemosyne [the goddess of memory and mother of the Muses], recollection and a gradually developed inwardness, *the remembrance of essence that formerly was directly present*" (emphasis added). At this point, the song becomes universal and more important than the minstrel or artist and now expresses "inner essence" rather than particular goings-on. Thus, "the 'pathos' that they now express is no longer personal, individual, or idiosyncratic" (*PS* §§723, 726–27, 729, 733).

During the classical period, it was through the epic poem that the poet worked to move the community from a group of individual self-conscious consciousnesses, or what Howard Kainz described as a "loose confederation of diverse spirits under one commander," closer to a single, self-conscious consciousness (a collective consciousness). Much of this work is done through the hero's narratives, but because the gods in the epic *need* the heroes in order to attain selfhood, they remain incomplete. The tragedy, however, makes the unity of the spirits possible because the content of the tragedy is not imagined but essential/real: the spectators can relate to the drama that is taking place on the stage. Equally important, the actors in the tragedy *know* "their rights and purposes," and speak them. They know that their power and will are not contingent (particularistic), "but the pathos of 'universal individuality.'" Throughout the drama, the chorus recognizes and articulates the struggle of individuals (especially the hero) against fate. But ultimately the hero in the tragedy is trapped between "'self-certainty and . . . objective essence,'" and the reality is that he is "doomed to destruction."[7]

Finally, the comedy/comic actor eliminates the fatalism of the tragedy by exposing all the usual rules of conduct as fraudulent. The comic makes fun of everybody—perhaps especially the gods and the government—and reveals the hypocrisy of all the proclamations, customs, and traditions that have been maintained in their names. With all the "masks" finally off, the conscious now understands that its fate is not to exist with no object (in the "great void of negation"); rather, its object is itself, and, thus, "the self is Absolute Being," itself as subject rather than substance.[8]

For the soul's complete development to Spirit, however, there has to occur a reconciliation of the finite self (Absolute Being) and the infinite Absolute. This reconciling occurs in Hegel's "Revealed Religion," where there is revelation (rather than redemption). The revelation is that "*All* men and women are incarnations of God." Absolute Being, an "immediate existence," vanishes, and "'the universal self-consciousness of the community' is born." Thus, in Hegel's "Revealed Religion," God is no longer alien (external; out there, somewhere): "God is Spirit and Spirit is us, nothing more."[9]

Despite two centuries of debate about Hegel's personal religious beliefs, a number of ideas are clear in *Phenomenology*. Among them, art is a form/expression of religion; one can witness the experience and development of individual and collective consciousness through art and religion; and art/religion can provide a path to Absolute Knowledge. In *The Souls of Black Folk*, and in nineteenth-century America, the art was that of the slave—Du Bois' "Sorrow Songs," the spirituals, in particular; it was the religion of that folk that provided the clearest illustration of Soul's journey to Spirit; and, perhaps, it was even the art and religion of the souls of black folk that provided evidence of Absolute Knowledge.

Part I: The Art and Religion of *Souls* and Hegel's "Experience of Consciousness"

> Music charms us, although its beauty only consists in the harmonics of numbers and in the reckoning of the beats or vibrations of sound-ing bodies, which meet at certain intervals, reckonings of which we are not conscious and which the soul nevertheless does make.
> —Gottfried Wilhelm Leibniz[10]

Although most scholars relate Du Bois' discussion of religion to the more obvious historical centrality of religion in black people's lives, "Of the Faith of the Fathers" is also part of an important philosophical discussion about the experience of consciousness and the philosophy of spirit. While Du Bois' chapter is a complete statement about the history of black religion in America, its total relevance in the context of Hegel's teleology is spread across several chapters and has to be pieced together. Still, suggesting from the beginning of his chapter on religion the whole process that the reader will ultimately witness, Du Bois immediately introduced "the Preacher, the Music, and the Frenzy." These three entities have special significance in the context of Hegel's experience of consciousness: they correspond to his minstrel/poet or Self-Consciousness, Absolute Art, and Absolute Being.

Du Bois' "preacher" recalls Hegel's "torchbearer" who emerges from the cult and becomes its leader. In *Phenomenology*, Hegel described this leader (the minstrel or poet) as "the smooth elaboration and fluent energy of all the participants. He is an inspired and living work of art that matches strength with its beauty; and on him is bestowed, as a reward for his strength, the decoration with which the statue was honoured, and the honour of being, in place of the god in stone, the highest bodily representation among his people of their essence" (*PS* §725). Du Bois described the black preacher similarly. In addition to his being "the most unique personality developed by the Negro on American soil," he was a "leader, a politician, an orator, a 'boss,' an intriguer, an idealist,—all these he is, and ever, too, the center of a group of men. . . . The combination of a certain adroitness with deep-seated earnestness, of tact with consummate ability, gave him preëminence, and helps him maintain it."

As was the case for Hegel, Du Bois' "frenzy" is more than the "meaningless stammer of Bacchic frenzy" but is rather part of the process through which "the artist has worked his way out of the initial enthusiasm, originating wholly from substance, into a [definite] shape" which is "his *own* existence," or Absolute Being, a "self-conscious soul." And Du Bois' Sorrow Songs represent Hegel's Absolute Art, in which "his [man's] *own* existence which, in all its stirrings and impulses, is permeated and accompanied by self-conscious soul; . . . the content is universal, for in this festival which honours man there vanishes the one-sidedness of the statues which contain only a national Spirit, a specific character of the divine nature." While some of the slave songs, like Hegel's early forms of art, reflect "the particular life, the demands, the needs, and customs of nation [the cult]," as Hegel continued, eventually the cult "is . . . no longer conscious . . . of its particularity but rather of having laid this aside, and is conscious of the universality of its human existence" (*PS* §726).

The foregoing description uses Hegel's "living work of art" to point out the literary and philosophical significance of Du Bois' early characterization of the preacher, the frenzy, and the music. But after introducing us to this trio, Du Bois went on to discuss "Negro religion as a development, through its gradual changes from the heathenism of the Gold Coast to the institutional Negro church of Chicago." He made it clear that *this* history (of religion and consciousness or Soul) is *America's* history: "the study of Negro religion is not only a vital part of the history of the Negro in America, but an interesting part of American history."

As one might, by now, expect, black American religion in Du Bois' description traveled the same path as Hegel's religion, beginning with the religion of "the *underworld.*" For Hegel, "It is the belief in the terrible, unknown night of Fate and in the Eumenides of the *departed spirit*: the former is pure negativity in the form of universality, the latter the same negativity in the form of individuality" (*PS* §674). Although Du Bois called what he described "natural religion," he actually blended Hegel's early "religion of the underworld" and "natural religion." In Du Bois' narrative, the black American's religion began in Africa where "[h]is religion was nature-worship, with profound belief in invisible surrounding influences, good and bad, and his worship was through incantation and sacrifice." The international slave trade relocated many of these Africans, but it did not immediately transform these practices. The master supplanted the chief, to be sure, and the plantation replaced the family/clan, but the priest and medicine man continued to supply other aspects of leadership, and

> the transplanted African [continued to live] in a world animate with gods and devils, elves and witches; full of strange influences,—of Good to be implored, of Evil to be propitiated. Slavery, then, was to him the dark triumph of Evil over him. All the hateful powers of the under-world were striving against him, and a spirit of revolt and revenge filled his heart. He called up all the resources of heathenism to aid,—exorcism and witchcraft, the mysterious Obi worship with its barbarous rites.

Eventually, however, the slaves submitted to Christianity, and their "exquisite native appreciation of the beautiful became an infinite capacity for dumb suffering. The Negro, losing the joy of this world, eagerly seized upon the offered conceptions of the next; the avenging Spirit of the Lord enjoining patience in this world, under sorrow and tribulation until the Great Day when He should lead His dark children home,—this became his comforting dream."

The slave's (new) religion, like Hegel's religion of the Middle Ages, was a fatalistic religion in that the believer must die in order to achieve unity with Spirit. As Du Bois noted, "all fatalistic faiths" can lead to that conclusion. But the American Revolution gave birth to abolitionism in the North and slave revolts in the South, and "for fifty years," Du Bois wrote, "Negro religion thus transformed itself and identified itself with the dream of Abolition." The abolition of slavery indeed "seemed to the freedman a literal Coming of the Lord." But with freedom came "the inevitable Age of Reaction" and, thus, what Hegel described as a "crisis of Spirit." The crisis for *both* Hegel and Du Bois related, as Du Bois said, to "*the soul-life of [the] nation*" (emphasis added). At its heart in nineteenth-century America was "the 'Negro Problem.'"[11]

Du Bois scholars have rarely seen any upside to this problem. But we should remember that there is consciousness present, which is very important. And being conscious of conscious (self-conscious) can be painful.[12]

But having self-consciousness (perhaps especially painful self-consciousness) is necessary to the eventual realization of spirit. Indeed, Du Bois' "double consciousness" and Hegel's "unhappy consciousness" are different names for the same state of consciousness. This painful self-consciousness is the necessary "bridge" that allows consciousness to connect to spirit and ultimately, one presumes, to reach Absolute Knowing. But consciousness has to reach Absolute Being before it can reach Absolute Knowing, and in order to illustrate Absolute Being, Du Bois had to invoke Hegel's chapter on "Spirit," which he did in naming "the Negro problem" and the difficult condition of "double consciousness."

Du Bois' "double consciousness" could easily have been a reference to the psychological diagnoses related to multiple personalities, which has become the basis of many discussions of his work.[13] But Du Bois' double consciousness was also, and especially important, the nineteenth-century American example of what Hegel described in "The world of self-alienated Spirit." Spirit suffers this alienation or confusion because it is caught up in an "ethical world" of laws and customs and business that contradict "the essence of the ethical," or divine law.[14]

For Hegel, it was the Enlightenment (during which religion and reason separated) that triggered this alienation, and for Du Bois it was slavery and the development of the color line. Before emancipation, the abolitionists in the North and the slave rebels in the South served as examples of those directly engaged in the battles of consciousnesses. The difficulty they endured resulted not only from the contradiction in the two sets of laws or ethics—slavery and race prejudice existing in a post-Revolutionary era of freedom and liberty—but also because any action taken by a member of either "alienated" group (slave or free) violated one law or the other, and, violating either the laws of the material or the spiritual world created extreme internal turmoil. In detail, Du Bois wrote:

> It is difficult to explain clearly the present critical stage of Negro religion. First, we must remember that living as the blacks do in close contact with a great modern nation, and sharing, although imperfectly, the soul-life of that nation, they must necessarily be affected more or less directly by all the religious and ethical forces that are to-day moving the United States. These questions and movements are, however, over-shadowed and dwarfed by the (to them) all-important question of their civil, political, and economic status. They must perpetually discuss the "Negro Problem,"—must live, move, and have their being in it, and interpret all else in its light or

darkness. . . . From the double life every American Negro must live, as a Negro and as an American, as swept on by the current of the nineteenth while yet struggling in the eddies of the fifteenth century,—from this must arise a painful self-consciousness, an almost morbid sense of personality and a moral hesitancy which is fatal to self-confidence. The worlds within and without the Veil of Color are changing, and changing rapidly, but not at the same rate, not in the same way; and this must produce a peculiar wrenching of the soul, a peculiar sense of doubt and bewilderment. Such a double life, with double thoughts, double duties, and double social classes, must give rise to double words and double ideals, and tempt the mind to pretence or to revolt, to hypocrisy or to radicalism.[15]

Viewing this problem as significantly more than a black problem, Du Bois described it as "*the writhing of the age* translated into black," in which the "false culture" of the day ("the Lie") triumphed (emphasis added). Just as the church leaders of the Renaissance Age turned black strength into weakness to justify the slave trade, giving life to the Lie, black churches of the nineteenth century often ignored the Lie and became "large social and business institutions catering to the desire for information and amusement of their members, warily avoiding unpleasant questions both within and without the black world, and preaching in effect if not in word: *Dum vivimus, vivamus* [while we live, let us live]." But, clearly, this was not living any more than the poor, black Dougherty County residents' Saturday trip to town was. For Du Bois' complete discussion of the reconciliation of the two consciousnesses in the context of religion, we must continue to navigate back and forth between the two chapters—on religion and songs—and examine his version of "religion in the form of art" in nineteenth-century America. It is important to note here that Du Bois ultimately discussed *three* types of songs, which have not yet been clearly distinguished one from another. Distinguishing them here not only reveals the movement of art as Hegel described it, from the particular to the universal, but demonstrates that Du Bois added one more important step.

The first work of art in Hegel's construct, "The Living Work of Art," is "abstract" and refers to "immediate" and "objective" art that is particularly individualistic. One can see both the in-itself and the of-itself of this art, but the two are not yet united. This art (like Hegel's statues and obelisks) is simply art. Du Bois' songs that fit this characterization are those that are personal, particular, and seem more like narrations about specific (personal) circumstances. The song of the ploughmen, for example, details "monotonous toil and exposure." The "bowed and bent old man" sang, "O Lord, keep me from sinking down." Coastal slaves insisted, "Michael, haul the boat ashore." Lines about the cold ("Winter'll soon be over") bespoke logical concerns for people regularly described (including by Du Bois) as "tropical." "The sudden wild thunderstorms of the South" became the voice of God ("My Lord called me . . . by the thunder"). There can be no mistaking the point of the old woman in the Sea Islands who began to sing "Nobody knows the trouble I've seen" upon learning that government officials had reversed their recently established policy to rent and sell confiscated and abandoned Sea Island land to the freedpeople who had worked it as slaves. And in the words, "my soul wants some thing that's new, that's new," we see what Du Bois described as "soul-hunger" and "restlessness." One can easily see the creativity and art in these songs; but one can also see examples of Hegel's art that is "objective" and "individualistic," generally reflecting "immediate" circumstances.

Importantly, however, Du Bois' nineteenth-century history of the experience of consciousness did not end with the "practical" songs. The musical epigraphs that opened each of his chapters are important to this aspect of his discussion. Although Du Bois at first left many readers wondering about the songs whose notes introduced his chapters, he alerted us that "[t]he words that are left to us are not without interest." They were the voice of the "unvoiced [which I maintain is not the 'powerless' slaves and former slaves—the easy interpretation—but the 'voice' of soul/consciousness] longing toward a truer world, of misty wanderings and hidden ways." And when one reads *The Souls of Black Folk* and finally arrives at the last chapter, where most of the songs that headed the earlier chapters receive titles, all the mysterious musical phrases make sense. As if to emphasize the importance of the literal meaning of the words to these songs and their practical work in behalf of soul's (or consciousness's) movement toward freedom, Du Bois highlighted what he described as ten "master songs," all of which are, not surprisingly, spirituals (as opposed to hymns). Eight of the ten are among the fourteen songs that head the chapters and relate directly to the conditions described in each chapter.[16]

"Swing Low, Sweet Chariot," which Du Bois described as "the cradle-song of death," begins the chapter on the life and death of Alexander Crummell. "The Meaning of Progress" begins with "the song of groping—'My way's cloudy.'" "My Lord, What a Mourning" opens the chapter "The Dawn of Freedom." Although diverse versions of the songs, including caricatures, had appeared over time, Du Bois described the original songs as very serious commentaries about exile and homelessness and relentless drudgework, with rest—death—only at the end of it all. Making connections between the titles of and words to the songs and the story told in the chapters is not a difficult task. But the meaning is also universal; they represent part of (Hegel's) "the living work of art."[17]

Religion, art, and aesthetic are all obvious in these songs. But Hegel urged us to think about art as more than "an instrument or a vehicle of expression which sometimes *happens* to be used for religious feeling." He also insisted that art was not "'aesthetic'" and was more than "craftsmanship." For Hegel, as already noted, "art is spiritual expression," spirit expressing *itself*, and the artist need not be aware of that.[18] Art is the vessel of Spirit's pathos and the evidence of pathos struggling for freedom/unity. Thus, in Du Bois' "master songs" we see the individual (as in the more personal songs) "vanish" as Hegel put it, and the appearance of the "universal song" that no longer simply reflects the daily goings-on—the individual circumstances and particular struggles of everyday life—but, instead, "inner essence" and "pathos" freed from "accidents of circumstance and personal idiosyncrasies" (PS §733). Du Bois' ten "master songs" were his example of Hegel's Absolute Art.[19]

As was the case for Hegel's Absolute Art, these songs have spiritual work to do. Almost as soon as the chapter on the songs opened, Du Bois began to reveal that accomplishment by reminding us that Fisk University's Jubilee Hall was "the great temple builded of these songs." The Jubilee Singers, "four half-clothed black boys and five girl-women—led by a man with a cause and a purpose," sang their way halfway around the world and raised $150,000, Du Bois said, "to found Fisk University." While it would be easy to read this as "practical work"—after all, an important school got built (at least in part) by the efforts of these singers and the songs—Du Bois' clever double metaphor suggests something more important. First, the "great temple," as he labeled Jubilee Hall, calls to mind the Roman temple dedicated to *all* gods. But second, and more important, the "pantheon" to which Hegel referred and Du Bois alluded was not of brick and mortar but of people and Soul, and Du Bois suggested that these songs accomplished this aspect of spiritual work.[20] From Nashville, he wrote,

North to Cincinnati they rode. . . . They stopped at Wilberforce. . . . and ever the magic of their song kept thrilling hearts, until a burst of applause in the Congregational Council at Oberlin revealed them to the world. They came to New York. . . . So their songs conquered till they sang across the land and across the sea, before Queen and Kaiser, in Scotland and Ireland, Holland and Switzerland.[21]

The singers toured the Western world for two years, and their songs and their efforts did more than build a school. They helped to create a community, a pantheon or collective consciousness, not just among black or freed people or even Americans, but also in the world. Thus, Du Bois' Sorrow Songs, his "master songs" in particular, easily represent an example of Hegel's spiritual work of art in the creation of collective consciousness.[22]

When Du Bois described "the Negro folk-song" as "the singular spiritual heritage of the nation," he was making a much more compelling and audacious claim than has heretofore been revealed. It went far beyond words, music, aesthetics, craftsmanship, and the social/cultural contribution that this art represented. It also exemplified something significantly greater than the sorrow in the souls of black folk. These songs, created between the early national and Civil War eras, compare to the (simultaneous) compositions of Verdi during the creation (unification) of modern Italy and those of Wagner during nineteenth-century efforts to organize the diverse central European principalities into "Germany." And so, to view Du Bois' appreciation and appropriation of Wagner (in his story about John Jones) as evidence of a celebration of German nationalism is, again, to see the tree but not the forest and, thus, to miss the point entirely.[23] It is instead that Wagner's compositions (as did Verdi's) symbolized art as the vessel through which Hegel's "pantheon," the race/nation (collective self-) consciousness was manifested, that Du Bois appreciated. The simultaneous creation of the Sorrow Songs, therefore, represents an addition to Hegel's elucidation of the history of World Soul or Consciousness. This very important manifestation of a collective self-consciousness came from the souls of black folk and represented a significant part of an addition—the nineteenth-century American addition—to Hegel's history of the experience of consciousness.

Du Bois' art was very much a part of the religion of the souls of black folk, but it is necessary to look more directly at religion to see that Du Bois also provided a nineteenth-century American example of what Hegel called "Revealed Religion." Du Bois' chapter on religion, "Of the Faith of the Fathers," begins in a way that suggests it will be a simple, straightforward narrative about a young New England sophisticate's first (shocking) encounter with black religion in the rural southern Bible Belt.

It was out in the country, far from home [Massachusetts], far from my foster home [Fisk University/Nashville], on a dark Sunday night. The road wandered from our rambling log-house up the stony bed of a creek, past wheat and corn, until we could hear dimly across the fields a rhythmic cadence of song,—soft thrilling, powerful, that swelled and died sorrowfully in our ears. I was a country school-teacher then, fresh from the East, and had never seen a Southern Negro revival.

As his party approached "the little plain church," they met an "air of intense excitement that possessed that mass of black folk." Du Bois reported that inside,

> A sort of suppressed terror hung in the air and seemed to seize us,—a pythian madness, a demoniac possession, that lent terrible reality to song and word. The black and massive form of the preacher swayed and quivered as the words crowded to his lips and flew at us in singular eloquence. The people moaned and fluttered, and then the gaunt-cheeked brown woman beside me suddenly leaped straight into the air and shrieked like a lost soul, while round about came wail and groan and outcry, and a scene of human passion such as I had never conceived before.

Du Bois predicted that if you have never been to a Negro revival, you would have a hard time imagining the "the religious feeling of the slave." He added, "as described, such scenes appear grotesque and funny, but as seen they are awful."

The last statement has regularly misled scholars in their discussions of Du Bois' ability (sometimes concluding, *his inability*) to identify with "the folk." Cornel West, for example, quoting from the above paragraphs and others, compared Du Bois' observations to that

> of an anthropologist visiting some strange and exotic people whose rituals suggest not only the sublime but also the satanic. The "awfulness" of this black church service . . . signifies for him both dread and fear, anxiety and disgust. In short, a black ritualistic explosion of energy frightened this black rationalist. It did so not simply because the folk seem so coarse and uncouth, but also because they are out of control, overpowered by something bigger than themselves. This clearly posed a threat to him.

West believed that Du Bois, "owing to his Puritan New England origins and Enlightenment values—found it difficult not to view common black folk as some degraded 'other' or 'alien'—no matter how hard he resisted."[24]

Du Bois' remarks, however, reveal just the opposite. Consider, again, the critical phrase: *"as described, such scenes appear grotesque and funny, but as seen they are awful*" (emphasis added). First, and most obvious, he said "but," not "and." And so, there is contradiction rather than agreement between the two independent clauses. Du Bois used "awful" here as in "awe filled." The scenes were "commanding awe" and "filled with awe," and "awe" reflects "fearful veneration or respect."[25] Second, and more to the point, what Du Bois witnessed was awe-full because he witnessed the powerful union of the finite and the infinite—the evidence of Absolute Being—spirit knowing spirit. This scene also suggests Hegel's "Revealed Religion"—in which "[a]ll men and women are incarnations of God" (spirit knowing itself as spirit).[26]

Du Bois' summary of the terror, madness, and possession, that it "lent a terrible reality to song and word," suggests that these individuals transcended the phenomenal (experience) and reached "the real" (Spirit). It was the religion and the art of the folk that created the possibility for and the realization of the union that allowed spirit to know itself as spirit, all of which is further developed in the next section.

Part II: The Songs of *Souls* and Hegel's "Philosophy of Spirit"

> I have seen a whole congregation of negroes at night, as they were worshipping in their church with some wild song or other and swaying to and fro with the ecstasy and glory of it, abandon as by one consent the semitone that should come according to the civilized modus, and sing in its place a big lusty whole tone that would shake any man's soul. —Sidney Lanier[27]

> Whoever wishes to comprehend the true nature of actual things, should turn his attention to these things, the numbers and proportions, because it is by them that everything is made clear. —Aristotle[28]

In "Of the Sorrow Songs," Du Bois wrote about a song that his great-great-grandmother sang to his great-grandfather.

> Do bana coba, gene me, gene me!
> Do bana coba, gene me, gene me!
> Ben d' nuli, nuli, nuli, nuli ben d' le.

Across 200 years, Du Bois wrote, "[w]e sing it to our children, knowing as little as our fathers what its words may mean." They sang the song anyway, "knowing well the meaning of its music."

It should not be totally unexpected that the philosopher would know "well the meaning of [this] music." Philosophers have traditionally paid a great deal of attention to sound: until relatively recently, as often that of music as of language.[29] But in a passage that James Monroe Trotter, writing in 1881, attributed to Bertini is a suggestion of an inherent (even an a priori) relationship between humans and music.

I would fain know what music is. I seek it as a man seeks eternal wisdom. Yesterday evening I walked, late in the moonlight, in the beautiful avenue of lime-trees on the bank of the Rhine; and I heard a tapping noise and soft singing. At the door of a cottage, under the blooming lime-tree, sat a mother and her twin-babies: the one lay at her breast, the other in a cradle, which she rocked with her foot, keeping time to her singing. In the very germ, then, when the first trace of life begins to stir, music is the nurse of the soul: it murmurs in the ear, and the child sleeps; the tones are the companions of his dreams; they are the world in which he lives. He has nothing; the babe, although cradled in his mother's arms, is alone in the spirit: but tones find entrance into the half-conscious soul, and nourish it as earth nourishes the life of plants.[30]

Both Bertini and Du Bois invoked an ancient philosophical principle of "knowing" that is distinct from what we generally think of as "learning." The suggestion of the potency of sound/music, regardless of one's ability to understand, literally, the meaning of words, not only creates an opportunity for us to think about Du Bois' mothers' song but also the use of music throughout *Souls* as a part of a philosophical discussion.[31]

To consider the music in this way is not to ignore the cultural or historical significance of the songs, which, ultimately, is intimately related to their philosophical importance; and the words, where they are known, are indeed significant. For one important example, we should consider David Levering Lewis's noting that the phrase "Gene me, gene me!" from Du Bois' mothers' song, bears some resemblance to Wolof words that translate "'Get me out, get me out!'"[32] Although Du Bois later changed some of the details of the story of his foremother's life, in *Souls* he said she "was seized by an evil Dutch trader two centuries ago; and coming to the valleys of the Hudson and Housatonic, black, little, and lithe, she shivered and shrank in the harsh north winds, looked longingly at the hills, and often crooned a heathen melody to the child between her knees."[33] It is not difficult to imagine that, beginning with her (or any person's) capture, through the middle passage, and throughout her enslavement, to get out, to be free, body and soul, would have been a logical desire of this mother.

But, as Du Bois moved on to talk about the larger category of slave songs, he explicitly cast the discussion in terms that encourage us to think about the music rather than the words, and in terms similar to, but moving beyond, those of Bertini:

> What are these songs, and what do they mean? I know little of music and can say nothing in technical phrase, but I know something of men, and knowing them, I know that these songs are the articulate message of the slave to the world.[34]

In that statement, Du Bois moved the discussion of the songs from one about "the experience of consciousness" and *learning* to one about the "philosophy of spirit" and *knowing*.

Du Bois' representation of black folks' relationship to the "Kingdom of Culture" was far more sophisticated than the obvious discussion of the words of the songs and their relationship to the chapter they headed.[35] And so the first goal of this section is to show that the "Sorrow Songs" were an example of something that went far beyond black religion and culture. Although Du Bois, like Bertini, claimed to know little about the technical aspects of the music, a careful reading (admittedly, *between* the lines) of the chapter on the Sorrow Songs betrays his modesty. The *science* of the sounds produced by these souls, even more than the words, held, as Du Bois insisted concerning the songs in general, a message for the world. But the science necessary to reveal that message is not one of the "new" sciences of the turn of the century, which are much too narrow (philosophers might say too abstract) to demonstrate the message fully. Consequently, this section pays particular attention to Du Bois' suggestions of old-fashioned metaphysics, the discussion of which is the second goal of this section.

Hegel's "Experience of Consciousness," his phenomenology, addressed that which could be discerned through the senses. Metaphysics, which views these phenomena as "appearances," seeks to explain what is real, some might say that which lies behind those appearances, does not rely on the senses for confirmation, and cannot be pointed to as matter. Such were "concepts," first causes, what is always true. Whether one interprets this as God (Leibniz) or a kind of God consciousness in man (Hegel), the idea here is that there is a form of knowledge that does not depend on matter as evidence. This "knowing" is an internalized, almost pre-theorized, knowledge of the idea itself (rather than the image of the idea).[36] In this context, deciphering the "message" that Du Bois mentioned does *not* depend on our knowing the titles of, or the words to, the songs, which might be why he did not include them in the musical epigraphs that began each of his chapters. And so, by giving us the opportunity to *hear* the music first, indeed by giving us no choice in the matter, Du Bois went beyond the history and evolution of the music (both of which this section explores as a third goal) and provided the foundation for a discussion based on the science of this music that came from the souls of black folk and represented, for Du Bois, an articulate message for and in Hegelian or, more generally, idealistic terms, a message *from*, the world.[37] Doing so provided more than a useful and appropriate conclusion to *Souls*. It also did more than add black people and the evidence of their "gift" to American culture. It allowed Du Bois to complete the nineteenth-century addition to Hegel's *Phenomenology*, which, in the case of the souls of black folk, included potential evidence of Absolute Knowledge. These four topics, neither totally discrete nor exactly in this order, are the subjects of this section. They begin with the assumption that, as Du Bois told us in the last line of his first chapter, we should "*listen* to the striving in the souls of black folk" (emphasis added).[38]

In his study of Hegel, philosopher Robert Solomon asked, "what[,] apart from decoration and a peculiarly profound form of entertainment, should the arts be?" Robin Maconie later applied the question explicitly to music: "[I]f music were not about 'music' as it is usually understood, what would it be about?" And almost one hundred years before either man posed his important question, Du Bois asked about the Sorrow Songs, "What are these songs, and what do they mean?"[39]

As already noted, Robert Solomon recognized that, "for Hegel, the arts were not at all 'aesthetic,' much less simple craftsmanship." Art was "spiritual expression" (spirit expressing *itself*).[40] And in that context, relating Du Bois' Sorrow Songs to Hegel's larger discussion of Soul's striving for Spirit, infinite knowledge or truth, is not as far-fetched as it might at first seem. Still, as Maconie noted (taking him out of context), "making a case for the existence of a world independent of words and their meanings" is indeed a struggle "for thinkers whose primary mode of discourse is words and their meanings."[41] It is, nevertheless, necessary for considering the possibility that Du Bois used the Sorrow Songs to illustrate Hegel's Absolute Knowledge and thus provided an important addition to Hegel's philosophy of spirit beyond adding America, black people, and the nineteenth century to it.

For the details, however, we have to go beyond the ten "master songs" Du Bois discussed, which Eric Sundquist has analyzed and which I have posited as evidence of Absolute Art and, along with religion, as an important manifestation of collective self-consciousness. Instead, we must consider the third group of songs in Du Bois' chapter on the Sorrow Songs, the implications of which have not yet received sufficient scholarly attention.[42]

In his very brief note about the history and evolution of the Sorrow Songs, Du Bois discussed eight songs, which he divided into three groups, and only two of the songs are among his ten "master songs." Based on early comments in his chapter, his mothers' song ("Gene Me, Gene Me") belongs in the first group, to which he added, "You May Bury Me in the East," which leads the chapter on the two Johns and is a "master song." The second group includes "March On," which heads the sixth chapter, and "Steal Away," which heads the chapter on the Sorrow Songs and is also among the ten "master songs." The third group includes "Bright Sparkles," "Dust, Dust, and Ashes," "My Mother's Took Her Flight and Gone Home," and "I Hope My Mother Will Be There" which, appropriately, heads the chapter, "Of the Passing of the First Born." Du Bois characterized the three groups thus: "The first is African music, the second Afro-American, while the third is a blending of Negro music with the music heard in the foster land. The result is still distinctively Negro and the method of blending original, but the elements are both Negro and Caucasian." The placement of these songs into this genealogical arrangement not only reflects the history of the music and provides another of many triadic constructs that Du Bois deployed throughout the book, but, reading *between* the lines, we can draw on important aspects related to the science of the music to relate this arrangement to Hegel's elusive Absolute Knowing.[43]

Nineteenth-century scores are available for two of the four songs Du Bois placed in the third category of (blended, Negro American) songs. "Bright Sparkles" and "Dust, Dust, and Ashes" are in the F-major key.[44] Both songs are in diatonic (seven-note) scales, typical of romantic (classical) and popular Western music. And F-major, and the G-major scale of "I Hope My Mother Will Be There," are among the most commonly used key signatures in Western popular music. "Bright Sparkles" even has a section of "horn fifths," very characteristic of eighteenth- and nineteenth-century European music, and it includes octave phrases (a unison created between female or treble clef and male or bass clef voices sounding the same note an octave apart). The song is, generally, very linear and predictable in its tones. "Dust, Dust and Ashes" is even more profoundly hymnal, and there are no notes outside the key: no "accidentals." When Du Bois described these songs as "distinctively Negro" despite the clear Caucasian influences, he was perhaps referring to the two-voiced texture of critical phrases in the verse that move in parallel thirds.[45]

The songs of the middle group, "March On" and "Steal Away," are both in the key of F-major.[46] Considering Du Bois' description of them (as Afro-American as opposed to blended, Negro American), one would expect to hear fewer Western traditions in these songs than in the two just discussed, and one would not be disappointed. "March On," for example, has *none* of the characteristics of the hymns discussed above. First, it is in 2/4 time rather than common (4/4) time. Common time has a rhythm of strong beat, weak beat, semi-strong beat, weak beat. The 2/4 rhythm is strong beat, weak beat, repeated in each bar. Although sometimes characterized as militaristic, this alternating, two-beat rhythm is easily a work-song rhythm. The song is also constructed in an unmistakable call-and-response format: an explicitly unison voice calls, "Way over in Egypt's land"; and a clear four-part harmonic chorus responds, "You shall gain the victory." "Steal Away," on the other hand, is in common time. Though not in a call-and-response form, it does have both octave and three-part harmony phrases. But what is particularly odd in this song is not its rhythm or its structure but the tones themselves. The F-major scale "naturally" includes B-flat, but in this song, B-natural, not part of this scale, appears and would be considered an "accidental" in Western music theory. B-natural, the leading tone of the key of C, shows up unexpectedly in this song that is in the key of F, thus disturbing and destabilizing the melody. There is, ironically, something particularly rational and real about this surprise and the disappearance of a particular (expected) tone in a song about escape, a point to which I shall return.

Finally, there are the two songs among the eight that Du Bois described as African. First is that mysterious tune in common (4/4) time, which I have been calling "Gene Me, Gene Me," and which Du Bois' mothers sang perhaps (more of which shortly) in the sorrow-full B-flat minor key. Du Bois used his mothers' song to begin his history of the music and his effort to sort out "the siftings of centuries." He described the song as "a heathen melody." Because he claimed to have no understanding of the meaning of the words to the song, we have to interpret "heathen" literally (and by nineteenth-century standards): the song was simply of a non-Christian source.[47] But second, given that he provided us no translation of the words to the song, we have to conclude, again, that it really is tones/sounds—the importance of the music—he is emphasizing here, rather than words.[48] Du Bois described the music as "primitive African music," adding, "it may be seen in larger form in the strange chant ("You may bury me in the east") which heralds [the chapter titled] 'The Coming of John.'"

Although Du Bois saw these two melodies as "African" music, the two songs are, in some ways, very different.[49] Only one ("You May Bury Me in the East") is actually in a minor key, although both songs start out in minor keys. Historians and others have made much of the minor key and its relationship to African American music. Most typically, these discussions focus on the so-called blue note, the flatted third, which is utilized in "You May Bury Me in the East."[50] One might also assume the presence of a pentatonic scale, a decisively ancient scale, and many would say a decidedly African scale, to which Du Bois alluded.[51] But "You May Bury Me in the East" is in a seven-note (diatonic) scale. And although "Gene Me, Gene Me" starts out in a pentatonic scale, at the very end, it oddly becomes diatonic. There are other unexpected turns in both songs. First, about midway through "You May Bury Me in the East," the song shifts from the C-minor key to its relative major E-flat. The song, however, utilizes "the major sixth [A-natural] in the minor mode," which is dramatically unexpected and uncharacteristic in this key. "Gene Me, Gene Me" is even more unusual. With its five flats, it appears to be in the key of B-flat minor, and, considering Du Bois' suggestive remarks about the song, perhaps that is how he read this music. But the song's ending, a final cadence with a leading tone of C, reveals that the song is actually in the key of D-flat major (the relative key of B-flat minor). In one way, this ending might make this song appear a little more "Western" than Du Bois might have known, but the unexpected changes, the nonlinearity, and all the other unusual aspects in the two songs make it easy to accept his characterization of them as African. Certainly, compared to the others, there is little in them that is characteristically European.

There is, however, another difference related to the sound of these songs compared to the others. The key of each, as one might expect, has a sound, a "spirit," perhaps. Both are heavy (enormous) sounds, but they are different. Whether one considers "Gene Me, Gene Me" as in B-flat minor or its relative key, D-flat major, both keys produce a despondent, oppressive, almost unbearable tone. The heaviness of the C-minor key of "You May Bury Me in the East," however, is usually strong, powerful, and profoundly heroic; its *piano Lento* notation further suggests a very calm seriousness. John Jones's brave struggles, and perhaps especially his decision to die rather than escape Altamaha, could not have been better framed than with a song in that deliberate (self-conscious?) C-minor key. And neither could the slave mothers' weariness have been demonstrated more profoundly than in B-flat minor/D-flat major.

Du Bois, it seems, knew precisely what he was doing when he distinguished these eight songs from his ten "master songs" and arranged them the way he did. His genealogical arrangement makes obvious good sense in terms of social/cultural adaptation. But perhaps Du Bois' knowledge of music was even more advanced than this. There is an aspect of the science of the sound of the Sorrow Songs that can actually take us as far back into the history and the science of music as we can reasonably go—to Pythagoras (or the Pythagoreans)—who gave us our first important theories related to science, music, and the science of music.[52]

A brief discussion of Pythagoras's musical/scientific determinations can move the discussion of the Sorrow Songs beyond some of its current limitations. First, it provides a way of seeing Du Bois' discussion of the songs as something that serves a significantly larger agenda than one defined (almost exclusively) by cultural nationalism, as important a cultural tradition as they were. Pythagoras's conclusions also help to challenge the reduction of nineteenth-century discussions of the songs to the creation of an illusion, the "magical, musical Negro," and as designed to mark the music as "other" and inferior (to European music). And, finally, the science of this music can move us beyond the tendency to reduce Du Bois' discussion to another example of racial essentialism. As already noted, the "essence" of Du Bois' discussion was not "race" but Soul.[53]

And so, the obvious question relates to whether the science of music can reveal an "observable" relationship to the mysterious, metaphysical concept of Soul. The most emphatic critics of Romantic characterizations of spirituals turn the discussions of the songs into sloppy sentimentalism (to put it mildly).[54] While it is true that the efforts of nineteenth-century Romantics were somewhat feeble (*hobbled* might be a better word, given the difficulty of describing sound with words, especially when that sound is dramatically different from what one is accustomed to hearing), we should remember that Romanticism included two important goals: first, to discern the relationship and the unity between man and nature (also described as "origins") and, second, to reunite art and science.[55] And so, their efforts were important even if ultimately unsuccessful. Hegel concluded that the sciences (biology and physics, in particular) could never reveal the internal, only the external. But perhaps the science of some of *these* songs really can transform what others have written off as sloppy sentimentalism into the *real* and reveal the possibility of Du Bois' having illustrated Infinite Knowledge.

According to lore, Pythagoras was intrigued by the sound of hammers hitting an anvil in a blacksmith's shop. His curiosity about the degree of difference (the interval) between two consonant or harmonious sounds led him to conduct a series of experiments, including one using a monochord (imagine something like a guitar fingerboard with only one string and a moveable bridge). When he shortened the string by half (without changing the tension), the shortened string produced a sound an octave higher than the sound of the full-length string. Shortening the string by a third (making the string two-thirds its original length) raised the sound by a fifth (from the original note or tone), and shortening it by a fourth produced a sound that was a fourth higher. The mathematical ratios represented by these intervals are 2:1 for the octave, 3:2 for the fifth, and 4:3 for the fourth. The remarkable pattern in the simple whole-number ratios is obvious. (The decimal equivalents ascending the scale are 1.000, 1.333, 1.500, and 2.00; in one scale they would correspond to d, g, a, d^1.) But if we add the next two intervals of a fifth within the octave, 1.125 and 1.778, they would complete a pentatonic scale, with the notes d, e, g, a, c, d^1. The pentatonic scale is an ancient scale, and it tends to be the scale of much folk music throughout the world. For a popular example, "Nobody Knows the Trouble I've Seen" is in this scale. Continuing in intervals of a fifth within this scale to add 1.185 and 1.688 creates a diatonic (7-note) scale (d, e, f, g, a, b, c, d^1) in the Dorian mode. Within this scale, all the intervals are either 9/8 or 256/243. The interval of the larger ratio, 9/8 or 1.125, is a tone, and the smaller ratio (256/243 or 1.0535) is a semitone.[56] The seven-note scale is the most commonly used scale today (our common scale starts at C, but, using the same math, we could start anywhere and produce a 7-note scale).

It was important enough that Pythagoras had determined the ratio intervals for a series of harmonious tones. But in determining the mathematical ratios that corresponded to these harmonious sounds, Pythagoras had also found the mathematical intervals for the musical notes (and, ultimately, scales) that people already sang, and, in doing so, revealed "a connection between arithmetic and aesthetics." As physicist Ian Johnston noted, people already sang those notes because they *liked* the sound, and the sound was "good." Whether or not connecting arithmetic and aesthetics was Pythagoras's aim, and Socrates seems not to have thought so, in addition to discovering the correlation between harmonious sounds and simple number ratios, Pythagoras had, in fact, illustrated a connection "between the natural world and the human soul."[57] The two notes an octave apart (2:1) typically represent the notes "men and women sing" when singing the same song in unison. Although it will sound as if they are "singing the same note," the interval separating the notes is a full octave. The 4:3 interval, "the perfect fourth," also represents one of "the most fundamental intervals in musical harmony." The interval of a fifth (3:2), called "the perfect fifth," is also a natural interval—sometimes the range between the two typical male voices, tenor and bass, or the typical female voices, soprano and alto. Ian Johnston wrote that "[u]ntrained singers will often find themselves singing a fifth apart without being aware of it." Johnston added: "Again there is a perception of sameness about the two notes separated by this interval—not as much as with the diapason [octave], rather it is a feeling of blending together."[58]

Determinations of the relationship between music and mathematics did not end with the Pythagoreans. In the second century, the astronomer Claudius Ptolemaeus (Ptolemy) identified the major third. That is, one could bridge or stop the hypothetical Pythagorean monochord a "fifth of the way from one end," creating an interval of a third (the major third) and a mathematical ratio of 5:4 between the sound of the unstopped string and the shortened string. The Greeks generally considered this interval discordant (not harmonious). But, one only has to add notes that are intervals of a third and a fifth higher to any note (the root) to produce *a major triad* and, thus, the foundation of harmonics. Moreover, continuing from that original note to the point of creating a seven-note scale by raising or lowering the note by a fifth would result in notes on a staff that look like the Pythagorean (Dorian) scale. Checking the actual distance between the notes (the interval) with a calculator, however, would consistently reveal a small difference. These notes would (to a keen ear) produce a slightly different sound (compared to the Dorian scale) because the whole tones and semitones in this scale are minor tones. Ptolemy, like Pythagoras, had demonstrated another "connection between the aesthetic quality of music and the simple logic of arithmetic." Centuries later, Johannes Kepler, considering aspects of Copernicus's heliocentric theory of the universe, rightly suggested that one could continue the mathematical process of adding notes infinitely.[59]

Conclusions about the sound of these determinations (related to the intervals of a third, fourth, and fifth, triads, chords, scales, major and minor modes, whole tones and semitones) were based, in large measure, on what one could hear. In 1886, Heinrich Hertz successfully measured the frequency of radio waves, making it possible to define intervals precisely, to create the "equal tempered scale" (a scale in which every semitone in an octave is equal to every other), and subsequently to place A^4 (A in the common, C, scale) at exactly 440 Hz. Indeed, it was finally possible to determine the precise position/interval of every note/tone, based not on sensual perception (hearing), which is often incorrect, even if only slightly, but on exact science. At least, that seemed to be the case.

When, however, nineteenth-century listeners heard the slave songs about which Du Bois wrote, they were hearing something that went quite beyond their ability to define in precise, scientific terms. Fanny Kemble, the English actress who was unhappily married to Georgia planter Pierce Butler, described the music she heard on his plantation as "semi savage," characterizing some of what she heard as "barbaric chants." Robert R. Moton, then an officer at Hampton Institute and later Booker T. Washington's successor at Tuskegee, referred to the songs as "priceless," "rude," and "wild" practically in the same sentence.[60] Thomas Wentworth Higginson, the white Civil War commander of the First South Carolina Volunteers (Colored Troops), upon hearing his soldiers singing "Wrestling Jacob," a retelling of the biblical story of Jacob's all-night wrestling match with the angel, concluded that the song had "a mystical effect and a passionate striving throughout." He added, "The Scriptural struggle between Jacob and the angel, which is only dimly expressed in the words [of the song], *seems all uttered in the music*" (emphasis added).[61] Mary Boykin Chesnut was so moved by a melodic prayer she heard during a church service near Camden, South Carolina, in 1861 that she said, "I would very much have liked to shout, too." She described the prayer, led by Jim Nelson, a "driver" whom she described as "a full-blooded African," as musical, but she recorded no notes or words. Indeed, she concluded that "[t]he words had no meaning at all." She instead noted handclaps, "a shrill shriek," a "minor key," and the likeness of a trumpet. Ultimately, the best she could do was to conclude: "*It was all sound*" (emphasis added).[62]

Individuals who had sufficient skills to chart the music, and interest enough to attempt it, provided more detail, if not more clarity, about these sounds. Despite their possessing some training in music, the transcribers were candid about their inability to place the notes correctly on the staff. One listener/transcriber wrote: "The voices of the colored people have a peculiar quality that nothing can imitate; and the intonations and delicate variations of even one singer cannot be reproduced on paper. And I despair of conveying any notion of the effect of a number singing together, especially in a complicated shout. . . . There is no singing in *parts*, as we understand it, and yet no two [singers] appear to be singing the same thing."[63] There was really no need for this person, or others, to apologize. When most of these observers were transcribing this music (1860s–80s), science had not yet yielded a precise way of measuring intervals of sound, and even once it was possible (after 1887), the Western musical staff simply did not have the space for recording all the notes that slaves sang. Still, there is a way in which these and other observers got it precisely right: despite all their apprehensions, they rightly recognized that there was more going on in these songs than words, and more going on in the music than mere notes.

When Du Bois described his short musical epigraphs that headed each of his chapters as a "haunting echo of these weird old songs," he simply reflected what many others had already noted. Allen, Ware, and Garrison, for example, characterized their best effort to transcribe the music/sounds as yielding "but a faint shadow of the original."[64] Lucy McKim (Garrison), the Hampton Institute teacher, was more precise. She acknowledged that "mere musical notes and signs" would not do justice to the music: "The odd turns made in the throat, and the curious rhythmic effect produced by single voices chiming in at different irregular intervals, seem almost as impossible to place on the score as the singing of birds or the tones of an Æolian Harp." Allen, Ware, and Garrison reminded readers that "[w]hat may appear to some to be an incorrect rendering, is very likely to be a variation; for these variations are endless." After a detailed effort to describe the tones, and only slightly paraphrasing McKim's earlier notation, Allen, Ware, and Garrison reported "sounds that cannot be precisely represented by the gamut, . . . 'slides from one note to another, and turns and cadences not in articulated notes.'" Thomas Fenner, also of Hampton, recognized that slaves sang tones for which there were "no musical characters to represent." He noted the flat seventh as an example, but he also indicated that in some songs (individual) tones could range "through an entire octave . . . according to the inspiration of the singer." Fenner, finally, offered a summary and a solution: the songs were simply "impossible to explain . . . in words, and to those who wish to sing them, the best advice is that [which is] most useful in learning to pronounce a foreign language: *Study all the rules you please; then—go listen to a native*" (original emphasis).[65]

Of all of the uniquenesses, the flat seventh deserves special attention. McKim, Fenner, and others heard it, pointed it out, and recognized it as both odd and impressive. They did not know (or did not note) how profoundly important it really was to the history and science of music or the science of the Sorrow Songs in the realm of philosophy. Antonín Dvořák, at least, knew that it was special. His *New World* (or, *From the New World*) *Symphony* includes an homage to slave music (the second movement, "Largo") that employs both this "new" note and scale.[66] Du Bois only casually noted the minor tones of the songs. But John Wesley Work of Fisk University, writing just a few years later and clearly influenced by *Souls*, provided important detail. Work saw the pentatonic scale and the flat seventh as the virtual "foundation" of the music that the Negro had built.

> The scale is peculiarly his own, and consequently satisfies his nature. Through it his nature manifests itself to the world. The spirit of the music is a common possession which takes outward form according to the nature of the possessor. The Negro in his primitive nature expressed his musical scale 1-2-3-5—6. Why? That was all the world meant to him. But the American Negro has gone one step further and added one more note, flat seven, an addition which goes a long way toward expressing the effect of added experience brought to him by a new life in a New World. This flat seven expresses a wild and overwhelming surprise at the utter strangeness of things. . . . *All this feeling of the African's awe was injected into that little flat seven,* America's contribution to the Negro's scale. (emphasis added)[67]

Du Bois would probably have agreed with Work's conclusions about nature, being, and intervals, but he might have seen one thing slightly differently. Based on the chapter on the Sorrow Songs, Du Bois would probably have seen the flat seventh not only as America's contribution to the Negro, but the new scale it made as the Negro's contribution to America. The African/American slave "found" a new note and created a new scale. Perhaps she did not know, empirically, that the new note was flatted; that its interval ratio (on a fixed-pitch instrument, in a C-major, equal tempered scale) was 9:5; that depending on the instrument, one might not be able to chart it precisely on a traditional staff. Indeed, the decimal equivalent for the *sounded* note could range anywhere between 1.78 and 1.68, and the frequency of the note could lay somewhere (anywhere) between 440 Hz (the frequency for A-natural) and 466.16 Hz (the frequency for B-flat). The frequency for the flat seventh was so peculiar, so imprecise, and so changeable that one simply COULD NOT place it *uniformly* in megahertz.[68] Still, just as Pythagoras identified the perfect fifth and the natural fourth and Ptolemy identified the major third, American slaves caught hold of that very important but only apparently not-quite-perfect-or-natural minor seventh and created a new scale and the foundation of a new music. They liked the sound; and it was good.

There was, however, more to this "new" music than its notes and scale. According to Lucy McKim, there were "also apparent irregularities in the time, . . . [that were] no less difficult to express accurately" than the tones. Lydia Parrish noted that slaves broke all the laws of linguistics, ignoring "spelling, pronunciation, and punctuation," making it impossible to illustrate their vocalizations on charts. John Wesley Work observed that "[e]xtravagant postamenta [portamento?], slurs, and free use of extra notes serve to mystify the collector of these songs who strives for accuracy." Work, who clearly understood a thing or two about music and philosophy, recognized these different rhythms as "idiomatic and . . . as essential to the body of our music as pure red blood is to the human body." Those odd, added syllables—consider the line "Lord I want to be a Christian *in-a-my-heart*," or Du Bois' master song, "Been a-Listening," or "I'm a-Rolling," which heads his ninth chapter—examples of Work's "free use of extra notes," reflected, for him, "perfect beauty in movement." Allen, Ware, and Garrison encouraged musicians not to be

> repelled by any difficulty in adapting the words to the tunes. The negroes keep exquisite time in singing, and do not suffer themselves to be daunted by any obstacle in the words [which Sterling Brown later described as the tyranny "of meter and rhyme"]. The most obstinate Scripture phrases or snatches from hymns they will force to do duty with any tune they please, and will dash heroically through a trochaic tune at the head of a column of iambs with wonderful skill.

The compilers did their best to arrange the words to the music, but "for the rest," they acknowledged, "one must make them fit the best he [*sic*] can, as the negroes themselves do."[69]

The complicated patterns people heard and the difficulty they had arranging words to notes obviously relate to what we generally think of as rhythm. It was of a nature that, combined with the tones, Thomas Wentworth Higginson admitted, would draw even the most "contemptuous . . . into the vortex erelong." On St. Simon's Island, three distinct simultaneous rhythms could be heard in "the melody, hand clapping, and tapping of the feet or heels on the floor." John Wesley Work, who also described the music as contagious, noted, "When the Negro sings *with the 'Spirit and the understanding'* not only with his voice does he sing, but with his body as well" (emphasis added). Fredrika Bremer's reflection on a service she witnessed in South Carolina in 1850 provides a useful summary of these observations: "They sang . . . with all their souls and with all their bodies in unison; for their bodies wagged, their heads nodded, their feet stamped, their knees shook, their elbows and their hands beat time to the tune and the words which they sang with evident delight." She added: "One must *see* these people singing if one is rightly to understand their life" (emphasis added).[70]

The rhythms of these songs were, without a doubt, complex. Writers even described individual singers in a group starting and stopping according to their own inclination, singing in different octaves, obviously in different rhythms, and sometimes even different songs. William Allen concluded that the result was, nevertheless, "a marvellous complication and variety . . . with the most perfect time, and rarely with any discord."[71]

Traditionally, when we talk about harmony, or this lack of discord, the point relates to diverse voices singing different but compatible tones (or, perhaps, blending soprano, alto, tenor, and bass tones). These writers, however, described the blending of diverse but concordant melodies with diverse and equally concordant rhythms, and, consequently, they also described the phenomenon of *harmonic rhythm*. In doing so, they had also reconnected (on more than one level) the art and science of music as the slaves regularly did in their daily lives (and which had grown farther and farther apart in the mainstream since the seventeenth-century scientific revolutions, eventually becoming completely separate). Philosophically, however, these songs accomplished even more. John Wesley Work not only saw these complex slave rhythms as "idiomatic," or especially common in black America, but suggested philosophical significance by relating them to the rhythm of the planets and the seasons. Further, he wondered, as a philosopher might, about the relationship of this music to Creation.[72]

When Work speculated about the philosophical meaning of these songs and their creation, it was more than sloppy sentimentalism that his words reflected. And perhaps nineteenth-century Romantics should not be faulted because they had no adequate sound-words to describe what they heard or because they understood "harmony" in such narrow dimensions. With more understanding than some of his predecessors, Work, literally related the creation of this music to the ancient philosophic idea of "the harmony of the universe," as he put it, the best-known classical account of which appears in Plato's dialogue *Timaeus*, in which Timaeus, a Pythagorean, explained the Demiurge's creation of World Soul.[73] By Timaeus's account,

> From an essence impartible, and always subsisting according to sameness of being, and from a nature divisible about bodies, he [the Demiurge; the creator god] mingled from both a third form of essence, having a middle subsistence between the two. And again, between that which is impartible and that which is divisible about bodies, he placed the nature of same and different. And taking these, now they are three, he mingled them all into one idea. But as the nature of

different could not without difficulty be mingled in same, he harmonized them together by employing force in their conjunction.

But after he had mingled these two with essence, and had produced one from the three, he again divided this whole into becoming parts; at the same time mingling each part from same, different, and essence. But he began to divide as follows:—In the first place, he received one part from the whole. Then he separated a second part, double of the first; afterwards a third, sesquialters of the second, but triple of the first: then a fourth, double of the second; in the next place a fifth, triple of the third; a sixth, octuple of the first; and lastly a seventh, twenty-seven times more than the first. After this, he filled up the double and triple intervals, again cutting off parts from the whole; and placed them so between the intervals, that there might be two mediums in every interval; and that one of these might by the same part exceed one of the extremes, and be exceeded by the other; and that the other part might by an equal number surpass one of the extremes, and by an equal number be surpassed by the other. (*Timaeus*, §35a–36a)

It is impossible to miss the representation of musical intervals, scales, triads, and chords in the above quotation. But the Demiurge continued to divide the whole into intervals, lengths, and circles, each type individually complete, different, and interconnected. The single external circle subsisted in a motion of sameness. But among the internal circles (there are seven), some revolved left (those "partaking of sameness") and some revolved right (those partaking of difference). The seven interior circles (of different sizes, moving in different motions and at different speeds) coursed "contrary to each other" while maintaining "order and proportion in their circulations." The external (undivided) circle maintained dominion (*Timaeus*, §36c–d).

After, therefore, the whole composition of the soul was completed according to the intention of its artificer, in the next place he fabricated within soul the whole of a corporeal nature; and, conciliating middle with middle, he aptly harmonized them together. But soul being every way extended from the middle to the very extremities of the universe, and investing it externally in a circle, at the same time herself revolving within herself, gave rise to the divine commencement of an unceasing and wise life, through the whole of time. And, indeed the body of the universe was generated visible; but soul is invisible, participating of a rational energy and harmony, and subsisting as the best of generated natures, through its artificer, who is the best of intelligible and perpetual beings.[74] (*Timaeus*, §36e–37a)

Thus, in Plato's account, the Demiurge forced sameness and difference together with essence and created the substance of World Soul. That substance (World Soul) was dispersed throughout and wrapped around the universe. And then by making a series of divisions in the substance, the Demiurge created the cosmos. Christopher Bamford described cosmos as "more than just the universe." It represented a "principle of unity . . . [reflecting] the harmony, sympathy, and kinship of all things—a universal interrelationship and interdependence: a harmony, which in the broadest sense we may take to be the void of God, the *a priori* law and divine order, incomprehensible in itself but presiding over all things."[75]

Timeaus's discussion of the Demiurge's construction of World Soul revealed a universal harmony in which all the parts of this universe are in constant concert. Plato, in *The Republic*, remarked simply that "there was a siren sitting on each of the planets singing." In the New Testament pronouncement (which Du Bois borrowed), it became "the morning stars sang together." But according to Timaeus, all the diverse parts of the universe made sounds as they moved in their circles, spheres, and lengths, and because they moved at different speeds and in different directions, and were different shapes, their sounds were different. These sounds, nevertheless, were in "ratios of musical consonances," or in harmony. The assumption is that humans can hear these sounds at birth, but lose the ability over time; and we indeed become less able to hear certain frequencies as we age. But for classical philosophers, the sounds were nevertheless there and this harmony existed (remained, some would say) in the soul, and through reason/thought (consciousness?) we could realize it again. Although scholars today would conclude that there is little (if any) "science" in this grand theory, Goethe saw these harmonies as eternal, and therefore concluded that they "did not require validation in the phenomenal world."[76]

But if we think of these discussions as efforts to make sense of the universe, to create order out of apparent chaos, and as a way of relating the material world to the spiritual world (or even man and nature, art and science), Du Bois' Sorrow Songs could become Hegel's "actual" (what others translate as "real") that is rational—Absolute Knowledge, even if music is, as Leibniz (in the first epigraph in this chapter) maintained and Jamie James paraphrased, a "hidden arithmetical exercise of a soul unconscious that it is calculating."[77]

And so, finally, we return to the question of what, besides art, music, or Sorrow Song was being created, and why it matters so much here. In ancient traditions, music was always about much more than sound. Music, in the words of Jamie James, often related to a "cosmic harmony that . . . constituted the universe" and reflected "the deep-seated human need to feel a connection with the Absolute, to transcend the phenomenal world."[78] Thomas W. Higginson's description of slave singing in Savannah as "a stimulus to courage and a tie to heaven" suggested something more literal than metaphorical. Higginson's earlier description of his soldiers' rendition of "Wrestling Jacob" as "a mystical effect and a passionate striving" also takes on additional meaning. His characterization of the small group of young singers in Savannah singing themselves "into the sublime scenery of the Apocalypse" is, likewise, more than literary flourish (even if that was the limit of his intention). Former slave Jacob Stroyer, though describing the tragedy of being sold south, nevertheless provided an appropriate characterization of this phenomenon: "The colored people cried out with one voice as though the heavens and earth were coming together." Du Bois alluded to this effect when he described the black church scene of the "Frenzy of 'Shouting,' when the Spirit of the Lord passed by, and, seizing the devotee, made him mad with supernatural joy." For Du Bois, the slaves' "stamping, shrieking, and shouting, . . . the weeping and laughing, the vision and the trance," were neither confounding nor embarrassing. They were, as he said, as "old as religion, as Delphi and Endor." And, he added, they were so much a part of black life "that many generations firmly believed that without this visible manifestation of the God there could be no true communion with the Invisible."[79]

Du Bois accomplished more in his discussion of the Sorrow Songs than premiering them as an important art form and religious symbol. He used them in a way that connected the souls of black folk to Hegel's "Philosophy of Spirit"—as evidence of Soul's development toward knowledge of the Infinite. Slaves demonstrated this absolute connection to the Infinite (to knowing) not in the "Frenzy," which, as noted, at best suggests Hegel's Absolute Being, but in the creation of this new music that regularly accompanied it. In this creation spirit not only meets, *and knows*, spirit, but, ultimately, knows itself as spirit. It is, to borrow words from Edward A. Lippman, "in the march of Hegel's spirit" that "art is superseded by pure thought, which can directly know the Ideas."[80] This "idea" was outlined in Timeaus's explication of the creation of World Soul in which the Demiurge "mingled" all the various parts of the universe (sameness, difference, and essence) "into one idea." Put yet another way, the creation of this music revealed the

The Religion and Songs of *Souls* 145

reconciliation of thought and being (double consciousness?), manifesting Infinite or Absolute Knowledge. Part III shows, more clearly, how.

Part III: The Songs of *Souls* and Hegel's "Absolute Knowledge"

[W]e discover that these sounds are obtained by vibrations, whose numbers and relations to each other are strictly calculable, can be expressed, indeed, in terms of logarithms. Music, then, is under law. It is founded on abstruse calculations. Man did not make these laws. He finds them there, ready-made and waiting for him. —J. Brierley[81]

No part of knowledge can stand wholly disconnected from other parts of the universe of thought. —J. Stanley Jevons[82]

In a very detailed description of a religious event that Fredrika Bremer attended in New Orleans in 1851, she reported that at some point a woman began to preach back to an "exhorter" who had been preaching to her. Eventually, the woman began to move around so much that it took "three other women" to control her, "as if to hold her still on the earth." The woman "fell and rolled" and "groaned" and walked around the church, waving her arms and shouting "'Halleluiah!'" Sometime after the woman's shouting subsided, "Her appearance was now calm, earnest, and really beautiful." And when congregants went to move her from near the altar where she lay prostrate, her body was rigid. Bremer continued:

When, by degrees, she had recovered consciousness, her glance was still fixed, but it seemed to me that it was directed rather inwardly than outwardly; she talked to herself in a low voice, and such a beautiful, blissful expression was portrayed in her countenance, that I would willingly experience that which she then experienced, saw, or perceived. It was no ordinary, no earthly scene. Her countenance was as it were transfigured. As soon as, after deep sighs, she had returned to her usual state, her appearance became usual also. But her demeanor was changed; she wept much, but calmly and silently.

As seriously as Bremer seemed to have taken this event, she also admitted "to having been thoroughly amused by the frolic." Nevertheless, she was sure that despite the "chaotic state," there was "the element of true African worship" in it. She added:

Give only intelligence, order, system to this outbreak of the warm emotions, longings, and presentiments of life, and then that which now appears hideous will become beautiful, that which is discordant will become harmonious. The children of Africa may yet give us a form of divine worship in which invocation, supplication, and songs of praise may respond to the inner life of the fervent soul!

The "intelligence, order, [and] system," the beauty and the harmony were already there. And so was the "divine worship" that Bremer predicted black Americans might eventually provide. They appeared in the "invocation, supplication, and songs of praise," which she failed to recognize were, indeed, a response "to the inner life of the fervent soul" of the spirit-filled woman.[83]

Aspects of the slaves' religious rituals, as already suggested, regularly moved and sometimes inspired outside observers. Thomas Wentworth Higginson was impressed enough by a ring shout he witnessed that he recorded details about it in his journal. He described a "glimmering fire, round which the dusky figures moved in the rhythmical barbaric dance the negroes call a 'shout,' chanting, often harshly, but always in the most perfect time, some monotonous refrain." While journalist Edward Pollard recognized the possibility of something important in what he observed, he stopped short of explicit confirmation. "[T]he idea we get of the negro's religion is not always ludicrous," Pollard wrote to a friend in the North. "Their hymns, or religious chants, might furnish a curious book. The words are generally very few, and repeated over and over again; and the lines, though very unequal, are sung with a natural cadence that impresses the ear quite agreeably."[84]

Despite limited understanding, the powerful impressions these rituals clearly made were no doubt enhanced by the fact that "church" in America, by this time, had become a rather sedate affair. And as Shane White and Graham White recently observed, deviations from the more stolid traditions were generally unacceptable to church leaders, who therefore vigorously discouraged chanting, dancing, and shouting.[85] But to extrapolate from the words of music historian Benjamin Farrington, and to move closer to Du Bois' philosophical concerns, the misunderstandings (misinterpretations) that readily occurred, causing people to view what they witnessed as wild, barbaric, hideous, curious, or bizarre, and worse, as a "frolic," should perhaps be thought of as a consequence of misplaced knowledge. Farrington wrote:

[T]here is no human knowledge which cannot lose its scientific character when men forget the conditions under which it originated, the questions which it answered, and the function it was to serve. A great part of the mysticism and superstition of educated men consists of knowledge which has broken loose from its historical moorings.[86]

According to ancient traditions, music was a sacrificial offering necessary to "conjure up and communicate with" the spirits/gods. (Sound was an indication of presence/being.) For Orpheus, the legendary musician and poet in Greek mythology, one sang "to invoke the Gods" because music was "the medium of communication with spirits." Music, chanting, and dancing, in the Orphic tradition, heightened sense-perception and led to a kind of awareness/knowing which, according to the Pythagoreans (and Platonists), was actually remembering—what the soul (conscious) already knows—that it *is*.[87] As alien as these ideas about music, remembering, and knowing might seem to us today, it remains the case that probably all spiritual rituals (especially "church") begin with some sort of incantation, whether a prayer, a chant, or a song, and whether or not people today know why they do it. The ancient goal was the union of substance and subject, the phenomenal and the spiritual, the visible and the invisible, the finite and the infinite.

Nineteenth-century Romantics constantly searched for evidence of this unity, the achievement of which would prove the unity of man and nature, that life was not a series of "accidents." Achieving this unity also represents part of the completion of Hegel's study of World Soul; it suggests the completion of Soul's necessary quest for knowledge or the journey to philosophy/Spirit. Metaphysicians maintained that this knowledge "has its source within us, in our understanding's attending to itself." And "what remembers is the understanding . . . which is that part of the soul having its source and essence in the divine spirit." A good portion of Plato's *Phaedo* is devoted to this idea that true knowledge resides in the soul, that soul (and knowledge) preexist birth, and therefore that (true) knowledge is actually something remembered. In *Phaedo*, required reading when Du Bois studied philosophy at Fisk, Cebes maintained that Socrates' favorite doctrine was that such "knowledge is simply recollection."[88]

Despite recent conclusions that reject any systematic relationship between *Phenomenology* and *Souls*, Du Bois' volume not only offers what can easily be interpreted as an addition to Hegel's experience of consciousness and philosophy of spirit by focusing on the nineteenth century and America, but within that construct, the Sorrow Songs represent the culmination of soul's/consciousness's education from the notion (appearance) of knowledge to true knowledge, truth, or science/philosophy. As Tom Rockmore has written, "the series of configurations which consciousness goes through along this road is, in reality, the detailed history of the *education* [*Bildung*] of consciousness itself to Science" (philosophy, or knowledge).[89] Fredrika Bremer's (earlier quoted) description of the nineteenth-century church-woman's experience perhaps provides an illustration of Hegel's description of the process: "In pressing forward to its true existence, consciousness will arrive at a point at which it gets rid of its semblance of being burdened with something alien, with what is only for it, and some sort of 'other,' at a point where appearance becomes identical with essence, so that its exposition will coincide at just this point with the authentic Science [knowledge] of Spirit. And finally, when consciousness itself grasps this its own essence, it will signify the nature of absolute knowledge itself" (*PS* §89). Pauline Watts described this effect in music as the "aware *major self,*" and perhaps Higginson heard some hint of it in the "monotonous refrain" of the soldiers' ring shout. Perhaps it also exists in the seemingly static, repetitious measure of music in Du Bois' mothers' song, and in the bass line of "You May Bury Me in the East," both of which are in the first group of Du Bois' musical genealogy.[90]

At the meeting of the experience of consciousness and the education or philosophy of spirit, and in the slaves' rituals and songs, we can see consciousness's shift from "a love of knowing" to Absolute Knowing and thus to Hegel's "science" or philosophy. This Absolute Knowledge reflects the successful outcome of Soul's (conscious's) journey/education that began with perception and moved to and through consciousness, self-consciousness, and reason to spirit. Tom Rockmore has characterized this process in terms of the science of cognition and described it as "the cognitive process [which leads to] the subject['s] . . . know[ing] its object as itself."[91]

Du Bois provided more than enough detail for us to see the conclusion of a process in which subject and object coincide or in which "the object as it is and the object as it appears coincide within consciousness."[92] S. K. Heninger Jr., however, has suggested the profound shift we might have to make in our thinking in order to succeed in recognizing this. It is a shift that is also necessary in order to see precisely how Du Bois, again, focusing on music rather than words, connected these songs and the knowledge they reflected in the context of World Soul and the individual and collective journey to Spirit. Writing on Pythagorean cosmology during the Renaissance era, Heninger personally rejected the validity of many aspects of Pythagorean doctrine, as most people today would. But he maintained that, in order to make any sense of the work of the Renaissance poets who accepted it, "it is important to shed our own equally delimiting assumptions." Heninger insisted, we have little chance of entering the renaissance mind if we confine ourselves to the inductive process. For example, astrology is folly unless we accept the notion of cosmos, the premise that all things in the universe are interrelated; and metempsychosis is superstitious unless we recognize the *anima mundi*, the world soul from which the individual soul emerges and to which it returns. There is no empirical evidence to support either of these beliefs. But once the fact of cosmos is granted, then deductive logic prescribes that astrology and metempsychosis must obtain.[93]

In this same light, we do not need to judge the metaphysical claims and conclusions in *The Souls of Black Folk* to see what Du Bois accomplished and how. The important thing here is to show that, through the Sorrow Songs and the a priori syntheses of metaphysics, it is possible to see evidence of Absolute Knowledge via the souls of black folk.

Embedded in Du Bois' discussion was a muted understanding of the science of the songs that revealed the slaves' creation as evidence of their and the music's connection to World Soul and what I have interpreted as a demonstration of Absolute Knowledge. To understand that, however, we have to set aside, for the moment, the visible, material aspects of the lives of black folk, which, without a doubt, help to illustrate the "experience of consciousness," and notice Du Bois' use of apriorities. The examples of a priori synthesis have always been controversial and difficult to accept because although apriorities are evidence based on reasoning, the reasoning is deductive (thought-based) rather than inductive (perceptual).

Du Bois' use of a priori synthesis was evident throughout *Souls*. At the risk of belaboring the obvious, the first suggestion of it is his apparent adaptation of *Phenomenology* (or at least its system/theory) as a model. But within *The Souls of Black Folk*, Du Bois' first explicit example appears within the first few pages of his volume where he characterized his mothers' song ("Gene Me, Gene Me") in terms of generations of family members' ignorance of the meaning of the words, while "knowing well the meaning of its music." How could they have known? Du Bois also posited an example of a priori synthesis in his opening the chapter on the songs with the important observation that "[e]ver since I was a child these songs have stirred me strangely. They came out of the South unknown to me, one by one, and yet *at once I knew them* as of me and of mine" (emphasis added). Again, one should ask, how is this possible?

Scholars have variously interpreted these remarks (and others) as Du Bois' somewhat nationalistic effort to connect himself, a "Talented Tenth" elite, to the songs and to "the folk" who created them. The interpretation is only partly (and probably only minimally) correct. Du Bois graduated from Fisk University at a time when less than 5 percent of Americans even graduated from high school. As a member of Harvard's 1890 graduating class, Du Bois was one of the commencement speakers. He shortly thereafter went off to Germany, where he pursued the social sciences (among other courses) practically at the time and in the place of their inception as scholarly fields. He was the first black person to earn a Ph.D. from Harvard (conferred in 1895), and, within a year, his dissertation became the first volume in Harvard University Press's Harvard Historical Studies series. Du Bois was not trying to pass as one of the folk, not even metaphorically. And he had no difficulty accepting how different he was from "the folk." But if Hegel's *Phenomenology* was his model, or even if the Platonic concept of World Soul held any value for him, Du Bois would also have understood that he and "the folk" were inter-related parts of the single unity that was World Soul. Consequently, he would have had no need to contrive a connection to them: he would have known that he and they were already connected.

Du Bois' "knowing" the songs, his and his family's "understanding" of "Gene Me, Gene Me," and even the former slaves' creation of this body of "weird" and wonderful sound evoke the same aspects of the Demiurge's creation of World Soul and the implied cosmology in Plato's report of its creation that was ultimately characterized as "the harmony of the spheres."[94] Du Bois could recognize these sounds, and black folks could effortlessly produce them, because, as a manifestation of Soul and a part of World Soul, this knowledge was already in their minds. Put another way, "the innate consciousness of humanity is total."[95] As Walter Burkert wrote, "there is a kind of knowing which penetrates to the very core of the universe, which offers truth as something at once beatific and comforting, and represents the human being as cradled in a universal harmony."[96] In the slaves' and former slaves' connecting to this Infinite Knowledge, in Du Bois' knowing, is the idea that they simply recalled the tones, intervals, rhythms that were part of the universe—the harmony of the universe—of which they were a part.

Still, unlike Solomon and Maconie, both of whom went on to answer the question each posed about art and music, Du Bois did not directly answer the questions that began his chapter on the Sorrow Songs ("What are these songs, and what do they mean?"). Du Bois, like Arnold Schoenberg a generation later, shunned any effort to delve into the construction of this music. Schoenberg wrote to a friend in 1932: "I cannot warn often enough against the overvaluation of these analyses, since they lead only to what I have always fought against—the recognition of how the piece is *made*; whereas I have always helped my students to recognize—what it is!"[97]

But, we, as phenomenological observers, can use the material to get to the spiritual. And in that light, although Du Bois' Sorrow Songs certainly reflect art, religion, and culture, beyond the perceptual things, themselves, the songs are ultimately evidence of slaves' having transcended the phenomenal/material world, or experience, and connected to the real (Spirit). And, as Du Bois insisted after demurring that he knew nothing of music but something of men, "these songs are the articulate message of the slave to the world." That message, to be sure, was literally the voice of black folk and came from the souls of black folk. But given that these souls were part of and, *in essence*, indistinguishable from that from which they originated, the songs were also the voice of the soul of the universe and reflected the unity and wholeness that World Soul is. And ultimately, the Sorrow Songs not only represent the completion of Soul's journey to Spirit but an example of Absolute Knowing, which Hegel either could not or would not point to at the end of the eighteenth century. For Hegel, absolute religion could lead believers to the idea that "the divine nature is none other than human nature," but "it cannot *demonstrate* it."[98]

Because Du Bois did not explicitly explain the connection and simply accepted it a priori, the most obvious question is whether or not it is possible to show this inductively—that is, whether we can "*demonstrate*" it. In obvious defiance of Schoenberg's warning, I think so. Hegel insisted that the "insight" necessary to demonstrate the union required philosophy, "the 'absolute science (*Wissenschaft*).'" But, equally important, and perhaps more important for us, as Heninger suggested, one would still have to accept the premise of the grand theory of the harmony of the universe (and World Soul) to do so. In that context, the creation of these songs reflects what was most important about much of ancient and classical philosophical thinking, the central point of which, as Pythagoras taught, concerned "the interrelatedness of all human knowledge." Plato's *Timaeus* insisted that "there is only one universe." And as insecure as Plato sometimes seemed about Pythagorean ideas, he nevertheless accepted the idea of "a musical universe based upon mathematical principles of harmony." Boethius concurred that "the soul of the universe is united by a musical concord," and "that we ourselves are united according to this same principle of similarity." For all three thinkers, the universe was "ruled by perfect, mathematical music." Although this music and its harmony is symbolic of a broader, universal harmony, we can and must refer back to the math to demonstrate this unity in Du Bois' Sorrow Songs beyond his useful and evocative musical genealogy.[99]

As already noted, one of the most perplexing aspects of the Sorrow Songs to some of the early listeners was that the tones they heard produced the harmonies they did. Some of the combinations of notes/tones heard in these songs under ordinary circumstances would have been described as discordant; often, they were not notes that one would normally hear sounded together. Yet, as the above observers noted, rather than discord, which music theory would have predicted, the notes produced agreeable sounds.

Musicologist Henry Krehbiel provided an excellent example of this in his description of the spiritual "Great Camp Meeting," which happens also to be the head-song for Du Bois' chapter on Booker T. Washington. Although Krehbiel described aspects of the sound as forceful (he used the words "barbaric force"), he provided an interesting description of the music: "Here the first section of the melody closes with a perfect cadence in the key of E-flat; the second section begins abruptly with an apparently unrelated shout on D-flat—'Gwine to mourn, and nebber tire'—which leads directly, as the effect shows, into the key of A-flat, the subdominant of E-flat. The transition has a singularly bright and enlivening effect and the return to the original key is easy and natural." Although Krehbiel did not say so, these two keys are normally deeply depressing and melancholy. Perhaps this is why he puzzled over the tones and particularly the keys of the song for another full page. Ultimately, he concluded that "the harmonization"—the concord—in the music to the song came from "Mr. Fenner [who published it], who has not told us to what extent he received hints from his singers."[100] Fenner's own words, some of which are quoted above, indicate that he could not have explained it because, as he admitted, he did not know how to. Perhaps we should think of the "bending" of notes—the creation of flatted thirds, fifths, and sevenths, so common in blues, jazz, and black spiritual music—as illustrative of the very thing that Plato described. His creation story, in which the Demiurge employed force, or movement ("bending," in this case), to unite sameness, difference, and essence into one harmonious thing, indicates these creators' simply having connected to that/their infinite knowledge.[101]

It is difficult to imagine anything that would illustrate that knowledge and the connection of the Sorrow Songs and their singers to it more clearly or profoundly than the slave's use of the flatted seventh in some of their songs. Krehbiel refused to speculate as to whether its use sometimes related "to an innate harmonic sense on the part of its users, which sometimes discloses itself very markedly in an evident feeling for the subdominant relationship, or is purely a melodic factor (as in Gregorian music)."[102] But if we consider the flatted seventh from a philosophical perspective, perhaps it loses its mystery and reflects truth/philosophy the way some metaphysicians understood it—as Absolute Knowledge. And we might no longer have to guess, as Krehbiel did, about the mystery of the subdominant relationship in the tones of the slaves' music.

As John Wesley Work noted, black Americans added the flatted seventh to a scale that had already dropped the fourth tone. The new scale Work described was 12356–7. The obvious question is to what extent do the missing fourth and the added flat seventh matter? In a traditional, natural, seven-note scale (whether major or minor) the fourth tone is the subdominant tone. Eliminating a subdominant is, itself, symbolically significant. But, even more, dropping the subdominant transforms the status (for lack of a better word) of some of the remaining notes. In particular, in a scale that has dropped the fourth (subdominant) tone, the fifth tone, which would normally be the dominant, loses that characteristic. That is, where the subdominant disappears, no dominant remains. And there is yet another important characteristic of this "new" scale. Although in natural major and minor scales, all seven tones are equal in degree, (they are half steps or semitones,) in this new, minor scale, the degree for the seventh interval (the added flatted seventh) is a whole step (rather than a half step) below the tonic (first tone). When the seventh tone was half a step below the tonic (that is, equal in degree to all the other tones in the scale) it (the seventh) was a leading tone. The seventh tone is called a leading tone not because of its grandeur; on the contrary, its sound creates the feeling of wanting to/needing to move up to (to lead to) the tonic (the first tone), a half-step higher. In other words, it seems/is incomplete. But in ending this "new" scale with the added flatted seventh—one of those "big lusty whole tone[s]" that Sidney Lanier (in the epigraph) said "would shake any man's soul" (especially, I would add, if that man expected another half step)—it has already moved up, is whole and no longer needy, and has connected to the first tone.

But this is mostly math (along with some sensual perception). And as Socrates and Aristotle complained of aspects of Pythagoreanisms, it should have a more explicit relationship to the human soul and, as I have suggested above, World Soul. The symbolism of the discussion of the flatted seventh should be clear enough where the idea of the harmony of the spheres is understood as something more than a theory of sound but also symbolic of nature, order, and human relationships. And probably no better parallel in human relationships exists to the new musical scale's dropping the subdominant and thereby eliminating the dominant than the struggle between Hegel's Lord and Servant (Du Bois' master and slave/landlord and tenant), in which each at first depends on the other for his status, but both have to realize their wholeness in and for themselves. What is less obvious is how this symbolism (appearance) manifests as real in the music of *The Souls of Black Folk*. We can, in fact, further transform examples of deductive, a priori, synthesis to inductive, a posteriori, evidence.

In "Steal Away," one of the songs from Du Bois' "middle" group of eight songs, the subdominant (fourth tone) disappears, which causes the elimination of the dominant and its power, and the seventh tone is transformed from a needy, desirous half-tone to a fully independent whole tone, no longer reaching for wholeness but *being* whole. It should not surprise us, given the subject of the song—the human/slave drive toward freedom, liberty, and wholeness. The dramatic modulation in "You May Bury Me in the East" (a song in the first group of Du Bois' genealogical arrangement) reflects the same transformation, making it an especially appropriate song, not only in terms of its words but in the science of the music for heading the chapter about the choices of John Jones's sovereign self/soul. The musical result of mathematical alterations (or the mathematical result of musical alterations) occur in music created by folk who were presumably unaware (in terms of "learning") of the science of either.[103] Thus, here it suggests Absolute Knowledge; it is as though they knew without having had to learn.

Du Bois ultimately characterized this music in a most provocative way:

[T]he Negro folk-song—the rhythmic cry of the slave—stands today not simply as the sole American music, but as the most beautiful expression of human experience born this side [of] the seas. It has been neglected, it has been, and is, half despised, and above all it has been persistently mistaken and misunderstood; but notwithstanding, it still remains as *the singular spiritual heritage of the nation* and the greatest gift of the Negro people. (emphasis added)

Du Bois' words about the significance of this music easily leads to conclusions about romanticism, fantasia, "race" talk, and implicitly, hyperbole. But for one framing a metaphysical discussion, the greater significance is, literally, that some of these songs reflected America's only example of soul's/consciousness's development to Spirit, philosophy (science), and Absolute Knowledge.[104]

In these songs and the rituals or the context (experience) in which they often appeared—church services, ring shouts, prayer meetings—the singers were "able to know by understanding itself the ideas that [they have, becoming] . . . knowers in actuality, that is, producers of genuine knowledge." Christopher Bamford continued "that through which the mind understands is one with that through which the world is created, so that knowledge of mind is knowledge of creation." For Plato, whose thinking was at least partly influenced by the Pythagoreans, "The soul's self-knowledge in pure thought thus becomes its knowledge of the universe."[105] Hegel put it slightly differently: "Spirit has made its existence identical with its essence; it has itself for its object just as it is, and the abstract element of immediacy, and the separation of knowing and truth, is overcome" (*PS* §37). In the context of Timeaus's dialogue the songs reflect evidence of the Demiurge's mingling *all* parts of the universe into "the idea"—the World Soul/the harmony of the spheres. Philosophers related this potential "knowing" to Idealism. This connection between self-knowledge (Soul) and knowledge of the universe (Spirit) was manifested in a "new song" as in times past—Psalms—and similarly addressed, as the Fisk University Jubilee Singers demonstrated, to all the nations.[106]

———

Scholarly attention to black art and culture during the 1960s reintroduced us to the significance of Du Bois' Sorrow Songs and simultaneously led us away from what might have been most important about them. In the case of the former, much of this attention appropriately focused on the art and creativity of the music and its performance. Slaves' fashioned instruments out of wood, dried vegetables, and animal skins; created complex, driving rhythms by stomping, slapping, snapping, and clapping body parts; and produced unmatched harmonies with their rhythms and voices. The words of the songs were, without a doubt, a creative/poetic means of slaves' preserving their thoughts about their general environment and circumstances. And Du Bois' pairing the musical epigraphs with verses from Byron, Shakespeare, Browning, Tennyson, Whittier, and others easily suggested that the art of the slaves was as important as that of people commonly recognized as paragons of the literary arts.

More recent scholarly examinations of the Sorrow Songs, including efforts to explain what we cannot see or hear (or translate/understand), certainly began to move us beyond phenomena. But ultimately, even this attention came to focus on the words, even though they were often missing or unrecognizable. David Blight and Robert Gooding-Williams, for example, saw a parallel between Du Bois' leaving out the words to the musical epigraphs and "slaves' clandestine creation and expression of this music." In the most thoroughgoing examination of the songs to date, Eric J. Sundquist, who acknowledged that "the musical epigraphs demonstrate [that] the words are in some sense secondary," also related the lack of understanding of the words in Du Bois' mothers' song to "the loss of ancestral language . . . remaining a secret language that cannot be correctly translated even by those who remember and repeat it." For Sundquist, the meaninglessness of the words calls attention to "the decimation of African culture under slavery." Most recently, Sandra Adell surmised that "Du Bois' complaint, like that of Plato, is that in the western tradition the voice—the words—have become subordinate to something else."[107]

In fact, Du Bois himself subordinated the words, and in doing so he silently echoed *and* addressed the classical (Platonic) criticisms of the Pythagoreans who failed to pay enough attention to the meaning of the sounds. Du Bois' chapter on the songs encourages us to think about music in an early philosophical tradition, especially during Plato's and Aristotle's time, when "'musikē' . . . signified *the* vocal art of declamation to which grammar, rhetoric, poetry, and other literary studies were subservient musical arts."[108] Accepting, in this case, that the "language" was music and that the music was the message, Du Bois' "articulate message of the slave to the world," that the nineteenth-century example of Absolute Knowing—America's *singular Spiritual* achievement to that point—came from the souls of black folk, is, however, impossible unless one accepts deductive reasoning—apriorities—as evidence in *The Souls of Black Folk*, which Du Bois did.

At the outset of his discussion of the songs, Du Bois introduced them in both deductive and inductive terms, or forms of knowledge. The philosopher, who "knew" the songs from the very moment he heard them (without ever having heard them before), was also the modern scholar who recognized "the songs . . . [as] the siftings of centuries"—a reflection of hundreds of years of history. In this statement, Du Bois evoked aspects of both Hegel's philosophy of spirit and his experience of consciousness by deftly connecting the one issue of "knowing," in the metaphysical tradition, to "learning" (experience) in the more modern material/empirical tradition. His also noting that "the music is far more ancient than the words" was probably deliberate and definitely compelling. It was a good way, if not the only way, to situate this nineteenth-century music in a much longer and more important trajectory (of the history of experience) than what was represented in the beginning-of-the-twentieth-century environment of vaudeville and minstrelsy or even Du Bois' brief description of the music's evolution. He could also have described the music as ancient because of its African antecedents. But there was no practical way for him to fix *the origin* of the sound or the music in Africa: certain aspects of the sound could just as easily have been Asian/"Middle Eastern" or, in nineteenth-century parlance and, more broadly, "oriental." And so, perhaps Du Bois' remark about the ancient nature of the music was an allusion to the idea of cosmic harmony, the harmony of the spheres, and World Soul. As Du Bois did in many other instances, and as the ancient/classical philosophers regularly did, he left this to us to discern. Indeed, as already noted, he did not even directly answer the most important questions about the songs that he, himself, had posed. Du Bois, however, knew that in the popular and scholarly imagination, "Africa was left without culture and without history" (an allusion to Hegel?).[109] Thus, it was important to provide a history and genealogy of this music. As a philosopher, it was equally important to connect this history (experience) to the principles of World Soul and Spirit.

Ultimately, the same intellectual shift that resulted in psychology's supplanting philosophy in discussions about the soul also solidified the break between art and science and science and religion. And over time, science came to focus on the practical/technical, while the big, seemingly unanswerable, questions, (e.g., man's place and purpose in the universe, man's relationship to nature) were left "to the philosophers and theologians." Music's functions narrowed as well, becoming mostly social (entertainment). Discussions about music came to focus on rather pedantic dichotomies such as "sacred versus profane, high art versus folk art, traditional versus progressive, upper-case Classical versus Romantic, lower-case classical versus pop," and corresponding ideas about the importance of listening to "the right music." Music thus lost its role in helping "to elucidate the fundamental unities that explain the function and thus the meaning of the phenomenal world," which had been a goal of ancient science. Jamie James saw a revival in such interests in music in "the compositions of the twentieth-century avant-garde, . . . and . . . in what might be called the folk culture of the occult underground."[110] Du Bois, I think, understood that the "fundamental" unities and the big, imponderable, universal questions were actually still being addressed and answered *throughout* the nineteenth century—in the songs of the slaves.[111]

CONCLUSION

"O World of Worlds, How Shall Man Make You One?"[1]

The abbreviators of works do injury to knowledge and to love. . . . Of what value is he who, in order to abbreviate the parts of those things of which he professes to give complete knowledge, leaves out the greater part of things of which the whole is composed? . . . Oh human stupidity! . . . You don't see that you are falling into the same error as one who strips a tree of its adornment of branches full of leaves, intermingled with fragrant flowers or fruit, in order to demonstrate that the tree is good for making planks. —Leonardo da Vinci[2]

If now once this great ground principle is fixed, that negroes are men,—an indivisible part of that great humanity which works and aspires,—then what are the ideals of life that interest them in common with other men? To ask that question is to answer it. They are the same. They, with all men, strive to know and to do, to organize and to dream, to fight in that great battle of the west in the glow of the setting sun.
—W. E. B. Du Bois[3]

Upon its publication in 1903, *The Souls of Black Folk* made an immediate impression on its readers. Jessie Redmon Fauset, who would ultimately become an important writer in her own right, wrote: "I am glad, glad you wrote it—we have needed someone to voice the intricacies of the blind maze of thought and action along which the modern, educated colored man and woman struggles." She asked Du Bois an important question; she also answered it. "It hurt you to write that book, didn't it? The man of fine sensibilities has to suffer exquisitely, just simply because his feeling is so fine."[4] A twenty-four-year-old working-class Russian Jewish immigrant wrote of buying the book, based purely on its title, in a Delancey Street (New York) book store. Reading it forced him to overcome his "natural shyness and conscious ignorance of style and form" and to write to Du Bois about the (elegantly) conflicting emotions that the book created in him. "I was over powered by a peculiar pain that was so much akin to bliss," he wrote. The book made him indignant, furious, ashamed, and disgraced, "yet, from underneath all this, up swelled a keen sense of inner delight." *Souls* evoked for him a "Satanic blending of both pain of a bleeding heart and joy [of] the gods." Mr. Tabak prayed that Du Bois would continue to pursue his "noble work" and would live long enough "to see those ghastly social injustices to be completely and forever abolished."[5]

Few written responses to Du Bois' book were more insightful than these two. The twenty-four-year-old working-class immigrant apologized in case he "failed in any degree to pay the respects due to a man of [Du Bois'] position and learning." But, he concluded, "I feel you are bigger than ordinary," and consequently he rightly reckoned that Du Bois would not be offended by this letter from a "poor, ignorant working man" and that he could speak to Du Bois as an equal. And despite Fauset's narrow focus on "modern, educated" black men and women (which would later be a criticism of her novels and was, here, something of a misread of Du Bois' volume), the eighteen-year-old black, female college undergraduate recognized what was at the heart of Du Bois' volume—a study of black being and doing or, in Fauset's words, "thought and action."[6]

The public reception of Du Bois' book was not uniformly as insightful or supportive. Although it is true that his powerful use of the ideas of veils, the color line, and double consciousness resonated with most black readers, some people had difficulties accepting one part or another of the study. Some believed that double consciousness, as they understood it, perfectly characterized their existence, and others lamented that the idea pathologized black people. Even though the idea of the veil(s) was meaningful to most black people, the reasons—religious, metaphorical, and/or literal— easily differed from one person to another. And while some black people fought tirelessly for the elimination of the color line, others believed that black people *could* thrive behind it, and should.

White readers recognized that the book was for and about them, too, and their responses covered the range of possibilities. Among them, W. D. Hooper, a southern (and liberal by southern standards) educator, was in part defensive, insisting that he was not like the southern whites Du Bois described and had never done anything to offend black people. But parts of the book made Mr. Tabak, who was more fully empathetic, ashamed "of being white colored." While William James, Du Bois' undergraduate adviser at Harvard, complained about the book's general negativity,

Du Bois' former graduate adviser, Albert Bushnell Hart, recognized the book as "'the only literature published by a Harvard Graduate in forty years.'" George Foster Peabody, while insisting that he was sympathetic, proffered the thought that Du Bois was too smart and too important "to indulge" black people as he had in *Souls*, concluding that Du Bois had damaged the reputation he was leaving to "[his] family and [his] people"; Max Weber, by contrast, asked for permission to translate the volume into German. After reading the copy of the book sent to him by his brother William, Henry James was moved to ask: "How can everything so have gone that the only 'Southern' book of any distinction published for many a year is *The Souls of Black Folk*, by that most accomplished of members of the Negro Race, Mr. W. E. B. Du Bois?"[7]

In the more than one hundred years that have passed since the publication of *The Souls of Black Folk*, neither interest in nor efforts to analyze the volume have subsided. Despite all the attention, old and new, *Souls* was (and remains) the phenomenon it was for reasons that have only partly (or not at all) been uncovered. Discovering some of these nuggets is possible, first, if one considers *Souls* as a whole, coherent work, shaped as much by Du Bois' foundation in philosophy as by his training in history, sociology, and political economics; second, if we view Du Bois' effort as one designed to establish black people—a striving people of soul and spirit—as a world-historical people, fit for inclusion among others generally recognized as such, even (perhaps especially) as black people were being characterized as not yet fit for full citizenship or, in the worse cases, even for fully human status; and, third, if we consider this effort as one that ultimately had the effect of adding the nineteenth century, America, and the souls of black folk to Hegel's narratives of the philosophy of history.

In *Souls*, Du Bois completed a discussion that he began in the early lecture/essay that launched his career as an activist scholar, "The Conservation of Races" (hereafter, "Conservation"), which also began his (public) excursion into Hegelian phenomenology and metaphysics.[8] In that essay, Du Bois' use of the words "race," "blood," "inheritance," and other similarly ambiguous terms easily led twentieth-century thinkers in particular down the wrong path. Adding late twentieth-century developments in DNA research to the discussion resulted in a real quandary. But when Du Bois wrote and presented "Conservation," a microscope that allowed the observation of cells was more than a decade away from development, and molecular biology was barely imaginable and would not come to fruition until the 1930s. And so Du Bois seems to have "failed" to reconcile his discussion of "race" with modern "science" in the "Conservation" essay for a good reason. His discussion was grounded in philosophy rather than biology or physiology. Du Bois' presentation of "Conservation" at the inaugural meeting of the American Negro Academy simply laid out practical and ideal (the material and the spiritual) rationales for the organization's existence and potential directions for its future work. He began by surveying "the whole question of race in human philosophy" and by recognizing "that any striving, no matter how intense and earnest, which is against the constitution of the world, is vain." Du Bois had, thus, begun this lecture with a significant suggestion of the idea of World Soul.[9]

Reminiscent of Herodotus's characterization of "Greekness," Du Bois defined "race" as "a vast family of human beings, generally of common blood and language, always of common history, traditions and impulses, who are both voluntarily and involuntarily striving together for the accomplishment of certain more or less vividly conceived ideals of life."[10] He recognized the saliency of notions of "blood, color and cranial measurements" in contemporary efforts to organize human groups but ultimately eschewed them in favor of the "spiritual" and "psychical" characteristics that he said transcended physical characteristics. He believed that black Americans had "a distinct mission as a race" that could only be accomplished as a race, and their destiny was *not* in their "absorption by the white Americans" but in "stalwart originality which shall unswervingly follow Negro ideals." In the *Academy Creed* that he proposed in the lecture, Du Bois described that mission/destiny, or ideal, as the realization of human brotherhood. Black Americans had to use their energy, intellect, and organizations to insist on "that broader humanity which freely recognizes differences in men, but sternly deprecates inequality in their opportunities of development."[11]

It was not merely in the first chapter of *Souls* but the whole book, published just a few years after the appearance of "Conservation," where these ideas found the space for more complete development.[12] Importantly, however, at some point between the two discussions, the "*conservation of race*" became the "*conservation of soul*" (emphasis added).[13] The *destiny* of the race was unchanged—"to attain self-conscious manhood" without Africanizing America or whitening blackness.[14] And the ultimate goal in *Souls*, more nuanced but unchanged, was "the ideal of human brotherhood, gained through the unifying ideal of Race; the ideal of fostering and developing the traits and talents of the Negro, not in opposition to or contempt for other races, but rather in large conformity to the greater ideals of the American Republic, in order that some day on American soil two world-races may give each to each those characteristics both so sadly lack."

In the Hegelian tradition, with its commentary about World Soul, all world historical peoples had an important contribution to make to the functioning of the whole. And *The Souls of Black Folk* is an illustration of the striving of one of those groups to fulfill its destiny. As historian Joel Williamson has aptly written, "Du Bois, like Hegel, sees the history of the world as the spirit of freedom rising to realize itself through specific world historical peoples. Consciousness is not achieved individually and one by one, but rather through the people, each people rising to a consciousness of itself, pursuing its 'Volksgeist' its spirit, its soul, its genius. It is as if God implanted in each people a distinct seed, and that essence, that spirit struggles with its opposite (matter) for life. As the spirit struggles, as it exercises its will, it rises and matures, unfolding the full promise always there, pre-formed, latent in the seed. . . . 'The History of the World,' declared Hegel, 'is none other than the progress of the consciousness of Freedom.'"[15] *The Souls of Black Folk* was a text for the nineteenth-century segment of that history.

Samuel Taylor Coleridge once wrote: "'Grant me a nature having two contrary forces, one of which tends to expand infinitely, while the other strives to apprehend or find itself in this infinity, and I will call up the world of intelligences with the whole system of their representation to arise up before you.'" Despite his own serious personal difficulties, Coleridge also understood that if we get over our "obsession with matter, the need for Matter as datum," we could realize that "'the idea of creation alone remains.'"[16]

Du Bois' graduate training certainly encouraged him to create a data-driven study of turn-of-the-century black urban life. As he later phrased it, "I determined to put science into sociology through a study of the condition and the problems of my own group. I was going to study the facts, any and all fact, concerning the American Negro and his plight, and by measurement and comparison and research, work up to any valid generalization which I could."[17] An early result was undoubtedly *The Philadelphia Negro*.

Perhaps the tepid (at best) public (white?) response to the study (and the snub by the University of Pennsylvania administration) helped Du Bois to overcome the near obsession with data that he had certainly adopted during the course of his historical studies with Albert Bushnell Hart at Harvard and his pursuit of political and historical economics with Gustav Schmoller and Adolph Wagner in Berlin. Perhaps, even, Du Bois simply remembered something that nineteenth-century German scientific materialists taught: "that there was a difference between science (*Wissenschaft*) and naked knowledge (*das blosse Wissen*)." What is clear is that in *Souls* Du

Bois returned to his broader foundation in philosophy. It was a study that began at Fisk; continued at Harvard with his first academic adviser William James, with the then-committed Hegelian idealist Josiah Royce, and with George Santayana, with whom Du Bois took a course that included the study of "German Philosophy from Kant to Hegel"; and it concluded (formally) in Berlin, where he studied under, among others, the devout neo-Hegelian historian Heinrich von Treitschke, whom Du Bois later described as "by far the most interesting of the professors" he had in Germany.[18]

When Du Bois wrote in mid-twentieth-century correspondence that his Harvard philosophical guides provided him "a philosophy which [had] served [him] since," he suggested that his study of philosophy did not impede but enhanced his subsequent historical analyses.[19] In his posthumously published *Autobiography*, Du Bois further explained that his historical studies with Albert Bushnell Hart inspired his "first steps toward sociology as the science of human action," but he also described his movement to history as having enabled him to conceive "the idea of applying philosophy to an historical interpretation of race relations."[20] There does not exist a better characterization of *The Souls of Black Folk*. That philosophically influenced "historical interpretation of race relations" is a simultaneous illustration of the two contentious forces (material/spiritual) that Coleridge described.

Some contemporary and subsequent readers of *Souls* were understandably uncomfortable with what appeared to be Du Bois' substitution of emotion for evidence. And *Souls* is, without a doubt, a passionate book. But the appearance of a problem results, ironically, not from Du Bois' having abandoned empiricism—"the facts, any and all fact"—but by his having returned (returned, when one considers the Philadelphia study) to philosophy. The new social science methods allowed Du Bois to illustrate and explain what everyone could already see, if they would only look. Metaphysics helped to show what lay behind it (philosophers might say, what it really was), its relationship to the whole, and its consistency to other forms of being—a goal of philosophy—the search for absolutes. And it is not an unreasonable conjecture that Hegel's *Phenomenology of Spirit* provided a model for this project. Du Bois was a true intellectual, and as Errol E. Harris observed, "At the end of the nineteenth century and in the early decades of the twentieth, Hegel was perhaps the most influential, the most revered, and the most closely studied philosopher of the western world."[21]

The methods Du Bois chose were consistent with methods chosen by other intellectuals at the time who were addressing some of the biggest and most confounding questions of the day (even of the century). As Walter Isaacson has recently shown, Einstein pursued his special and general theories of relativity empirically *and* philosophically, and he refused to accept the conclusion of either as valid until the conclusions of both pursuits matched. Although it took fifteen more years to provide the empirical proof for the general theory, physicist Max Born recognized it as "'the greatest feat of human thinking about nature, the most amazing combination of philosophical penetration, physical intuition and mathematical skill.'" Brian Greene added, "'General relativity provides the choreography for an entwined cosmic dance of space, time, matter and energy.'" Born and Greene thus described Einstein's laws in ways that certainly suggest the ancient philosophical principle of cosmic harmony—the complete and yet interrelated nature of the diverse parts of the universe. What is even more important here, ALL of Einstein's greatest scientific discoveries began as deductions.[22]

Hegel, Du Bois, and Einstein all illustrated what A. E. Taylor argued around the time Du Bois was writing *Souls*—that "[t]he various sciences differ primarily, not as dealing with different *parts* of the world of reality, but as dealing with the whole of it so far as can be brought under different *aspects*." These different sciences simply approached the facts from different perspectives. Although we would be hard pressed to characterize certain aspects of metaphysics as science as we define it today, nineteenth-century and early twentieth-century intellectuals, particularly physicists and philosophers, conscientiously pursued knowledge and truth through theoretical/deductive processes, which, for them, was perfectly logical (no pun intended). Metaphysics allowed, as Taylor put it, a study of "any absolute ['applicable to all things'] principles which are assumed or put forward in the study of other sciences." Moreover, because metaphysics was "a science of being *qua* being" as Aristotle put it, philosophers considered it to be "the foundation of all science." Metaphysics, a study of first principles ("the general conditions to which all reality, as such, conforms"), includes ontology ("the study of being"), cosmology ("the structure of the universe"), and epistemology (a study of knowledge). Metaphysicians sought, ultimately, to develop "general laws" that connect all phenomena, and, for some of them, "[e]mpiricism was but the beginning, the lowest level of reasoning, at the top of which philosophy reigned."[23] Thus, Du Bois did not evade philosophy; at least not in *The Souls of Black Folk*. He dove, head first, into it, and embraced every major aspect of it.[24]

Du Bois pursued both what Hegel described as "the actual" (which scholars have written as "the real") through philosophy and "the rational" through empiricism. If the outcomes of the pursuits were successful, we would be able to see, in the words of Hegel, that "what is rational is actual, and what is actual is rational" (or, what is rational is real and what is real is rational). The experience of consciousness and the philosophy or science of spirit would lead to the same place—knowledge. It has been difficult for scholars to see both pursuits as scientific even where science is understood simply as the quest for knowledge. Consequently, some of the metaphysical aspects of *Souls* have easily been reduced to "mysticism" in a way that raises suspicion. But mysticism was a well-established scholarly tradition. Mystics sought to account for that which cannot be seen, that which cannot be observed through the senses; in this case, the different "shapes" or characteristics of consciousness, or soul. Mysticism should not be confused with nineteenth-century spiritualism, which involved efforts to communicate with the dead. Du Bois' nineteenth-century writing style, often described as Victorian, and his concerns with Spirit and "Spiritual Striving," perhaps caused some scholars to conflate spiritualism and mysticism, resulting in the appearance that Du Bois somehow veered off the scholarly/scientific course in *The Souls of Black Folk*.[25]

The idea that Du Bois made a mess of the science in his early works might also result from viewing science in narrow (twentieth-century) terms and can hold only (and then just barely) if one limits "science" to biology and/or physiology. Despite Du Bois' using some language in *Souls* that evokes these sciences, it is extremely doubtful that he would have allowed himself to be lured into a debate about blood, brain weight, and skull size—which, at the time, was itself somewhat muddled "science."[26] Instead, Du Bois used all the new (rational/empirical) methods of the social sciences to document the material life and environment in which the souls of black folk moved (what Hegel called the context and experience), while *also* using metaphysics to explore the spiritual world (the development of consciousness), and, together, to deliver, in fact, the most complete discussion that had been offered to that time about the history and experience of the souls of black folk in nineteenth-century America.

Modern understandings of science relate to methods of experimentation that were not fully organized until the twentieth century. Du Bois' system of study was based partly on classical Greek science, which, until the Renaissance and beyond it for many, especially philosophers and physicists, held "that the world was a kosmos, an ordered and harmonious structure" rather than the mechanical system of independent parts that Newton proposed (and Einstein's theories and subsequent empirical proofs worked to modify). According to the ancient understandings, this cosmos was "a living organism" in which all parts "had an innate purpose to contribute to the harmonious functioning of the whole." Those parts, without outside interference, "moved naturally toward their proper places in the universe." It was this idea that buttressed Du Bois' Talented Tenth ideal, which was not an argument designed to promote one segment of black America over another but an idea offered in the interest of a harmonious, well-functioning universe in which all parts (people) received the support (Hegel's "ladders") necessary for them to make their own self-determined contributions to it. All groups required that their most able members receive the most extensive training available (in whatever areas they pursued) and that they work to support and encourage the endeavors of the rest of the group. The "problem of the color-line" was obviously that this external phenomenon interfered with that process, creating discord, lies, revolt, and revenge. But even more important for Du Bois, and as Aristotle maintained, such interference could make it impossible "to reveal the essence of phenomena." In the case of black folk, this interference (the color line) created results (poverty, illiteracy, etc.) that the larger society regularly misrepresented as real. Because in the universe/cosmos, Soul—"that which perceives and knows"—was the source of all living, because individual souls were both "part of the force that moves the entire universe" and "part of a universal process of knowing," these obstructions could not be destructive of any part of the universe (the souls of black folk) without also being destructive of the whole—*anima mundi* or World Soul—and America.[27]

Remembering Du Bois' philosophical foundation helps to resolve ironically competing conclusions about his work in which a major aspect of some of the general complaints turn out to be a point of celebration for others. In the case of the former it appears that Du Bois essentialized blackness/race, and in the case of the latter he celebrated race/nationalism. Du Bois neither essentialized nor valorized blackness. Rather, Essence itself, or Soul, was his focus, along with its source, Spirit. Showing that consciousness in the context of the lives of black folk traveled the same course it traveled in the historical contexts of all other "world-historical peoples," Du Bois demonstrated the essential unity of the souls of black folk with the rest of humankind. His goal was not to make black folk different or exceptional, not even in their unbelievable suffering (as he noted, American slavery was *not* the worst the world had known), but to show that they, in their loving and living and longing, in their doing and being, were no different from (*essentially*, in and of the same Spirit as) the other folks whose history and experience Hegel's study illustrated.

Confusion in our interpretative efforts results also from an incomplete view of Du Bois' relationship to Enlightenment thought. Like Hegel, he was not so thoroughly enamored of Enlightenment ideas as one might imagine. On one hand, Enlightenment thought (and its eighteenth- and nineteenth-century manifestations—material empiricism and philosophical positivism, along with early developments in social scientific methods) made it important for Du Bois to demonstrate black accomplishments since emancipation and to show the systemic barriers (the color line, among them) to further achievement. He also showed that where black folks' efforts were stymied, the whole community was stunted in its development as well. But Enlightenment-era thinkers had also put the proverbial elephant in the room. As Michel-Rolph Trouillot has pointed out, Enlightenment thought formally introduced the idea of race into the most important philosophical question, "what is man?" in ways that suggested that Africans were undeniably humans, but of an inferior sort.[28] Given the subsequent flood of literature that introduced a variety of hierarchies of human beings in which black people often fell somewhere between humans and animals, in the *tertium quid* category, not even the biblical notion of the unity of humankind stood much of a chance. And so Du Bois did something that has persistently caused confusion: while using Enlightenment views of science, and especially nineteenth-century notions of empiricism, to make as complete a case as possible about the *experience* of the souls of black folk, Du Bois simultaneously *challenged* other Enlightenment-era (and prevailing) views by demonstrating the essential humanity of black people.[29]

Enlightenment views of science, and the subsequent new social sciences, in particular, demanded a certain kind of evidence—"the rational." In that environment, metaphysics is an easy target. Most people readily accept Plato's first four ways of knowing/identifying an object—"by name, by definition, by image, or by knowledge to which mind and right opinion are added" (the latter of which is more popularly characterized as that about which we have all agreed is fact). "But the fifth, Being itself . . . 'that which is the object of knowledge and truly exists,'" really does sound like a variant of what Einstein, describing quantum entanglement, labeled "spooky action at a distance." Perhaps no one made the critique of metaphysics more powerfully during the eighteenth-century rise of science than David Hume, who concluded:

> If we take in our hand any volume; of divinity or school metaphysics, for instance; let us ask, Does it contain any abstract reasoning concerning quantity or number? No. Does it contain any experimental reasoning concerning matter of fact? No. Commit it then to the flames: for it can contain nothing but sophistry and illusion.[30]

We have long since become accustomed to a form of research in which one reaches general scientific conclusions from the patterns created by compiling diverse specific examples of directly observable evidence. Such explicit empirical evidence is substantial in *The Souls of Black Folk*, especially in the middle chapters of the book. Du Bois' specific examples of the number of homes and acreage purchased by black Americans, the number of individuals who achieved literacy, higher education, and/or graduate and professional education, the work these individuals did after achieving this education, proved their contribution to the development of the nation and led to fairly obvious conclusions about the potential of the larger group were it not for the existence of the color line. Du Bois showed the striving, the material outcomes of the striving, the failures of the striving, and the reasons for the failures in urban and rural settings. He showed that absentee landlordism and industrial capitalism as they operated throughout the South were devastating for the whole South, not just sharecroppers and tenant farmers. He consistently showed the denial of the premise of the Declaration of Independence and the threat the denial posed for the development of the country as a whole. He also pointed out, however briefly, that these traditions knew no boundaries and were having devastating consequences throughout the world. For most of us, this inductive reasoning resonates—we can see the examples/evidence that produced the conclusions.

We should also consider the pattern Du Bois repeatedly pointed out involving "revolt and revenge," assimilation or sycophancy ("living the Lie"), and, ultimately, under the best of circumstances, self-determination or wholeness/freedom as additional and compelling empirical evidence as well. In the Hegelian construct, these are evidence of Consciousness's movement to "new true object[s]" through experience, which was the "dialectic process which consciousness executes on itself—on its knowledge as well as on its object—in that sense that out of it the new and true object arises."[31] In all of Du Bois' examples in *Souls*, among slaves and former slaves, in John Jones, Crummell, and even Du Bois himself (the episode with the tall, newcomer girl), we see the pattern of revolt and revenge, assimilation/sycophancy, and the ultimate struggle to reach wholeness/freedom and self-determination. They are not only examples of Hegel's Self-Consciousness, Reason, and Spirit, they are also useful adaptations of Aristotle's desire/appetite, reason/thought, and spirit.

One should, in fact, also view Du Bois' framework of work, culture, and liberty as another adaptation of the Aristotelian triumvirate; as a more accessible, modern iteration of the ancient ideals. This adaptation would have been recognizable to those who were literate in either classical or modern Continental philosophy. But they were terms that also resonated in the turn-of-the-twentieth century "progressive" ethos in America even if the reader had never read Aristotle or Hegel.

Work, culture, and liberty, and Du Bois' more obvious dialectical arrangement of revolt and revenge, assimilation and sycophancy, and self-determination or freedom, both reveal evidence of what Hegel called the experience of consciousness. But what is even more important than that illustration is what it means. It did *more* than document black life and experience in nineteenth-century America. Hegel's history of the experience of consciousness took us from the customs and traditions of Greek civilization to the law and politics of Roman civilization, and from the law and politics of the Romans to the humanism of the Renaissance, and from the humanism of the Renaissance to the individualism of the Enlightenment.[32] *The Souls of Black Folk*, then, took us from the individualism of the Enlightenment to the materialism of nineteenth-century industrial capitalism and, thus, added the nineteenth century and America to Hegel's universal history of the experience of consciousness.

Quite possibly, however, the rational, Hegel's "experience of consciousness," Du Bois' history and social science, was merely the detail. Although detail is undeniably important for a scientist, detail alone was not enough for some philosophers. As Errol E. Harris reminds us,

Analysis [empiricism] by itself presents us only with the separated details devoid of their bearing and dependence upon one another, and as their intrinsic character usually, if not always, depends on their mutual interrelation, isolating them from the context from which they have been dissected distorts our understanding of the whole.

Harris continues with a quote from R. G. Collingwood:

"One cannot abstract without falsifying. To think apart of things that severance makes no essential difference to their inner nature is only to erect falsification into a principle."[33]

Not surprisingly, Du Bois, like Hegel *and* Einstein, was interested in more than the details.[34] Philosophers sought "the real." Hegel's illustration of "the real"—what we cannot observe through the senses—is explored through the "philosophy of spirit." Spirit, which is the goal/object of Soul's striving, is the ultimate realization of truth or knowledge.

Throughout *Souls* this quest *appears*, almost consistently, as an overt discussion of education and a focus on schools and schooling. From the discussion of the post–Civil War era creation of free public schools for black and white southern youths in the first two chapters of *Souls*, through the chapters on Booker T. Washington, Dougherty County, Atlanta, John Jones, and Crummell, Du Bois demonstrated what he said white southerners always understood—that "education among all kinds of men always has had, and always will have, an element of danger and revolution, of dissatisfaction and discontent." Throughout his discussion, Du Bois evoked the idea of Soul's constant quest for knowledge/truth, and its dissatisfaction until reaching that ultimate/universal truth (Spirit/the real). As he so aptly put it, "men strive to know."[35]

Josie, her sister, and her brothers, in the middle section of the book, epitomized the danger of awakening this consciousness. These siblings were struggling for the details, even if they did not yet know why. But Du Bois ultimately characterized Josie, who merely "longed to learn," and her brothers, as having had their "young appetites . . . whetted to an edge by school and story and half-awakened thought." Because of that, it became impossible for them to be *content* "born without and beyond the World." Du Bois understood that they could not be content because the truth/real was that they were in and of that world, but the color line kept them "without and beyond" it. Leaving the dichotomy unresolved was dangerous.[36]

Perhaps the most revealing example of this aspect of Soul's necessary striving for truth/knowledge appears in the chapter "Of the Coming of John." The example is not so much, as one might think, John's return to school and performing well upon his return. The best example came after John's totally humiliating "homecoming" presentation at church in Altamaha. When John fled from the church, he was followed by his little sister, Jennie. In anguish herself over John's embarrassment, she cried on his shoulder but managed to ask, "'does it make every one—unhappy when they study and learn lots of things?'" John "paused and smiled" and answered, "'I am afraid it does.'" Jennie then asked, "'Are you glad you studied?'" to which John responded "slowly but positively." After thinking for a moment, Jennie spoke again: "'I wish I was unhappy,—and—and,' putting both arms about his neck, 'I think I am, a little, John.'" Du Bois gave us no direct clues about the meaning of this truncated "dialogue." But if we take Hegel's study as our model, this awakened soul/consciousness was already on the path to Absolute Knowledge, real truth, and being in and of itself, or spirit.

Each of Hegel's chapters focuses on particular aspects of Soul's development toward that end. Although obviously not always as explicit, Du Bois' volume roughly follows the chapter-to-chapter example, as my preface to chapter 5 illustrates. Du Bois, like Hegel, also demonstrated some movement through these stages *within* most of his individual chapters. This is especially evident for each of the first three and four of the final five chapters of *Souls*. And while across the individual chapters in the final section one can see evidence of consciousness's developing toward its full potential, in the final chapter on the songs we see the complete Hegelian process. Du Bois takes us from the general, individual, everyday songs (Hegel's living work of art), which reflect consciousness and self-consciousness (spirit meeting spirit), to the ten master songs (the spiritual work of art), which reflect reason (spirit knowing spirit), to, reading *between* the lines, the creation of a "new song" in which spirit knows itself as spirit.

Through the songs, Du Bois not only extended Hegel's discussion of Soul's journey to Spirit through the nineteenth century by focusing on America and the souls of black folk, he provided an important example of Absolute Knowing, which Hegel did/could not. In using the souls of black folk to accomplish *this* important nineteenth-century American addition to *Phenomenology*, Du Bois, again, achieved much more. As other scholars have correctly pointed out, very near the opening statement of the book Du Bois added black people to Hegel's six world historical peoples. And as now commonly accepted, the Sorrow Songs contributed much to his placing them there. But the songs were much more than an aspect of African American culture and black people's "gift" (contribution) to American culture, both being somewhat obvious, empirical/materialistic conclusions about the significance of the songs. And given the context in which the book appeared, one in which turn-of-the-century urban reformers were touting the "gifts" of immigrants in order to make their presence more palatable to a nervous white Anglo-Saxon Protestant America, the suggestion that black folks' gift was this cultural contribution resonates. But the "real" gift of black folks, not just to America but to the world, was not this obvious material manifestation, a song, but was rather spiritual—the manifestation of the ancient idea of the wholeness and coherence of World Soul—the connection to Absolute Knowledge that the creation of the "new song" represented. During the nineteenth century, it was black people in America who provided this evidence of "knowing" and who, therefore, joined the Egyptian and Indian, the Greek and Roman, the Teuton and German as the seventh son. And so, implicitly, black folk, by their knowledge and their creation, also represented one of the seven rings in Plato's/Timaeus's explication of the Demiurge's creation of World Soul.

The rise of individualism during the period after the French Revolution created real fear for Hegel in part because most of the old "grand theories" (such as World Soul) that had provided some coherence to ideas about the nature of the universe and man's place in it seemed to be invalidated. The comparable crisis of spirit for Du Bois was caused by industrial capitalism, which as Julius W. Friend and James Feibleman later concluded (about industrialism) confused means as ends. Friend and Feibleman described industrialism as "a human tool which has lost its utile function and achieved an independent meaning." They surmised that industrialists "have brought their allegiance to an abstraction from the world of matter," and "[h]umanity, which industrialism was to have served, has become its slave instead." They advocated the creation of a new, human centered cosmology. But they also recognized the possibility of its being viewed derisively, as little more than "mind spinning" philosophy.[37]

Philosophers have regularly apologized for their "mind spinning" discussions. Even Hegel, in the famous preface to *Phenomenology*, wrote, "any attempt to expound the system of Science from this point of view is unlikely to be favourably received." He was heartened by the fact that some of the most important ideas of Plato and Aristotle had been challenged at different times. This made it possible for Hegel to maintain hope that his "attempt to vindicate Science for the Notion, and to expound it in this its proper element, will succeed in winning acceptance through the inner truth of the subject-matter" (*PS* §71).

Du Bois *ended* his text with the same somewhat-skeptical hope: his "Afterthought."

Hear my cry, O God the Reader; vouchsafe that this my book fall not still-born into the world-wilderness. Let there spring, Gentle One, from out of its leaves vigor of thought and thoughtful deed to reap the harvest wonderful. (Let the ears of a guilty people tingle with truth, and seventy millions sigh for the righteousness which exalteth nations, in this drear day when human brotherhood is a mockery and a snare.) Thus in Thy good time may infinite reason turn the tangle straight, and these crooked marks on a fragile leaf be not indeed

The End.

It is not too much to note first that in Du Bois' prayer it is the reader to whom he referred as an infinite spirit ("God the Reader")—another allusion to *Being*, in and of itself. He hoped his study would not be lost but would fall in fertile ground. And he appealed to Absolute Knowledge ("infinite reason"). In accepting that this knowledge would come *in its own time* ("in Thy good time"), he provided the final Hegelian expression in his book. Hegel's effort "to vindicate Science" insisted, "We must hold to the conviction that it is the nature of truth to prevail when its time has come, and that it appears only when this time has come, and therefore never appears prematurely, nor finds a public not ripe to receive it" (*PS* §71).

Despite Du Bois' tremendous personal, intellectual accomplishment in writing *The Souls of Black Folk*, given Soul's goal of being free, whole, and harmonious, there remained a pressing crisis of spirit symbolized by the persistence of the color line in America and its global counterpart, imperialism/colonization. Du Bois' "problem of the color-line" statement has never lacked attention. But, finally, there is another important, related, question to consider.

Du Bois opened the first chapter of *The Souls of Black Folk* with the following paragraph:

> Between me and the other world there is ever an unasked question: unasked by some through feelings of delicacy; by others through the difficulty of rightly framing it. All, nevertheless, flutter round it. They approach me in a half-hesitant sort of way, eye me curiously or compassionately, and then, instead of saying directly, How does it feel to be a problem? they say, I know an excellent colored man in my town; or, I fought at Mechanicsville; or, Do not these Southern outrages make your blood boil? At these I smile, or am interested, or reduce the boiling to a simmer, as the occasion may require. To the real question, How does it feel to be a problem? I answer seldom a word.

In addition to all the other things Du Bois accomplished in *Souls*, in this volume-opening question he also launched a classical philosophical dialogue, a thought experiment through which, theoretically, reason/mind would ultimately lead to truth/knowledge. In our contemplation of this idea, we should consider Walter Burkert's caution about dialogues:

> It will take more than Plato's dialogues and teaching to have a final "system," made up out of non-contradictory rules and terms. For not even knowledge firmly grasps its object. Plato is not satisfied with

elegant "principia mathematica," he asks for the Good—not in the sense of an "ought" imposed by some authority, but as the goal of all striving, the prop and meaning of existence. This can only be perceived in an individual experience similar to religious revelation. But the only way to it is the common quest of indefatigable dialogue, which necessarily leads to the most stringent rules of dialectic, to logic and mathematics.[38]

The Souls of Black Folk is itself a dialogue. But as Burkert continued about dialogues in general, there is no neat, clear end to the dialogic process that "can be taken down on paper or papyrus." And so, predictably, Du Bois' "dialogue" seems to end appropriately, as other, classical, dialogues end—with no explicit answer to the question. But in the tradition of the classical dialogue, the teacher/philosopher and his students begin with one of those big unanswerable questions ("How does it feel to be a problem?"). And the classical dialogue, as a thought experiment, also has a hypothesis. Du Bois' hypothesis was that "[t]he *problem* of the Twentieth Century is the problem of the color-line" (emphasis added). The dialogue (*Souls*) takes the students (readers) through all the possible ways of examining or thinking about the hypothesis in order to prove or invalidate it. Du Bois explored the theory through history, art, sociology, psychology, political science/economics, anthropology, philosophy, and theology, and he examined the relationships between and among men and between men and their government(s). And all of the evidence led to a conclusion that we will have to infer because the classical dialogue allows/demands that one reach one's own conclusion based on the evidence and one's own understanding of it. Based on all this diverse and extensive nineteenth-century evidence, the so-called "Negro problem" was not the problem: "The problem of the Twentieth Century [was] the problem of the color-line."

Throughout the nineteenth century, black Americans embodied World Soul's continual striving for the good—harmony, wholeness, self-determination, and freedom; for the beautiful—life; and for the true—knowledge, all of which Soul seeks and the color line persistently impeded.[39] And World Soul's journey is still not complete. Despite all the striving of the souls of black folk, and their material and spiritual accomplishments, the two large (material and spiritual) forces that Coleridge described had not yet been fully reconciled by the principle of the third (the souls of black folk?) in either America or the world. But Du Bois did not leave us "there." Just before his "Afterthought," Du Bois closed the book by, almost inexplicably, inserting a sheet of music. And people whom he described as "my children, my little children" sang his volume to its (apparent) close, their voices wafting up to his office window, "let us cheer the weary traveler along the heavenly way." In Du Bois' ending the volume with children's singing, and this particular song no less, we should be reminded that sound is an announcement of presence, *Being*, and so song serves, again, to invoke and communicate with Spirit. Consequently, as was the case for Hegel, there is hope.[40]

NOTES

Introduction

1. Quotation from G. W. F. Hegel, *The Phenomenology of Mind*, translated and introduced by J. B. Baillie, 2d rev. and corrected ed. (1910; New York: Humanities Press, Inc., 1971), 19–20.

2. Douglass's discussion of the slaves' songs and its appearance in *Souls* has been well documented. Anna Julia Cooper's writing has not. Among many obvious parallels between *Souls* and *A Voice from the South*, Cooper offered glimmers of Du Bois' eventual Talented Tenth throughout the book. She saw Crummell as a prophet (she actually used the word) before Du Bois wrote his allegory. On the failure of people to heed Crummell's advice on the education of black women, Cooper wrote: "They have had both Moses and the Prophets in Dr. Crummell and if they hear not him, neither would they be persuaded through one came up from the South" (herself). In Cooper's voice, black women were "confronted by both a woman question and a race problem" ("double consciousness"?). She saw in the race "a quickening of its pulses and a glowing of its self-consciousness." According to Cooper, "each race has its badge, its exponent, its message . . . which is its own peculiar keynote, and its contribution to the harmony of nations." She believed "in allowing every longing of the human soul to attain its utmost reach and grasp." She believed that "the laws of matter determine the laws of intellect." She invoked Voltaire, critiqued Hume, crushed Comte, and was skeptical (no pun intended) of a series of philosophical positivists—all of whom also made appearances in *Souls*. See Anna Julia Cooper, *A Voice from the South; by a Black Woman of the South*, introduction by Mary Helen Washington (1892; New York: Oxford University Press, 1988), quotations on 24, 144, 152, 259, 288. There are more than a few other parallels between Cooper's *Voice* and Du Bois' *Souls*, and a detailed textual analysis is sorely needed. For a different sort of example, her critique of Comte is biting (more than Du Bois' later critique in *Dusk of Dawn*). She described him as "a half-crazy French schoolmaster" who "would have been as harmless as any other lunatic" had his views not evolved into a "philosophy of *natural science*" that was taken up by "John Stuart Mill, Herbert Spencer, G. H. Lewes, and a noble army of physicists, naturalists, physiologists, and geologists." She sampled some of their words. "'We have no knowledge of anything but phenomena, and the essential nature of phenomena and their ultimate causes are unknown and inscrutable to us'"(Mill). "'All phenomena without exception are governed by invariable laws with which no volitions natural or supernatural interfere'" (Comte). "'Final causes are unknown to us and the search after them is fruitless'" (Comte) (292–93). Cooper was born in 1858 in North Carolina. Her mother was a slave and her father was their owner. She earned B.A. and M.A. degrees from Oberlin College and her Ph.D. from the University of Paris. For more details

of her life, see Mary Helen Washington's introduction to *Voice* and Louise Daniel Hutchinson, *Anna Julia Cooper: A Voice from the South* (Washington: Smithsonian Institution, 1982).

3. Classicist Page duBois, in *Out of Athens: The New Ancient* (Cambridge, MA: Harvard University Press, 2010), has made a compelling case for some level of tolerance among classicists when today's nonclassicists appropriate classical literature in their theory and criticism and fail to get it all quite right. It is important to note here that Du Bois' theoretical application of Plato's design probably does not require any special indulgence, was undertaken more than a century ago, and was particularly effective. On Du Bois' marginalization, see Aldon Morris and Amin Ghaziani, "Du Boisian Sociology: A Watershed of Professional and Public Sociology," *Souls: A Critical Journal of Black Politics, Culture and Society* 7 (2005), 47–54, quotation on 47. This marginalization continued after Du Bois' death. For a discussion of the ten-year struggle to have his homeplace recognized as a historic site, see Amy Bass, *Those About Him Remained Silent: The Battle over W. E. B. Du Bois* (Minneapolis: University of Minnesota Press, 2009).

4. Stephen Jay Gould, *Hen's Teeth and Horse's Toes: Further Reflections in Natural History* (New York: W. W. Norton and Co., 1994), 11. For discussions of some of the public celebrations of the anniversary of *Souls* see, Manning Marable, "Celebrating *Souls*: Deconstructing the Du Boisian Legacy," in Alford A. Young Jr., Manning Marable, Elizabeth Higginbotham, Charles Lemert, and Jerry G. Watts, *The Souls of W. E. B. Du Bois* (Boulder: Paradigm Publishers, 2006), 6–28. In Spring 2005, *Public Culture* issued a special edition entitled *100 Years of the Souls of Black Folk: A Celebration of W. E. B. Du Bois*, which Robert Gooding-Williams edited. In 2005, *Souls* issued a special edition entitled "Critical Perspectives on W. E. B. Du Bois." In 2004, Cambridge University Press initiated *Du Bois Review: Social Science Research on Race*.

5. Historians were among the first scholars to recognize Du Bois' importance in the scholarly canon. Later, social scientists (especially sociologists and political scientists/theorists) began to incorporate his work into their standards. Although philosophers also recognize Du Bois' contribution to their field, often through Jamesian social psychology, philosophical pragmatism, and political philosophy and/or ethics, discussion of the extent of his contribution to philosophy has barely scratched the surface. This study takes seriously Lucius Outlaw's insistence that scholars (*including nonphilosophers*) "give Du Bois's work the kind of careful consideration that is cultivated in attending to the world of canonical figures in philosophy." Lucius T. Outlaw (Jr.), *On Race and Philosophy* (New York: Routledge, 1996), 6.

6. The development of both possibilities has recently begun with the publication of two major studies of Du Bois' religious thought. Ironically, they take nearly opposing views. See Edward J. Blum, *W. E. B. Du Bois: American Prophet* (Philadelphia: University of Pennsylvania Press, 2007); and Jonathon S. Kahn, *Divine Discontent: The Religious Imagination of W. E. B. Du Bois* (Oxford: Oxford University Press, 2009). One should, however, also consider Manning Marable, "The Black Faith of W. E. B. DuBois: Sociological and Political Dimensions of Black Religion," *Southern Quarterly* 23 (Spring 1985), 15–55; and Reiland Rabaka, "The Prophet of Problems:

Du Bois's Philosophy of Religion, Sociology of Religion, Critique of the Black (and White) Church, and Critical Theory of Liberation Theology," in *Du Bois's Dialectics: Black Radical Politics and the Reconstruction of Critical Social Theory* (Lantham, MD: Lexington Books, 2008), 119–58. A brief but pointed response to Blum is Kevin M. Schultz, "Spiritual Yes; But Religious? A Review Essay," *Historically Speaking: The Bulletin of the Historical Society* (September 2009), 37–38.

7. James L. Christian, *Philosophy: An Introduction to the Art of Wondering*, 4th ed. (New York: Holt, Rhinehart and Winston, 1973), 161. For a significant and substantial biography of Hegel, one that considers his writings and the works and history that influenced his thinking, see Terry Pinkard, *Hegel: A Biography* (Cambridge: Cambridge University Press, 2000).

8. Du Bois to Herbert Aptheker, January 10, 1956, in Herbert Aptheker, ed., *The Correspondence of W. E. B. Du Bois* (Amherst: University of Massachusetts, 1973), 3:394–96, quotation on 396. Obviously, this would not be the first interpretation linking Du Bois' work to possible intellectual predecessors for which there is no direct evidence. Most recently, see Anne E. Carroll, "Du Bois and Art Theory: *The Souls of Black Folk* as a 'Total Work of Art,'" *Public Culture* (Spring 2005), 235–54. Carroll relates *Souls* to Wagner's music theory. She writes, "There is little evidence in his published writing to link the book to these concepts about the arts. But there is significant cultural and textual evidence that suggests the relevance of the idea of the total work of art to *Souls*. . . . Wagner and his theories about the unity of the arts were widely disseminated and hugely influential in Germany in the years when Du Bois lived there as a graduate student." Carroll's essay ends with a reminder of "the magnitude of [Du Bois'] intellect" and by urging scholars to "to continue to explore the full range of the allusions in his work." See esp. 236–40, quotations on 236–37, 254. J. G. A. Pocock, in a study of both political thought and political discourse, discusses some of the problems inherent in trying to establish an author's intentions when there is no direct evidence. It often leads to our becoming "imprisoned in the hermeneutic circle" and to our critics' constructing even more such circles in an effort to disprove an offered interpretation. Pocock raises important questions about the possibility of the (original) author's isolating his/her own intentions, which often "come into being only as they are effected in the text." See Pocock, *Virtue, Commerce, and History: Essays on Political Thought and History, Chiefly in the Eighteenth Century* (Cambridge: Cambridge University Press, 1985), 1–50, quotations on 4.

9. While Zamir notes the parallels between the first chapter of *Souls* and the middle section of *Phenomenology*, Zamir does not see Du Bois' discussion as teleological or metaphysical at all. See Shamoon Zamir's *Dark Voices: W. E. B. Du Bois and American Thought, 1888–1903* (Chicago: University of Chicago Press, 1995), esp. 113–19, 248 (n. 2). Also recognizing a relationship between the two texts is Russell A. Berman, "Du Bois and Wagner: Race, Nation, and Culture between the United States and Germany," *German Quarterly* 70 (Spring 1997), 123–35. David Levering Lewis, in *W. E. B. Du Bois: Biography of a Race, 1868–1919* (New York: Henry Holt and Co., 1993), 139–40, makes clear the connections but does not explore them. Joel Williamson, *The Crucible of Race: Black/White Relations in the South since Emancipation* (New York: Oxford University Press, 1984), 399–413, recognizes Hegelian

influences in *Souls,* but does not explicitly link them to *Phenomenology.* Anthony Monteiro, in "W. E. B. Du Bois and the Study of Black Humanity: A Rediscovery," *Journal of Black Studies* Online (April 6, 2007), sees Du Bois as having created a new phenomenology based on Hegelian traditions and suggests a material metaphysics in Du Bois' work. Ross Posnock, *Color & Culture: Black Writers and the Making of the Modern Intellectual* (Cambridge, MA: Harvard University Press, 1998), 111–21, sees Du Bois as both a pragmatist and a Hegelian idealist and concludes that Du Bois adapted (rather than adopted, which I maintain) *Phenomenology.* Other studies that make connections between Du Bois' work and Hegel's *Phenomenology* are cited below in appropriate places. None of these other sources provides a systematic analysis of a potential relationship between *Souls* and Hegel's *Phenomenology.* And most make the connection between Hegel and Du Bois through Du Bois' 1897 *Atlantic Monthly* essay "Strivings of the Negro People," which, with revisions, became the first chapter of *Souls.* The connection made by these scholars relates more generally to philosophy of history.

10. Louis Menand, *The Metaphysical Club* (New York: Farrar, Straus and Giroux, 2001), 263; Williamson, *The Crucible of Race,* 407; William E. Burghardt Du Bois, "Bismarck," Commencement speech delivered at Fisk University, June 1888, The Papers of W. E. B. Du Bois, University of Massachusetts, Amherst, reel 80; and "Ferdinand Lassalle, German Socialist (1825–64)," www.1902encyclopedia. com/L/LAS/ferdinand-lassalle.html. The last paragraph of Du Bois' address, which includes the Lassalle-Schopenhauer-Hegel line, is crossed out in the manuscript, suggesting that Du Bois did not deliver these words. On the typescript, he separated the crossed-out lines from the rest of the text and labeled them: "(Cut from Speech)." The manuscript copy of the speech is in bad condition, and there is a hole where "Schopenhauer" was written on the typescript that was prepared in 1933. It appears that Du Bois corrected all the typographical errors on the typescript and filled in the words that the typist found illegible and for which empty spaces appeared in the typed copy. But Du Bois was apparently not certain by this time that Schopenhauer was the name that was in the original address, and so he put a question mark after the written-in name in the parentheses. It does, however, make sense that Schopenhauer was the missing name. (Terry Pinkard, in *Hegel: A Biography,* 11, 465, reported that Schopenhauer "harbored a lifelong passionate dislike for Hegel" and "thoroughly detested" him. And he is not the first to come to that conclusion.) The final lines of the "Bismark" manuscript are not legible at all in the microfilm copy of the papers. They were added by hand on the typed copy, suggesting they might not have been legible for the typist either (by 1933), but are mostly illegible there as well at this point.

11. I do realize that the jury is still out as to whether Hegel's *Phenomenology* supports metaphysics. For example, although very helpful to my efforts, Robert C. Solomon, *In the Spirit of Hegel: A Study of G. W. F. Hegel's Phenomenolgy of Spirit* (New York: Oxford University Press, 1983), 8, finds metaphysics, "culminating in the ultimate ontological assurance—'the Absolute,'" to be "the very antithesis of the spirit of Hegel." Terry Pinkard came to this same conclusion in *Hegel's Phenomenology: The Sociality of Reason* (Cambridge: Cambridge University Press, 1994).

Although I see the study as both phenomenology and metaphysics, it should be noted that my study is not an attempt to analyze *Phenomenology* but to relate Du Bois' *Souls* to it.

12. There is considerable disagreement among Hegel scholars about what Hegel's "system" is and where *Phenomenology* fits within it. Some of this disagreement probably results from the title(s) of the study. The original title was *Science of the Experience of Consciousness*. Hegel changed the title to *Phenomenology of Spirit*, which was clearly to be a part of a larger work. Some of the first copies of the book bore the larger title *System of Science. Part One: Phenomenology of Spirit*. I am in agreement here with Werner Marx, *Hegel's Phenomenology of Spirit: Its Point and Purpose—A Commentary on the Preface and Introduction*, trans. Peter Heath (New York: Harper and Row, Publishers, 1975), which concludes that, regarding the historical debate as to whether Hegel's study is "a 'Science of the Experience of Consciousness,' or a 'Phenomenology of Spirit,'" it is both. Although my reading of Marx greatly enhanced my still-limited understanding of Hegel, I don't see the two discussions taking place sequentially, as Marx does, but simultaneously.

13. One of the best expressions of this idea I have seen is A. E. Taylor, *Elements of Metaphysics* (London: Methuen, 1961), 106 and n. 1. Taylor wrote: "[W]e must carefully avoid falling into the mistake of thinking of the Reality and the world of its appearances as though they formed two distinct realms. In a systematic unity, we must remember, the whole can exist only in so far as it expresses its nature in the system of its parts, and again the parts can have no being except as the whole expresses itself through them. To the degree to which this condition is departed from by any of the types of system familiar to us, those systems fall short of being perfectly systematic. Reality, then, being a systematic whole, can have no being apart from its appearance, though neither any of them taken singly, nor yet the sum of them thought of collectively, can exhaust its contents. And though no appearance is the whole of Reality, in none of them all does the whole Reality fail to manifest itself as a whole. The whole is truly, as a whole, present in each and every part, while yet no part is the whole." In the note, Taylor reminds us that it is "not the sum of" the parts that he is describing as the whole. "[T]he systematic whole of Reality is not a sum but a single experience."

14. Although most people use the thesis-antithesis-synthesis motif to describe Hegelian dialectics, I have instead used the words Hegel used (abstract-negative-concrete) rather than Kant's terms.

15. Robert Gooding-Williams, "Philosophy of history and social critique in *The Souls of Black Folk*," *Social Science Information* 26 (June 1987), 99–114, sees *Souls* as an incomplete (or only partly successful) representation of philosophy of history because it is not a universal history. I see Du Bois' effort as completely successful in that Du Bois was *adding* the nineteenth century to Hegel's universal history. Following Hegel's lead, I have capitalized the terms "Consciousness," "Self-Consciousness," "Reason," and "Spirit" when using them as "forms" of consciousness.

16. Frank M. Kirkland, "How Would Hegel's *Phenomenology of Spirit* Be Relevant Today?" *Logos* (online) (Winter 2008), 1–10. Kirkland refers to Robert Pippin's "On Not Being a Neo-Structuralist."

17. Georg Wilhelm Friedrich Hegel, *The Philosophy of History*, trans. J. Sibree, rev. ed. (New York: Wiley Book Co., 1900), 98–99. The absence of a particular type of state government, characteristics of religion, and the organization of society prevented Hegel's including Africa in his philosophy. An intense and sustained critique of Hegel's *Philosophy*, published in the 1830s, is based primarily on its treatment of most of the world's people of color, who remained outside the philosophy of history for one reason or another. And some scholars even maintain that Hegel continues to "haunt" philosophy with regards to Africa. On this final point, see Olufemi Taiwo, "Exorcising Hegel's Ghost: Africa's Challenge to Philosophy," *African Studies Quarterly* 1, no. 4 (1998), http://www.africa.ufl.edu/asq/v1/4/2.htm.

18. The discussions of China and India are located at Hegel, *The Philosophy of History*, 61–63, 111–72. The latter pages are part of a larger discussion on "The Oriental World," including areas we would now identify as Near and Middle Eastern. "Threshold" remark on page 99. And see Du Bois' explicit remarks on Indian, Chinese, and black people in n. 10 of my conclusion. Important questions and answers developed at hegel.net by Paul Trejo, Maurizo Canfora, and Kai Froeb concluded that Hegel's comments about Africa (in *Philosophy of History*) were not race based. In defense of this position, they point to Hegel's dismissal of physical characteristics as evidence of spirit/knowledge in *Phenomenology*. I consulted this site on January 27, 2011. The most detailed discussion of this debate is provided in Pinkard, *Hegel*, esp. 489–93. Pinkard, focusing on Hegel's *Philosophy of Right*, explores the charges that the work valorized European culture, a conclusion that Hegel emphatically rejected along with "all doctrines of racial superiority floating around Europe at the time." Pinkard discusses Hegel's work in ways that make the traditional misinterpretations of it apparent. He also offers a clear caution against reading Hegel so simplistically in German/nationalistic terms. And finally, see Babacar Camara, *Reason in History: Hegel and Social Changes in Africa* (Lanham, MD: Lexington Books, 2011). Camara insists that Hegel's larger discussions have been misread and that his Africa comments have been taken out of context. Camara finds Hegel's conclusions about sub-Saharan Africa entirely appropriate and not racist.

19. Quotation from Hegel, *Philosophy*, 86–87. According to Hegel, states that oppressed great segments of its population never achieved the highest level of development.

20. This study assumes, as Shamoon Zamir wrote, that Du Bois was both "an empirical scientist building a scientific basis for reform and higher understanding of the problems of race" and "an idealist philosopher of history." Zamir, *Dark Voices*, 6. In general, I am building on Zamir's idea that in "Sociologist Hesitant," Du Bois attempted to bridge the developing chasm between philosophy and the new empirical sociology. (See especially Zamir, 68–109.) In some ways, Zamir and I end up at the same place, if by slightly different routes. Zamir writes: "'Conservation' seeks to place the African-American and African peoples on the world stage," and "*Souls*'s appeal to sympathy is a plea for their humanity" (109). Zamir, however, does not see Du Bois' study as teleological or metaphysical. A study that takes seriously Du Bois' use of metaphysics is Dan S. Green and Edwin D. Driver, "W. E. B. DuBois: A Case in the Sociology of Sociological Negation," *Phylon* 37, no. 4 (1976), 308–33.

Although these authors are primarily concerned with other issues, they recognize that Du Bois' work often took "a middle of the road approach between metaphysical meandering at one extreme and a tangled mass of statistics at the other." I think, as Green and Driver say, and as I will show later, that "DuBois saw a unity between all scientific endeavor" and deeply and consistently engaged metaphysics (318). More decisively recognizing Du Bois' efforts to construct a metaphysical system is Emily R. Grosholz, "Nature and Culture in *The Souls of Black Folk* and *The Quest of the Silver Fleece*," in *W. E. B. Du Bois on Race and Culture: Philosophy, Politics and Poetics*, ed. Bernard W. Bell, Emily R. Grosholz, and James B. Stewart (New York: Routledge, 1996), 177–90. Axel R. Schäfer describes the "German historical school of economics" (which influenced Du Bois' scholarship) as reflecting "Hegelian metaphysics, Kantian epistemology, and Herderian historicism" but as also rejecting "all *a priori* assumptions." Schäfer writes that instead of "*a priori* laws of nature," ethical goals of this school were embedded "in specific economic, social, political, and cultural environments." See, "W. E. B. Du Bois, German Social Thought, and the Racial Divide in American Progressivism, 1892–1909," *Journal of American History* 88 (December 2001), 925–49, quotations on 934–35. Recently, the tendency has been to reject outright Du Bois' reliance on metaphysics. For a vigorous and sustained anti-metaphysical argument, see Jonathon S. Kahn, *Divine Discontent*, which insists throughout that "Du Bois's religious voice is decidedly antimetaphysical" (10). Anthony Monteiro, in "W. E. B. Du Bois and the Study of Black Humanity," describes Du Bois' efforts, generally, as phenomenological "rather than" metaphysical (6). Barrington S. Edwards, in "W. E. B. Du Bois Between Worlds: Berlin, Empirical Social Research, and the Race Question," *Du Bois Review: Social Science Research on Race* 3 (2006), 395–424, maintains that Du Bois rejected metaphysics "because its aim did not entail the unity of knowledge" (399). Edwards's study does not consider *The Souls of Black Folk*.

Much has been made of Du Bois' Philosophy IV course at Harvard, no doubt because of the existence of his examination booklets from the class. While Du Bois was there, however, Josiah Royce taught Philosophy II, Metaphysics. George Herbert Palmer pointed out (much later) that although William James (Du Bois' undergraduate adviser) was "forever exposing the follies of the idealists" (Royce and Palmer), at least once James and Royce taught the metaphysics course together (each teaching one semester). And, once, James also ended up teaching Royce's portion for six weeks. Palmer's memoir also pays some attention to his own study of Hegel, though he says, "I never became an Hegelian" and in fact went on to describe himself as an anti-Hegelian. All of this suggests that Du Bois, who studied the works of or studied with all three men, had a mind of his own. George Herbert Palmer, *The Autobiography of a Philosopher* (1930; New York: Greenwood Press, 1968), 47–48, 52–54, 68–70. A good, accessible overview of this relationship and that among the Cambridge philosophers generally is Bruce Kuklick, *A History of Philosophy in America, 1720–2000* (Oxford: Clarendon Press, 2001), part II.

21. Quotation from W. E. B. Du Bois, *The Souls of Black Folk*, introductions by Nathan Hare and Alvin F. Poussaint (New York: New American Library, 1969), 45.

This paragraph benefitted from my reading of Jacob Needleman's *The American Soul: Rediscovering the Wisdom of the Founders* (New York: Jeremy P. Tarcher/ Putnam, 2003), especially chapters 1–4. Needleman used "the common cosmic Selfhood" (8) rather than "World Soul," which I have interpreted as synonymous. I have put "really" in quotation marks above only because of the popular use of "real" for what Hegel characterized as "actual." Also note that central to my discussion throughout this volume is that Du Bois' double consciousness was not the debilitating psychological condition of multiple personalities. Although "double-consciousness" as a psychological term/condition was known to American intellectuals before the turn of the century, the technical use of the term gained currency with American intellectuals just after Du Bois published *Souls*. Pierre Janet, a French philosopher/ physician/psychologist who is credited with coining the terms "dissociation" and "subconscious," gave a series of important lectures at Harvard in 1906 and published *The Dissociation of a Personality*. Also important to the developing understanding of the psychological condition of double consciousness was Morton Prince, a Tufts University physician and medical researcher who specialized in abnormal psychology and especially multiple personalities.

22. On the leadership class broadly, see Adolph L. Reed Jr., "Stratification, Leadership and Organization: The Role of the Black Elite," in *W. E. B. Du Bois and American Political Thought: Fabianism and the Color Line* (New York: Oxford University Press, 1997), 52–70. Most scholarship currently focuses not on the Talented Tenth or a general leadership class but an "intellectual elite." Introducing, but not developing, the parallel in Plato's Philosopher Rulers, see Joy James, *Transcending the Talented Tenth: Black Leaders and American Intellectuals* (New York: Routledge, 1997), 19. James writes: "Du Bois's academic training in Greek classicism infuses his 1903 model of Negro leadership with a Platonic hierarchy of enthroned philosopher kings/queens." James's chapter considers both of Du Bois' presentations on this topic and concludes that "it took [him] nearly half a century to democratize the Talented Tenth in the militant spirit of [C. L. R.] James's radical observations made in the 1950s" (17). I understand James's point, but maintain that the first (1903) presentation by Du Bois was more radical (if less explicitly so) than believed. In ways similar to James, Reiland Rabaka sees Du Bois' second Talented Tenth essay (1948) as a eulogy for the Talented Tenth in its announcing a "Guiding Hundredth" and as a retreat from the leadership of the "philosopher kings and queens" and the birth of "revolutionary democratic socialist group leadership." See "The Du Bois-Washington Debate: Social Leadership, Intellectual Legacy, and the Lingering Problematics of African American Politics," in *Du Bois's Dialectics*, 81–118, quotations on 113–14. And for an explicitly philosophical interpretation of Du Bois' Talented Tenth proposal, see Rabaka, "W. E. B. Du Bois's Evolving Africana Philosophy of Education," *Journal of Black Studies* (March 2003), 399–449. An intriguing essay that explicitly sees Du Bois' Talented Tenth theory as Hegelian is Dominic J. Capechi Jr. and Jack C. Knight, "W. E. B. Du Bois's Southern Front: Georgia 'Race Men' and the Niagara Movement, 1905–1907," *Georgia Historical Society* (Fall 1999), 479–507.

23. The definition of "spiritual" is from M. B. Foster, *The Political Philosophy of Plato and Hegel* (1935; Oxford: Clarendon Press, 1968), 26. In *Phenomenology*,

§§42–46, a very difficult discussion on the efficacy of using math to determine the thing in itself, Hegel seems to say that it is not possible because the proof remains external to the thing. I think one can relate the mathematics of this music to nature, as my fifth chapter attempts to show. The observations of the nineteenth-century writers are detailed in chapter 5 of this book. The most well-known of those publications is William Francis Allen, Charles Pickard Ware, and Lucy McKim Garrison, comp., *Slave Songs of the United States* (1867; New York: Peter Smith, 1951). Where the scholarly discussions of this music focus on the words of the nineteenth-century listeners, they practically credit those listeners with creating the music through their words. Ronald Radano, in *Lying up a Nation: Race and Black Music* (Chicago: University of Chicago Press, 2003), like Du Bois, understands that this music shares some characteristics of white music in the South (and provides a useful analysis of Du Bois' discussion of the Sorrow Songs in its final pages (the "Epilogue"), but an implication of Radano's larger discussion is that this music was at least partly created by the descriptions of it. Although there is much more than this to Radano's study, he maintains that the transcribers' inability to chart the music (and what they wrote about it) helped to create "an imagined realm cast in the romantic language of race" (228). Their words "invented" a "'Negro sound'" (229). Radano characterizes these efforts as "modern fantasies" that are "derived from a positivist musicology that presumes art to exceed the social meanings that inevitably contain it" (2). Radano's conclusions are clearly influenced in part by Paul Gilroy's *The Black Atlantic: Modernity and Double Consciousness* (Cambridge, MA: Harvard University Press, 1995), esp. 72–110. My study shares Gilroy's conclusions about the transnational intellectual world which Du Bois' writings reflected and to which they contributed (see esp. ibid., 111–45). Gilroy's discussion of the Jubilee Singers (and Du Bois' Sorrow Songs) decenters the text/words, as does my study (though very differently); and like Gilroy I recognize Du Bois' appreciation of "the vernacular" (the folk). But our approach to and conclusions about the music are very different. My discussion attempts to explain this music as something "real" and as something that fails "to exceed the social meanings" (to use Radano's paraphrasing of Gilroy) only because we have not looked very far beyond the social meanings. I attempt to push understandings of this music beyond Romantic *rhetoric*. One scholarly work that provides important metaphysical insights into this spiritual music is James Cone, *The Spirituals and the Blues: An Interpretation* (New York: The Seabury Press, 1972). Cone's metaphysics is religious (ontological), and he sees this music as reflecting "black people's deepest aspiration and devotion" and as demonstrating "the meaningfulness of black experience," black "humanity," and the "affirmation of life" (6–12). Quoting Howard Thurman (another important black theologian), Cone reminds us that the creators of these songs were slaves—property—making their declarations of their humanity even more significant. The songs were about "the somebodiness of their being" (16), an affirmation of personhood (21). Cone insists that this was not "art for art's sake" but a "community's view of the world and its existence in it" and their struggle to be free. Cone adds that, without having studied philosophy, they knew their enslavement was not "rational" and that "[a]s with all ontological assumptions, the truth of a presuppositional assertion [that their enslavement contradicted God's will] is found in the givenness of existence itself and not in theory" (72–73). In a suggestion of Hegel's discussion of "Lordship and Bondage," Cone notes that these slaves were able "to view black humanity independently of their oppressors," and that their eschatology, in which they freed themselves, was "jarringly non-historical" (100).

24. The first of the contemporary reviews of *Souls* to suggest a sense of incoherency was W. H. Johnson, review of *Souls, The Dial* 34 (1903), 299–302, which concludes that although all the essays relate to the book's title, the essays "do not present a formal unity." Everett S. Lee, "W. E. B. Du Bois: *The Souls of Black Folk*," in *Landmarks of American Writing*, ed. Hennig Cohen (New York: Basic Books, 1969), 228–39, describes "the organization of the essays into a book [as] forced" (235). Numerous others, although not seeing the assemblage as incoherent, do see the essays as "compiled" as a consequence of a request from a publisher and thus miss the opportunity to see how the essays, most of which were previously published in one form or another, work together in monographic form. An exception to the image of pulled-together essays is Robert Stepto, "The Quest of the Weary Traveler: W. E. B. Du Bois's *The Souls of Black Folk*," in *From Behind the Veil: A Study of Afro-American Narrative* (1979; Urbana: University of Illinois Press, 1991), 52, which provides an archeological exploration of the evolution of the essays, characterizing the book as "not merely an assembled text, but also an orchestrated one."

25. As noted in the acknowledgments, I am indebted to Robert Harris for his question at a 2003 special AHA session on "*The Souls of Black Folk* after 100 Years: W. E. B. Du Bois and the Twentieth Century." Recognizing that our papers and comments had focused on America and its southern states, Harris asked if Du Bois' volume had not also commented on the world. None of us had an adequate answer. Harris's question helped me to grasp the importance of Hegel's discussion of world-historical subjects and events in Du Bois' masterwork.

26. To be born with a veil, in the folk tradition, is to be born with special gifts and powers. This idea is discussed in detail in chapter 1.

27. While most of these traditional labels reflect some aspect of identity politics, one should see Ross Posnock, *Color and Culture*, which characterizes Du Bois' thought as an example of cosmopolitanism, in the Greco-Roman tradition of one's relationship to the world. Posnock utilizes a very useful characterization of Du Bois—"an anti-race race man." Du Bois' own words about his travels in Europe suggest as much: "I met men and women as I had never met them before. Slowly they became, not white folks, but folks. The unity beneath all life clutched me. I was not less fanatically a Negro, but 'Negro' meant a greater, broader sense of humanity and world fellowship. I felt myself standing, not against the world, but simply against American narrowness and color prejudice, with the greater, finer world at my back." *The Autobiography of W. E. B. Du Bois: A Soliloquy on Viewing My Life from the Last Decade of Its First Century*, introduction by Werner Sollors (Oxford: Oxford University Press, 2007), 99.

28. Du Bois, *Dusk of Dawn: An Essay Toward an Autobiography of a Race Concept* (1940; New Brunswick: Transaction Publishers, 1991), 38; William James to Du Bois, February 9, 1891, in Aptheker, *Correspondence of W. E. B. Du Bois*, 1:10;

Reed, *W. E. B. Du Bois and American Political Thought*, 107; and E. Franklin Frazier, "The Du Bois Program in the Present Crisis," quoted in Dolan Hubbard, *The Souls of Black Folk One Hundred Years Later* (Columbia: University of Missouri Press, 2007), 282–83.

29. Stephen G. Hall, *A Faithful Account of the Race: African American Historical Writing in Nineteenth-Century America* (Chapel Hill: University of North Carolina Press, 2009).

30. For a useful interpretation of Du Bois' likely view of art and the actual use of art in *Souls*, see Carroll, "Du Bois and Art Theory: *The Souls of Black Folk* as a 'Total Work of Art.'" My point here, however, relates to *Souls* as a total work of which the art was a part.

31. For the definitive biographies of Du Bois, see David Levering Lewis, *W. E. B. Du Bois: Biography of a Race, 1868–1919*, and *W. E. B. Du Bois: The Fight for Equality and the American Century, 1919–1963* (New York: Henry Holt and Co., 1993 and 2000). One should also consult Du Bois' own autobiographical writings, particularly *Dusk of Dawn* and *The Autobiography of W. E. B. Du Bois*.

Chapter 1

1. Quotations from W. E. B. Du Bois, *The Souls of Black Folk*, edited by Nathan Hare and Alvin F. Poussaint (New York: New American Library, 1969). All quotations from this work are taken from this edition unless otherwise noted. There are, to date, more than one hundred editions of *The Souls of Black Folk*. Except for editions reproduced in the original form, it is unlikely that any have the same pagination. For that reason, and because of the large number of direct quotations from *The Souls of Black Folk* in this book, I have not documented the source of direct quotes in the notes. In most instances, the chapter from which the quotation comes is evident. When I have found it necessary to include a note, I have cited the volume as Du Bois, *Souls*, and will, hereafter, refer to the work as *Souls* in the text.

2. David Levering Lewis, *W. E. B. Du Bois: Biography of a Race, 1868–1919* (New York: Henry Holt and Co., 1993), 283.

3. Arnold Rampersad, *The Art and Imagination of W. E. B. Du Bois* (1976; New York: Schocken Books, 1990), 70, 79; Eric Sundquist, *To Wake the Nations: Race in the Making of American Literature* (Cambridge, MA: Belknap Press of Harvard University Press, 1993), 485; and Adolph L. Reed Jr., *W. E. B. Du Bois and American Political Thought: Fabianism and the Color Line* (New York: Oxford University Press, 1997), 91. Gerald Early describes this passage as "One of the most famous quotations in American literature, and probably the most famous in all African American literature" in Early, ed., *Lure and Loathing: Essays on Race, Identity, and the Ambivalence of Assimilation* (New York: Penguin Press, 1993), xvii. Wilson J. Moses characterizes the reprinting of the double consciousness passage in terms of "stupefying frequency" in "Culture, Civilization, and Decline of the West: The Afrocentrism of W. E. B. Du Bois," in *W. E. B. Du Bois on Race and Culture*, ed. Bernard W. Bell, Emily R. Grosholz, and James B. Stewart (New York: Routledge, 1996), 243. Bernhard Ostendorf, "Black Poetry, Blues, and Folklore: Double Consciousness in

Afro-American Oral Culture," *American Studies/Amerika Studien* 20 (1975), 209–59, concludes that "Dubois's [*sic*] imaginative metaphor [double consciousness] has become a belabored common denominator for recent Black Studies theory. It has staled for us by too much repetition and has lost its explanatory power by rampant hypostatization. However, the phenomenon has persisted and has been rechristened by various disciplines, both synchronic and diachronic" (212). On Du Bois' use of the term, Dickson D. Bruce Jr., in "W. E. B. Du Bois and the Idea of Double Consciousness," *American Literature* 64, no. 2 (June 1992), 299–310, looks at it from both a psychological and philosophical perspective and concludes that Du Bois' use of the term reflected some part of all of the previous uses, culminating in a new use. And for an analysis of the different ways this term has been interpreted, see Ernest Allen Jr., "Du Bosian Double Consciousness: The Unsustainable Argument," *Massachusetts Review* 43 (Summer 2002), 217–53.

4. Examples that include but do not focus on *Souls* include Ostendorf, "Black Poetry, Blues, and Folklore"; Virginia M. Burke, "The Veil and the Vision," *Black American Literature Forum* 11 (Fall 1977), 91–94; William B. Gravely, "The Dialectics of Double-Consciousness in Black American Freedom Celebrations, 1808–1863," *Journal of Negro History* 67 (Winter 1982), 302–17; David W. Blight, "Up from 'Twoness': Frederick Douglass and the Meaning of W. E. B. Du Bois's Concept of Double Consciousness," *Canadian Review of American Studies* 21(Winter 1990), 301–19; Onita Estes-Hicks, "Cross-Cultural Explorations of Du Boisian Double-Consciousness: Jean Rhys and Jean Toomer," *Contributions in Black Studies* 9/10 (1990–92), 6–16. The terms themselves (veils, double consciousness) have also inspired many other works not related directly to Du Bois or *Souls*.

5. I consider the 1896 Supreme Court ruling in *Plessy v. Ferguson* as marking the institutionalization of the color line.

6. While a major point of my study is completely opposite the premise of Eugene Victor Wolfenstein's psychoanalytic discussion of Du Bois' work, I agree that "the greater part of the scholarly literature [on *Souls*] has been focused on various of its parts rather than the whole, specific themes rather than the narrative they comprise, its principal concepts (such as the Veil, two-ness, and double consciousness) rather than their deployment within the text." Eugene Victor Wolfenstein, *A Gift of the Spirit: Reading "The Souls of Black Folk"* (Ithaca: Cornell University Press, 2007), 1–2.

7. This essay sees Du Bois' remark as suggesting something skeletal or not yet complete in his use of the word "outline" rather than "indefinite," as Rampersad, *Art and Imagination*, 70, sees it. It will become more apparent later (beginning in chapter 4) how profoundly Hegelian Du Bois' volume is. Here, it is useful to note that his opening with a "vague, uncertain outline" recalls Hegel's preface, in which he characterized his description of the education his book detailed as "a history . . . delineated in faint outline." See G. W. F. Hegel, *The Phenomenology of Mind*, trans. and intro. by J. B. Baillie (1910; London: George Allen and Unwin, Ltd., 1971), 90. In A. V. Miller, trans., *Hegel's Phenomenology of Spirit* (Oxford: Oxford University Press, 1977), §28, Miller translates it as "in a silhouette." It is possible that both examples should be read more literally as an indication that Du Bois' "Forethought"

and Hegel's "Preface" are simply introductions to what will be a complete development in their texts.

8. See Carroll Y. Rich, "Born with the Veil: Black Folklore in Louisiana," *Journal of American Folklore* 85 (1976), 328–31. Richard Cullen Rath, in "Echo and Narcissus: The Afrocentric Pragmatism of W. E. B. Du Bois," *Journal of American History* 84 (September 1997), 461–95, provides a very useful discussion of the terms "veil" and "caul" and the evolution of their use (484–88). Also see Cynthia D. Schrager, "Both Sides of the Veil: Race, Science, and Mysticism in W. E. B. Du Bois," *American Quarterly* 48 (December 1996), 575, which characterizes double consciousness similarly to the way that people usually characterize the veils: "[D]ouble consciousness is not a debilitating state of being; it is a privileged locus of knowing." A review of *The Souls of Black Folk* by "J.C." in the *Times Literary Supplement*, October 18, 1996, summarizes most of the earlier descriptions of the veil, describing it as "the central metaphor of the book" (31). The review ultimately sees the veil as negative, reflecting "a social system of separation," "a psychological screen," and a concept powerful enough to divide not only whites but different groups of blacks, "finally perverting the black man's idea of himself."

9. Thomas C. Holt, "The Political Uses of Alienation: W. E. B. Du Bois on Politics, Race, and Culture, 1903–1940," *American Quarterly* 42 (June 1990), 301–23. Holt contends that Du Bois' life work involved developing "a theory of society interactively with and through social and political practice ('work, culture, liberty') in order to achieve enlightenment *and* emancipation." He later added: "For Du Bois, 'work, culture, liberty' continued to be the keys to unlocking the paradox of race and class" (320). My essay is in agreement with Holt's conclusions but sees work, culture, and liberty as not just central to Du Bois' or anyone's life work, but as at the heart of the discussion of *The Souls of Black Folk.*

10. See Stanley Brodwin, "The Veil Transcended: Form and Meaning in W. E. B. Du Bois' 'The Souls of Black Folk,'" *Journal of Black Studies* 2 (March 1972), 305–6. Offering a similar interpretation to the one suggested in the Brodwin quote is Robert Gooding-Williams, "Philosophy of History and Social Critique in *The Souls of Black Folk,*" *Social Science Information* 26 (March 1987), 107. In fairness to Gooding-Williams, it should be noted that his description suggests *both* race and the color line. In one sentence he describes the veil "as a metaphor for the social practice of Jim Crow," but the next sentence suggests that the veil ("the Negro's veil") is another word for "race." Williams continues, Du Bois "also implies that this veil would prevent the Negro from obtaining insight into the white world which excludes him, were it not for a gift of second-sight, which gift makes palpable what the veil would otherwise render remote." Ernest Allen Jr. used the term "color curtain," thus also joining the color line and the veil in a way extending both in "Ever Feeling One's Twoness: 'Double Ideals' and 'Double Consciousness' in *The Souls of Black Folk,*" *Contributions in Black Studies: A Journal of African and Afro-American Studies* 9/10 (1990–92), 55–69, quotation on 56. The first significant use of the phrase "color curtain" of which I am aware is Richard Wright's *The Color Curtain: A Report on the Banung Conference* (1956) in which he wrote of his observations of this meeting of representatives of African and Asian nations to discuss race and colonialism.

11. Wilson Moses, "The Poetics of Ethiopianism: W. E. B. Du Bois and Literary Black Nationalism," in *Critical Essays on W. E. B. Du Bois*, ed. William L. Andrews (Boston: G. K. Hall & Co., 1985), 100–101.

12. Also noting the empowering (in this case, equalizing) aspect of the veil in the biblical scene of rending the veil in Matthew 27:51 (and also in Mark and Luke) is Jerold J. Savory, "The Rending of the Veil in W. E. B. DuBois's 'The Souls of Black Folk,'" *College Language Association Journal* 15 (March 1972), 334–37. Until the rending of the veil only the high priests could speak directly to God. After the event, all people gained access.

13. From my own perspective, this "shadow of the veil" is perhaps the most elegant metaphor in the book, given that, ultimately, neither shadows nor veils (where the veil is the color line and where both are considered in the context of Hegelian Idealism) are "real." Du Bois' most poignant use of the shadow occurred when he spoke of his dead child: "And thus in the Land of the Color-line I saw, as it fell across my baby, the shadow of the Veil." He continued: "I saw the shadow of the Veil as it passed over my baby, I saw the cold city towering above the blood-red land." On dwelling "above the veil," Ross Posnock suggests not simply that color was irrelevant "above the veil," but that color did not exist there. See Posnock, *Color and Culture: Black Writers and the Making of the Modern Intellectual* (Cambridge, MA: Harvard University Press, 1998).

14. Robert Gooding-Williams, "Philosophy of History and Social Critique in *The Souls of Black Folk*," 107. I will show later that black folks see their own "other" rather than themselves as "other." Gooding-Williams subsequently wrote, "I now reject the thesis that second sight is inherently negative," in *In the Shadow of Du Bois: Afro-Modern Political Thought in America* (Cambridge, MA: Harvard University Press, 2009), 286 (n. 44). Recognizing second sight as a "gift" that mitigates the potential negativity of double consciousness is Nahum Dimitri Chandler, "Originary Displacement," *Boundary* 2 (Fall 2000), 272–73. A summary of some of the uses of "double consciousness" and its contemporary contexts are provided in Reed, *W. E. B. Du Bois and American Political Thought*, esp. 91–99. And see Tom Lutz, *American Nervousness, 1903: An Anecdotal History* (Ithaca: Cornell University Press, 1991), esp. 261–75. In Lutz's discussion of neurasthenia, the source of double consciousness is represented as being a free American and an unfree black person. He compares *Souls* to the writings of Henry James. Also looking at the diverse possible meanings of "double consciousness" in Du Bois' work is Dickson D. Bruce, "W. E. B. Du Bois and the Idea of Double Consciousness," which concludes that the term is spiritual and denotes a contest between African and American consciousnesses rather than two characteristics of a single consciousness. Bruce does, however, rightly see Du Bois' argument as antimaterialist. And see David W. Blight, "Up from 'Twoness,'" which characterizes double consciousness in less pathological terms, as do I, but in terms of "cultural biformity" (303). And although I also agree that Du Bois was writing about the psychological damage that racism causes, Du Bois was calling for more than the freedom Blight described, but also for liberty, which this essay demonstrates was not a synonym. Also on double consciousness, see Ernest Allen Jr., "On the Reading of Riddles: Rethinking DuBoisian 'Double Consciousness,'" in

Lewis R. Gordon, ed., *Existence in Black: An Anthology of Black Existential Philosophy* (New York: Routledge, 1997), 49–68.

15. Adolph L. Reed Jr. recognized that "Du Bois and others. . . . understood that disfranchisement and loss of civil rights could ultimately destroy black aspiration." Reed framed this idea primarily in the context of opposition to Booker T. Washington's philosophy rather than as a central message of Du Bois' book. See Reed, *W. E. B. Du Bois and American Political Thought*, 61.

16. Rath, "Echo and Narcissus," 470, makes the point directly: "The 'striving' was the point."

17. Most scholars follow some version of Du Bois' introductory suggestion about history, sociology, and life "within the veil." See Rampersad, *Art and Imagination*, 70, and Manning Marable, *W. E. B. Du Bois: Black Radical Democrat* (Boston: Twayne Publishers, 1986), 47. Paul Gilroy, *The Black Atlantic: Modernity and Double Consciousness* (Cambridge, MA: Harvard University Press, 1993), 122–25, is among works viewing the parts differently. Eric J. Sundquist, *To Wake the Nations*, 492, delineates four overlapping sections: freedom and black leadership (chapters 1–3); leadership and education (chapters 4–6); "the economy and geography of the postwar South" (chapters 4–9); and "life 'within the veil' and the meaning of black culture" (chapters 10–14). Robert Stepto, in "The Quest of the Weary Traveler: W. E. B. Du Bois's *The Souls of Black Folk*," in *From Behind the Veil: A Study of Afro-American Narrative* (1979; Urbana: University of Illinois Press, 1991), 52–91, accepts Du Bois' own division and views the first nine chapters as being about black people in a white world and the last five chapters as on the black world. Hazel Carby echoes this characterization in *Race Men* (Cambridge, MA: Harvard University Press, 1998). And, finally, see Stanley Brodwin's structure in "The Veil Transcended," 307, which holds that the book has three major parts: "The first phase is that of revolt and freedom—the whole Civil War complex (. . . chs. 1 and 2)—the second phase is that of moral, intellectual, and economic adjustment, attendant with all the temptations of the white man's values for blacks, passivity in the face of white power, and the effect of personal tragedy on Du Bois' own strivings (. . . chs. 3–11); the third phase deals with the necessity to affirm life in the face of tragedy as seen through Alexander Crummell, 'John Jones,' and the sorrow songs themselves (. . . chs. 12–14)."

18. The idea of a savant is another important one that scholars have passed on the opportunity to analyze. It reinforces or repeats points that Du Bois made throughout the volume, including those related to the veil and the color line. A savant is usually an extraordinarily gifted or talented person who also has equally profound social disabilities. Ernest Allen Jr., saw Du Bois' examples as evidence of the "twinned collapse of specified 'double ideals.'" And Robert Stepto noted that Du Bois' use of the artisan as one example was both evidence of "the double aimed struggle" and a commentary on Booker T. Washington's idea of the black yeoman. See Allen, "On the Reading of Riddles," 52; and Stepto, "The Quest of the Weary Traveler," 83.

19. For a recent, brief account of the Washington/Du Bois relationship see Raymond Wolters, *Du Bois and His Rivals* (Columbia: University of Missouri Press, 2002), 40–76. Also see Francis L. Broderick, *W. E. B. Du Bois: Negro Leader in a*

Time of Crisis (Stanford, CA: Stanford University Press, 1959), 62–75; Elliott M. Rudwick, "The Overture to Protest: Beginnings of the Du Bois-Washington Controversy," in *W. E. B. Du Bois: Voice of the Black Protest Movement* (Urbana: University of Illinois Press, 1982), 54–76; and Basil Mathews, "The Continuing Debate: Washington vs. Du Bois," in *W. E. B. Du Bois: A Profile*, ed. Rayford W. Logan (New York: Hill and Wang, 1971), 183–209. Alolph L. Reed Jr. distinguished between some of the older and newer discussions related to the debate between the two men in *W. E. B. Du Bois and American Political Thought*, 127–38. One early essay, Everett S. Lee, "W. E. B. Du Bois: *The Souls of Black Folk*," in *Landmarks of American Writing*, ed. Hennig Cohen (New York: Basic Books, 1969), 233, describes the chapter on Washington as the "chapter that gave to the book an instant and lasting importance." One of the first reviews of the book predicted that this chapter would be "the centre of interest" for many readers. See Carl Kelsy, review of *The Souls of Black Folk*, *Annals of the American Academy of Political and Social Science* 22 (1903), 230–32, quotation on 231. Sundquist, *To Wake the Nations*, 465–66, sees the chapter as helping to "subvert the authority of Booker T. Washington" and calls this "attack" on Washington, "the notorious centerpiece of his [Du Bois'] critique of African American leadership." David Levering Lewis rightly saw the chapter more broadly as an attack on "the ethos, science, and propaganda of racial dehumanization as much as Bookerite compromises" and an attack on the possibility that dehumanization and brutalization might become "officially sanctioned instruments of racial subjugation." He nevertheless suggested a similar anti-Washington interpretation later when he wrote that "Of the Wings of Atalanta" (*Souls*, chapter 5) protested "Washington's turning the black world upside down so that the starring roles went to peasant farmers, skilled mechanics, and domestics, forcing the Talented Tenth off stage." David Levering Lewis, *W. E. B. Du Bois: Biography of a Race*, 275–76, 290–91. Playthell Benjamin wrote about the Washington chapter: "I believe that there does not exist another essay in which so much of consequence is said in a mere seventeen and a half pages—or said so well." Stanley Crouch and Playthell Benjamin, *Reconsidering the Souls of Black Folk* (Philadelphia: Running Press, 2002), 130. And see Hazel V. Carby, *Race Men*, 38–41, which also sees Du Bois' framing of Washington "as evidence of a stunted or deformed manhood, a masculine style incompatible with the incorporation of the race into the modern nation-state." Kevern Verney, "The Realist and the Dreamer? Booker T. Washington and W. E. B. Du Bois," in *The Art of the Possible: Booker T. Washington and Black Leadership in the United States, 1881-1925* (New York: Routledge, 2001), 79–93, compares the two men and sees Du Bois as more conservative than most people see him in comparison to Washington. And Verney reminds us that Washington was still trying to hire Du Bois at Tuskegee as late as 1902 and invited Du Bois to dinner at his home shortly after *Souls* was published. Also seeing the differences between the two men in terms of degrees is Thomas E. Harris, *Analyses of the Clash over the Issues between Booker T. Washington and W. E. B. Du Bois* (New York: Garland Publishing, 1993). A good summary of the history and development of the Talented Tenth is Rampersad, *The Art and Imagination of W. E. B. Du Bois*, 91–115.

20. Although Du Bois had called for both higher education and industrial education in his original essay, the year after the article on the Talented Tenth appeared (perhaps in response to the criticism it attracted for its opposition to Washington), Du Bois published a paper insisting that black Americans had to have both higher education and industrial education. See Du Bois, "The Development of a People," *International Journal of Ethics* 14 (April 1904), 292–311.

21. David Levering Lewis, *W. E. B. Du Bois: Biography of a Race*, 288. The idea of "slavery and civic death" has since been explored in detail in Orlando Patterson, *Slavery and Social Death* (Cambridge, MA: Harvard University Press, 1982). One of the most balanced reviews of *Souls*, which pays particular attention to this issue, is Arthur P. Davis, *Journal of Negro History* 39 (April 1954), 140–42.

22. Atalanta is the heroine from Greek mythology who promised to marry any man who could beat her in a footrace. All who challenged her failed except Hippomenes who repeatedly tossed golden apples (provided by Aphrodite) ahead of her, which she stopped to admire. The first two times he passed her, but she caught up. The third time they were close to the finish line, and the apple bounced off the course causing Atalanta a longer delay. Hippomenes passed her and won the race. A more detailed analysis of Du Bois' chapter on Atlanta, comparing *Souls* to Henry James's *The American Scene* in its critique "of the excesses of the Gilded Age," is Kenneth W. Warren's *Black and White Strangers: Race and American Literary Realism* (Chicago: University of Chicago Press, 1993), 109–30, esp. 112–20, quotation on 116.

23. Among those interpreting the ideas related to the Talented Tenth as a reaction to the lost status of the better educated are David Levering Lewis, *W. E. B. Du Bois: Biography of a Race*, 290–91, who cautiously wrote: "[i]f the concept of status anxiety had validity, then the Talented Tenth experienced it as farmers, preachers, peddlers, grocers, and hairdressers formed up behind the wizard [Washington] for a march into prosperity"; and Adolph L. Reed Jr., who, in "Du Bois's 'Double Consciousness': Race and Gender in Progressive Era American Thought," *Studies in American Political Development* 6 (Spring 1992), 93–139, described Du Bois as a part of a turn-of-the-century cohort of educated East Coast intellectuals on a "search for order" (117). Reed's characterization included but was not limited to status anxiety. Also see second Lewis quote in n. 19, above.

24. This broad definition was probably best articulated, to that time, by Edward Burnett Tylor, in *Origins of Culture*, vol. 1 of *Primitive Culture: Researches into the Development of Mythology, Philosophy, Religion, Art and Custom* (1871; Harper and Row, 1958), 1, where he wrote: "Culture or Civilization, taken in its wide ethnographic sense, is that complex whole which includes knowledge, belief, art, morals, law, custom, and any other capabilities and habits acquired by man as a member of society." And note Tylor's general use of "culture" and "civilization" as synonyms, which might speak to the debates on whether Du Bois' use of "civilization" was elitist. It is possible that Du Bois' contemporaries would have seen the terms in a more benign way than we see them now. Tyler also quoted in "Culture," *International Encyclopedia of the Social Sciences*, ed. David L. Sills (New York: Macmillan Co. and Free Press, 1968), 3:527, in an essay that also traces the development of the concept of culture across time and as used in a multidisciplined literature. Also see n. 27 below.

25. Explicitly on the development of the prison system in the South, see David M. Oshinsky, *"Worse Than Slavery": Parchman Farm and the Ordeal of Jim Crow Justice* (New York: The Free Press, 1996); Mary Ellen Curtin, *Black Prisoners and their World, Alabama, 1865–1900* (Charlottesville: University Press of Virginia, 2000).

26. On black people's struggle for work, land ownership, and general self-determination, and the corresponding development of debt and debt peonage, see Du Bois' own *Black Reconstruction in America, 1860–1880*, introduction by David Levering Lewis (1935; New York: Simon and Schuster, 1995); Edward Magdol, *A Right to the Land: Essays on the Freedmen's Community* (Westport, CT: Greenwood Press, 1977); and Gerald David Jaynes, *Branches without Roots: Genesis of the Black Working Class in the American South, 1862–1882* (New York: Oxford University Press, 1986).

27. See the discussion of "folk," "*kulture*," and "*Volksgeist*," for example, in Wilson J. Moses, "Culture, Civilization, and Decline of the West," 245–47. Moses fruitfully assesses the expressions "folk soul" and "people's spirit" somewhat synonymously. Most often, definitions of soul are implied and must be inferred. And the explanations are wide ranging. Rampersad, *Art and Imagination*, 74–75, 88, appropriately views "folk" as a synonym for "nation," but sees "souls" in the title of the book "as a play on words, referring to the 'twoness' of black Americans," thus, seeming to focus simply on the plurality of the word. Rampersad does later, however, draw parallels between Du Bois' use of "soul" and turn-of-the-century psychologists' use of "consciousness." Dickson D. Bruce Jr. placed "soul" in the context of Transcendentalist double consciousness in "W. E. B. Du Bois and the Idea of Double Consciousness," 300–301. Although an implication of Bruce's discussion is that "soul" relates to self-realization, with which I agree, "soul" and "spirit," which I see as different, also appear to be synonyms in his essay. Eric Sundquist seemed to impose a 1960s popular culture understanding on "soul" without defining it when he wrote that Du Bois replaced Washington's "philosophy of the toothbrush with a philosophy of black soul and [transfigured] the narrow conception of labor and nation building in Washington's program into a broad, exhilarating call for the labor necessary to construct a black American wing in the 'kingdom of culture.'" He also emphasizes the way Du Bois appropriated the Sorrow Songs' "core expression of African-American culture, their *soul*, in order to create a foundation for modern African American culture as an extension of slave culture." See Sundquist, *To Wake the Nations*, 466 and 458, respectively. Shamoon Zamir relates Du Bois' use of "folk" and "soul" to the transcendentalist thought of Gottfried von Herder and Franz Boas in Zamir, *Dark Voices: W. E. B. Du Bois and American Thought, 1888–1903* (Chicago: University of Chicago Press, 1995), 105–6. Also on Herder's use of "folk" and Du Bois' appropriation of it in both national and racial terms is Ernest Allen Jr., "On the Reading of Riddles," esp. 60–62. Although not focusing on *The Souls of Black Folk*, and more implicit than explicit, also see Alton B. Pollard III, "The Last Great Battle of the West: W. E. B. Du Bois and the Struggle for African America's Soul," in Early, *Lure and Loathing*, 41–54. Gooding-Williams, *In the Shadow of Du Bois*, 4, distinguishes Du Bois' use of "folk" from "masses." The masses were an "aggregate of uncultured, premodern"

black people, and the folk comprised "a group united by a collectively shared ethos or spirit." Also see ibid., 140–47.

28. Even in the transitioning of aspects of eighteenth-century philosophy (the philosophy of the mind, based largely on Aristotelian and Platonic principles) into science (psychology), there was still much in this theory of the mind to assist Du Bois in exposing the southern way of life. Eighteenth-century British philosophers held that "the mind is composed only of sensations and mental images[,] . . . that all complex precepts or ideas are formed through associations, and that all trains of thought arise through associations." The chapters in *Souls* represented here as being about culture succeed in showing what black folk could not help but learn, as a consequence of sensation and association, in the post-Reconstruction South. It was *not* the kind of education for which Du Bois argued in the chapter about Atlanta (chapter 5). Although by the time Du Bois completed his formal training in philosophy, Darwinism (biology) had disrupted the primacy of sensationism and associationism, the rise in influence and misuse of Darwinism would probably also have encouraged him to look back to the philosophy foundations for support of his ideas. Quotations in the note and the text from *Dictionary of Philosophy and Psychology*, s.v. "Soul," 557–58; *The Encyclopedia of Philosophy*, 2nd ed., s.v. "Psychology," 15; *Encyclopaedia of Religion and Ethics*, s.v. "Soul," 741. Also seeing the importance of "potential," see George Armstrong Kelly, "Notes on Hegel's 'Lordship and Bondage,'" in *Hegel: A Collection of Critical Essays*, ed. Alasdair MacIntyre (Notre Dame: University of Notre Dame Press, 1976), 203, in which Kelly suggests "spirit in potential," by describing Hegel's conception of Soul as "life on the margin of consciousness." One should note the parallels between ideas related to (James's) associationism and sensationism discussed here and the broad definition of culture in n. 24, above. For more detail about aspects discussed here, also see chapters on "association" and "sensation" in William James, *The Principles of Psychology*, 3 vols. (Cambridge, MA: Harvard University Press, 1981). Also see "Psychology," *Encyclopedia of Philosophy*, vol. 7, ed. Paul Edwards (New York: Macmillan Publishing Co., and The Free Press, 1967).

Finally, it is important to note that although Christian writing (i.e., Old and New Testaments) used "soul" and "spirit" as synonyms, early Greek philosophy did not. A discussion of the evolution of the term "soul" may be found in "Ancient Theories of Soul," *Stanford Encyclopedia of Philosophy*, at http://plato.stanford.edu/entries/ancient-soul/; the survey includes the uses of "soul" in many of the texts consulted here (e.g., Plato's *Phaedo* and *The Republic*, Aristotle's *On the Soul*). Consulted on 3/25/2005. The essay was revised on 4/22/2009, and the later version is signed Hendrik Lorenz.

29. Although recent interpretations of Du Bois' work appropriately equate "identity" and "self-consciousness," it is important to note here that a philosopher would have easily equated "consciousness" and "soul," and Du Bois was well aware of this common concept.

30. Rampersad, *Art and Imagination*, 75, describes the incident as John Jones's discovering John Henderson "playfully attempting to kiss" Jones's sister. In a later essay Rampersad described Henderson as "a would-be white seducer." See "W. E. B. Du Bois as a Man of Literature," *American Literature* 51 (March 1979), 63. Other

scholars conclude that Henderson was attempting to rape Jennie. What is clear is that Jennie was resisting John Henderson. Du Bois wrote: "There was only a black man hurrying on with an ache in his heart, seeing neither sun nor sea, but starting as from a dream at the frightened cry that woke the pines, to see his dark sister struggling in the arms of a tall and fair-haired man."

31. Rampersad, *Art and Imagination*, 76, makes this point of joint destiny especially clear.

32. Shamoon Zamir, "'The Sorrow Songs'/'Songs of Myself': Du Bois, the Crisis of Leadership, and Prophetic Imagination," in Werner Sollors and Maria Diedrich, *The Black Columbiad: Defining Moments in African-American Literature and Culture* (Cambridge, MA: Harvard University Press, 1994), 145–66; and Sundquist, *To Wake the Nations*, 466. Also see Stepto, *From Behind the Veil*, 57, which echoes this notion that this "section turns out to be not so new after all, primarily because it may be seen as a remarkable embellishment full of various narrative modes," that Du Bois expressed in other publications several years earlier.

33. See Jacob Needleman, *The American Soul: Rediscovering the Wisdom of the Founders* (New York: Jeremy P. Tarcher/Putnam, 2003), esp. 139–72, quotation on 144. The detail of Needleman's discussion focuses on the Bill of Rights and its relationship to the Constitution, but, importantly, it is also a discussion of Jeffersonian vs. Hamiltonian perspectives of government and spiritual vs. material perspectives. Needleman's discussions of rights, freedom, liberty, and property are especially useful here.

34. Without the Thirteenth Amendment states still had the constitutional power to establish slavery. And so the amendment not only abolished slavery but abolished the power of states to establish it.

35. Although my detailed discussion of the relationship between Hegel's work and *Souls* begins in chapter 4, some of the proto-Hegelian implications of the Declaration should be clear.

36. An 1883 Supreme Court decision overturned the Civil Rights Act of 1875, which had banned discrimination in public accommodations, and the 1896 *Plessy* decision institutionalized the principle of legalized segregation.

37. Words from the Declaration of Independence make clear why Du Bois relied upon it rather than the Constitution. All of the following charges that the colonists leveled against George III find parallels in the post-Reconstruction South, some of which are detailed in the middle chapters of *Souls*.

> He has refused his Assent to Laws, the most wholesome and necessary for the public good. . . .
>
> He has refused to pass other Laws, for the accommodation of large districts of people, unless those people would relinquish the right of Representation in the Legislature, a right inestimable to them and formidable to tyrants only. . . .
>
> He has dissolved Representative Houses repeatedly, for opposing with manly firmness his invasions on the rights of the people. . . .
>
> He has erected a multitude of New Offices, and sent higher swarms of Officers to harass our people, and eat out their substance. . . .

He has combined with others to subject us to a jurisdiction foreign to our constitution, and unacknowledged by our laws; giving his Assent to their Acts of pretended legislation: . . .

For imposing Taxes on us without our Consent:

For depriving us in many cases, of the benefit of Trial by Jury: . . .

For taking away our Charters, abolishing our most valuable Laws, and altering fundamentally the Forms of our Governments:

For suspending our own Legislatures, and declaring themselves invested with power to legislate for us in all cases whatsoever. . . .

In every stage of these Oppressions, We have Petitioned for Redress in the most humble terms: Our repeated Petitions have been answered only by repeated injury. A Prince whose character is thus marked by every act which may define a Tyrant is unfit to be the ruler of a free people.

David Waldstreicher, *Slavery's Constitution from Revolution to Ratification* (New York: Hill and Wang, 2009), provides an extensive discussion that can be used to explain further Du Bois' reliance on the rhetoric and rationales of the Declaration of Independence rather than the Constitution.

38. Thomas Paine, *Common Sense*, in *Thomas Paine: Political Writings*, ed. Bruce Kuklick (Cambridge: Cambridge University Press, 1989), 32.

39. One should also notice that Paine's section entitled "Thoughts on the Present State of American Affairs" ends with an appeal for freedom using the image of "the weary traveler."

O ye that love mankind! Ye that dare oppose, not only tyranny, but the tyrant, stand forth! Every spot of the world is overrun with oppression. Freedom hath been haunted round the globe. Asia, and Africa, have long expelled her.–Europe regards her like a stranger, and England hath given her warning to depart. O! receive the fugitive, and prepare in time an asylum for mankind.

[Thomas Paine], *Common Sense: Addressed to the Inhabitants of America on the Following Interesting Subjects* . . . (Philadelphia: James Carey, 1796), 17. Paine's "fugitive" is freedom and relates to the colonists' relationship to their (British) government. Du Bois ended the third section of his volume, proposed here as being about liberty, and the book, with the words and music to "Let us cheer the weary traveler . . . along the heavenly way." Du Bois' "fugitive" (the weary traveler) is liberty. There have been numerous interpretations of Du Bois' reference to the weary traveler. Some scholars viewed it literally and wrote about the physical and spiritual exhaustion an activist experiences. See Sundquist *To Wake the Nations*, 538. Shamoon Zamir recognized the "philosophical traveler" as a common entity in romantic writing and linked Du Bois' appropriation of it to William Blake's poem, "The Mental Traveller." See Zamir, *Dark Voices*, 186–99.

One should also compare Paine's opening of "The Age of Reason: Being an Investigation of True and of Fabulous Theology, Part First" (1794), titled "The Author's

Profession of Faith," to Du Bois' "Credo" written in 1904. The entire text of Paine's essay on his religious beliefs may be found in Kuklick, *Thomas Paine: Political Writings*, 205–57; the "Credo," on 207–8.

40. The idea of individual rights is generally a modern conception, best expressed during the French Revolution, when the term "Equality" gained the kind of influence of "liberty" and "liberties," which were more like "rights." The Greek idea of liberty related to "protection of the group from attack" and "the ambition of the group to realize itself as fully as possible." Moreover, "[i]n such an organic society the concept of individual liberty was virtually unknown." Aristotle saw liberty as impossible without equality. See "Liberty," in *Encyclopedia of the Social Sciences*, 2d ed., ed. David L. Sills (New York: Macmillan Company and The Free Press, 1972), 9:442–47, quotation on 442; and "Civic Humanism," *Stanford Encyclopedia of Philosophy*, http://plato.stanford.edu/entries/humanism-civic/, consulted October 10, 2002. A very useful exploration of "civic humanism" is James Hankins, ed., *Renaissance Civic Humanism: Reappraisals and Reflections* (New York: Cambridge University Press, 2000). On Renaissance Era developments, also see J. G. A. Pocock, *The Machiavellian Moment: Florentine Political Thought and the Atlantic Republican Tradition* (Princeton: Princeton University Press, 1975). Final quotes in the text are from Needleman, *The American Soul*, 49, 156. Recent discussions among literary theorists on the rhetoric of rights often characterize "rights" in ways that resemble my description of liberty. One such discussion is Anita Haya Goldman, "Negotiating Claims of Race and Rights: Du Bois, Emerson, and the Critique of Liberal Nationalism," *Massachusetts Review* 35 (Summer 1994), 169–201. For another useful discussion of liberty, liberalism, individualism, republicanism, and other related ideas, see Kwame Anthony Appiah, *The Ethics of Identity* (Princeton: Princeton University Press, 2005).

Throughout *Souls*, Du Bois regularly referred to America as a *republic* rather than a *nation*. Nationalism, being more individualistic, would actually constrain the kind of development that Du Bois advocated. Given that, as Du Bois used the terms, republican liberty directly opposes "liberal nationalism," I would look to classical literature for the source of Du Bois' allusions throughout this book and to Renaissance "civic humanism" for additional influence. Moreover, as discussed in chapter 2, it was the *soul* that Du Bois saw as *sovereign*, which paralleled the discussion of republican liberty. Vincent Harding, in "W. E. B. Du Bois and the Black Messianic Vision," *Freedomways: A Quarterly Review of the Freedom Movement* 9 (Winter 1969), 44–58, is unconvinced that Du Bois ever referred to himself as a "'Negro Nationalist'" and indeed on one occasion he cautioned against his views being placed in that category" (44).

From the pre–American Revolutionary Era one should consider Cato's Letters, which contained much more detail on liberty than the writings of Thomas Paine. Letter #59 (December 30, 1721), for example, seeks to prove that liberty is "the unalienable Right of All Mankind" and that "the Good of the Society" is the purpose of government. Cato viewed all men as born free and saw "liberty" as "a Gift . . . from God." In Letter #62 (January 20, 1721) Cato described liberty as "the Power which every Man has over his own Actions, and his Right to enjoy the Fruits of his Labour,

Art, and Industry, as far as by it he hurts not the Society, or any Members of it, by taking from any Member, or by hindering him from enjoying what he himself enjoys." He adds that every man has a right to assistance from others in the protection of his property, otherwise one group will take that of every other group. And certainly reflecting some of Du Bois' thoughts about the problem of Booker T. Washington's leadership, Cato wrote: "There is not, nor can be, any Security for a People to trust to the mere Will of one, who, while his Will is his law, cannot protect them if he would. The Number of Sychophants and wicked Counsellors, that he will always and necessarily have about him, will defeat all his good Intentions, by representing Things falsely, and Persons maliciously; by suggesting Danger where it is not, and urging Necessity where there is none; . . . by sacrificing particular Men to their own Revenge, under pretence of public Security; and drawn by engaging him and his People in dangerous and Destructive Wars, for their own Profit or Fame; by throwing public Affairs into perpetual confusion, to prevent an Enquiry into their own behavior; and by making him jealous of his People; and his People of him, on purpose to manage and mislead both sides." Also important, Cato added, "True and impartial Liberty is therefore the Right of Every Man to pursue the natural, reasonable, and religious Dictates of his own Mind; to think what he will, and act as he thinks, provided he acts not to the Prejudice of another; to spend his own Money himself; and to Labour his own Way; and to labour for his own Pleasure and Profit." See John Trenchard and Thomas Gordon, *Cato's Letters; or Essays on Liberty, Civil and Religious, and other Important Subjects*, 3rd ed. (New York: Russell & Russell, 1969), 2:214–25, 244–55. "Cato" was an earlier pseudonym for two British writers. An American whose identity has never been confirmed took this pseudonym in the 1780s.

It is possible that my distinguishing freedom and liberty as the difference between relations to government and society is the same as Jacob Needleman's "two democracies," which he describes as internal and external or spiritual and material. The former is not possible without the latter, but his point is that both are necessary. The purpose of government (the external democracy) is to create and protect the conditions that allow the internal democracy (conscience) to develop. Needleman writes that "external democracy without spiritual democracy will otherwise inevitably destroy itself and the people within it," an idea reflected in Plato's critique (in *The Republic*) of democratic forms of government, which often led to "the tyranny of the majority" because they reflected desire, rather than higher forms of thought (which would focus more on the whole). See especially Needleman, *The American Soul*, 170–72.

41. Kwaku Larbi Korang, "As I Face America: Race and Africanity in Du Bois's *The Souls of Black Folk*," in *W. E. B. Du Bois and Race*, ed. Chester J. Fontenot Jr. and Mary Alice Morgan, with Sarah Gardner (Macon, GA: Mercer University Press, 2001), 166–86, quotation on 184–85.

42. Du Bois' thinking had changed over time. In his 1897 lecture/essay, "The Conservation of Races," he challenged those who would tout the promises of the Declaration of Independence as a symbol of freedom, and he insisted that "We, who have been reared and trained under the individualistic philosophy of the Declaration of Independence and the 'Laisserfaire" [*sic*] philosophy of Adam Smith, are loath to see and loath to acknowledge this patent fact of human history. We see the

Pharaohs, Caesars, Toussaints and Napoleons and forget the vast races of which they were but epitomized expressions. We are apt to think in our American impatience, that while it may have been true in the past that closed race groups made history, that here in the conglomerate America *nous avons changer tout cela*—we have changed all that and have no need of this ancient instrument of progress." He concluded that "a careful consideration of history" would not validate the conclusion that the course of history was determined by "closed race groups." See "The Conservation of Races," reprinted in David Levering Lewis, *W. E. B. Du Bois: A Reader* (New York: Henry Holt & Co., 1997), 20–27, quotation on 21–22.

Although it is clear that the idea that people have "natural rights" is, in political theory, highly debatable, and that the origin of the idea of "natural rights" is equally debatable, I don't think it is unreasonable to suspect that, by 1903, Du Bois carefully distinguished between these two political documents and found the Declaration of Independence more suitable than the Constitution for the reasons I suggest in the text. Moreover, I think it is possible that the Declaration of Independence, because it is more directly related to what we now think of as "natural rights" (primarily because of the language in it), would be the document more related to Spirit and Reason, more in the classical rather than the Enlightenment sense. A good discussion of the evolution of the idea of natural rights (before Locke and Hobbes), is Brian Tierney, "Origins of Natural Rights Language: Texts and Contexts, 1150–1250," *History of Political Thought* 10 (Winter 1989), 615–46. Tierney's article will make clear why we should not assume Du Bois' language is exclusively Enlightenment language, even though it is impossible to separate the Declaration of Independence entirely from Enlightenment thinking and particularly the notion of "rights." A discussion that provides the bases for arguing for *and* against my position is "Rights" (chapter 4) in Fred D. Miller Jr., *Nature, Justice, and Rights in Aristotle's Politics* (Oxford: Clarendon Press, 1995), 87–139, the broad subject of which is "Are there any 'rights' in Aristotle?" I am grateful to the leaders of the Seminar on Human Dignity/Human Rights at the National Humanities Center (1995–96), who included these essays in their readings, and to Harlan Beckley, a member of the seminar, who shared his copies of their readings with me, while I participated in a different seminar.

43. Most scholars see black American religion this way. Wilson Jeremiah Moses, in *Afrotopia: The Roots of African American Popular History* (Cambridge: Cambridge University Press, 1998), saw Du Bois' interpretation of black religion as a modification of African traditions over time by an infusion of Christian traditions. Alain Locke, however, taking his cue from Du Bois, made this point more clearly, even, than Du Bois in *Souls*. Locke wrote: "'The spirituals are really the most characteristic product of race genius as yet in America. But the very elements which make them uniquely expressive of the Negro make them at the same time deeply representative of the soil that produced them. Thus, as unique spiritual products of American life, they become nationally as well as racially characteristic. It may not be readily conceded now that the song of the Negro is America's folk song; but if the spirituals are what we think them to be, a classic folk expression, then this is their ultimate destiny.'" Locke quoted in Gilroy, *The Black Atlantic*, 91. Perhaps no book demonstrates the Americanness of black art better than Albert Murray's *Blue Devils*

of Nada: A Contemporary American Approach to Aesthetic Statement (New York: Pantheon Books, 1996), especially his discussions of Duke Ellington and Louis Armstrong. But also see yet another Alain Locke quote on 90–91: "'If after absorbing the new content of American life and experience, and after assimilating new patterns of art, the original (Afro-American) artistic endowment can be sufficiently augmented to express itself with equal power in more complex pattern and substance, then the Negro may well become what some have predicted, *the artist of American life.*'"

44. Sundquist, *To Wake the Nations*, 4.

45. At the beginning of the book, Du Bois wrote that after being snubbed by his white, female schoolmate, he decided not to "tear down that veil, to creep through." He "held all beyond it in common contempt, and lived above it in a region of blue sky and great wandering shadows." Du Bois' greater interest, however, became seeing that *all* folk have "the chance to soar in the dim blue air above the smoke."

46. In *Dusk of Dawn: An Essay Toward an Autobiography of a Race Concept* (1940; New Brunswick: Transaction Publishers, 1984), 27, Du Bois provided a parallel from his own life. He criticized his earlier scholarly/literary focus on "the relation of my people to the world movement" when he should have been questioning "the world movement." He later understood more fully that "I and people like me and thousands of others who might have my ability and aspiration were refused permission to be part of this world."

Chapter 2

1. Spinoza's *Tractatus Theologico-Politicus*, quoted in Robin Maconie, *The Science of Music* (Clarendon Press: Oxford, 1997), 65.

2. W. E. B. Du Bois, *Dusk of Dawn: An Essay Toward an Autobiography of a Race Concept* (1940; New Brunswick: Transaction Publishers, 1991), 139–40.

3. Du Bois, *The Philadelphia Negro: A Social Study* (Philadelphia: University of Pennsylvania Press, 1899). See Du Bois' subsequent discussion of *The Philadelphia Negro* in *Dusk of Dawn: An Essay Toward an Autobiography of a Race Concept*, 59, where he wrote: "It was as complete a scientific study and answer as could have then been given, with defective facts and statistics, one lone worker and little money. It revealed the Negro group as a symptom, not a cause; as a striving, a palpitating group, and not an inert, sick body of crime; as a long historic development and not a transient occurrence." He later noted in his autobiography that despite a lack of support or subsequent recognition for the work, he "made a study of the Philadelphia Negro so thorough that it has withstood the criticism of 60 years." Du Bois, *The Autobiography of W. E. B. Du Bois: A Soliloquy on Viewing My Life from the Last Decade of its First Century*, introduction by Werner Sollors (1968; New York: Oxford University Press, 2007), 125–27. Recent explorations of the work on the 100th anniversary of its publication maintain that this is still true. See Michael B. Katz and Thomas J. Sugrue, eds., *W. E. B. Du Bois, Race, and the City: The Philadelphia Negro and its Legacy* (Philadelphia: University of Pennsylvania Press, 1998).

4. Aldon Morris and Amin Ghaziani, "Du Boisian Sociology: A Watershed of Professional and Public Sociology," *Souls* 7 (2005), 47–54. On the importance of

sociology to Du Bois during the early years of his professional career, his use and discussions of it, see Dan S. Green and Edwin D. Driver, "W. E. B. Du Bois: A Case in the Sociology of Sociological Negation," *Phylon* 37 (1976), 308–33. On the reception of the Philadelphia study, see David Levering Lewis, *W. E. B. Du Bois: Biography of a Race, 1868–1919* (New York: Henry Holt and Co., 1993), 179–210, esp. 179–80, 188–90. On the influence of Du Bois' study in Germany on his becoming a sociologist and his desire that this kind of study be used to develop social policy, see Francis L. Broderick, "German Influence on the Scholarship of W. E. B. Du Bois," *Phylon* 19 (1958), 367–71. But also see Du Bois' own subsequent discussion in *The Autobiography of W. E. B. Du Bois*, esp. 124–27. On the failure of the sociological profession to recognize Du Bois' contribution (up to the 1990s), see Charles Lemert, "A Classic from the Other Side of the Veil: Du Bois's *Souls of Black Folk*," *Sociological Quarterly* 35, no. 3 (August 1994), 383–96. In this essay, Lemert describes his participation on a committee of social theorists of "distinguished accomplishment," each of whom was charged with identifying a scholar "whose scholarly work had redefined sociology's official canon of theoretical classics." His suggestion that the group name a project for Du Bois was rejected because, according to members of the group, Du Bois had never done "anything that mattered anyhow." Another example appears in Green and Driver, "W. E. B. Du Bois," 324, where they refer to a 1974 letter to them from the American Sociological Association in which the president rejected "a proposed session on Du Bois for the Annual Meetings" because he "did not know anything about [Du Bois'] contributions to sociology." Green and Driver recognized Du Bois' belief that it would be empirical data, knowledge provided by scientific study (sociology), that would solve the race problem. Also contributing to this discussion, see in Robert W. Williams, "The Early Social Science of W. E. B. Du Bois," *Du Bois Review* 3 (Fall 2006), 365–94.

5. Even Du Bois had warned, in the extremely social scientific *Philadelphia Negro*, against relying on statistics as foolproof. In one instance, he wrote: "The best available methods of sociological research are at present so liable to inaccuracies that the careful student discloses the results of individual research with diffidence; he knows that they are liable to error from the seemingly ineradicable faults of the statistical method, to even greater error from the methods of general observation, and above all, he must ever tremble lest some personal bias, some moral conviction or some unconscious trend of thought due to previous training, has to a degree distorted the picture in his view. Convictions on all great matters of human interest one must have to a greater or less degree, and they will enter to some extent into the most cold-blooded scientific research as a disturbing factor.

"In a house-to-house investigation there are, outside the attitude of the investigator, many sources of error: misapprehension, vagueness and forgetfulness, and deliberate deception on the part of the persons questioned, greatly vitiate the value of the answers; on the other hand, conclusions formed by the best trained and most conscientious students on the basis of general observation and inquiry are really inductions from but a few of the multitudinous facts of social life, and these may easily fall far short of being essential or typical." *The Philadelphia Negro: A Social Study*, introduction by Elijah Anderson (1899; Philadelphia: University of Pennsylvania Press, 1996), 2–3.

Maria Farland, in "W. E. B. Du Bois, Anthropometric Science and the Limits of Racial Uplift," *American Quarterly* 58 (December 2006), 1017–44, esp. 1017–18, 1035–36, concludes that it was the Labor Department's rejection and destruction of Du Bois' study of Lowndes County, Alabama, along with the general rejection of social settlement work (such as that which *The Philadelphia Negro* represents) that caused Du Bois "to substitute 'human souls for statistics,' as he put it in *Souls*." She also notes his move into fiction rather than philosophy. He did publish *The Quest of the Silver Fleece* in 1911, but most of Du Bois' fiction (books, at least) appeared during the 1920s and might rather reflect the literary renaissance of the time. A different interpretation is presented in Morris and Ghaziani, "Du Boisian Sociology," 52–54, which maintains that after *The Philadelphia Negro* failed to yield the public-policy results that Du Bois hoped the empirical study would trigger, he "plunged headfirst into public sociology." The authors trace this work through his Atlanta University studies and his work in the NAACP, especially on *Crisis*. They also consider the American Negro Academy and the Pan-African Congress as a part of this commitment. All of this suggests that Du Bois never fully left sociology. He did, however, consistently reject the "grand theorizing found in the works of Comte, Spencer, Giddings, and Sumner" as "biological analogy" and "a new analysis" that "implies knowledge but does not supply it" (48). Morris and Ghaziani conclude that sociologists, including those currently urging public sociology, have, after one hundred years, caught up with Du Bois. And see Earl Wright II, "Using the Master's Tools: The Atlanta Sociological Laboratory and American Sociology, 1896–1924," *Sociological Spectrum* 22 (January 2002), 15–39, in which Wright points out that "the first American school of sociology" (15) was not the Chicago School (1915–30) but the Atlanta Sociological Laboratory (1896–1924), which had produced two major studies before Du Bois' arrival there in 1897. Du Bois' own explanation for leaving this science behind was very explicit: First, after the lynching of Sam Hose, he could no longer be "a calm, cool, and detached scientist." And second, there was no interest in "scientific work of the sort that I was doing." See Du Bois, *Dusk of Dawn*, 67.

6. W. E. B. Du Bois, "Sociology Hesitant," *Boundary* 2 (Fall 2000), 37–44, quotations on 39. Jstor.org/stable/303733. Accessed 3/12/2000. This essay is an important representative among Du Bois' early critiques of scientism. The essay was probably written in 1905, the year after the meeting of the Congress of Arts and Sciences at the 1904 St. Louis World's Fair (Universal Exposition). The "rediscovery" of this essay resulted in this special issue of *Boundary* 2, edited by Robert Judy.

7. Du Bois, review of "*The Souls of Black Folk*," *The Independent*, November 17, 1904, 1152. The column in the *Independent* in which this review appeared is entitled "Every Man His Own Reviewer." It was a column in which authors, by invitation, reviewed their own work. In his review, Du Bois insisted that the book did have "a clear central message," but for many readers "a penumbra of vagueness and half-veiled allusion" made them "especially impatient." He pointed out that there was "a unity of purpose in the distinctively subjective note that runs in each essay" and that "[t]hrough all the book runs a personal and intimate tone of self-revelation." He offered no apology for the confusion, saying people's conclusions about the book were ultimately "a matter of taste." Even his own evaluation of it changed from time

to time. He concluded: "Sometimes I think very well of it, and sometimes I do not." (The larger, philosophical significance of this subjective tone and the idea of self-revelation will become more evident beginning in my fourth chapter.)

8. See chapter 1, nn. 3, 4, 8, 10–14.

9. See Philip J. Swoboda, foreword to S. L. Frank, *Man's Soul: An Introductory Essay in Philosophical Psychology*, trans. by Boris Jakim (Athens: Ohio University Press, 1993), xiv–xv. Seymon Frank was one of a number of Russian anti-materialists who "converted" from Marxism to neo-idealism. Suggesting how independent Du Bois' own thinking was, Frank's description easily fits people such as William James, Du Bois' first academic adviser at Harvard, and the person whose work scholars often point to as his intellectual model.

10. Du Bois, *Dusk of Dawn*, 26. The line is slightly different in Du Bois' later-published *Autobiography*. In either case, one can only wonder whether this "sociology of human action" comment was an allusion to the 1904 Congress in St. Louis, which was heavily advertised and included the people considered to be leaders on the various topics. (Du Bois was not invited.) Ronald A. T. Judy provides some detail on the meeting in an essay that focuses on Du Bois' "Sociology Hesitant." See Judy, "On W. E. B. Du Bois and Hyperbolic Thinking," *Boundary* 2 (Fall 2000), 1–35. Jstor.org/stable/303773. All the papers of the St. Louis meeting, including a history of its development, have been published and are available at various on-line sites.

11. In an extreme example of Du Bois' concerns about scholars who wrote about black folks from no real knowledge base, Du Bois wrote to Charles Francis Adams after two such articles by him appeared in *Century Magazine*. Du Bois informed Adams that "one of the most unfortunate things about the Negro Problem is that persons who 'do not for a moment profess to be informed on the subject' insist on informing others. This, for a person who apparently boasts of advanced scientific knowledge is most deplorable and I trust that before publishing further matter on the race problem, you will study it. To this end, I am sending you some literature." See Du Bois to Adams, November 23, 1908, and the subsequent exchanges in Adams to Du Bois, November 28, 1908, and Du Bois to Adams, December 15, 1908, in Herbert Aptheker, ed., *The Correspondence of W. E. B. Du Bois* (Amherst: University of Massachusetts Press, 1973), 1:142–44. Also see David W. Blight, "W. E. B. Du Bois and the Struggle for American Historical Memory," in *History and Memory in African-American Culture*, ed. Geneviève Fabre and Robert O'Meally (New York: Oxford University Press, 1994), 66 (n. 2).

12. Perhaps the best survey of the interpretations of double consciousness in literature on *Souls* and Du Bois is Adolph L. Reed Jr., "DuBois's 'Double Consciousness': Race and Gender in Progressive-Era American Thought," *Studies in American Political Development* 6 (Spring 1992), 91–125. A detailed study of the idea itself is Dickson D. Bruce Jr., "W. E. B. Du Bois and the Idea of Double Consciousness," *American Literature* 64 (June 1992), 299–309. In an essay on the various popular uses of the term and Du Bois' ultimate failure to make sense of it, see Ernest Allen Jr., "Du Boisian Double Consciousness: The Unsustainable Argument," *Massachusetts Review* 43 (Summer 2002), 217–53. A useful explanation of

Du Bois' use of double consciousness that reflects the influence of Hegel is Ernest Allen Jr., "Ever Feeling One's Twoness: 'Double Ideals' and 'Double Consciousness'" in *The Souls of Black Folk*," *Contributions in Black Studies: A Journal of African and Afro-American Studies* 9/10 (1990–92), esp. 59–60. For an extraordinary discussion of double consciousness in the context of (double) displacement, see Nahum Dimitri Chandler, "Originary Displacement," *Boundary* 2 (Fall 2000), 249–86. Chandler applies the idea to major historical works on American slavery. And see Robert Gooding-Williams, *In the Shadow of Du Bois: Afro-Modern Political Thought* (Cambridge, MA: Harvard University Press, 2009), 66–95.

13. Wilson Jeremiah Moses, *Afrotopia: The Roots of African American Popular History* (Cambridge: Cambridge University Press, 1998), 156–57; Allen, "Du Boisian Double Consciousness: The Unsustainable Argument," 37 (n. 68). Lewis, *W. E. B. Du Bois: Biography of a Race*, 292, reveals Hayford as a fan of Du Bois who described *Souls* as a "great work" that would contribute to the resolution of "'the race problem.'"

14. Examining double consciousness from the perspective of social psychology is Stanley O. Gaines Jr., "Perspectives of Du Bois and Fanon on the Psychology of Oppression," in *Fanon: A Critical Reader*, ed. Lewis R. Gordon, T. Denean Sharpley-Whiting, and Renée T. White (Malden, MA: Blackwell Publishers, 1996). And see Shanette M. Harris, "Constructing a Psychological Perspective: The Observer and the Observed in *The Souls of Black Folk*," in *The Souls of Black Folk: One Hundred Years Later*, ed. Dolan Hubbard (Columbia: University of Missouri Press, 2003), 218–50. Offering a psychoanalytic approach is Eugene Victor Wolfenstein, *A Gift of the Spirit: Reading "The Souls of Black Folk"* (Ithaca: Cornell University Press, 2007).

15. Here I have gone one step further than Chandler in "Originary Displacement," who proposes that double consciousness, where read as the condition of being an American and a Negro, "confound[ed] the ultimate premise of racial distinction." Chandler sees this as not necessarily a negative condition. He proposes that "the Negro in Africa might conceivably have a place in human history, perhaps even tangentially in America" even though mainstream constructs of "America" allowed no room for this idea (273–74). I take up this idea in some detail beginning in chapter 4.

16. Although I will discuss Du Bois' volume in the context of Hegel's *Phenomenology* more fully in the second half of this volume, it is useful to point out here that in Hegel's text, "reflection" is an important part of consciousness's effort to discover (and realize) what it is.

17. Joe Sachs, trans., *Aristotle's "On the Soul" and "On Memory and Recollection"* (Santa Fe, NM: Green Lion Press, 2001), 9. And see Richard L. Schacht, "Hegel on Freedom," in *Hegel: A Collection of Critical Essays*, ed. Alasdair MacIntyre (Garden City, NY: Doubleday and Co., 1972), 292. Schacht describes the Aristotelian "distinction between potentiality and actuality" in terms of "'coming-to-be' generally: . . . 'for coming-to-be necessarily implies the pre-existence of something which *potentially* 'is,' but *actually* 'is not'; and this something is spoken of both as 'being' and as 'not-being.'" And, finally, see George Armstrong Kelley, "Notes on 'Lordship and Bondage,'" in MacIntyre, *Hegel: A Collection of Critical Essays*, 203, which describes Hegel's conception of Soul as "life on the margin of consciousness." Relating this

idea to music, see Robin Maconie, *The Science of Music* (Oxford: Clarendon Press, 1977), 103–4, which quotes Alan Towey: "'Aristotle classifies acts of perceiving, including hearing, as activities complete at any moment, in which respect they are to be distinguished from movements. (He) uses the term *kinesis* rather than *metabole* in his account of hearing. He elsewhere defines *kinesis* as "the actuality (*entelechia*) of what potentially (*dynamei*) is, as such," a definition which seems designed to capture the distinctive feature of a process that is ongoing, rather than the end-result of that process.'"

18. Related to this topic, see Ian Hacking, *Rewriting the Soul: Multiple Personality and the Sciences of Memory* (Princeton: Princeton University Press, 1995). In this study that evolved from an effort to understand and explain contemporary diagnoses of multiple personality disorder, Hacking concluded that "a new science, a purported knowledge of memory, quite self-consciously was created in order to secularize the soul. . . . Hence spiritual battles are fought, not on the explicit ground of the soul, but on the terrain of memory, where we suppose that there is such a thing as knowledge to be had" (5). Hacking adds, "I am preoccupied by attempts to scientize the soul through the study of memory" (6). And see page 165, which describes dédoublement in nineteenth-century France as partly a "battle between the old school and the new school, the eclectic spiritualists and the positivists. The positivists were ranged on the anticlerical, republican side of the New Third Republic" and were among groups and individuals who saw the "German- and English-speaking worlds" excelling in science over France. A study that explicitly puts Du Bois among anti-positivists is Cynthia D. Schrager, "Both Sides of the Veil: Race, Science, and Mysticism in W. E. B. Du Bois," *American Quarterly* 48 (December 1996), 551–86.

19. One also finds this three-part (desire, reason, spirit) description of Soul in *The Republic*, §§435–45, 580–81. This was not the first time Du Bois used this framework. In his review of Washington's *Up from Slavery*, Du Bois wrote about the response of "imprisoned" people taking three forms (the classic dialectical formation): "a feeling of revolt and revenge; an attempt to adjust all thought and action to the will of the greater group; or, finally, a determined attempt at self-development, self-realization, in spite of environing discouragement and prejudice." Du Bois, "The Evolution of Negro Leadership," *Dial* 31 (July 16, 1901), quotation on 53–54. Eugene Victor Wolfenstein, in *A Gift of the Spirit*, 2–3, sees the three parts differently and does not see them achieving the kind of unity described here. Wolfenstein writes: "At least as I read it, *Souls* grows out of an aesthetic/affective configuration consisting of *a situation of insult and injury both personal and racial; anger as the native and direct response to the humiliating wound; and, when anger is suppressed, a melancholy retreat from the site of the injury.*" Paul Gilroy, in *The Black Atlantic: Modernity and Double Consciousness* (Cambridge, MA: Harvard University Press, 1993), 127, transforms the classical three-part arrangement in his reading of *Souls*, maintaining that "[d]ouble consciousness emerges from the unhappy symbiosis between three modes of thinking, being, and seeing." For Gilroy, the three modes are, respectively, "racially particularistic," "nationalistic," and "diasporic or hemispheric, sometimes global and occasionally universalist."

20. Winfried Siemerling, using the same quote in "W. E. B. Du Bois, Hegel, and the Staging of Alterity," *Callaloo* 24 (Winter 2001), 325–33, views Douglass rather than Washington as the example of assimilationists. See page 328.

21. In *Dusk of Dawn*, Du Bois insisted that his grievance was not personal but philosophical, and that the appearance of a split after the publication of *Souls* was mostly manufactured by a group he referred to as "the Tuskegee Machine." It is clearly the case that even after Du Bois' critique of Washington in his review of *Up from Slavery*, Washington continued to try to convince Du Bois to come to Tuskegee to work. To be sure it could have been the tactic of keeping one's friends close and one's enemies closer, and it does appear that the attack on Du Bois in the *Colored American* after the publication of *Souls* was Washington inspired, given that he had considerable financial interest in the paper if not total editorial control. The *Colored American* reported that were it not for the chapter on Washington, Du Bois' book would have gone unnoticed. See Everett Lee, "W. E. B. Du Bois: *The Souls of Black Folk*," in *Landmarks of American Writing*, ed. Hennig Cohen (New York: Basic Books, 1969), 235. For additional detail on this issue, see Francis L. Broderick, *W. E. B. Du Bois: Negro Leader in a Time of Crisis* (Stanford: Stanford University Press, 1959), 62–75; and Lewis, *W. E. B. Du Bois: Biography of a Race*, 238–64.

22. Most scholars point to the potential negative material consequences of Washington's position given the archaic nature of vocational training in this rapidly industrializing age. They also note that the problem was compounded by the fact that labor unions formally excluded black membership, and land was difficult to buy and to keep.

23. A few pages earlier, Prosser, Turner, and Vesey were in the third category, and here it appears that they are in the first. Considering carefully the wording here, however, it is the descendants of these militants (emigrationists) who are in the first, lower, group. Also note that the hopelessness of this course was suggested by American actions in Hawaii, the West Indies, and the Philippines (other "weaker and darker peoples" in the world) at the time Du Bois was writing.

24. While this seems like the ultimate irony, given that Du Bois would eventually become a citizen of Ghana, he accepted Ghanaian citizenship *after* the United States refused to renew his passport. Du Bois had historically insisted upon self-determination *in* America, and he consistently objected to mass-emigrationist schemes. See David Levering Lewis, *W. E. B. Du Bois: The Fight for Equality and the American Century, 1919–1963* (New York: Henry Holt and Co., 2000), 569.

25. Many of Du Bois' details about this family relate to Josie's commitment to their independence and her own desire for self-development: "Best of all I loved to go to Josie's, and sit on the porch, eating peaches, while the mother bustled and talked: how Josie had bought the sewing-machine; how Josie worked at service in winter, but that four dollars a month was 'mighty little' wages; how Josie longed to go away to school, but that it 'looked like' they never could get far enough ahead to let her; how the crops failed and the well was yet unfinished; and, finally, how 'mean' some of the white folks were."

26. Although much has been made of Du Bois' elitism, the sensitivity with which he described Josie's family is probably unparalleled. He similarly admired the Burkes,

who also lived in Wilson County. "They used to have a certain magnificent barbarism about them that I liked. They were never vulgar, never immoral, but rather rough and primitive, with an unconventionality that spent itself in loud guffaws, slaps on the back, and naps in the corner." And, finally, in a later chapter, his characterization of the folk who gathered in town (Albany) on Saturdays was no different. "They are black, sturdy, uncouth country folk, good-natured and simple, talkative to a degree, and yet far more silent and brooding than the crowds of the Rhine-pfalz, or Naples, or Cracow. They drink considerable quantities of whiskey, but do not get very drunk; they talk and laugh loudly at times, but seldom quarrel or fight." They are all people who simply lack the opportunity for further self-development.

27. See John Burnet, "The Socratic Doctrine of Soul," The Second Annual Philosophic Lecture, *Proceedings of the British Academy, 1915–1916* (London: Oxford University Press), 240–41. Burnet added on page 243, "no doubt Socrates held that the conviction of ignorance was the first step on the way to salvation."

28. Irwin Edman, ed., *The Works of Plato* (1928; New York: Modern Library, 1956), xxxvii.

29. During the Middle Ages, the liberal arts included seven courses in two divisions. The lower division, or trivium, included grammar, logic, and rhetoric. The higher division, or quadrivium, included arithmetic, geometry, astronomy, and music.

30. Du Bois' shift from "The Conservation of Races" (1897) to "the conservation of soul" represents another important idea that has escaped detailed analysis by Du Bois scholars. Scholarly critiques that conclude that he essentialized race (which will be discussed later) are based partly on his 1897 essay and fail to take into account that just a few years later, in *Souls*, 118, Du Bois moved from "race" to "soul."

31. Du Bois' discussion of Atlanta and his appropriation of Atalanta are both related to Wagner's *Das Reingold* in that it is also about gold, greed, and power. In Wagner's opera, the gold ends up being a curse to all who possess it.

32. Burnet, "The Socratic Doctrine of Soul," 243.

33. Plato, *Apology*, in Edwin, *The Works of Plato*, 74–75.

34. Robert Gooding-Williams, *In the Shadow of Du Bois*, distinguishes between "the masses" and "the folk." Gooding-Williams sees Du Bois as viewing the masses as "defective" (using various synonyms throughout the book) because of their distance from modernity and the folk as "a group united by a self-expressive, self-clarifying collective and collectively shared spirit" (140). Gooding-Williams identified Du Bois with the folk, not "with the aggregate of uncultured and largely illiterate individuals [the masses] whose acculturation is the central aim of his politics of self-development" (143). Gooding-Williams also described the masses in terms of "nonsovereign souls" while John Jones, because of his education, is a "sovereign soul" (143). I agree that Du Bois identified with the folk and understand Gooding-Williams's use of the Herdian distinction between the two groups, but I don't see this dichotomy so clearly in *Souls*. In my view, "the folk" with whom Du Bois identified were themselves largely "uncultured" and "illiterate." And, clearly, I see all souls as sovereign and, as the next few pages will show, John Jones's becoming ensouled as only coincidentally related to his schooling.

35. Du Bois' characterization of certain churches should be distinguished from his thinking about religion. He clearly and regularly was disparaging of the big, established, urban churches whose leaders and congregants did little to change the world for the better or to improve life for all black people. But in *Souls*, at least, Du Bois' discussion of the religion and churches of the folk is very different, which I discuss in more detail below in chapter 5.

36. Du Bois complained about "the passionate belief" of some people "that somewhere between men and cattle, God created a *tertium quid*, and called it a Negro,—a clownish, simple creature, at times even lovable within its limitations, but straitly foreordained to walk within the Veil." Note also Du Bois' use of Omar Khayyám's poem in the epigraph to chapter 6 ("Of the Training of Black Men), which calls it a shame, given the capabilities of Soul, that it has to live "crippled" in a "clay carcass."

37. These categories also correspond to Hegel's Consciousness, Self-Consciousness, Reason, and Spirit, and will be discussed below.

38. My characterization here is consistent with Paul Gilroy's conclusions about black writing in the nineteenth century, in which the Hegelian struggle between master and slave was rewritten and the slave chose to fight to the death rather than endure bondage. The most well-known account is Frederick Douglass's choosing to do battle with the slave breaker Covey (an act of "self-creation and self-emancipation"). In Hegel's discussion, the slave concludes (thoughtfully) that to live rather than to die is the objective. (But in the Hegelian form, the slave is not quite as dependent in choosing to live as Gilroy suggests.) In discussing the slave's choice to fight, Gilroy provides an important statement from Du Bois that should be related to the Du Bois epigraph above my conclusion: "'This the American black man knows: his fight here is a fight to the finish. Either he dies or wins. If he wins it will be by no subterfuge or evasion of amalgamation. He will enter modern civilization here in America as a black man on terms of perfect and unlimited equality with any white man, or he will not enter at all. Either extermination root and branch, or absolute equality. There can be no compromise. This is the last great battle of the West.'" Gilroy, *The Black Atlantic*, 41–71, quotations on 69, 71.

39. Eric J. Sundquist, *To Wake the Nations: Race in the Making of American Literature* (Cambridge, MA: Belknap Press of Harvard University Press, 1993), 457–539.

40. The most complete analysis of the opera in the context of Du Bois' chapter that I have seen is Russell Berman, "Du Bois and Wagner: Race, Nation, and Culture between the United States and Germany," *German Quarterly* 70 (Spring 1997), 123–35, esp. 127–31. Berman's conclusion is possible, but in the opera, the swan is Gottried, Elsa's brother who had been lost to his family, having been turned into a swan by Ortrud's magic. Thus, though the parallel is not complete, it would make more sense to conclude that John Jones is the swan, and Elsa is Jennie, his sister whom he rescued from her assailant.

Kwame Anthony Appiah takes the idea of Du Bois' attachment to German nationalism one step further to make a point about Du Bois' (complete) cosmopolitanism in "Ethics in a World of Strangers: W. E. B. Du Bois and the Spirit of Cosmopolitanism," in *The Berlin Journal* 11 (Fall 2005), 23–26, and the coexistence/

simultaneity of cosmopolitanism and nationalism that Du Bois exemplified. Gilroy in "'Cheer the Weary Traveller:' W. E. B. Du Bois, Germany, and the Politics of (Dis) placement," in *The Black Atlantic*, 139–40, sees the story of John Jones as a warning for those who would become educated and forget from whence they came, and alienate the very people they hope to uplift. On Wagner, in particular, Gilroy writes: "The story [of John] unconvincingly transposes some of Du Bois's own experiences in Berlin onto his protagonist's discovery of Wagner's music in a New York concert hall." In Keith E. Byerman's, *Seizing the Word: History, Art, and Self in the Work of W. E. B. Du Bois* (Athens: University of Georgia Press, 1994), 33, John's hearing "Song of the Bride" as he died suggests a kind of "deracination" that resulted from "Du Bois's theme of the value of black education in Eurocentric culture."

41. J. Brierley, *Studies of the Soul* (1898; New York: Thomas Whittaker, 1903), 62. Earlier, Brierley maintained that the "realm" of the "ordered harmony" of creation is "ready to our hands" in music. He described music as "sounds. . . . obtained by vibrations, whose numbers and relations to each other are strictly calculable, can be expressed, indeed, in terms of logarithms. Music, then, is under the law. It is founded on abstruse calculations. Man did not make these laws. He finds them there, ready-made and waiting for him." Brierley ultimately described it as "a pre-existent intellect" (60–62).

42. Brierley's volume was published in May of 1898 and had its fifth and sixth printings in April and August of 1903. *Souls* was first published in April that year.

43. A useful interpretation of music in *Souls* and Du Bois' use of Wagner (theoretically) throughout the book, including in the John Jones chapter, is Anne E. Carroll, "Du Bois and Art Theory: *The Souls of Black Folk* as a 'Total Work of Art,'" *Public Culture* (Spring 2005), 235–54.

44. In Wolfenstein, *A Gift of the Spirit*, 115, the chapter on John Jones is "as at once the capstone of the text's narrative arch and its phenomenological kernel." Jones becomes, in Wolfenstein's view, Du Bois' alter ego. Chester J. Fontenot Jr. posits that the chapter, through a dual mind/body voice, demonstrates the South's habit of "cannibaliz[ing] its sons" in "Du Bois's 'Of the Coming of John,' Toomer's 'Kabnis,' and the Dilemma of Self-Representation," in Hubbard, *The Souls of Black Folk: One Hundred Years Later*, 148. Gilroy, *The Black Atlantic*, 115, sees Du Bois, generally, as restricted by the traditional methods, disciplines, and styles in his effort to "convey the intensity of feeling" that his "exploration of racialised experience demanded."

45. Plato, *Crito*, in Edman, *Works of Plato*, 92–95, 100. The dialogue in *Crito* takes place in the prison to which Socrates has been committed. Crito begs Socrates to escape, informs him that "there are persons who are willing to get you out of prison at no great cost" (93) and that there were many other places where he (Socrates) could live and would be welcome. In Plato's *Apology*, Socrates explains why he is on trial and what he has done. He is aware that he can escape but he insists that to leave out of a fear of death would be to deny the philosopher's mission. Moreover, if he were to escape, it would make all his teaching a lie. He finally concludes, "Men of Athens, I honour and love you; but I shall obey God rather than you, and while I have life and strength I shall never cease from the practice and teaching of philosophy, exhorting any one whom I meet" (59–88, esp. 73–76, quotation on 74).

46. Plato's *Phaedo*, in Edman, *Works of Plato*, 186. This entire dialogue (100–189) is about the soul, what it is, where it comes from, and what happens to it upon the death of the body. It was required reading when Du Bois studied at Fisk.

47. There is, however, another possible metaphor in the song Jones heard as he was about to die. We might also consider Jones's hearing "Song of the Bride," which is more popularly known today as "Here Comes the Bride," as a stunning Christian metaphor of Jesus' (the bridegroom's) execution, which allowed his union with God. In this context, Jones's physical death allowed the union (in a religious context) that Soul/consciousness is constantly seeking and ultimately achieves with this Infinite Spirit upon death. For a general theological discussion of this idea, see Howard Thurman, *Deep River* and *The Negro Spiritual Speaks of Life and Death* (1945; Richmond, IN: Friends United Press, 1975). In Robert Gooding-Williams, *In the Shadow of Du Bois*, 124, John Jones's death is tragic and Du Bois' ending is "a note of pessimism without consolation." This conclusion is tied to the musical epigraph heading the chapter, "You may bury me in the east." But, as Gooding-Williams acknowledges, the verse is actually triumphant in the Christian context. ("You may bury me in the East, / You may bury me in the West, / But I'll hear that trumpet sound / In that morning" [124]).

Chapter 3

1. Rev. W. V. Tunnell, "The Necessity of the Higher Education," *AME Church Review* 6 (October 1889), 174. William Victor Tunnell gave the opening prayer at the 1895 memorial service for Frederick Douglass at the Fifteenth Street Presbyterian Church. Tunnell was a member of the faculty at Howard University from 1891 to 1928.

2. W. E. Burghardt Du Bois, "The Talented Tenth," in *The Negro Problem: A Series of Articles by Representative American Negroes of To-Day* (New York: James Pott & Company, 1903), 33–75. Hereafter cited as Du Bois (1903).

3. W. E. B. Du Bois, "The Talented Tenth," typescript, speech before the Sigma Pi Phi Boulé, Wilberforce University, August 11–13, 1948, 20, W. E. B. Du Bois Papers, University of Massachusetts, Amherst, reel 80. There are two typescript copies of the 1948 speech in the microfilm. Quotations in this book are from the copy marked "exactly as delivered." Hereafter cited as Du Bois (1948). The scholarly work that, in the most detail, posits Du Bois' theory as anti-Washington is August Meier, *Negro Thought in America, 1880–1915* (Ann Arbor: University of Michigan Press, 1968). For a history of the Boulé, see Charles Wesley, *History of Sigma Pi Phi, First of the Negro-American Greek-Letter Fraternities* (Washington, D.C.: Association for the Study of Negro Life, 1954). According to Wesley, among the six founding members of the fraternity, five were physicians (one of them also a pharmacist), and one was a dentist. In 1948 when Du Bois gave this presentation, among 440 members, there were 152 in medicine (presumably physicians), 105 teachers, 46 dentists, 45 attorneys, 23 ministers, 20 businessmen, 9 college presidents, 7 engineers, 4 social workers, 4 judges, 3 college deans, 3 pharmacists, 1 journalist, 1 professional chemist, 1 architect, 3 retirees, and 8 unknown. In terms of income, 80 earned less than $5,000 per year, 199 earned between 5 and $9,000, 111 earned between 10 and $24,000, 16

earned more than $25,000. (Ibid., 5, 316–17.) The national income average that year was less than $3,000 and was less than half of that for black Americans.

4. See Adolph L. Reed Jr., *W. E. B. Du Bois and American Political Thought: Fabianism and the Color Line* (New York: Oxford University Press, 1997), 53. In addition to the scholars Reed cites as arguing that Du Bois abandoned his idea of the Talented Tenth, one could also add the discussion by Joy James, entitled "Du Bois' Rejection of Black Elite Leadership," in *Transcending the Talented Tenth: Black Leaders and American Intellectuals* (New York: Routledge, 1997), 18–27. James, like David Levering Lewis, discusses Du Bois' eventual embrace of the working class. James, however, also importantly makes clear that her study is about an *intellectual* elite. Another study that seems to equate the Talented Tenth today with an intellectual elite and with those who achieve a certain type of education is Henry Louis Gates Jr., "Parable of the Talents," in Gates and Cornel West, *The Future of the Race* (New York: Alfred A. Knopf, 1996), 1–52. And see in the same volume, Gates, "W. E. B. Du Bois and 'The Talented Tenth,'" 115–32, which is followed by a copy of the 1903 article. Gates called the 1903 essay "a coda to *The Souls of Black Folk*" (119). And see David Levering Lewis, *W. E. B. Du Bois: The Fight for Equality and the American Century, 1919–1963* (New York: Henry Holt and Co., 2000), 538, which maintains that by the time of the Wilberforce speech, Du Bois "had come now to abjure the very idea of the Talented Tenth." Also related, Everett Lee wrote for a 1969 volume, "An aristocrat at heart, Du Bois had little faith in the masses. Moreover he felt personally threatened by Washington and his 'Tuskegee Machine,' and he despised Washington's submissiveness and moralizing." Still, Lee sees Du Bois as fair to Washington. Everett Lee, "W. E. B. Du Bois' *The Souls of Black Folk*," in *Landmarks of American Writing*, ed. Hennig Cohen (New York: Basic Books, 1969), 234. Robert Gooding-Williams, *In the Shadow of Du Bois: Afro-Modern Political Thought in America* (Cambridge, MA: Harvard University Press, 2009), sees Du Bois' Talented Tenth as a much more dominating class than I do. Gooding-Williams sees these members as reigning "over the benighted, ignorant" masses "who can socially integrate their lives by obeying the directives of their betters" (34). This characterization is evident throughout the volume, but see pages 31–36. This domination is somewhat tempered by the fact that the political philosophy includes a group leadership in which the leaders share the ethos of the folk.

5. The conclusion that the Talented Tenth theory favored elites results partly from misreadings of the text. For one example, Patricia L. Hill wrote, "Du Bois continuously stresses his individual tenets of culture and liberty by urging higher education for the black elite and by insisting upon full political and civil rights for all." As already indicated, this is not an isolated interpretation. But Du Bois was urging higher education not *for* the elite but in order *to create* an elite or an educated leadership class. See Hill, "American Popular Response to W. E. B. Du Bois's '*The Souls of Black Folk*,'" *Western Journal of Black Studies* 2 (Spring 1978), 54–55. Among those not concluding that the theory was designed for or would have the effect of protecting elites, Thomas C. Holt appropriately sees the Talented Tenth (which he acknowledged as composed of black intellectuals) in terms of their "special duty to their race," which Holt rightly concludes renders "the struggle for black self-realization . . . a

struggle for all people." See Holt, "The Political Uses of Alienation: W. E. B. Du Bois on Politics, Race, and Culture, 1903–1940," *American Quarterly* 42 (June 1990), 305.

6. Du Bois' application to Harvard reveals that most of his coursework at Fisk was in these fields, but he also studied French, German, science, and math. This application also indicates that his secondary school preparation included six years of Latin and five and a half years of Greek. W. E. B. Du Bois application to Harvard College, Harvard University Archives, Pusey Library, Cambridge, Mass.

7. Du Bois, *Dusk of Dawn: An Essay Toward an Autobiography of a Race Concept* (1940; New Brunswick: Transaction Publishers, 1991), 38–39.

8. James, *Transcending the Talented Tenth*, 19, notes the relationship between Du Bois' theory and this ancient text but does not develop it. Eugene Victor Wolfenstein, *A Gift of the Spirit: Reading The Souls of Black Folk* (Ithaca: Cornell University Press, 2007), 40, recognizes Platonic (*The Republic*) influences in *Souls* but ultimately attributes Du Bois' ideas about the Talented Tenth to Carlyle who wrote, for example, " 'We must have more Wisdom to govern us, we must be governed by the Wisest, we must have an Aristocracy of Talent!' " Although I will not discuss it in this book, one should also consider the relationship between Du Bois' Talented Tenth discussions and Hegel's emphasis on "the German ideal of *Bildung*"—"the ideals of education, art, culture, and the formation of cultivated taste." This would be especially important for those who would become educators in the emerging "modern" university system that was built on intellectuals rather than clerics or the politically connected. This ideal in the context of Hegel's life and pursuits is discussed throughout Terry Pinkard, *Hegel: A Biography* (Cambridge: Cambridge University Press, 2000), 49–50. Importantly, Pinkard also distinguished between merely gaining an education (learning?) and the self-development required to represent the ideal of *Bildung*, which went substantially beyond "learning." Moreover, this pursuit was not limited to elites, and it did not make one an elite. The ideal of *Bildung* was decidedly antibourgeois.

9. This very brief description of the education process is detailed in Plato, *The Republic*, trans. and ed. Desmond Lee, 2nd ed. (New York: Penguin Books, 2003), Parts III and VII. Aspects of my description of the educational process are also from Jamie C. Kassler, *Music, Science, Philosophy: Models in the Universe of Thought* (Aldershot: Ashgate, 2001), 165–70, quotation on 168. And see Plato's *Laws*. Hereafter, for direct quotations from Plato's *The Republic*, I will give the citation in the text, enclosed in parentheses, using the abbreviation *PR* followed by the paragraph number. Citations to the editor's or translator's remarks will be given in the notes.

10. Du Bois, *Souls*. The statement in *Souls* was much more developed than the original iteration in Du Bois (1903), 63, where he simply said, "I insist that the object of all true education is not to make men carpenters, it is to make carpenters men." What has been consistently lost in discussions of Du Bois is that his characterization of the purpose of work (perhaps his reading of "Lordship and Bondage") is very similar to at least one aspect of Karl Marx's conclusions, which were also adapted from Hegel. Although Marx's idea of the industrial proletariat's alienation from the product of his labor is better known, for Marx and Du Bois work had a product other than (in addition to) a material one; an outcome/product of work was

also objective man. Also note that in "The Development of a People," *International Journal of Ethics* (April 1904), 292–311, Du Bois insisted: "I care not what his [the leader's] vocation may be—preacher, teacher, physician, or artisan." He knew that any of them had the potential to "solve the Negro problem" (307).

11. Du Bois (1903), 46, 60–63.

12. Ibid., 61–66.

13. Ibid., 55, 58, 63, 45, respectively.

14. These conclusions are based on *The Republic*, Parts IV and VI. Plato insisted that "'if we want to pick the best Guardians, we must pick those who have the greatest skill in watching over the community'" (412c), and "'we must choose from among our Guardians those who appear to us on observation to be most likely to devote their lives to doing what they judge to be in the interest of the community, and who are never prepared to act against it'" (412e). He added, Rulers (philosophers), "if they were to do their job properly, should have no houses or land or any other possessions of their own, but get their daily bread from others in payment for their services, and consume it together in common" (464b–c). Philosophers "will be self-controlled and not grasping about money. Other people are more likely to worry about the things which make men so eager to get and spend money" (485e). Suggesting that philosophers do not seek power, Plato discussed having to "force" philosophers to become rulers at 499c–d. He believed that because the demand for philosophers' service is just, they will ultimately accept the responsibility as an "unavoidable necessity" (520d–e). Philosophers "would despise all present honours as mean and worthless, and care most for doing right and any rewards it may bring; and they would regard justice as being of paramount importance, and, throughout their reorganization of society, serve and forward it" (540d–e). Finally, Plato insisted that there were two things "which our Guardians must at all cost prevent from slipping unobserved into our state." The two things were "wealth and poverty" (421e–422a).

15. Although most scholars who have addressed this topic over the last twenty or so years focus on the intelligentsia, Fiona Spiers recognized the significant problem in the scholarship of defining the Talented Tenth: "for when Du Bois first used the phrase he was postulating an altruistic élite who would donate its talents to racial uplift, not describing the style or structure of any existing leadership group. Yet his words were eagerly received by the educated few, who found an identity and a cohesion in this concept." Spiers adopted a very "useful distinction between the 'intelligentsia,'" who generally were college-educated and/or professionals, "and the intellectuals, a much smaller group who contribute directly to the creation, transmission and criticism of ideas." Fiona E. Spiers, "The Talented Tenth: Leadership Problems and the Afro-American Intellectuals, 1895–1919," *Bulletin of the John Rylands University Library of Manchester* 61 (Autumn 1978), 229, 214, respectively. Seeing the Talented Tenth more broadly, and exploring the early implementation of the idea in Georgia, see Dominic J. Capeci Jr. and Jack C. Knight, "W. E. B. Du Bois's Southern Front: Georgia 'Race Men' and the Niagara Movement, 1905–1907," *Georgia Historical Quarterly* (Fall 1999), 479–507. And see n. 24 below.

16. Quotations from Du Bois (1948), 1. A general discussion and interpretation of Du Bois' economic thought with some emphasis on his Talented Tenth theory

is Juliet E. K. Walker, "Racial Capitalism in a Global Economy: The 'Double Consciousness' of Black Business in the Economic Philosophy of W. E. B. Du Bois," in Chester J. Fontenot Jr. and Mary Alice Morgan, with Sarah Gardner, eds., *W. E. B. Du Bois and Race* (Macon, GA: Mercer University Press, 2001), 70–96. Reiland Rabaka makes clear that Du Bois was a pioneer in critical race theory, particularly in his critiques (implicit and explicit) of Marxism, some of which are contained in the second Talented Tenth address. See Rabaka, *Du Bois's Dialectics: Black Radical Politics and the Reconstruction of Critical Social Theory* (Lantham, MD: Lexington Books, 2008), esp. 109–15.

17. Du Bois (1948), 2–3, 4, 5, 11.

18. Ibid.; Reed, *W. E. B. Du Bois and American Political Thought*, 68, mistakenly concludes that Du Bois proposed starting with the college fraternities. Reed wrote: "After identifying undergraduate fraternities . . . as providing a basis for a large race organization among the enlightened elite, he strove to impress the emerging generation with the need to adopt an 'ideal of plain living and high thinking.'" In fact, Du Bois concluded that "[t]he undergraduate fraternities, even with their graduate chapters, have probably a constituency too young and too busy trying to make a living. Then too, they are dominated by rather youthful ideals of the mis-called college spirit. I turn then to this fraternity [the Boulé]." Du Bois (1948), 11.

19. Du Bois (1948), 12–15, quotation on 12. Wesley's summary of the survey reported that 1 member was under 30 years old, 311 were between 30 and 60, and 128 were over 60. (Wesley, *History of Sigma Pi Phi*, 316.)

20. Du Bois (1948), 17.

21. Ibid., 15, 16. And see Spiers, "The Talented Tenth," 212, where she concludes that "it was not to be a closed caste, but rather the pinnacle of a meritocracy."

22. Du Bois (1948), 11–12, 13, 14, 20.

23. On Du Bois' sitting alone after the address, see Lewis, *W. E. B. Du Bois: The Fight for Equality and the American Century*, 538. Lewis proposed that Du Bois' being alone was perhaps the first indication of his declining influence among people who once identified (or were identified) so closely with him. But it is important to note, also, that the words in the above quote were the last words of the speech, thus increasing their sting. Wesley's *History of Sigma Pi Phi*, 302–16, reports on this meeting. But the only hint of any problems this expressed sentiment might have caused is the ambiguous statement: "This address was the occasion of controversy and discussion throughout these sessions" (301–11).

24. As suggested above, the scholarly debate seems to have shifted from "the talented tenth" to the "intellectual elite" and, sometimes, the public intellectuals, which one has to assume are even smaller groups than Du Bois proposed. James, *Transcending the Talented Tenth*, xxi, outlines the debate and clearly describes "African-American intellectuals—as the postmodern Talented Tenth." She and Adolph Reed, however, both realize that we should not automatically assume that intellectuals are/were members. Fiona E. Spiers, "The Talented Tenth," 207, is explicit: "The Talented Tenth was never coterminous with either the upper or the middle class, and was, in principle at least, open to all satisfactory aspirants, admission being on the grounds of proven ability and a willingness to assume the responsibilities of utilizing

that ability to help ameliorate the condition of the less fortunate of the race." David Levering Lewis, *W. E. B. Du Bois: Biography of a Race: 1868–1919* (New York: Henry Holt and Co., 1993), 289–90, recognizes that "the majority of those who matched the Talented Tenth profile [did not] consider themselves part of the movement" as a consequence of their fear of Washington, "but those who were members fit the profile" in terms of "family, education, profession, region, and urban dwelling."

25. Du Bois was not far off the mark. Wesley's history of the organization makes clear that their purpose was not "to visit the sick and bury the dead" (like most fraternal and beneficial societies at the time of this group's founding) "but to bind men of like qualities, tastes, and attainments into close sacred union, that they might know the best of one another." Wesley also noted that the organization had historically opposed expansion. They saw their purpose as "the enrichment of the personal life of its members, in the binding of men of like qualities, tastes and attainments into close, sacred and fraternal unions." He recognized that these men were "not separated from the masses for they were dependent upon them," but that that dependence did not seem to result in a fraternal relationship with them. Wesley, *History of Sigma Pi Phi*, [i], 27.

26. Du Bois (1948), 11, 12, 18–19. According to Wesley's history, national officers included the "Grand Sire Archon, the Grand Grammateus, the Grand Thesauristes, the Grand Leading Archon, [and] the Grand Lecturing Archon." This is according to the 1908 constitution, reprinted on page 60 of Wesley's work. Some of these titles, appropriately modified, were repeated in the individual organization chapters. Wesley gives some of the history of the titles (and their evolution) in Greek history, and the relationship between them and the titles used in this organization on pages 38–39.

27. Quotations from Du Bois (1948), 15, 17, 20.

28. Henry George, *Progress and Poverty: An Inquiry into the Cause of Industrial Depressions, and of Increase of Want with Increase of Wealth—The Remedy* (San Francisco: W. M. Hinton & Co., 1879); and Edward Bellamy, *Looking Backward, 2000–1887* (Boston: Ticknor & Co., 1881). Du Bois later said he "'revered'" Bellamy's book when he read it as a youngster. See Reed, *W. E. B. Du Bois and American Political Thought*, 107. A work exploring numerous nineteenth- and twentieth-century communitarian societies is Donald E. Pitzer, ed., *America's Communal Utopias* (Chapel Hill: University of North Carolina Press, 1997).

29. Du Bois (1948), 9–10.

30. Holt, "The Political Uses of Alienation," 310–311; Spiers, "The Talented Tenth," 212. Holt sees Du Bois' radicalization (probably Fabianist rather than Leninist) as having occurred during or by the late 1920s and early 1930s.

31. Du Bois (1903), 50–51, reports that there were 2,304 black college graduates in the United States in 1899, and *The Twelfth Census of the United States—1900* reports the black population as 8,845,789. Using those numbers, the percentage of the black population that had graduated from college was about 3/100 of 1 percent. The percentage of black college graduates among those twenty years and older (4,347,809) was about 5/100 (or one-twentieth) of 1 percent. Lewis Perry, *Intellectual Life in America: A History* (New York: Franklin Watts, 1984), 283, reports that

there were (only) 238,000 students in undergraduate school in 1900 in the entire country and fewer than 6,000 in graduate school. Moreover, across the nineteenth century, less than 5 percent of the national population went to college.

32. Du Bois (1903), 45.

33. Although ancient Athens is regularly described as the birthplace of democratic forms of government, it is also the case that out of a population of 200,000–300,000, the voting population (adult men of a certain status) totaled only 35,000–45,000. See *The Republic*, xxvii. Also note that Plato thought that most people were not wise enough to choose leaders who would best represent their interests and would instead choose based on popularity. He believed that politicians under democracy worked not in the interest of the general public but for themselves and, more generally, for the wealthy. Ultimately, Plato concluded that democracy led to tyranny. See *PR*, 555d–576.

34. See U. S. Bureau of the Census, *Statistical Abstract of the United States: 1986* (Washington, D.C., 1985), 134. (See table 218, "Years of School Completed, by Race, Sex, and Age: 1984.") The statistic is based on persons at least twenty-five years old as of March 1984. My thanks to Kenneth Hamilton for pointing out this statistic to me.

35. Lewis, *W. E. B. Du Bois: The Fight for Equality and the American Century*, 550, implies this kind of expansion, writing, "If representative Negroes were in short supply for the Du Bois cause, those who did not fit the classic Talented Tenth profile began to show their support." Lewis also links Du Bois' efforts to "the left, blacks and whites, labor, students, and church people."

Du Bois' move away from the college trained if not the Talented Tenth as the potential leaders by the 1950s is also suggested in Dan S. Green in "W. E. B. Du Bois' Talented Tenth: A Strategy for Racial Advancement," *Journal of Negro Education* 46 (Summer 1977), 358–66, which discusses Du Bois' seeing more leadership potential in the working class than the college educated and his belief that it would remain that way until black educational institutions were "'rescued from [their] sycophantic and cowardly leadership'" (364; quoting Du Bois' *In Battle for Peace: The Story of My 83rd Birthday*). The most convincing discussion of this movement is contained in Reiland Rabaka, *Du Bois's Dialectics*, esp. 93–115.

36. Du Bois (1948), 9, 17.

Chapter 4

1. Reverdy C. Ransom, "A Programme for the Negro," *AME Church Review* 16 (April 1900), 423–30, quotation on 423. Although Ransom is not usually mentioned in discussions of Rauschenbusch, Gladden, and other important Social Gospelers, he was nevertheless a very important part of this movement. Ransom was also among the founding members of the NAACP. For a biography of Ransom, see Annetta L. Gomez-Jefferson, *The Sage of Tawawa: Reverdy Cassius Ransom, 1861–1959* (Kent, OH: Kent State University Press, 2002).

2. For a detailed discussion of Crummell as an inspiration and mentor to Du Bois, see David Levering Lewis, *W. E. B. Du Bois: Biography of a Race, 1868–1919* (New York: Henry Holt and Company, 1993), esp. 161–74. Robert Gooding-Williams, in

"Du Bois's Counter-Sublime," *Massachusetts Review* 35 (Summer 1994), 202–3, an essay on Du Bois' Crummell chapter, sees Du Bois establishing "himself as the founding father of modern African American thought." In *In the Shadow of Du Bois: Afro-Modern Political Thought in America* (Cambridge, MA: Harvard University Press, 2009), 162–209, Gooding-Williams sees Du Bois as constructing himself as Douglass's intellectual heir. Eric J. Sundquist in *To Wake the Nations: Race in the Making of American Literature* (Cambridge, MA: Belknap Press of Harvard University Press, 1993), 514–17, saw Crummell as a father figure for Du Bois and also posited that Du Bois' choosing Crummell to write about further undercut Booker T. Washington's leadership position. The definitive biography of Crummell is Wilson Jeremiah Moses, *Alexander Crummell: A Study of Civilization and Discontent* (New York: Oxford University Press, 1989).

3. W. E. B. Du Bois, *The Souls of Black Folk*, ed. Henry Louis Gates Jr. and Terri Hume Oliver (New York: W. W. Norton & Company, 1999), 135 (n. 2). The most extensive discussion of the "symbolic geography" of *Souls* is in Robert B. Stepto, *From Behind the Veil: A Study of Afro-American Narrative*, 2d ed. (1979; Urbana: University of Illinois Press, 1991), esp. 66–82. Robert Gooding-Williams provides a detailed discussion of Du Bois' use of Bunyan and other sixteenth- and seventeenth-century Protestant texts in *Souls* in "Du Bois's Counter-Sublime."

4. Lewis, *W. E. B. Du Bois: Biography of a Race*, 166.

5. I refer here to the canonical, rather than the professional, prophets of religion. The professional prophets, often described as psychics, sorcerers, soothsayers, and diviners, prophesied for a living. Old Testament scholar E. W. Heaton called them "the 'yes-men' of government circles" who gained "an official status because they lent a halo of sanctity to the projects of the party in power." They regularly assured employers that everything was fine "when, in fact, the state was verging on a moral and political collapse." He characterized their actions as "'flattering divination.'" E. W. Heaton, *The Old Testament Prophets* (Baltimore: Penguin Books, 1961), 34–54, quotations on 37. The status of the canonical prophets derived from their relationship to God. Jeremiah described the word of professional prophets compared to real messages from the Lord as the straw (chaff) to the wheat (Jer. 23:25–28). Another way to think about the difference between the two types of prophets is provided in Donald E. Gowan, *Theology of the Prophetic Books: The Death and Resurrection of Israel* (Louisville, KY: Westminister John Knox Press, 1998), 2, which notes that although people regularly equate prophecy with predictions of the future, "to be 'prophetic'" relates to taking the "lonely stance for truth and justice, against popular opinion." Gowan describes prophets as "lonely individualists who stood for spiritual religion and against organized religion's ritualistic observances, which were devoid of concern for justice." Edward J. Blum, *W. E. B. Du Bois: American Prophet* (Philadelphia: University of Pennsylvania Press, 2007) frames Du Bois as a prophet in this tradition. Distinguishing between jeremiadic and prophetic speech in African American history is David L. Chapell, *A Stone of Hope: Prophetic Religion and the Death of Jim Crow* (Chapel Hill: University of North Carolina Press, 2004). For a detailed discussion of the jeremiad tradition in African American history (one that includes Du Bois' writings), see David Howard-Pitney, *The African American*

Jeremiad: Appeals for Justice in America, rev. ed. (Philadelphia: Temple University Press, 2005). The standard study of the jeremiad in American history is Sacvan Bercovitch, *The American Jeremiad* (Madison: University of Wisconsin Press, 1978). A useful critique of Bercovitch's conclusion, especially in view of African American jeremiads, is Jonathon S. Kahn, *Divine Discontent: The Religious Imagination of W. E. B. Du Bois* (Oxford: Oxford University Press, 2009), 68–90. Kahn concluded that "Bercovitch's account of the American jeremiad . . . swallows the African American jeremiad whole" (90).

Also on canonical prophets generally, see R. B. Y. Scott, *The Relevance of the Prophets* (New York: Macmillan Company, 1944), 2–12; and Sheldon H. Blank, *Understanding the Prophets* (New York: Union of American Hebrew Congregations, 1983), 35–46. On prophetic writings (the message rather than the man) see John F. A. Sawyer, *Prophecy and the Prophets of the Old Testament* (New York: Oxford University Press, 1987), 61–125; and Heaton, *The Old Testament Prophets*, 17–33. Heaton also details the significance of the people the prophet presumes to lead on pages 55–89. The prophet's purpose was to look after and guide the people and to make "the nation a people fit for God's own possession and purpose" (1 Peter 2:9).

6. Although in Judaism, Christianity, and Islam there are many recognized prophets, it is also the case that Moses, Jesus, and Mohammad are recognized in all three as canonical. One can find equally compelling parallels in Buddhism and Confucianism, but neither Buddha nor Confucius ever claimed to be direct messengers of God, as was the case for the others. Indeed, the distinction between prophets and what Abraham J. Heschel calls "prophetic personalities" is that the former hear from God and speak for God, while "divines" (for example) interpret nature. See Heschel, "Prophets Throughout the World," in *The Prophets* (n.p.: The Jewish Publication Society of America, 1962), 447–82.

7. Wilson Jeremiah Moses has provided clear evidence of Crummell's difficult personality throughout *Alexander Crummell* and more compactly in "W. E. B. Du Bois's 'The Conservation of Races' and its Context: Idealism, Conservatism and Hero Worship," *Massachusetts Review* 34 (Summer 1993), 275–94. Old Testament scholars indirectly make a compelling case for a reexamination of Crummell's work and writing. Biblical scholars point out, for example, that because prophets traditionally serve in a time of great moral crisis, their demands of the people and the nation regularly made them appear to be troublemakers. They were "disturbers of the peace." The messages were urgent, the tone unequivocal, which often created tension between the prophet and his people. Some scholars distinguish priests (i.e., ministers) from prophets by describing priests as reassuring and soothing as they minister to "the eternal and changeless . . . in man's life." Prophets, on the other hand, are more concerned with the moment, which explains the urgency and crisis in their tone. Prophets are less concerned with conventional religion than with "social transformation." They seek to change "the *ethos* of the community." See Blank, *Understanding the Prophets*, 48, and R. B. Y. Scott, *The Relevance of the Prophets*, 12–17, 41–49. Abraham J. Heschel noted that although prophets begin their speech with "*a message of doom*," they usually "conclude *with a message of hope*." Moreover, "[i]nstead of showing us a way through the elegant mansions of the mind, the

prophet takes us to the slums." Heschel, *The Prophets*, 3–4, 7, 12. E. W. Heaton, *The Old Testament Prophets*, 50, 60, adds that prophets risk everything in doing this work: they regularly lose their friends, family, property, health, and reputation. All of these general characterizations of prophets make Crummell's contemporaries' characterizations of his personality worthy of reexamination (while also making Du Bois' framing him as a prophet more understandable). For one especially fitting piece reflecting all of these characteristics, see Crummell, "The Destined Superiority of the Negro," in J. R. Oldfield, ed., *Civilization and Black Progress: Selected Writings of Alexander Crummell on the South* (Charlottesville: University Press of Virginia, 1995), 43–53.

8. Eugene Victor Wolfenstein, in *A Gift of the Spirit: Reading "The Souls of Black Folk"* (Ithaca: Cornell University Press, 2007), 95, made this point differently and in a way useful to the conclusion here. He wrote that Du Bois "places before us one of the varieties of religious experience without asking us to believe in it." In a chapter on Du Bois that focuses on the evidence of religion in his writings, Wilson Jeremiah Moses wrote that even though Du Bois had "abandoned at least organized religion" by the time he was thirty years old, he clearly continued to use Christian symbols in his writing well beyond that. Moses later quoted Du Bois' saying that when he graduated from Fisk he was "still a 'believer' in orthodox religion." *Afrotopia: The Roots of African American Popular History* (Cambridge: Cambridge University Press, 1998), 139, 141. In W. E. B. Du Bois, *Prayers for Dark People*, ed. Herbert Aptheker (Amherst: University of Massachusetts Press, 1990), Aptheker wrote that Du Bois did not regularly attend any church, "but he was well aware of the enormous influence of the church upon the history and lives of Black people and upon his own life." Aptheker added that "Du Bois disliked denominational religion and detested that 'Christianity'. . . became an excuse for the status quo—whether slavery or racism or war" (vii, viii). Still, Aptheker insisted that Du Bois never became an atheist. Jonathon S. Kahn, in *Divine Discontent*, views Du Bois as "irreligious." Taking a nearly opposite position, and understanding religion as more than theology or orthodoxy, is Edward J. Blum, *W. E. B. Du Bois: America Prophet*.

9. This definition of "allegory" is provided at http://www.tnellen.com/cybereng/lit_terms/allegory.html.

Old Testament scholar E. W. Heaton described allegory as "a device for combining an ancient authority with a current belief—without appearing to sacrifice either." He pointed to the Song of Solomon as the most creative use of biblical allegory, in which "secular love songs . . . speak of Christ and his Church." He discussed the use of allegory by Jewish philosophers who presented Hebrew Scriptures to people who were essentially pagans and in terms of New Testament writers' attempts to present Christian gospel to people brought up under Judaism. See Heaton, *The Old Testament Prophets*, 12–14.

10. Although Crummell's life was undoubtedly *personally* important for Du Bois, *The Columbia Electronic Encyclopedia* (Columbia University Press, 2004), in its definition of "allegory," notes, "The characters in an allegory often have no individual personality but are embodiments of moral qualities and other abstractions." See http://www.reference.com/browse/columbia/allegory.

11. See Heaton, *The Old Testament Prophets*, 15. Probably most of the best-known students of philosophy during the medieval age were clerics or monks. Through their prodigious translation work, ancient philosophical texts were made more accessible and provided a useful bridge for the modern philosophers. French philosopher, mathematician, and scientist René Descartes (1596–1650) is credited with initiating the split between philosophy and religion. For a very useful discussion of the relationship between the two traditions and their eventual divergence, see Francis MacDonald Cornford, *From Religion to Philosophy: A Study in the Origins of Western Speculation* (1912; Atlantic Highlands, NJ: Humanities Press, 1980).

With specific regard to Du Bois, despite sometimes intense debates about his religiosity, Allen Dwight Callahan, in "Introduction: Figures in the True," in *African American Religious Life and the Story of Nimrod*, ed. Anthony B. Pinn and Allen Dwight Callahan (New York: Palgrave MacMillan, 2008), 7, using Zora Neale Hurston and James Baldwin as examples, points out the importance of recognizing black writers' acceptance of "the Christian church as an important cultural development, but without acceptance of its theological stance." Also see 10–11 (n. 22), which, quoting Thomas J. J. Altizer's *The Gospel of Christian Atheism*, points out the deep roots of the Christian prophetic tradition in the works of "a Blake, a Hegel, a Marx, a Dostoevsky, and a Nietzsche." Callahan quotes Nietzsche's observation that "'what . . . really triumphed over the Christian god was Christian morality itself.'" Certainly one can see Du Bois' writings in this light.

12. As an undergraduate at Fisk University, Du Bois took courses in the Philosophy Department on "Logic of Christian Evidence" and "Natural Theology." See W. E. B. Du Bois, admission application to the Harvard College Committee of the Faculty on Admissions from other Colleges, Faculty of Arts and Sciences folder, Harvard University Archives, Pusey Library, Cambridge, Massachusetts.

13. An analysis of the historical antagonism between philosophers and theologians is Lou H. Silberman, "Prophets and Philosophers: The Scandal of Prophecy," in *Interpreting the Prophetic Tradition: The Goldenson Lectures, 1955–1966*, introduction by Harry M. Orlinsky (Cincinnati: The Hebrew Union College Press and New York: KTAV Publishing House, 1969), 81–100. This proposal of ways of reconciling the two groups was the 1958 lecture.

14. "Science of the Experience of Consciousness" was the original title of Hegel's volume. And some scholars have said the first part of *Phenomenology* is just that, while the last part is a philosophy of history. See especially Werner Marx, *Hegel's Phenomenology of Spirit: Its Point and Purpose—A Commentary on the Preface and Introduction* (New York: Harper & Row, Publishers, 1975), x–xi and notes. Although I am focused on Du Bois, I view Hegel as having done both, with the two discussions taking place simultaneously even though I have separated them in places for the sake of clarity.

Hereafter, for direct quotations from A. V. Miller, trans., *Hegel's Phenomenology of Spirit* (Oxford: Oxford University Press, 1977), analysis and foreword by J. N. Findlay, I will give the citation in the text, enclosed in parentheses, using the abbreviation *PS* followed by the paragraph number. Citations to Findlay's analysis or other translations will be given in the notes by page number. I will also capitalize Hegel's "forms" of consciousness (Consciousness, Self-Consciousness, Reason, Spirit) when using them as he used them.

15. Dewey M. Beegle, *Moses, The Servant of Yaweh* (Grand Rapids: William B. Eerdmans Publishing Company, 1972), 53.

16. See E. Dinet and Sliman Ben Ibrahim, *The Life of Mohammad the Prophet of Allah* (Paris: The Paris Book Club, n.d.), [5]-9. The nurse was unlikely because she was so poor herself and because she was unable to nurse. After choosing Mohammad, however, her breasts filled with milk and her family subsequently prospered. Joseph Campbell called the phenomenon of remarkable beginnings a "'monomyth'" and described it as common to folk tales and mythologies since the ancient world. Campbell's *The Hero with a Thousand Faces* quoted and discussed in Blum, *W. E. B. Du Bois: American Prophet*, 25–26

17. Some Bible scholars report this story as an appropriation of the legend of Sargon I, from 1,000 years earlier, for the specific purpose of creating this remarkable beginning for Moses. Others point to equally plausible explanations. For example, there is an etymological similarity between the name Moses and the Hebrew word for "to draw out" (as from the water). They are Mosheh and mashah. Also note, however, that the word "moses" is the Egyptian word for child or son (e.g., Thutmoses and Ramoses), and he was rescued by an Egyptian princess. See Beegle, *Moses*, 50–55; and Elias Auerbach, *Moses*, trans. and ed. by Robert A. Barklay and Israel O. Lehman (Detroit: Wayne State University, 1975), 17.

18. Dinet and Ibrahim, *The Life of Mohammad*, 9–10.

19. For theological and practical discussions of each of these temptations, see Dean Howard Thurman, *Temptations of Jesus: Five Sermons Given by Dean Howard Thurman in Marsh Chapel, Boston University* (San Francisco: Lawton Kennedy, 1962). The three temptations are common to all the major world religions and to the mythology of ancient cultures as well.

20. This one example suggests the difficulty of attributing some of Du Bois' allusions to either Old or New Testament traditions. Important parts of these instructions to the Ephesians (6: 10–17) were also uttered in one of the most important of the Old Testament prophetic books, Isaiah (59: 16–20), in which, when others failed to do the necessary work, God went to work to redeem Zion, a "lost" community full of liars, injustice, violence, and general iniquity, after shielding Himself with a breastplate of righteousness, "helmet of salvation," "garments of vengeance," and a cloak of zeal.

21. One wonders what Du Bois intended to suggest in his reporting that Crummell "stretched forth his hands eagerly." Presumably, he was reaching for the hand that reached out in Isaiah 59:1, in which we are reminded that (despite the sins of Israel) God's "hand is not shortened, That it cannot save."

22. The apparent failure of the prophet is not uncommon. Judah collapsed under the watch of Jeremiah; he failed to reform Judeans, and they went into exile in Egypt. Ezekiel, who received his call in Babylon (during the exiles' first deportation) never returned to Palestine. Heaton, *Old Testament Prophets*, 28–29. Also see George W. Coats, *Moses: Heroic Man, Man of God*, Supplement Series 57, *Journal for the Study of the Old Testament* (Sheffield: Sheffield Academic Press, 1988), [213], where Coats

reminds us that this seeming paradox is exactly what the prophet is supposed to model to his people—a type of "integrity [in which he is the] . . . hero, the authentic man, [and] the suffering servant of the Lord" all at once. This is a somewhat tragic figure in that despite his sacrifices for his people, they reject him. But he is also heroic in that "he maintained his intimacy with God and People" anyway. And see Coats, "The Failure of the Hero: Moses as a Model for Ministry," in *The Moses Tradition*, Supplement Series 161, *Journal for the Study of the Old Testament* (Sheffield: Sheffield Academic Press, 1993), 115–24.

23. God even warned Jeremiah of the opposition he would face from friends and family. And, indeed, Jeremiah constantly bemoaned the pits that other people dug for him.

24. Detailed analysis of the murmuring and whispering and the implications is in Coats, *Moses*, 109–24.

25. On the American Negro Academy, see Alfred A. Moss Jr., *The American Negro Academy: Voice of the Talented Tenth* (Baton Rouge: Louisiana State University Press, 1981). Also see Wilson Jeremiah Moses, "Tuskegee under Fire: The American Negro Academy, 1896–1898," in *Alexander Crummell: A Study of Civilization and Discontent*, 258–75; and see Crummell's address to the first meeting of the academy, "Civilization the Primal Need of the Race," in Oldfield, *Civilization and Black Progress*, 195–99.

26. For a brief discussion of second sight in the Old Testament that is distinct from "wizardry," see Sawyer, *Prophecy and the Prophets of the Old Testament*, 9–12, 14–16.

27. See Beegle, *Moses*, 261; Auerbach, *Moses*, 138–41.

28. Suggesting problems with this interpretation, Deuteronomy 34:7 reports that at the age of 120, at the time of his death, "his eyes were not dim nor his natural vigor abated." A detailed analysis of the Exodus story of the mask is provided in Auerbach, "Moses' Mask and the Teraphim," in *Moses*, 137–41, which concludes that the veil was a cultic mask, worn by a priest when consulting a deity.

29. In Coats, *Moses*, 138, the veil is similarly a symbol for a hero of "divine authority." "[H]is face shines with the transfiguration effected by God's presence." In Coats, *The Moses Tradition*, 70–71, the veil is a "symbol of . . . office" and "authority."

30. Some scholars believe that this idea of Moses with horns resulted from a bad translation of scripture (Exodus 34:29–35) in which the rays of light emanating from his face became translated as horns. In Hebrew, the word "keren" can mean either "radiated" or "grew horns." The interpretation has become somewhat fixed by Michelangelo's sculpture of Moses housed in the Basilica di San Pietro in Vincoli in Rome.

31. Heaton, *The Old Testament Prophets*, 135.

32. Moses, *Afrotopia*, 136–49, quotation on 148–49. In his essay, "W. E. B. Du Bois and Antimodernism," Moses elaborated on some of the contradictions in Du Bois' writing and life, coming to a conclusion opposite that of David Lewis on Du Bois' commitment to organized religion; as already noted, Moses, citing Du Bois, connected Du Bois to organized religion up to about the age of thirty but added that Du Bois' writings continued to reflect his religious upbringing and background at least until he was in his sixties. Given the similarities between the traditional

religious and philosophical concerns, which will become more apparent below, rather than attempt to define Du Bois' religious orientation, this essay focuses on the common theological and philosophical concerns.

33. Wolfenstein, *A Gift of the Spirit*, 131–32.

34. The scholarly work that links Du Bois' thinking at the turn of the century most thoroughly to the Progressive reforms of the era and intellectual traditions underpinning them is Adolph L. Reed Jr., *W. E. B. Du Bois and American Political Thought: Fabianism and the Color Line* (New York: Oxford University Press, 1997). One work that characterizes Crummell as an Idealist in the tradition of Cambridge Platonism is Moses, *Alexander Crummell*, esp. 275. Earlier studies that recognize the importance of Hegel to Du Bois' work include Stanley Brodwin, "The Veil Transcended: Form and Meaning in W. E. B. Du Bois' 'The Souls of Black Folk,'" *Journal of Black Studies* 2 (March 1972), 303–21. Brodwin describes Du Bois' essays as "a neo-Hegelian dialectic whose stage of synthesis carried him—and by extension, all those who would follow—into a spiritual realm of historical and racial understanding that does not merely rend, but transcends the veil of color. This literary strategy is at once relevant to both black and white man, giving the work its universal dimension" (306). And see Joel Williamson, *The Crucible of Race: Black-White Relations in the American South Since Emancipation* (New York: Oxford University Press, 1984), esp. 402–13, which recognizes Du Bois' essay "Strivings" as "fundamentally Hegelian" but adds that "[i]t would be fruitless to search for a one-to-one appropriation of Hegelianism in Du Bois' essay" (403). Subsequent studies that recognize the Hegelian influence in Du Bois' work, especially in *Souls*, include Robert Gooding-Williams, "Philosophy of History and Social Critique in *The Souls of Black Folk*," *Social Science Information* 26 (June 1987), 99–114; Paul Gilroy, *The Black Atlantic: Modernity and Double Consciousness* (Cambridge: Harvard University Press, 1993), esp. 134; David Levering Lewis, *W. E. B. Du Bois: Biography of a Race*; Sandra Adell, *Double-Consciousness/Double Bind: Theoretical Issues in Twentieth-Century Black Literature* (Urbana: University of Illinois Press, 1994), 11–28; Ernest Allen Jr., "On the Reading of Riddles: Rethinking Du Boisian 'Double Consciousness,'" in *Existence in Black: An Anthology of Black Existential Philosophy*, ed. Lewis R. Gordon (New York: Routledge, 1997), 49–68; and Richard Cullen Rath, "Echo and Narcissus: The Afrocentric Pragmatism of W. E. B. Du Bois," *Journal of American History* (September 1997), 461–95. Among these studies, only Lewis sees a detailed parallel.

35. See, in particular, Johann Gottlieb Fichte, *The Vocation of Man* (1800); Friedrich Wilhelm Joseph von Schelling, *System of the Whole of Philosophy and of Naturphilosophie in Particular* (1804); and Georg Wilhelm Friedrich Hegel, *Phenomenology of Spirit* (1807). "I" and "thou" are both subjective personal pronouns. "Myself" is a reflexive personal pronoun that is usually objective when it coincides with the subject. Thus, all of them seem to be carefully selected pronouns given that it is this very dualism that Idealism seeks to resolve, so that the "double consciousness" becomes a single united consciousness. It is also important that reflexive pronouns (myself) are bound by the antecedent (I, in this case), rather than an other (thou). A study of such subjectivities in the context of (American) slavery studies is Nahum Dimitri Chandler, "Originary Displacement," *Boundary* 2 (Fall 2000),

249–86. Chandler described his essay as a partial response to a former professor's encouraging him to consider slavery scholarship in the context of Hegel's writings. The result is an excellent theoretical construction and application that American and African American historians, particularly those who work on slavery, should read.

36. A very useful discussion of the phenomenologist (or the phenomenological observer) is Werner Marx, *Hegel's Phenomenology of Spirit*, 74–75, 78–97. On the subject of the phenomenologist, Hegel wrote that the sense-certain consciousness (the early stage of consciousness) merely apprehends the object, "therefore, *we* must step into its place and be the Notion which develops and fill out what is contained in the result." For details, see Findlay analysis, in Miller, *Hegel's Phenomenology of Spirit*, 513 .

37. See *PS* §§90–110. Also note that Du Bois described Crummell's apprehending "forms," the term Terry Pinkard insists is the proper translation of the term used in Hegel's study (as opposed to "shapes").

38. Here, one can see parallels between this discussion and Hegel's "Force and the Understanding" (the stage of consciousness after perception/sense-certainty), a stage foreshadowing Self-Consciousness, but not fully there. See *PS* §§132–65. This discussion resembles Hegel's "Perception: or the Thing and Deception," which is discussed more fully below (the preface to chapter 5) in the context of collective conscious's development.

39. Hegel's discussion of Lordship and Bondage is at *PS* §§178–96. Also see George Armstrong Kelly, "Notes on Hegel's 'Lordship and Bondage,'" in *Hegel: A Collection of Critical Essays*, ed. Alasdair MacIntyre (Garden City, NY: Doubleday and Co., 1972), 189–217.

40. In addition to the Hegel paragraphs, noted above, quotations are also from Findlay analyses in Miller, *Hegel's Phenomenology of Spirit*, 523–24.

41. The struggle is characterized in this manner in ibid., 524–25.

42. Ibid., 523.

43. On work, see *PS* §§218–33. On the crisis as the bridge, also see Hegel's discussion of Lordship and Bondage at *PS* §195–96 where he wrote that the bondsman's fear of the lord is what launched the bondsman's movement toward wisdom, and work enabled him to become "conscious of what he truly is." For the lord, desire was the formative activity, but for the bondsman it was work. The bondsman eventually realizes that the lord is dependent on him (the bondsman) for his (the lord's) identity, and with that understanding it is the consciousness of the bondsman rather than the lord's that is freed.

44. G. W. F. Hegel, *Phenomenology of Mind*, 2nd rev. ed., trans. J. B. Baillie (1910; London: George Allen Unwin, Ltd., 1971), 281; and *PS* §§253–308.

45. Hegel wrote, "The single individual is incomplete Spirit, a concrete shape in whose whole existence *one* determinateness predominates, the others being present only in blurred outline" (§28).

46. The wording I have used in this sentence is from Findlay analysis, in Miller, *Hegel's Phenomenology of Spirit*, 575–76. "Beautiful soul" is Hegel's characterization.

47. More of the details of this process of Reason's being raised to Spirit are provided in the preface to chapter 5 below and may be consulted fully at *PS* §§360–437.

For details of Crummell's work after returning from Africa, see Moses, *Alexander Crummell*, esp. 196–214.

48. Hegel, *Phenomenology*, 227.

49. Werner Marx, *Hegel's Phenomenology of Spirit*, 2–5.

50. Ibid., 28–29. Also see Miller, *Hegel's Phenomenology of Spirit*, §28, which begins: "The task of leading the individual from his uneducated [unscientific] standpoint to knowledge [science] had to be seen in its universal sense, just as it was the universal individual, self-conscious Spirit, whose formative education had to be studied."

51. Moses, *Afrotopia*, 144, 145.

52. On the basic philosophical idea of man as essentially good as opposed to the Calvinistic idea of man as inherently bad, see Jacob Needleman, *The American Soul: Rediscovering the Wisdom of the Founders* (New York: Jeremy P. Tarcher/Putnam, 2003), 145.

53. Moses, *Afrotopia*, 146.

54. For an example from Crummell that is similar to Du Bois', see Alexander Crummell, "The Dignity of Labour: and Its Value to a New People," in Oldfield, *Civilization and Black Progress*, 65–77. Although the essay slips into a rather traditional discussion of the dignity and value of all labor, the essay begins with a philosophically classical framing of "work." "There are two ways of knowing things in the world. The *one* is to know them in a crude, blind, uninformed and mechanical manner, i.e., by the senses merely, and the bodily power; somewhat as an animal knows a thing. This kind of knowing is altogether outward, and pertains mainly to our physical nature. But the *other* mode of knowing is the apprehension of principles and essences; the seeing into the very life of things; and the seizing upon the highest uses and advantages which they may offer" (65).

Also see Du Bois, *Prayers for Dark People*, in which Aptheker identifies the scriptural passages that served as the bases of Du Bois individual prayers. In one example, Du Bois wrote, "We should not be great but busy—not pious but sympathetic—not merely reverent, but filled with the glory of our Life—Work. God is Love and Work is His Revelation. Amen" (60). Aptheker refers to John 4:7–12. In another prayer that Aptheker relates to Ecclesiastes 2:4–11, Du Bois beseeches: "O God, teach us who are looking eagerly forward to the great play-time of the year to weigh wisely and well the seriousness of play. . . . We would learn, Our Father, to choose our recreations as thoughtfully as our duties—to bring them in and mingle them with our work—to make our life a oneness of work as rest-in-work, rest and work-in-rest and Joy in both" (10). And see the prayer on page 28, which, based on Ecclesiastes 11:1–7, includes the line "we must work if we would *learn* and *know*." Most of these prayers were directed to the students he lectured at Atlanta University.

Preface to Chapter 5

1. See A. V. Miller, trans., *Hegel's Phenomenology of Spirit*, analysis and foreword by J. N. Findlay (Oxford: Oxford University Press, 1977), 321–55. When possible, the source of quotations from *Phenomenology* will hereafter be given in the text as

PS, followed by the appropriate paragraph number, enclosed in parentheses. Thus, the source of this discussion of the unhappy consciousness would be cited as *PS* §§527–81. References to Findlay's analysis will be noted by page number. When referring to Hegel's "forms" of consciousness (Consciousness, Self-Consciousness, Reason, Spirit), I will capitalize them as he did.

2. Terry Pinkard's *Hegel's Phenomenology: The Sociality of Reason* (Cambridge: Cambridge University Press, 1994) gives the most (and most consistent) attention to the significance of the "social space" and the relationship of reason to the social world in the development of consciousness in Hegel's work. Although I have focused my discussion on *The Souls of Black Folk*, and it is my contention that Du Bois added America, the nineteenth century, and black folk to Hegel's *Phenomenology*, as the previous chapter reveals, I believe we can show the development of consciousness in Du Bois' volume on multiple levels—in individuals such as Crummell, among black folk as a group, and in America, in general, although each is (sometimes simultaneously) at a different place in development in his volume.

3. Quotation from Robert Gooding-Williams, *In the Shadow of Du Bois: Afro-Modern Political Thought in America* (Cambridge, MA: Harvard University Press, 2009), 285 (n. 37). Gooding-Williams's conclusion is not unlike that of Joel Williamson's in *The Crucible of Race: Black-White Relations in the American South* (New York: Oxford University Press, 1984), 403, where he wrote, "It would be fruitless to search for a one-to-one appropriation of Hegelianism in Du Bois' essay ['Strivings']." Eugene Victor Wolfenstein, *A Gift of the Spirit: Reading "The Souls of Black Folk"* (Ithaca: Cornell University Press, 2007) comes to the same conclusion. Gooding-Williams was responding to Shamoon Zamir, *Dark Voices: W. E. B. Du Bois and American Thought, 1888–1903* (Chicago: University of Chicago Press, 1995), which does see the parallels between the "Strivings" essay and *Phenomenology*.

4. In addition to Pinkard, *Hegel*, cited above, the most useful study for pursuing the relationships among these authors in particular, but many others as well, is Terry Pinkard, *German Philosophy, 1760–1860: The Legacy of Idealism* (Cambridge: Cambridge University Press, 2002).

5. The more one reads of Hegel's discussion of "the force," the more Du Bois' characterization of Washington resembles this medium, which is simultaneously soliciting and solicited. Each only exists in its relationship with the other and so neither has substance and "exists simply and solely in its *expression*, which at the same time is nothing else than a supersession of itself." See Miller, *Hegel's Phenomenology of Spirit*, §§139–43, quotation from §141.

6. Although this is not a unique idea, Hegel's characterization of every man taking what he can for himself is at least reflected, as already noted, in Du Bois' second Talented Tenth essay (1948), in which he apologized for not remembering (when he wrote the first Talented Tenth essay) that people in power regularly ended up in a "free-for-all, with the devil taking the hindmost and the foremost taking anything they could lay hands on." Also note that in the early Revolutionary Era, virtue required the sacrifice of individual desires for the greater good.

7. Early republicans in the era of the American Revolution saw virtue in classical terms. It involved the subordination of one's personal desires for the benefit of the

public. It demanded equality, but then also subordination (to the common good). See Perry Lewis, *Intellectual Life in America: A History* (New York: Franklin Watts, 1984), 161–204, esp. 163–65.

8. In addition to the noted Hegel references in the text, see Findlay analysis, in Miller, *Hegel's Phenomenology of Spirit*, 556.

9. This idea would not have been alien to Du Bois. Franz Boas published a very important article in 1901 entitled "The Mind of Primitive Man," *Journal of American Folklore* 14 (Jan.–March 1901), 1–11, which, in its conclusion, distinguished between "culture" and "mind" and viewed mind in a collective context and as relevant whatever the stage of culture. It was a pathbreaking article that changed the way people pursued anthropology, sociology, and other fields as well. Boas's book of the same title was published ten years later. And as I have noted elsewhere, particularly after science destabilized religion, culture became a substitute. But Du Bois knew that it was "culture" and "civilization" (taking it, uninvited, to areas of the world now called the global South and parts of the Near, Middle, and Far East as well) that was causing so much destruction throughout the world.

10. Quotations from Findlay analysis, in Miller, *Hegel's Phenomenology of Spirit*, 568.

11. The idea of "pure duty" as something of a substitute (or even an antecedent) for self-realization might give the work of racial uplift, especially where it was the mission of better-off and better-able black people with and on behalf of the less able, new meaning.

12. Du Bois had earlier reminded readers of other "moments" when no one could have imagined that Europe would ever represent a pinnacle of "civilization." And these souls (black folk) were barely a generation out of slavery. See chapter 5, n. 47.

13. Normally, the noumenal and the absolute represent the thing that can never actually be known but has to be inferred based on experience.

14. This brief discussion of "music and nature" is based on Pauline Watts, *Music: The Medium of the Metaphysical in E. T. A. Hoffman* (Amsterdam: Rodopi NV, 1972), 31–41, quotations on 34, 33, 31. Watts (Hoffman) characterized music in metaphysics as "the Will, the Absolute itself" (16). Although Hegel did not believe that we could use mathematics to demonstrate the unity of music and nature, Hoffman believed that "music and nature unite in sound, sight, and mathematical relationships to mediate the supernatural realm to sensitive, receptive people" (40).

Chapter 5

1. Arthur Schopenhauer, *The World as Will and Representation*, vol. 1, quoted in Peter Franklin, *The Idea of Music: Schoenberg and Others* (Houndmills: Macmillan Press, Ltd., 1985), 8.

2. Quotations from Robert C. Solomon, *In the Spirit of Hegel: A Study of G. W. F. Hegel's Phenomenology of Spirit* (New York: Oxford University Press, 1983), 582–83, 588–89. Also see Solomon's entire chapter, "The Secret of Hegel (Kierkegaard's Complaint): Hegel's Philosophy of Religion," 580–634. Solomon refers to James Hutchinson Stirling's *The Secret of Hegel: Being the Hegelian System in*

Origin Principle, Form and Matter (1865). For a discussion of Hegel's early writings and their anti-Christian, if not antireligion, slant, see Walter Kaufman, "The Young Hegel and Religion," in *Hegel: A Collection of Critical Essays*, ed. Alasdair MacIntyre (Garden City, NY: Doubleday and Co., 1972), 61–99, esp. 66–71.

Jonathon S. Kahn, *Divine Discontent: The Religious Imagination of W. E. B. Du Bois* (Oxford: Oxford University Press, 2009) discusses Du Bois' extensive use of religious rhetoric and his simultaneous rejection of religion (orthodoxy). The need to separate Du Bois' ideas from religion seems based on the premise that religion inherently (and perhaps exclusively) relates to one's relationship to God, and to representations of religion—churches, ministers, Christians, etc. Du Bois' persistent and vigorous critique of religion and religious symbols makes it easy to characterize his thought as anti-Christian and perhaps, as Kahn sees Du Bois, as "irreligious" and "antimetaphysical." But the conclusion that Du Bois was antireligion, a conclusion numerous others share as well, is probably based on too narrow a definition of religion. An alternative view to Kahn's is Edward J. Blum, *W. E. B. Du Bois, American Prophet* (Philadelphia: University of Pennsylvania Press, 2007), which looks at Du Bois' religiosity without equating religion to belief in a personal God.

3. These subheadings, provided by A. V. Miller, have been translated slightly differently (and possibly more usefully) by others. For example, Solomon translates Hegel's (Miller's) "Natural Religion" as "The Religion of Nature," and he uses "The Spiritual Work of Art" rather than "Religion in the Form of Art."

4. Solomon, *In the Spirit of Hegel*, 602–8, quotations on 602, 608. And see *PS* §§691–98.

5. Solomon, *In the Spirit of Hegel*, 606. And see *PS* §§701–2. Describing absolute art, Hegel, in §702, wrote: "Spirit transcends art in order to gain a higher representation of itself, viz. to be not merely the *substance* born of the self, but to be, in its representation as object, *this self*, not only to give birth to itself from its Notion, but to have its very Notion for its shape, so that the Notion and the work of art produced know each other as one and the same."

6. Hegel analyst Findlay wrote: "Language is the medium in which Spirit or social subjectivity exists. Through language one personal Ego recognizes the Ego-status of another personal Ego, and so transcends its separate individuality." See Miller, *Hegel's Philosophy of Spirit*, 575. And see Hegel's discussion at §652 where he describes "language as the existence of Spirit."

7. Howard P. Kainz, *Hegel's Phenomenology, Part II: The Evolution of Ethical and Religious Consciousness to the Absolute Standpoint* (Athens: Ohio University Press, 1983), 147; Tom Rockmore, *Cognition: An Introduction to Hegel's Phenomenology of Spirit* (Berkeley: University of California Press, 1997), 169–70. And see Solomon, *In the Spirit of Hegel*, 604–12; and *PS* §§733–35.

8. Kainz, *Hegel's Phenomenology*, 154–55.

9. Solomon, *In the Spirit of Hegel*, 611, 628–29; and *PS* §§759, 761, 763, 779, 781–84. Tom Rockmore, *Cognition*, 155, notes that "Hegel studies religion as a form of knowledge just 'below' absolute knowing, in effect as a defective form of philosophy." Based even on Rockmore's study of *Phenomenology*, I don't see it as "defective"

but as a complete, but not the final, step in the progression of philosophy or science/knowledge in the Hegelian sense.

10. The Leibniz quote from his 1714 essay, "Principles of Nature and Grace, Based on Reason," is from Jamie C. Kassler, *Music, Science, Philosophy: Models in the Universe of Thought* (Alderschot: Ashgate Publishing, 2001), 247 (n. 74). The entire text of Leibniz's essay can be found in Gottfried Wilhelm Leibniz, *Philosophical Papers and Letters*, trans., ed., and intro. by Leroy E. Loemker (Chicago: University of Chicago Press, 1956), 2:1033–43.

11. To this point, black religion traveled the route of religion in history. Du Bois' underworld paralleled Hegel's, which characterized the ancient Greek world. The pre-Enlightenment world was one dominated by a belief in heaven, which Hegel described as a useful substitute for the underworld. During the Enlightenment, however, Hegel's religion became a "religion of morality," another negative form in which, ultimately, spirit is not able to complete itself (*PS* §§673–76). Religion was useful to getting consciousness this far, but, according to Hegel, spirit can only be completed through philosophy/knowledge. See Rockmore, *Cognition*, 155–62.

12. Sandra Adell, *Double-Consciousness/Double Bind: Theoretical Issues in Twentieth-Century Black Literature* (Urbana: University of Illinois Press, 1994), 15, rightly proposes that "Du Bois' notion of double-consciousness seems to correspond to . . . consciousness as self-consciousness." But, as this essay will show, there is even more to it.

13. On double consciousness interpreted as a form of mental illness, scholars usually refer to the 1893 publication by Oswald Külpe, *Outlines of Psychology, Based upon the Results of Experimental Investigation*, trans. Edward Bradford Titchener (London: S. Sonnenschein & Co., New York: Macmillan and Co., 1895), cited in Arnold Rampersad, *The Art and Imagination of W. E. B. Du Bois* (New York: Schocken Books, 1990), 74, 302 (n. 14). Rampersad also recognizes the Emersonian/Transcendental use of the term that could also have influenced Du Bois. Dickson D. Bruce Jr., "W. E. B. Du Bois and the Idea of Double Consciousness," *American Literature* 64 (June 1992), 303–4, however, sees the term as at least seventy-five years older than the date of the appearance of Külpe's volume and as antedating Emersonian Transcendentalism. Bruce cites an 1817 article/report in *Medical Repository* of a case of "A Double Consciousness, or a Duality of Person in the same Individual." In this example, a woman awoke from a coma "with no memory of who she was and with a wholly different personality." After falling into this deep sleep again, she awoke as her former self. She moved between these two states for another fifteen or so years, at which point she permanently became the second person. She never had any memory of the other self. The editors of *Medical Repository* used the term "double consciousness" to describe her case. William James, one of Du Bois' intellectual mentors, used the term similarly. Bruce concluded that Du Bois used the term in these ways. Given, however, that in the medical example, the two selves did not know each other, it seems an unlikely example for Du Bois to model. An important characteristic of Hegel's "unhappy consciousness" is the awareness of, and struggle against, the other. Bruce also saw the struggle as between being African and American (305). And he concluded that Du Bois did not resolve the division in

the *Atlantic* article ("Strivings of the Negro People" (1897), which became the basis of the first chapter in *Souls*, and that "neither the Emersonian nor the psychological literature, despite the optimism of the latter, gave him much of a guide for how to do it" (306–7). My chapter obviously contends that Du Bois worked it out, but in Hegelian terms, as we shall see. Recent psychological analyses of Du Bois' *Souls* and double consciousness include Eugene Victor Wolfenstein, *A Gift of the Spirit: Reading "The Souls of Black Folk"* (Ithaca: Cornell University Press, 2007); and Shanette M. Harris, "Constructing a Psychological Perspective: The Observer and the Observed in *The Souls of Black Folk*," in *The Souls of Black Folk: One Hundred Years Later*, ed. Dolan Hubbard (Columbia: University of Missouri Press, 2003), 218–50. And see chapter 1, n. 14, and chapter 2, nn. 12–14, in this volume.

14. Hegel's complete discussion is located at *PS* §§438–581.

15. See *PS* §464–76 on the destruction of the ethical world, and §§477–83 on the conflict with legal status, which leads to the culture of self-alienated spirit. And on the self-alienation, see especially §486, in which Hegel wrote: "this Spirit constructs for itself not merely *a* world, but a world that is double, divided and self-opposed. The world of the ethical Spirit is its own *present* world; and therefore each of its powers exists in this unity, and in so far as they are distinct from one another they are in equilibrium with the whole. Nothing has the significance of being the negative of self-consciousness; even the departed spirit is present in his *blood*-relationship, in the *self* of the family, and the universal *power* of the government is the *will*, the self of the nation. Here, however, what is *present* has the significance only of an objective reality, the consciousness of which exists in a beyond; each single moment *qua* essence receives this, and with it actuality, from an 'other,' and so far as it is actual, its essence is something other than its own actuality. Nothing has a Spirit that is grounded within itself and indwells it, but each has its being in something outside of and alien to it. The equilibrium of the whole is not the unity which remains with itself, nor the contentment that comes from having returned into itself, but rests on the alienation of opposites."

Also note that where I have inserted ellipses in the Du Bois quote in the text, he addressed what he calls the "peculiar problem of their inner life," which concerned women, families, children, wealth, and crime. Hegel addressed this in §475.

16. The fourteen songs here are in the order of their appearance in *Souls*; master songs are preceded by an asterisk: *"Nobody Knows the Trouble I've Seen," *"My Lord, What a Mourning," "A Great Camp-Meeting in the Promised Land," *"My Way's Cloudy," *"The Rocks and the Mountains," "March On," "Bright Sparkles in the Churchyard," "Children, You'll Be Called On," "I'm a-Rolling," *"Steal Away," "I Hope My Mother Will Be There," *"Swing Low, Sweet Chariot," *"I'll Hear the Trumpet Sound" ("You May Bury Me in the East"), and *"Wrestling Jacob." The two remaining master songs (which do not appear as epigraphs) are "Roll, Jordan, Roll" and "Been a-Listening." Perhaps the best scholarly analysis that relates the slave songs to conditions of life across time is Miles Mark Fisher, *Negro Slave Songs in the United States* (1953; New York: Carol Publishing Group, 1990). But equally useful as a general history is John Wesley Work, *Folk Song of the American Negro* (Nashville: Fisk University Press, 1915; New York: Negro Universities Press, 1969).

17. For a more detailed discussion of the connection between the lyrics of these songs and the content of the chapters, see Eric Sundquist, "Swing Low: *The Souls of Black Folk*," in *To Wake the Nations: Race in the Making of American Literature* (Cambridge, MA: Harvard University Press, 1993), 457–539. A good overview of these songs is Harold Courlander, *Negro Folk Music, U.S.A.* (New York: Columbia University Press, 1963).

18. Solomon, *In the Spirit of Hegel*, 605.

19. These songs compare to the way Hegel wrote about the language of the tragedy: In the tragedy, "the language ceases to be narrative [which the earlier hymns represented] because it enters into the content, just as the content ceases to be one that is imaginatively presented" (*PS* §733).

20. My way of describing the creation of collective consciousness is related to, but in some ways different from, what Terry Pinkard characterizes as "the social world." See Pinkard, *Hegel's Phenomenology: The Sociality of Reason* (Cambridge: Cambridge University Press, 1994). There is probably no better study of the way this music, particularly as it evolved into blues and jazz, represented a "universal aesthetic statement" than Albert Murray's *The Blue Devils of Nada: A Contemporary American Approach to Aesthetic Statement* (New York: Pantheon Books, 1996). Murray sees art, in general, as "the ultimate extension, elaboration, and refinement of the rituals that reenact the primary survival techniques (and hence reinforce the basic orientation toward experience) of a given people in a given time, place and circumstance" (13). For Murray (describing the work of Hemingway), art "communicates the essence of subjective experience" (172). It concerns "what it means to be human" (11) and is very much concerned with self-realization. Murray sees the articulation of this blues/jazz (American) aesthetic in both the literary and visual arts as well.

21. Regarding this quote from *Souls*, Robert B. Stepto, *From Behind the Veil: A Study of Afro-American Narrative*, 2nd ed. (Urbana: University of Illinois Press, 1991), recalls Du Bois' words on this topic but interprets them more narrowly. Du Bois wrote:

> Then in after years when I came to Nashville I saw the great temple builded of these songs towering over the pale city. To me Jubilee Hall seemed ever made of the songs themselves, and its bricks were red with blood and dust of toil. Out of them rose for me morning, noon, and night, bursts of wonderful melody, full of the voices of my brothers and sisters, full of the voices of the past."

Stepto interprets this as an example of "symbolic geography; Jubilee Hall is not so much a local building as it is a locus-specific structure. . . . To *see* Jubilee hall is to know why the Sorrow Songs are alternately called Jubilee Songs, and to glimpse the Afro-American *genius loci*" (76).

A good reconstruction of the Jubilee Singers' early tours, with extensive contemporary reports on the concerts and published reviews of them, is Louis D. Silveri, "The Singing Tours of the Fisk Jubilee Singers: 1871–1874," in *Feel the Spirit:*

Studies in Nineteenth-Century Afro-American Music, ed. George R. Keck and Sherrill V. Martin (New York: Greenwood Press, 1988), 105–16. Also see John Wesley Work, "The Tour of the Original Jubilee Singers," in *Folk Song of the American Negro* (Nashville: Fisk University Press, 1915), 101–9. Contemporary histories of the singers include Gustavus D. Pike, *The Jubilee Singers and their Campaign for Twenty Thousand Dollars* (Boston: Lee and Shepard, 1873); and J. B. T. Marsh, *The Story of the Jubilee Singers* (London: Hodder and Stoughton, 1877). The most detailed study of the Jubilee Singers is Andrew Ward, *Dark Midnight When I Rise: The Story of the Jubilee Singers Who Introduced the World to the Music of Black America* (New York: Farrar, Straus and Giroux, 2000). A discussion of the Jubilee Singers that places their international travels in the context of enlightenment thought and the failures of modernity is Paul Gilroy, " 'Cheer The Weary Traveller': W. E. B. Du Bois, Germany, and the Politics of (Dis)placement," in *The Black Atlantic: Modernity and Double Consciousness* (Cambridge, MA: Harvard University Press, 1993), 87–93. Gilroy reminds us that the Jubilee Singers were competing with the popularity of minstrelsy at the time and regularly faced audiences disappointed in and confused by their performance. Also placing the songs and the Jubilee Singers in the context of contemporaneous minstrelsy are Scott Herring, "Du Bois and the Minstrels," *MELUS* 22 (Summer 1997), 3–17, which sees Du Bois "retaking black American music" from the distortions of minstrelsy (4), and Christopher A. Brooks, "The 'Musical' Souls of Black Folk: Can a Double Consciousness be Heard?," in Hubbard, *The Souls of Black Folk: One Hundred Years Later*, 269–83. Herring also views Du Bois' coupling the "high art stanzas to the 'low art' " examples at the head of each chapter as a way of weakening (or erasing) the boundary between the two. And in a similar characterization of the two kinds of music, Fredrika Bremer, *The Homes of the New World: Impressions of America*, trans. Mary Howitt (New York: Harper and Brothers, 1854), 1:394, writing about the music *before* the Jubilee Singers or Fisk University existed, pointed out "the so-called 'Sable Singers,' who travel about the country painted up as negroes, and singing negro songs in the negro manner, and with negro gestures, as it is said; but nothing can be more radically unlike, for the most essential part of the resemblance fails—namely, *the life*." Another discussion relating Du Bois' discussion of the Sorrow Songs to popular music is Tom Lutz, *American Nervousness, 1903: An Anecdotal History* (Ithaca: Cornell University Press, 1991), 267–75.

22. J. Brierley described the process of music's creating this "spiritual unity" thus: "Under the . . . moving, mighty harmony, a thousand separate men and women, gathered promiscuously and knowing nothing of each other, have ceased to be individuals. They are blended for the time into a huge common consciousness, which laughs and cries, exults or despairs, as one single soul. It is in the exaltation of such a moment that we realize the full force of Goethe's saying, that 'only mankind together is the true man, and the individual can only be joyous and happy when he feels himself in the whole.' " *Studies of the Soul* (1898; New York: Thomas Whittaker, 1903), 53.

23. Much of the criticism of Du Bois' use of Wagner includes discussions of the ways Wagner's music subsequently came to be used in the service of Nazism. Theodor W. Adorno, *Introduction to the Sociology of Music*, trans. E. B. Ashton

(New York: Seabury Press, 1976), provides a discussion of how easy it was for romanticism to slide into nationalism. There was, however, an important distinction. The romantics valued folk music; the nationalists manufactured it (for their own purposes). Adorno also makes clear that some of Wagner's works came at the very end of the romantic period. See Adorno's chapter entitled "Nations," 154–76.

24. Cornel West, "Black Strivings in a Twilight Civilization," in Henry Louis Gates Jr. and Cornel West, *The Future of the Race* (New York: Alfred A. Knopf, 1996), 59–60. Paul Gilroy, *The Black Atlantic*, 129, sees Du Bois' report of his visit to the church as an indication that "the buried social memory of that original terror" (of slavery) was revived in him. Gilroy, who recognizes the Hegelian influence in *Souls* (rather than West's earlier emphasis on Pragmatism in *The American Evasion of Philosophy* [London: Macmillan, 1977]), also notes that Du Bois appreciated these churches and preachers because they helped awaken the "common consciousness" but disliked them for their "anti-modern conservativism." Shamoon Zamir, "'The Sorrow Songs'/'Song of Myself': Du Bois, the Crisis of Leadership, and Prophetic Imagination," in *The Black Columbiad: Defining Moments in African-American Literature and Culture*, ed. Werner Sollors and Maria Diedrich (Cambridge, MA: Harvard University Press, 1994), 145–66, also describes Du Bois' relationship to ordinary black people as somewhat "ambivalent" (148) and his relationship to the songs as reflecting "representational hesitancy" (152), which Zamir attributes to the modeling Du Bois took from "Crummell's Episcopalianism" (158–59). Zamir was the first among these studies to characterize Du Bois' visit to the church service as spectacle, with an added voyeuristic aspect to it. Zamir writes, "The feelings of the young Du Bois reproduce the same exoticism that led the white middle-class reading public at the turn of the century to seek out works that revealed how 'the other half' lived" (148). If Du Bois' model was Hegel, and if we read Du Bois' words carefully, we will be able to come to different conclusions from some of these. In what is perhaps Hegel's most well-known critique of Christianity, "The Positivity of the Christian Religion" (1795), he described Christianity as a religion fit for slaves. He therefore advocated a folk religion, which, in his view, came from the hearts (soul?) of the people rather than authorities and espoused the common good rather than individual salvation. I think that is what Du Bois saw here—a folk religion that he appreciated and recognized as "real." It was the big "modern" urban churches, with their educated leaders and congregants, that worried him.

25. *The American Heritage Dictionary*, 2d college ed., s.v. "awful" and "awe." One should also note that in the Biblical sense, fear is not negative but reflecting reverence and respect.

26. Solomon, *In the Spirit of Hegel*, 628.

27. Quoted in Dena J. Epstein, *Sinful Tunes and Spirituals: Black Folk Music to the Civil War* (Urbana: University of Illinois Press, 1977), 294–95.

28. Aristotle's *Metaphysics*, quoted in Walter Burkert, *Lore and Science in Ancient Pythagoreanism*, trans. Edwin L. Minar Jr. (Cambridge, MA: Harvard University Press, 1972), 50.

29. For a collection of works excerpted to trace philosophical explorations of music from Plato through nineteenth-century romantics, see Joscelyn Godwin,

ed., *The Harmony of the Spheres: A Sourcebook of Pythagorean Tradition in Music* (Rochester, VT: Inner Traditions International, 1993). And see W. Oliver Strunk, ed., *Source Readings in Music History* (New York: W. W. Norton, 1950).

30. James M. Trotter, *Music and Some Highly Musical People . . .* (1881; New York: Johnson Reprint Corporation, 1968), 11. I am assuming it is Henri Bertini (1846–1933), the French composer, whom Trotter quoted.

31. The "Sorrow Songs" of Du Bois' final chapter have received considerable attention. The most detailed study of them is contained in Sundquist, *To Wake the Nations*, 457–539. Nearly all serious studies of Du Bois consider some aspects of Du Bois' chapter on these songs. Some of these sources are cited in part 1 of this chapter and below at appropriate places.

32. David Levering Lewis, *W. E. B. Du Bois: Biography of a Race, 1868–1919* (New York: Henry Holt and Company, 1993), 14–15. Note that Edward J. Blum, in *W. E. B. Du Bois: American Prophet*, 31, mistakenly reads "You may bury me in the east" as the translation of the words in Du Bois' mothers' song.

33. In Du Bois, *Dusk of Dawn: An Essay Toward an Autobiography of a Race Concept* (1940; New Brunswick: Transaction Publishers, 1991), 111, 114, he acknowledged that it could have been his great-grandmother, Violet, who came from Africa.

34. Though it certainly makes sense that Du Bois and Bertini would have used similar words to describe a feeling about music, it is also difficult to imagine Du Bois' not having read James Trotter's book. Trotter was well known within black and white elite circles in and around Boston. His son, William, was, like Du Bois, a member of the very small circle of black Harvard alums. William Trotter finished B.A. and M.A. degrees in 1895 and 1896. Du Bois finished B.A., M.A., and Ph.D. degrees in 1890, 1891, and 1895. The two were among the founding members of the Niagara Movement. Du Bois also wrote in his autobiographies about his relationship with the younger Trotter.

35. Du Bois' discussion of culture, generally, begs for more scholarly attention. During the nineteenth century "culture" became a substitute for (an alternative to) religion for some intellectuals, especially after the popularization of Darwin's theories. That is, if man could not count on theological propositions about the possible perfection of man, if evolution made natural selection somewhat accidental, man could at least demonstrate his development through the acquisition of (high) culture. This would certainly give new meaning to Du Bois statement "the price of Culture is a Lie." It might suggest his validation of the art and religion of the folk as "truth" (and, I think, "goodness" and "beauty," too). And it might also offer another indictment of some of those who were presumed members of the Talented Tenth. See Lewis Perry, "The Cultivated Class in the Late Nineteenth Century," in *Intellectual Life in America: A History* (New York: Franklin Watts, 1984), esp. 263–316. And see Terry Pinkard, *Hegel: A Biography* (Cambridge: Cambridge University Press, 2000), throughout, for its discussions of *Bildung*, which relates more to self-development than what we think of as "class."

36. Brierley, *Studies of the Soul*, 62, describes music as demonstrating something of "a pre-existent intellect." Very helpful studies of metaphysics in all its dimensions

are A. E. Taylor, *Elements of Metaphysics* (1903; London: Methuen Publishing, 1961); and Henry J. Koren, *An Introduction to the Science of Metaphysics* (St. Louis: B. Herder Book Co., 1955).

37. The idea of this being a message from the world is based on the philosophical principle that the parts and the whole are different but not distinct. Thus, a message from the souls of black folk is, equally, a message from the soul of the universe. Hegel quoted the Aristotelian idea from *Politics*, 1255b: "'The parts and the whole, like the body and the soul, have an identical interest.'" Quoted in George Armstrong Kelly, "Notes on Lordship and Bondage," in Alasdair C. MacIntyre, comp. and ed., *Hegel; A Collection of Critical Essays*, 195 (n. 14). One can see the basis of this idea in Plato's reporting of the Demiurge's creation of world soul, which is discussed below.

38. Although hearing is obviously sensual, the point, which was demonstrated in part 1 above and will become clearer below, is that the important message of the slave to the world, while certainly conveyed through the tones, is much more than what one hears (literally). Pauline Watts's discussion of E. T. A. Hoffman makes the case of "a spiritual element" of music clearly: "[F]ar from restricting itself to being an audible perception, perceived at the time of the physical production of the sound, music forms inexplicable human relationships which seem to have their source outside the spheres of time, space and the sound medium." See Watts, *Music: The Medium of the Metaphysical in E. T. A. Hoffman* (Amsterdam: Rodopi NV, 1972), 52.

39. Solomon, *In the Spirit of Hegel*, 605; Robin Maconie, *The Science of Music* (Oxford: Clarenden Press, 1997), xi. Also note Trotter's opening discussion in *Music and Some Highly Musical People*, 7–11, which begins, "what is music?" and in which he all but apologized for having to use words to explain music and for being unable to define it except in dictionary terms. Ultimately, Trotter described music as its own language.

40. Solomon, *In the Spirit of Hegel*, ibid.

41. Maconie, *The Science of Music*, vii–ix, quotations on ix.

42. Not only have these songs not undergone the scrutiny that the ten master songs have received, but in some instances the two lists are inexplicably conflated. For one example, Richard Cullen Rath, in "Echo and Narcissus: The Afrocentric Pragmatism of W. E. B. Du Bois," *Journal of American History* 84 (September 1997), 492–93, wrote about the "ten or so 'master songs'" (there were exactly ten) that "formed the core of African American racial identity." He continued, "Du Bois thought that in the master melodies 'we can trace here and there signs of development' by examining and interpreting the strata that had worn and accreted upon the melodic and rhythmic base of the sorrow songs." Rath described the master songs as reflecting "three stages" (African, Afro-American, and Negro American), which was actually Du Bois' characterization of a different group of songs that only slightly overlaps the master songs. Rath does, however, note that it was the music rather than the words that are most important in Du Bois' discussion of the Sorrow Songs. See ibid., 489–97.

43. Although Du Bois went on to add a fourth category consisting of white music influenced by black tradition, my analysis is based on the three groups he identified as black music.

44. The scores used for these two songs come from *Religious Folk Songs of the Negro as Sung on the Plantations* (1874; Hampton, VA: The Institute Press, 1909), 28–33, 79–83.

45. The two-voice textures suggest distance from a three-part harmony that songs of the middle group reflect and that ethnomusicologists see as stylistically European.

46. The version of "Steal Away to Jesus" used here is from *Religious Folk Songs of the Negro*, 152. Music for "March On" is from John W. Work, *American Negro Songs and Spirituals: A Comprehensive Collection of 230 Folk Songs, Religious and Secular* (New York: Crown Publishers, 1940), 204–5.

47. To interpret Du Bois' use of "heathen" as evidence of his elitism, which is a common interpretation, might be a bit of an overreach. This term, along with "civilization," which I discussed earlier, were commonly used in nineteenth-century histories of "progress," in which all "civilizations" rose and fell. Although one might be inclined to judge these different stages of development along a scale that goes from bad to good, I think Du Bois' point was much more complex and instructive than that. For details of nineteenth-century black historians' utilization of the progress mode in their studies, see Stephen Gilroy Hall, *A Faithful Account of the Race: African American Historical Writing in Nineteenth-Century America* (Chapel Hill: University of North Carolina Press, 2009). Du Bois' engagement of this scholarly tradition is, likewise, reflected in *Souls*, where he wrote:

> The silently growing assumption of this age is that the probation of races
> is past, and that the backward races of to-day are of proven inefficiency
> and not worth the saving. Such an assumption is the arrogance of peoples
> irreverent toward Time and ignorant of the deeds of men. A thousand years
> ago such an assumption, easily possible, would have made it difficult for the
> Teuton to prove his right to life. Two thousand years ago such dogmatism,
> readily welcome, would have scouted the idea of blond races ever leading
> civilization. So woefully unorganized is sociological knowledge that the
> meaning of progress, the meaning of 'swift' and 'slow' in human doing, and
> the limits of human perfectability, are veiled, unanswered sphinxes on the
> shores of silence. Why should Æschylus have sung two thousand years before
> Shakespeare was born? Why has civilization flourished in Europe, and
> flickered, flamed, and died in Africa? So long as the world stands meekly
> dumb before such questions, shall this nation proclaim its ignorance and
> unhallowed prejudices by denying freedom of opportunity to those who
> brought the Sorrow Songs to the Seats of the Mighty?

A useful discussion that provides succinct insights into diverse aspects (harmony, tone, vocalization, etc.) of African music, is Alan P. Merriam, "African Music," in

Continuity and Change in African Cultures, ed. William R. Bascom and Melville J. Herskovits (1959; Chicago: University of Chicago Press, 1970), 49–86. (Importantly, Dett arranged and published a substantial volume of black spiritual music in R. Nathaniel Dett, *Religious Folk-Songs of the Negro as Sung at Hampton Institute* [Hampton, VA: Hampton Institute Press, 1927].)

48. Suggesting, further, the importance of *sound* rather than words in Du Bois' thinking, Regennia N. Williams quotes a 1933 article by Du Bois in which he defended Nathaniel Dett's programming European music as the director of Hampton Institute's choir (over which Dett was apparently fired). Du Bois wrote:

> What it [the criticism of Dett] really means is that Negroes must not be allowed to attempt anything more than the frenzy of the primitive, religious revival. "Listen to the Lambs" according to Dett, or "Deep River," as translated by Burleigh, or any attempt to sing Italian music or German music, in some inexplicable manner, leads them off their preserves and is not "natural." To which the answer is, Art is not natural and is not supposed to be natural. And just because it is not natural, it may be great Art. The Negro chorus has a right to sing music of any sort it likes and to be judged by its accomplishment rather than by what foolish critics think that it ought to be doing. *It is to be trusted that our leaders in music, holding on to the beautiful heritage of the past, will not on that account, either be coerced or frightened from taking all music for their province and showing the world how to sing.*

Although I understand Williams's highlighting the final sentence, for the purpose of this chapter, I would emphasize: "Art is not natural and is not supposed to be natural. And just because it is not natural, it may be great Art." Clearly, this is another clue that Du Bois sees Art (with the capital "A") as Spirit. See Regennia N. Williams, "Robert Nathaniel Dett and African America's Christian Kingdom of Culture, 1926–1932," in *The African Diaspora and the Study of Religion*, ed. Theodore Louis Trost (New York: Palgrave MacMillan, 2007), 73–91, quotation on 87. (Du Bois' essay, "Our Music," appeared in the July 1933 issue of *The Crisis*.)

49. The music consulted for "You May Bury Me in the East" comes from Henry Edward Krehbiel, *Afro-American Folksongs: A Study in Racial and National Music* (1913; New York: Fredrick Ungar Publishing Co., 1962), 86. This volume includes another version of the song on page 31. I used Harry Burleigh's arrangement from his history of the Fisk Jubilee Singers. The other version Krehbiel reproduced is an arrangement by Arthur Mees for the (N.Y.) Mendelssohn Glee Club. "Gene me, gene me" comes from *Souls*.

50. In the key of C, the blue notes, the flatted third and seventh, are E-flat and B-flat, respectively. In C, the E and B are normally played as "naturals." When these notes are flatted, it is not always possible to indicate precisely where a particular (sounded) tone lies on a traditional western staff. In such a case, its approximate position might be suggested, for example, by a downward pointing arrow over the note on the staff, indicating that it should be played somewhat lower than the note on the

staff and that the interval is slightly smaller (diminished) than the note on the staff. Writers describe the sound, depending on the instrument, in terms of "'swoops, glides, slurs, smears, and glisses.'" See Harold Courlander, *Negro Folk Music, U.S.A.* (New York: Columbia University Press, 1963), 18–21. Alan P. Merriam, "African Music," in Bascom and Herskovits, *Continuity and Change in African Cultures*, 72, quotes Arthur Morris Jones, a British missionary and musicologist who published extensively on African music, saying in the more than twenty years he lived in central Africa, he "never heard an African sing the 3rd and the 7th degrees of a major scale in tune." Merriam believed this conclusion could not be applied to African music generally, perhaps related more to East rather than Central Africa, and that the use of the 3rd and 7th tones in diatonic scales there needed more study.

51. Although the pentatonic scale is not *uniquely* African, there is no doubt about its importance to African/African American music. A pentatonic scale is, as one would guess, a five-note scale. The most common one is played on the five black keys of a keyboard. There are, however, other (major and minor) scales that skip notes, representing "gapped systems." In such instances, particularly by dropping the 4th and 7th, a major scale can be transformed into a pentatonic scale, which happens often in the spirituals. See Courlander, *Negro Folk Music*, 15–16. A detailed discussion of these scales and variations of them may be found in Krehbiel, *Afro-American Folksongs*, 70–99.

52. Scholars generally refer to "the Pythagoreans" because most of what little is known of Pythagoras comes from them rather than from direct evidence left by him. My thanks to my colleague Greg Anderson for introducing me to important literature on the Pythagoreans and Pythagorean science.

53. An example of a nationalistic study of black music is Amiri Baraka, "The 'Blues Aesthetic' and the 'Black Aesthetic': Aesthetics and the Continuing Political History of a Culture," *Black Music Research Journal* (Autumn 1991), 101–9; and see LeRoi Jones [Amiri Baraka], *Blues People: Negro Music in White America* (New York: William Morrow & Co., 1963). One example of a detailed critique of the romanticization of black music is Ronald Radano, *Lying up a Nation: Race and Black Music* (Chicago: University of Chicago Press, 2003). The current tendency among critical theorists is to run (as quickly as possible) away from any suggestion of essentialism, which probably seems too much like superstition, religion, or even simple ignorance. Part of the problem may be that current critical theorists have not made the leap that Du Bois made a hundred years ago from "race" to "soul." For a useful example, see Michael Awkward, *Negotiating Difference: Race, Gender and the Politics of Positionality* (Chicago: University of Chicago Press, 1995), 186. In a chapter focusing on Michael Jackson, Awkward writes: "If we fail to interrogate essentialist constructions of blackness, we submit to a racial irrationality that heretofore marked blacks as less than human and continues to exert its influence upon what many of us hold as the most fundamental personal areas of our lives as Americans: our formulations of subjectivity and community." This example is particularly useful because of its focus on community and subjectivity, which are important to Hegel's study of Consciousness. Some critics of what they see as essentializing blackness remind us that black music is created out of a particular environment. In this regard,

see Gilroy, *The Black Atlantic*. Quoting Foucault, Gilroy accepts the idea of "soul" but seems ultimately to negate that acceptance: "'It would be wrong to say that the soul is an illusion, or an ideological effect. On the contrary it exists, it has a reality, it is produced permanently around, on, within the body by the functioning of power that is exercised'" (102). Because of this external power, Gilroy can easily conclude that "our understanding of antiphony [and other 'vernacular forms'] will have to change. . . . [W]e will have to remember that these communicative gestures are not expressive of an essence that exists outside of the acts which perform them and thereby transmit the structures of racial feeling to wider, as yet uncharted, worlds" (110). Gilroy's conclusion makes sense for a discussion of "race" but not for a discussion related to Soul, which he concedes is real.

54. See Rodano, *Lying up a Nation*. Rodano is not alone in this critique of romanticism, but he probably has the most detailed discussion of the way nineteenth-century writers' essentially created an "oversimplified phenomenology of blackness" (10) which more modern writers and thinkers have accepted, thus essentializing black music by situating it in a fantasy "of autonomous form" (2).

55. A good general entry into the historical critical debate about music is Theodor W. Adorno, "Public Opinion and Critics," *Introduction to the Sociology of Music*, 138–53. Adorno, while accepting critics and criticism, makes clear their limitations. "What is thought, said, and written about music, what views of it people express, does indeed often differ with its real function, with the actual effect it has on people's lives, on their consciousness and on their unconsciousness. Yet this function enters into opinion, whether in adequate or in distorted form, and conversely, opinion works back on the function and may even shape it. The factual role of music takes a good deal of its bearings from the reigning ideology" (138). Adorno's discussion also shows how criticism deprives art "of all claim to truth." It is a complex essay that explores both sides of the issue. And he makes the important point that very often the critic's work should begin where it instead ends. See ibid., 138, 142, 150.

Also useful here is Ernst Bloch, *Essays of the Philosophy of Music*, trans. Peter Palmer (Cambridge: Cambridge University Press, 1985), 210–11. Bloch notes the tendency to treat music as "a shapeless rushing or a warm bank of mist" (my sloppy sentimentalism characterization) rather than "a piece of mathematical logic." Discussions that are limited to mood ignore proportion and composition. He reminds us that music made it into the quadrivium because of the "Pythagorean mathematical-astronomical" theories. Moreover, as others have said, "a composer is a combination of a shaman and an engineer." Particularly because of the discrediting of "romantic exuberance," the greater, "more modern impression" is made by the engineer. Still, analyses of the notes/tones (what I have tried to do) eliminates the expressiveness of the craftsmanship. It removes the "I" from the composition. Bloch also suggests, contrary to my view, that relating the music to the cosmos separates it from Soul.

56. Ian Johnston, *Measured Tones: The Interplay of Physics and Music*, 2nd ed. (Bristol: Institute of Physics Publishing, 2002), 2–9; John G. Landels, *Music in Ancient Greece and Rome* (London: Routledge, 1999), 130–32.

57. Johnston, *Measured Tones*, 9. According to Landels, *Music in Ancient Greece and Rome*, 132, the "Pythagoreans do not seem to have been very interested in

discovering exactly why there was a relationship between string length and the pitches of notes. They contented themselves with forming mathematical theories about musical intervals which started from comparative physical measurements of string lengths." On Socrates' response to the Pythagoreans, see Plato, *The Republic*, 531a–c, where Socrates famously criticized the Pythagoreans for failing to go far enough beyond their important musical theories. He sarcastically described them as "people who torment the strings and try to wring the truth out of them by twisting them on pegs." He complained further that the Pythagoreans were no different from the astronomers: "'they look for numerical relationships in audible concords, and never get as far as formulating problems and examining which numerical relations are concordant [harmonious], which not, and why.'" The probable source of Socrates' ire is that he wanted the Pythagoreans to relate the mathematical ratios and the sounds to Soul and being—the Pythagoreans are empiricists.

Aristotle was apparently equally puzzled as to why the Pythagoreans would not have been interested in more than "perception." The Pythagoreans "'squander,'" Aristotle said, "their principles on this world of ours, as though there did not exist anything but what is perceptible, what the sky encloses." Quotation from Walter Burkert, *Lore and Science in Ancient Pythagoreanism*, trans. Edwin L. Minar Jr. (Cambridge, MA: Harvard University Press, 1972), 31. Especially useful here is the chapter entitled "Platonic and Pythagorean Number Theory," 15–96.

It is important to note here that most of Pythagoras's experiments have been proven incorrect. Moreover, Pythagoras's ideas were based not "on mathematics or on experimental physics" but on "'reverence' for certain numbers in their roles in music and cosmology." Still, the conclusions lay the groundwork for the foundation of the science of music. Plato's scale, in *Timeaus*, is not audible at all and rather represents "the numerically harmonic structural pattern of the world, the 'world soul,'" which is discussed below. Ibid., 372–73, 400. Burkert provides a detailed study of the development of "Pythagorean Musical Theory" (369, 400).

58. Johnston, *Measured Tones*, 2–4, and see 12–14, where Johnston concludes that "Pythagoras' discovery was that there is a mathematical relationship between lengths of vibrating string which produce pairs of notes which sound harmonious when played together." And see John Fauvel, Raymond Flood, and Robin Wilson, *Music and Mathematics: From Pythagoras to Fractals* (Oxford: Oxford University Press, 2003), 14–19.

59. Johnston, *Measured Tones*, 12–14, 21–24. These three tones of the triad would correspond to do-me-so (in the Solfège system) and a frequency ratio of 4:5:6. See Dave Benson, *Music: A Mathematical Offering* (Cambridge University Press, 2007), 155. (Benson's electronic book, which is updated regularly, was consulted on November 14, 2009, at http://www.maths.abdn.ac.uk/~bensonj/html/maths.music.html.

60. Frances Anne Kemble, *Journal of a Residence on a Georgian Plantation in 1838–1839*, ed. John A. Scott (New York: Alfred A. Knopf, 1961), 259–60; Robert R. Moton, introduction to *Religious Folk Songs of the Negro*, vi.

61. Thomas Wentworth Higginson, *Army Life in a Black Regiment* (1870; East Lansing: Michigan State University Press, 1960), 160. Indeed the "epic" wrestling match calls to mind Hegel's description of conscious's struggle with essence. "This

pure activity, conscious of its inalienable strength, wrestles with the shapeless essence. Becoming its master, it has made the "pathos" into its material and given itself its content, and this unity emerges as a work, universal Spirit individualized and set before us." See *PS* §702–4. In the Biblical account of Jacob's struggle, "the angel" is a man who, at one point, tried to convince Jacob to give up the fight, but Jacob refused to let go until the man blessed him. Ultimately God did bless Jacob because he "struggled with God and with man, and [has] prevailed." Gen. 32:28. It would probably not be inappropriate to relate this dual struggle to one with both matter and/or experience (man) and with philosophy or science/knowledge (spirit/ God). And, ultimately, Jacob *knows* that this blessing is his.

62. Chesnut quoted in Epstein, *Sinful Tunes and Spirituals*, 225–26. Epstein's volume provides numerous examples of contemporary reactions to the singing (220–29). Her chapter 17 addresses the publication of the songs, including alterations to the music during the process.

63. William Francis Allen, Charles Pickard Ware, and Lucy McKim Garrison, *Slave Songs of the United States* (1867; Bedford, MA: Applewood Books, 1995), iv–v.

64. Ibid., iv.

65. Ibid., iv–vi; Thomas P. Fenner, introduction to *Religious Folk Songs of the Negro*, iii–iv.

66. The reference here is to Dvořák's *Symphony Number 9 in E Minor*, also called *From the New World*. Although there is disagreement about what Dvořák's inspirations were, it is clear that Jeanette Thurber invited him to head the National Conservatory of Music, which she opened (in 1888) to black musicians. Dvořák is said to have immersed himself in "American" music (Henry Burleigh was among the students and worked as a transcriber for Dvořák for a time). Thurber was seeking some legitimacy for American music, and if the conservatory did not accomplish it, Dvořák's symphony certainly did. It became (and remains) an internationally celebrated composition. For a contemporary article about the work by the composer, see Antonín Dvořák, "Music in America," *Harper's New Monthly Magazine* 90 (February 1895), 428–34. John Wesley Work, *Folk Song of the American Negro*, 98–99, credits Dvořák with having said "that the only original music America could claim was the music of the Negro." Work also added Chadwick's "Second Symphony," Schoenfield's "Sunny South Overture," and Kœger's "Ten American Sketches" as also having taken great advantage of the music of the slave songs (33).

67. Work, *Folk Song of the American Negro*, 41–42.

68. These calculations represent the "normal" minor seventh. The harmonic minor seventh (7:4, 1.75) is very flat and considered "unusable in western music." The grave minor seventh figures are 16:9 and 1.782. Slaves used all the space between these two and slid below them. The flat seventh has been described as "the first major extension to traditional harmony." See Tom Ball, "The Tuning CD: 'Using Drones to Improve Intonation,'" www.dwerden.com/SoundFiles/IntonationHelper/ the_Tuning_CD_Booklet_free_version.pdf; and David Canright, "A Tour Up the Harmonic Series," http.redshirt.com/~dcanright/harmser/. Also see the discussion of the harmonic B-flat compared to the western tempered B-flat in Gerhard Kubik, *Africa and the Blues* (Jackson: University Press of Mississippi, 1999), 129.

69. Allen, Ware, Garrison, *Slave Songs of the United States* (1995), iv, vi; Lydia Parrish, *Slave Songs of the Georgia Sea Islands* (1942; Hatboro, PA: Folklore Associates, 1961), xv; John Wesley Work, *American Negro Songs and Spirituals*, 26; John Wesley Work, *Folk Song of the American Negro*, 38–39; and Sterling Brown, "Negro Folk Expression: Spirituals, Seculars, Ballads and Work Songs," *Phylon* 14, no. 1 (Winter 1953), 45–61, whose statement, only slightly paraphrased here, is on page 45.

70. Higginson, *Army Life in a Black Regiment*, 151; Lydia Parrish, *Slave Songs of the Georgia Sea Islands*, xiv; Fredrika Bremer, *The Homes of the New World: Impressions of America*, trans. Mary Howitt (New York: Harper and Brothers, 1854), 1:393–94; Work, *Folk Songs of the American Negro*, 38.

71. Allen, Ware, Garrison, *Slave Songs of the United States* (1995), v. The compilers wrote: "There is no singing in *parts*, as we understand it, and yet no two appear to be singing the same thing—the leading singer starts the words of each verse, often improvising, and the others, who 'base' him, as it is called, strike in with the refrain, or even join in the solo, when the words are familiar. When the 'base' begins, the leader often stops, leaving the rest of his words to be guessed at, or it may be they are taken up by one of the other singers. And the 'basers' themselves seem to follow their own whims, beginning when they please and leaving off when they please, striking an octave above or below (in case they have pitched the tune too low or too high), or hitting some other note that chords, so as to produce the effect of a marvelous complication and variety, and yet with the most perfect time, and rarely with any discord." James Weldon Johnson suggests that Allen failed to understand that what he described was, simply, harmony. Johnson described both unison and part harmony of slave songs; he viewed the songs as unique among the larger body of folk music in that slave songs were group songs sung in harmony. He quotes Carl Van Vechten's early studies of black music, which maintain that "'Negro folksongs differ from the folksongs of most other races through the fact that they are sung in harmony.'" James Weldon Johnson, *The Book of American Negro Spirituals* (New York: Viking Press, 1925), 35. Another discussion of harmony as unique to African American folk singing is reprinted in Parrish, *Slave Songs of the Georgia Sea Islands*, xiv, n. 10. Parrish quotes N. G. J. Ballanta who wrote: "'The aesthetic value of the Spirituals arises from the fact that they are conceived and sung in harmony. This fact has baffled many musicians, as the folksongs of other peoples are conceived in unison. The reason is that the Negro in singing, as his African brother, thinks not of a scale which is simply a succession of individual tones, and which forms the basis of the folksongs of other people, but of a chord where there are three distinct and individual tones sounding at the same time, and in combination producing a harmonious effect.'"

72. Work, *Folk Song of the American Negro*, 38–39. And see Robert R. Moton's introduction to *Religious Folk Songs of the Negro as Sung on the Plantations*, vi, where he wrote in this new edition, "Though the words are sometimes rude and the strains often wild, yet they are the outpourings of an ignorant and poverty-stricken people whose religious longings and ideals struggled for expression and found it through limited vocabularies and primitive harmonies. They are not merely poetry, they are

more than poetry, they are life itself—the life of the human soul manifesting itself in rude words, wild strains, and curious though beautiful harmonies."

73. Work, *Folk Song of the American Negro*, 39. Rodano, *Lying Up a Nation*, could be correct in viewing the nineteenth-century writers' labeling this music as "different" as a way of labeling it inferior. But I think some of them, particularly those interested in preserving as much of the sound as they could capture, recognized it as good (at least). Talking about it in the terms they did makes it even clearer that language, in spite of Hegel's seeing it as "soul existing as soul" (and the emphasis placed on language since then by critical theorists) is, by its nature, limiting.

74. Plato, *Timaeus*, as quoted in Godwin, *The Harmony of the Spheres*, 4–6; and see 403–6 (nn. 6–15), for musical translations/interpretations. Godwin uses Thomas Taylor, *The Works of Plato* (1804). I have modified paragraph breaks here.

75. Christopher Bamford, "Introduction: Homage to Pythagoras," in Bamford, ed., *Homage to Pythagoras: Rediscovering Sacred Science* (Hudson, NY: Lindisfarne Press, 1994). 27. Also see Jamie James, *The Music of the Spheres: Music, Science, and the Natural Order of the Universe* (New York: Grove Press, 1993), 41–59, on "Plato and the World Soul."

76. Maconie, *The Science of Music*, 37–42; James, *Music of the Spheres*, 190–91. And note that Arthur Schopenhauer saw music as more than representations of "'Ideas,'" but "the Will, the Absolute itself." See Watts, *Music: The Medium of the Metaphysical in E. T. A. Hoffmann*, 16. And for a more detailed, accessible discussion of Schopenhauer, see Peter Franklin, "Music, the Will and Ideas," in *The Idea of Music: Schoenberg and Others* (London: MacMillan Press, 1985), 1–17.

77. Leibniz quote in James, *The Music of the Spheres*, 180. Ancient Greeks looked for "harmonies in nature," of which music was an example. And Pythagoreans went beyond math, believing that "the planets, produced harmonious sounds as they moved in space. This is the 'music of the spheres,' a harmonious relationship of the heavenly bodies." Harvey E. White and Donald H. White, *Physics and Music: The Science of Musical Sound* (Philadelphia: Sanders College, 1980), 4. And see James, *The Music of the Spheres*, 20–40, on the Pythagoreans and harmony.

78. James, *The Music of the Spheres*, 16, 18.

79. Thomas W. Higginson, *Army Life in a Black Regiment*, 160, 172–73; Jacob Stroyer, *My Life in the South* (Salem, MA: Salem Observer Book and Job Print, 1885), 41. Endor is a Canaanite village in the Hebrew Bible and Old Testament, and Delphi is the site of the most important oracle (of Apollo) of Ancient Greece. Thus, here again, Du Bois deliberately mixed the message of religion. If, however, scholars are generally correct in seeing Alexander Crummell as the intellectual role model of Du Bois, and if Wilson Moses is correct in his conclusion that Crummell found "[t]he idea of 'gettin' saved,' based on the belief in communication with Jesus or the Holy Spirit after a frenzied dance, or 'ring shout,' or trancelike possession, . . . the height of absurdity," then, apparently, Du Bois would have disagreed with him, at least in part. See Wilson Jeremiah Moses, "Introduction: Alexander Crummell and the Destined Superiority of African People," in Trost, *The African Diaspora and the Study of Religion*, 7.

Walter Burkert, in *Lore and Science in Ancient Pythagoreanism*, 357, wrote on the possibility of Pythagoras's being a shaman. The discussion, based in a "pre-scientific [a priori] conception of order" in which "the idea of cosmic music has its roots," offers a possible explanation for what Du Bois here (and Fredrika Bremer in part 3 of this chapter witnessed). In his description, Burkert posited that "relationships that usually have their effect unconsciously, or only enter consciousness as the result of slow and patient reflection, become immediate, overwhelming experience in ecstasy. The soul that in ecstasy, or dream, or trance, travels to heaven, hears there the music of the universe, and its mysterious structure immediately becomes clear to him. . . . If Pythagoras was something like a shaman, who in ecstasy made contact with worlds 'beyond,' then the tradition that he personally heard the heavenly music surely preserves something of truth. When we look beyond the façade of analysis and explication of the harmony of the spheres, what we find is neither empirical nor mathematical science, but eschatology." Both the Pythagorean idea of numbers and the possibilities of this kind of transcendence are important to this chapter, even though Burkert seems to see the two as antithetical. A very different exploration of Du Bois' use of art and religion is Wilson Moses, "W. E. B. Du Bois on Religion and Art: Dynamic Contradictions and Multiple Consciousness," in *Creative Conflict in African American Thought: Frederick Douglass, Alexander Crummell, Booker T. Washington, W. E. B. Du Bois, and Marcus Garvey* (Cambridge: Cambridge University Press, 2004), 185–96.

It might be useful to consider Du Bois' "visible manifestation of the God" in the context of Hegel's distinguishing between objective and subjective religion, the latter of which concerns "what the people really believe and feel—and not the established doctrines that the theologians promulgate" (objective religion). Quotation from Terry Pinkard, *Hegel*, 39–40. And see Pinkard's discussion of religion through page 43.

80. Final quotation from Edward A. Lippman, *Musical Thought in Ancient Greece* (New York: Columbia University Press, 1964), 75. Lippman ends this discussion by saying, "The Ideas are reached by dialectic, which proceeds by reason alone, but the point of departure is sense and the route leads through harmonic theory." Also note that "infinite" here does not mean endless, as in mathematics ("because you never come to the last term"; i.e., 1.333 . . .). Rather, infinite, here, refers to "having an internal structure which is the harmonious and complete expression of a single self-consistent principle." The finite, on the other hand, is finite not because "it has a 'last term,' *i.e.* because there is something else outside it, but because the 'last term' is arbitrarily determined, *i.e.* determined by something other than the principles of its internal structure. In other words, the essential defect of the finite is that it is not solely determined by its own structural principle." See A. E. Taylor, *Elements of Metaphysics*, 9th ed. (London: Methuen and Co., 1930), 116.

81. Quotation from Brierley, *Studies of the Soul* 61. Brierley goes on to characterize music as "a pre-existent intellect" (62).

82. Jevons quoted in Kassler, *Music, Science, Philosophy*, vii.

83. Bremer, *The Homes of the New World*, 2:236–38.

84. Higginson, *Army Life in a Black Regiment*, 148; Edward A. Pollard, *Black Diamonds Gathered in the Darkey Homes of the South* (New York: Pudney & Russell, Publishers, 1859), 35–36. For an important historical discussion of the ring shout

see Sterling P. Stuckey, "Introduction: Slavery and the Circle of Culture," in *Slave Culture: Nationalist Theory and the Foundations of Black America* (New York: Oxford University Press, 1987), 3–97.

85. Shane White and Graham White, "Sing no hymns of your own composing," in *The Sounds of Slavery: Discovering African American History through Songs, Sermons, and Speech* (Boston: Beacon Press, 2005), 55–71. An earlier discussion of this is Dena J. Epstein, *Sinful Tunes and Spirituals*, 229–37. Fredrika Bremer often lamented that in some cases the singing, praying, and shouting would immediately cease when she and other whites arrived at church meetings. See Bremer, *The Homes of the New World*, 1: 290, 311, 314. And see the example of the one slave woman who refused to be deterred by the presence of whites when she was moved by the spirit and announced: "'Nebbah mind de wite folks! My soul's happy!'" Quoted in Newman White, *American Negro Folk Songs* (Cambridge, MA: Harvard University Press, 1928), 37–38.

86. See Benjamin Farrington, *Greek Science: Its Meaning for Us*, rev. ed. (1941; Harmondsworth: Penguin Books, 1961), 311. (Farrington's statement is a tribute to history as a science.) Farrington is misidentified as Harrington in Robin Maconie's *The Science of Music*, vii. My thanks to Kenneth Hamilton for providing me the best example of superstition's being something disconnected from its logic by reminding me that one should not walk under ladders because ladders sometimes fall, and things and people often fall off them, and it would be helpful to see them coming. He, thereby, forced me to think a lot harder about superstition than I probably would have.

87. Bamford, "Homage to Pythagoras," in *Homage to Pythagoras*, 17–20, 28. In addition to the possibility of chanting to increase sense perception, we might also consider that the "[p]ersistence of repeat in music, its ostinato of rhythm and obsession of form, signify in some way the reappearing gleam of the aware *major self.*" Quotation from Watts, *Music: The Medium of the Metaphysical in E. T. A. Hoffman*, 40. This effect is described especially in nineteenth-century descriptions of the slaves' religious songs. Lydia Parrish, *Slave Songs of the Georgia Sea Islands*, 228, described a rendition of "Do Remember" in which the singers repeated this phrase "an interminable number of" times. She estimated a version with eighteen or twenty repetitions. Eileen Southern, *The Music of Black Americans: A History* (New York: W. W. Norton & Company, 1971), 161, described ring shouts that could last for hours, in which the song became "a chant, a 'wild, monotonous chant,' and its text became the 'repetition of an incoherent cry.'" Thomas Wentworth Higginson described "quaint, monotonous, endless, negro-Methodist chants, with obscure syllables recurring constantly, and slight variations interwoven" in *Army Life in a Black Regiment*, 13. John F. Watson, in 1819, witnessed camp meetings during which the people "'sing for hours together, short scraps of disjointed affirmations, pledges, or prayers, lengthened out with long repetition *choruses.*'" Quoted in Epstein, *Sinful Tunes and Spirituals*, 218. Finally, James Weldon Johnson distinguished between spirituals and these "shout songs" in *The Book of American Negro Spirituals*, 33. He had observed these chants evolving out of what began (in performance) as a spiritual. It became "a wild, monotonous chant" in which "[t]he same musical phrase is

repeated over and over one, two, three, four, five hours. . . . The very monotony of sound and motion [the ring shout] produces an ecstatic state."

88. Bamford, *Homage to Pythagoras*, 28; Plato, *Phaedo*, in Irwin Edman, ed., *The Works of Plato* (1928; New York: Modern Library, 1956), esp. 129–41, quotation on 129. Du Bois' application to Harvard indicates that he read *Phaedo* in the original Greek. See W. E. B. Du Bois, [Application to] Harvard College. Committee of the Faculty on Admissions for other Colleges, Faculty of Arts and Sciences Folder, Harvard University Archives, Pusey Library, Cambridge, MA.

89. Tom Rockmore, *Cognition*, 27. And see *PS* §77–78. "Bildung" inside the brackets is original to the quote. It should be pointed out here that this is a significantly narrower use of the term than Terry Pinkard provides and is cited (and described) in the preface to this chapter, above.

90. See n. 87. Unfortunately, some of the early efforts to preserve slave songs were marred by the elimination of this very effect. One editor/compiler reported, "'I have used the pruning knife freely, removing ineffective stanzas, and trimming back most of the ever-present repetition.'" He went on to celebrate his effort to preserve the music "and to make it stand out a little more sharply on the printed page." Quoted in Fisher, *Negro Slave Songs in the United States*, 15. Lydia Parrish, *Slave Songs of the Georgia Sea Islands*, 45, recognized more inadvertent ways that the music was altered. She wrote: "In my experience transcriptions and records are both too susceptible to the biased interpretation of the musicians trained in the European idiom." Clearly, listening for particular sounds, and being unable to recognize the significance of other sounds because of training, culture, etc., affected all the transcriptions.

91. Rockmore, *Cognition*, 15–16; and see *PS* §36–37. For a recent discussion of the life and mind of the quintessential "Renaissance man," Leonardo da Vinci, viewed through the modern science of cognition, see Fritjof Capra, *The Science of Leonardo: Inside the Mind of the Great Genius of the Renaissance* (New York: Doubleday, 2007), 237–56, esp. 249–56.

92. Rockmore, *Cognition*, 15–16.

93. S. K. Heninger Jr., *Touches of Sweet Harmony: Pythagorean Cosmology and Renaissance Poetics* (San Marino, CA: Huntington Library, 1974), xv. Metempsychosis is reincarnation, or the notion that immortal human souls transmigrate and are reborn in other animals. A useful study of metaphysics that explains inductive and deductive science and provides ways of reconciling them include Jorge J. E. Gracia, *Metaphysics and Its Task: The Search for the Categorical Foundations of Knowledge* (Albany: State University of New York Pres, 1999), 83–93; and W. Stanley Jevons, *The Principles of Science: A Treatise on Logic and Scientific Method* (1877; New York: Dover Publications, 1958).

94. Cornel West was not the first to have had a difficult time seeing Du Bois connected to these folk—most scholars have. Eric Sundquist, who recognized Du Bois' unique ability to write about the folk, also concluded that there was some "ambivalence" that "kept Du Bois from any sort of comfortable unification with the folk consciousness epitomized by black spirituals." In a footnote, Sundquist reminded us of E. Franklin Frazier's much earlier, venomous characterization of Du Bois as

"'sensitive to every slight concerning the Negro and feeling on the other hand little kinship or real sympathy for the great mass of crude, uncouth black peasants with whom he was identified.'" Sundquist, *To Wake the Nations*, 460–61. This was, ironically, Du Bois' complaint about the Talented Tenth in the 1948 presentation. See chapter 3, above.

95. Quoted in Bamford, *Homage to Pythagoras*, 23, on "the basis of a Pythagorean theory of knowledge."

96. Burkert, *Lore and Science in Ancient Pythagoreanism*, 482. Although I use the term "science" as Hegel did, I am not unmindful of the difficulties attendant to this use. Burkert understood that it would be a mistake to call Pythagoras a scientist or even a philosopher (as we understand the terms). "But the fascination that surrounded, and still surrounds, the name of Pythagoras does not come, basically, from specific scientific connotations, or from the rational method of mathematics, and certainly not from the success of mathematical physics. More important is the feeling that there is a kind of knowing which penetrates to the very core of the universe, which offers truth as something at once beatific and comforting, and presents the human being as cradled in a universal harmony."

97. Arnold Schoenberg to Rudolf Kolisch, July 1932, quoted in Franklin, *The Idea of Music: Schoenberg and Others*, 91. Also revealing these aspects are the early letters between Schoenberg and the artist Wassily Kandinski. See Jelena Hahl-Koch, ed., *Arnold Schoenberg, Wassily Kandinsky: Letters, Pictures and Documents*, trans. John C. Crawford (London: Faber and Faber, 1983), especially Kandinsky to Schoenberg, January 18, 1911, and August 19, 1912, and Schoenberg to Kandinsky, January 24, 1911.

98. Terry Pinkard, *Hegel: A Biography*, 201. Although some scholars see the Sorrow Songs as further (material) evidence of double consciousness, it is useful to point out Kwaku Larbi Korang's resolving one aspect of the dilemma in "As I Face America: Race and Africanity in Du Bois's *The Souls of Black Folk*," in *W. E. B. Du Bois and Race*, ed. Chester J. Fontenot Jr. and Mary Alice Morgan, with Sarah Gardner (Macon, GA: Mercer University Press, 2001), 186. Korang described the Sorrow Songs as demanding "the passage of a soulful black aesthetic from its African priority to an American originality. Roots to fruits: Africa finds its consummation in America. Just as surely America finds its originality in the African self-presence within itself. Here in an aesthetic that is African American, African *and* American, Du Bois discovers an affirmative resolution, a transcendence of what is otherwise a pathological dilemma of double consciousness. A New World aesthetic in which Africa and America cohabit in a resolutive tension becomes a prophetic metaphor, an article of faith—that it may yet be possible to be both a Negro and an American."

99. Jamie James, *The Music of the Spheres*, 23, 44–45, 51, 142; Pinkard, *Hegel*, 201; Watts, *Music: The Medium of the Metaphysical in E. T. A. Hoffman*, 10–11.

100. Krehbiel, *Afro-American Folksongs*, 77–79.

101. The description of the movement (force) in this music adds yet another layer to Du Bois' earlier noted statement in the chapter on Washington ("It is as though Nature must needs make men narrow in order to give them force"). It also suggests,

even more, that Du Bois' understanding of music was deeper than he let on (or, in this context, than he even consciously knew).

102. Kreibhiel, *Afro-American Folk Songs*, 77.

103. Even without an analysis of the music, Ernest Allen put this nicely: "Du Bois . . . marveled at the intrinsic beauty of a music which had required neither composers, arrangers, nor performers of professional stature for its execution." See "On the Reading of Riddles," 60.

104. Although Kelly Miller did not argue directly for "Absolute Knowledge" in his essay "The Artistic Gifts of the Negro," he came very close. Miller wrote in part: "The pent-up energy within breaks through the aperture of sound while the slower and more accurate deliberations of the intellect are yet in process of formulation. . . . These weird, plaintive, lugubrious longings go straight to the heart without the intervention of cumbersome intellectual machinery." Describing the newness of this music, adapted by Work and fleshed out in Du Bois' remark in *Black Reconstruction*, the epigraph introducing this book, Miller wrote in part, "Negro melody has been called the only autochtonous music of the American Continent. . . . It was reserved for the transplanted African to sing a new song racy of the soil, which had been baptized with his blood and watered with his tears. This music is the spontaneous expression of the race soul under new and depressing environment. . . . These songs are not African, but American. The scene, circumstances and aspirations are not adapted to some distant continent, but to their new environment in a land, not of their sojourn, but of their abiding place. Shall they not immortalize the soil from which they sprang?" Miller, *Race Adjustment: Essays on the Negro in America* (New York: Neal Publishing Co., 1909), 236–37.

105. Bamford, "Homage to Pythagoras," 28.

106. Clement of Alexandria described the "new song" of early Christians in a way that would not be inappropriate for describing the slaves' songs: "'[T]his Eunomus of mine sings not . . . in Phrygian or Lydian or Dorian [scales]; but the new harmony, with its eternal nome that bears the name of God.'" Quoted in Watts, *Music: The Medium of the Metaphysical in E. T. A. Hoffman*, 12. My comparison here to the Psalms raises a related point. Although we normally think of the Psalms in terms of words because of how they are presented to most of us, singer-songwriter Leonard Cohen recently reminded us of these *songs* in his (recently) much-covered "Hallelujah," which focuses on the tones. The first verse of that song reminds us of the "secret chord" that David played that was pleasing to God. There is some debate today surrounding the authorship of the Psalms, about half of which have traditionally been attributed to David. Nevertheless, the idea of the newness of the sound of the songs of David has held.

John Wesley Work, *Folk Song of the American Negro*, 20–21, described the slave songs as a "new song" that was "new in thought and spirit." Work distinguished it from various kinds of African music, and from the music of Indians and Europeans, to which some nineteenth-century writers related it (26–33). Krehbiel, *Afro-American Folksongs*, 68–69, provides a useful way of revealing how new this scale was. Krehbiel noted that in the more than 500 songs he analyzed, there were "seven variations from the normal, or conventional, diatonic major and minor scales . . .

besides the songs which were set down as mixed or of vague tonality." The variations, some of whose roots he described as African, include: "1. the major scale, with the seventh depressed a semitone, *i.e.*, flatted; (2) the major scale, without the seventh or leadingtone; (3) the major scale, without the fourth; (4) the major scale, without either seventh of [*sic*, or] fourth (the pentatonic scale); (5) the minor scale, with a raised or major sixth; (6) the minor scale, without the sixth, and (7) the minor scale, with the raised seventh—the so-called harmonic minor." Also see the chapter, "Songs of the American Slaves," 11–28. And see Johnson, *The Book of American Negro Spirituals*, 35, which discusses a Carl Van Vechten article that addressed the uniqueness of the harmonies of the music.

Also see Alec Harman, with Anthony Milner and Wilfrid Mellers, *Man and His Music: The Story of Musical Experience in the West* (New York: Oxford University Press, 1962), 743–58, which describes Wagner's accomplishments, regardless of evaluations of "aspects of his personality," as "one of the supreme achievements of the human mind" in his creation of music that "evoke[d] the world of his inner life" (743). The authors describe parts of Wagner's *Lohengrin* as "a new sound, which tells us already that Wagner's dream will be realized not on the stage, but in the orchestra pit." They even conclude that Wagner himself was not yet aware of "[t]he precise nature of this new art" that he created (747).

107. W. E. B. Du Bois, *The Souls of Black Folk*, ed. David W. Blight and Robert Gooding-Williams (Boston: Bedford Books, 1997), 217 (n. 1); Sundquist, *To Wake the Nation*, 528; Sandra Adell, *Double-Consciousness/Double Bind*, 28. A useful examination of the songs that sees Du Bois as having deliberately distanced the words from the music is Virginia Whatley Smith, "They Sing a Song of Slavery: Frederick Douglass's *Narrative* and W. E. B. Du Bois's *The Souls of Black Folk* as Intertexts of Richard Wright's *12 Million Black Voices*," in Hubbard, *The Souls of Black Folk: One Hundred Years Later*, 85–129.

108. Kassler, *Music, Science, Philosophy*, 166.

109. Quotation from W. E. B. Du Bois, *Dusk of Dawn*, 98. I consider this statement an allusion to Hegel's *Philosophy of History*.

110. James, *The Music of the Spheres*, 3–19, quotations on 9, 11, 14–15, 5, 19. James provides a perfect description of this abandonment in terms of science "leaving behind the larger questions that had launched its great intellectual adventure, while . . . [music turned] its focus inward, concentrating on the emotional life of man rather than on the vast scheme of which it was always believed that he formed a part. . . . There would seem to be an inextinguishable yearning in the human soul, almost its defining characteristic, to form these connections, to find a meaningful order in the bewildering complexity of the perceptible universe" (18). Hegel himself ultimately decided that art lost that larger role during the post-Enlightenment period when art and religion separated. See James J. Sheehan, "Aesthetic Theory and Architectural Practice: Schinkel's Museum in Berlin," in David Wetzel, *From the Berlin Museum to the Berlin Wall: Essays on the Cultural and Political History of Modern Germany* (Westport, CT: Praeger, 1996), 11–29, esp. 12–14, 25–27.

Although it is not clear that James was referring to jazz musicians in his mentioning the avant-garde, jazz musicians have regularly sought and sometimes produced truly new music. See Robin D. G. Kelley, *Thelonious Monk: The Life and Times of an American Original* (New York: Free Press, 2009) for clear parallels between Kelley's and Monk's descriptions of various aspects of music and the above characterizations. Anecdotally, one might also consider Wingy Malone's action after passing a signboard in front of a 52d Street (NY) jazz club which announced: "Come in and Hear Dizzy Gillespi." Malone promptly returned to the club where he was playing and produced and placed a sign out front that announced "come in and Hear the Truth." See Patrick Burke, *Come in and Hear the Truth: Jazz and Race on 52nd Street* (Chicago: University of Chicago Press, 2008), 1. Malone's point was well made, but one could reasonably expect to find Monk inside the second club if one were in search of "the truth."

111. Thomas S. Hibbs has also recognized a special significance of the songs in "Subversive Natural Law: MacIntyre and African-American Thought" in *The Death of Metaphysics; The Death of Culture: Epistemology, Metaphysics, and Morality*, ed. Mark J. Cherry (Dordrecht and London: Springer, 2006), 135–50. Hibbs writes about "the transcendent spiritual appeal of the songs of the slaves." He adds, "[t]he paradox could not be more striking or the indictment more palpable. America's highest longings, indeed the noblest aspirations of human nature itself, reside in that portion of American humanity most reviled by mainstream America. . . . The sorrowful songs of the slaves embody the supreme virtues of the human creature" (147).

Conclusion

1. This line is from Du Bois' chapter on Crummell.

2. Quotation from Fritjof Capra, *The Science of Leonardo: Inside the Mind of the Great Genius of the Renaissance* (New York: Doubleday, 2007), 12.

3. Du Bois' 1905 essay, "The Negro Ideals of Life," is quoted in Ernest Allen Jr., "Du Boisian Double Consciousness: The Unsustainable Argument," *Massachusetts Review* 43 (Summer 2002): 230.

4. Jessie Fauset to Du Bois, December 22, 1903, in Herbert Aptheker, ed., *The Correspondence of W. E. B. Du Bois* (Amherst: University of Massachusetts Press, 1973), 1: 66. Du Bois seems to have borrowed Fauset's suggestion about "fine feelings" when he wrote in his *Independent* review (November 17, 1904) of the difficulties inherent in translating "the finer feelings of men into words." Jessie Redmon Fauset (1882–1961) not only became an important novelist during the 1920s, publishing *There Is Confusion* (1924), *Plum Bun: A Novel without a Moral* (1929), *The Chinaberry Tree: A Novel of American Life* (1931), and *Comedy: American Style* (1933), she also served as the literary editor of *The Crisis* under Du Bois from 1919 to 1926. Fauset was a 1905 graduate of Cornell University, where she studied classical languages.

5. D. Tabak to Du Bois, n.d., Du Bois, *The Souls of Black Folk*, ed. David W. Blight and Robert Gooding-Williams (Boston: Bedford Books, 1997), 260–61.

6. Ibid.

7. W. D. Hooper to Du Bois, September 2, 1909, in Aptheker, *Correspondence of W. E. B. Du Bois*, 1:152–53; D. Tabak to Du Bois, in Du Bois, *Souls*, ed. Blight and

Gooding-Williams, 260–61. The conclusion that William James viewed the book as despairing is based on Du Bois' response to him dated June 12, 1906, reprinted in ibid., 261–62, in which Du Bois insisted that rather than a "minor key," his volume conveyed "aggressive & unquenchable hopefulness." Hart quoted in David Levering Lewis, *W. E. B. Du Bois: Biography of a Race, 1868–1919* (New York: Henry Holt and Company, 1993), 294. George Foster Peabody to Du Bois, January 9, 1904, and Max Weber to Du Bois, May 30, 1905, in Aptheker, *Correspondence of W. E. B. Du Bois*, 1:69, 106–7; Henry James, *The American Scene* (1907; Bloomington: Indiana University Press, 1968), 418. Henry James's comment might have been designed, in part, to congratulate his brother, Du Bois' former advisee. In William James's letter to his brother that accompanied the book, he only said: "I am sending you a decidedly moving book by a mulatto ex-student of mine, Du Bois, professor of History at Atlanta (Georgia) negro College. Read chapters VII to XI for local color, etc." William James to Henry James, June 6, 1903, in Henry James, ed., *Letters of William James* (Boston: Atlantic Monthly Press, 1920), 2:195–96. The Henry James who edited these volumes is the son of William.

8. W. E. B. Du Bois, "The Conservation of Races," in David Levering Lewis, ed., *W. E. B. Du Bois: A Reader* (New York: Henry Holt and Company, 1995), 20–27. Scholars who relate the "Conservation" essay to Du Bois' subsequent work connect it to the first chapter of *Souls*. The point here is that the ideas raised in "Conservation" are developed across the entire text of *Souls*. Robert Gooding-Williams aptly described Du Bois' 1897 essay ("Conservation") as "a philosophical prolegomenon to *The Souls of Black Folk*, because it offers a theoretical promise that Du Bois only begins to fulfill in what eventually became the opening essay of *Souls*." See Gooding-Williams, "Outlaw, Appiah, and 'The Conservation of Races'" in Bernard W. Bell, Emily R. Grosholz, and James B. Stewart, *W. E. B. Du Bois on Race and Culture: Philosophy, Politics, and Poetics* (New York: Routledge, 1996), 39–56, quotation on 53. Thomas C. Holt, "The Political Uses and Alienation: W. E. B. Du Bois on Politics, Race, and Culture, 1903–1940," *American Quarterly* 42 (June 1990): 301–23, also compares the two essays, though in different ways. And see Holt's "W. E. B. Du Bois's Archaeology of Race: Re-Reading 'The Conservation of Races,'" in *W. E. B. Du Bois, Race, and the City: The Philadelphia Negro and Its Legacy*, ed. Michael B. Katz and Thomas J. Sugrue (Philadelphia: University of Pennsylvania Press, 1998), 61–76, which explores Du Bois' construction as an example of the politics of race. Another analysis of Du Bois' lecture/essay and a discussion of that first meeting of the Academy is Wilson J. Moses, "W. E. B. Du Bois's 'The Conservation of Races' and Its Context: Idealism, Conservatism and Hero Worship," *Massachusetts Review* 34 (Summer 1993): 275–94. Lucius Outlaw demonstrates fully the significance of the "Conservation" essay in "'Conserve' Races?" in Bell, Grosholz, and Stewart, *W. E. B. Du Bois on Race and Culture*, 15–39. Also see Outlaw, "On W. E. B. Du Bois's 'The Conservation of Races,'" in *Overcoming Racism and Sexism*, ed. Linda A. Bell and David Blumenfeld (Lanham, MD: Rowman & Littlefield Publishers, 1995), 70–102, which follows a reprint of Appiah's "The Uncompleted Argument." In Lucius T. Outlaw Jr., "Against the Grain of Modernity: The Politics of Difference and the Conservation of 'Race,'" *On Race and Philosophy* (New York: Routledge, 1996), 135–57,

esp. 151–57, Outlaw explores the "Conservation" essay as a philosophical text. I have inserted the word "public" above because Du Bois had clearly been grappling with the ideas in this essay since his Harvard days, which is demonstrated in his often cited "Philosophy IV" notebook. See, W. E. B. Du Bois, "Phil. IV," mss, Hugh Smythe Papers, box 12, Schomburg Center for Research in Black Culture, New York Public Library. But also see the complete development of this essay labeled "The Renaissance of Ethics: A Critical Comparison of Scholastic and Modern Ethics," Thesis in Philosophy IV, 1889, mss, W. E. B. Du Bois papers, James Weldon Johnson Memorial Collection, box 3, f. 57, Beinecke Rare Book and Manuscript Library, Yale University, New Haven, CT.

9. Quotations from Du Bois, "Conservation," 20. I obviously allude here, in the DNA statement, to the most well-known (and cited) discussion of Du Bois' failures regarding science, Kwame Anthony Appiah, "The Uncompleted Argument: Du Bois and the Illusion of Race," *Critical Inquiry* 12 (Autumn 1985): 21–37. Many scholars have taken direct issue with Appiah's conclusion, and I have cited some of them above. Kwaku Larbi Korang, in "As I Face America: Race and Africanity," in *W. E. B. Du Bois and Race: Essays Celebrating the Centennial Publication of The Souls of Black Folk*, ed. Chester J. Fontenot Jr. and Mary Alice Morgan, with Sarah Gardner (Macon, GA: Mercer University Press, 2001), 166–93, summarized the criticism of Du Bois as about his having created a "willful mystification to buttress a scientifically and ethically unsupportable race-feeling" (167) with which Korang disagrees (as do I). Richard Cullen Rath, "Echo and Narcissus: The Afrocentric Pragmatism of W. E. B. Du Bois," *Journal of American History* (September 1997), sees Du Bois as having premiered "historical events, not biological race" and as having given "biological racialism a place, but no formal function" in his study (466–69). Rath, however, sees Du Bois' metaphysics as African.

10. Herodotus characterized "'Greekness'" in terms of "'the common blood, the common language; the temples and religious rituals; the whole way of life we understand and share together.'" Herodotus quoted in Derek Heater, *A Brief History of Citizenship* (New York: New York University Press, 2004), 88.

While Du Bois' discussion of "race" in "Conservation" can be confusing, in addition to his having moved from "conservation of race" to "conversation of soul" by the time he wrote *Souls*, he had already recognized that "race" as a scientific construct was a nonstarter despite the myriad efforts of others to draw scientific conclusions about race. In the *Dusk of Dawn* chapter "The Concept of Race," he explained the process of his thinking in the context of his personal experiences. When he was in elementary school, race only came up in geography, which "pictured . . . Indians, Negroes and Chinese by their most uncivilized and bizarre representatives; the whites by some kindly and distinguished-looking philanthropist." By the time he reached high school, his "racial inferiority could not be dwelt upon because the single representative of the Negro race in the school [(himself)] did not happen to be in any way inferior to his fellows." At Harvard, he "began to face scientific race dogma." In one museum, "a series of skeletons arranged from a little monkey to a tall well-developed white man, with a Negro barely outranking a chimpanzee" was the model. In classes, the emphasis "was quietly transferred to brain weight and brain capacity, and last to the 'cephalic index.'" In his graduate classes (at Harvard and in Germany) the emphasis became culture, but the Chinese, Indians, and Negroes were left out of the discussions (which strongly suggests Hegel's *Philosophy*). As soon as he became comfortable with the idea of the survival of the fittest, with the provision that time was taken into account, the "science" changed again. He wrote: "I was skeptical about brain weight; surely much depended upon what brains were weighed. I was not sure about physical measurements and social inquiries. For instance, an insurance actuary actually published in 1890 incontrovertible statistics showing how quickly and certainly the Negro race was dying out in the United States through sheer physical inferiority. I lived to see every assumption of Hoffman's 'Race Traits and Tendencies' contradicted; but even before that, I doubted the statistical method which he had used. When the matter of race became a question of comparative culture, I was in revolt. I began to see that the cultural equipment attributed to any people depended largely on who estimated it; and conviction came later in a rush as I realized what in my education had been suppressed concerning Asiatic and African culture." After World War I, psychological tests "were quickly adjusted so as to put black folk absolutely beyond the possibility of civilization." Du Bois concluded that science became "the slave of caste and race hate." See *Dusk of Dawn: Autobiography of a Race Concept* (1940; New Brunswick, NJ: Transactions Publishing, 1991), 97–100.

11. Du Bois, "Conservation," 21–25.

12. See n. 8, above.

13. For Du Bois' "conservation of soul" remark, see *Souls*, 118. Recognizing changes in Du Bois' ideas is Joel Olson, "W. E. B. Du Bois and the Race Concept," *Souls* 7 (Summer-Fall 2005): 118–28, esp. 120–22. Olson sees the shift not from "race" (in "Conservation") to "soul" (in *Souls*) but from race as something physiological and historical to something anthropological or cultural (by the 1910s) to something totally socially constructed (by the 1930s). I agree with Olson's general conclusion but insist that Du Bois fully understood what we now call "the social construction of race" decades before the 1930s. An important element of Hegel's masterwork was, after all, that the development of consciousness was conditioned by history and experience.

14. Jay Parini concluded that Du Bois (and Crummell before him) believed "'that assimilation and acculturation into European American culture represented the only route for African Americans to acquire social equality and intellectual empowerment.'" Parini, *Promised Land: Thirteen Books that Changed America* (New York: Doubleday, 2008), 205. And see Shanette M. Harris, "Constructing a Psychological Perspective: The Observer and the Observed in *The Souls of Black Folk*," in *The Souls of Black Folk: One Hundred Years Later*, ed. Dolan Hubbard (Columbia: University of Missouri Press, 2003), 218–50, which Parini quotes.

15. Joel Williamson, *The Crucible of Race: Black-White Relations in the American South since Emancipation* (New York: Oxford University Press, 1984), 403–4.

16. Coleridge quoted in Christopher Bamford, ed., *Homage to Pythagoras: Rediscovering Sacred Science* (Hudson, NY: Lindisfarne Press, 1994), 21. Coleridge was responding to Descartes' remark: "give me matter and motion and I will construct

you a universe." For the original Coleridge statement, see *The Complete Works of Samuel Taylor Coleridge*, Biographea Literaria or Biographical Sketches of my Literary Life and Opinions (New York: Harper and Brothers, 1868), 3:357. And for a very useful and accessible discussion of Coleridge's ideas, particularly in the context of German metaphysics, see Louis Menand, *The Metaphysical Club* (New York: Farrar, Straus and Giroux, 2001), 245–67. (Samuel Taylor Coleridge should not be confused with Samuel Coleridge-Taylor.)

17. Du Bois, *Dusk of Dawn*, 51.

18. Du Bois' Harvard coursework is listed in Francis L. Broderick, "The Academic Training of W. E. B. DuBois," *Journal of Negro Education* (Winter 1958): 12–13. The quote on science is from Frederick Gregory, *Scientific Materialism in Nineteenth Century Germany* (Dordrecht: D. Reidel Publishing Company, 1977), 155. And see Du Bois' discussion of von Treischke, in *The Autobiography of W. E. B. Du Bois: A Soliloquy on Viewing My Life from the Last Decade of Its First Century*, intro. Werner Sollors (Oxford: Oxford University Press, 2007), 102–5.

19. Du Bois to Herbert Aptheker, January 10, 1956, in Aptheker, *Correspondence of W. E. B. Du Bois*, 3:394–96, quotation on 396. Quoted fully in the introduction to this volume.

20. Du Bois, *Autobiography*, 93.

21. Quotation from James L. Christian, *Philosophy: An Introduction to the Art of Wondering*, 4th ed. (New York: Holt, Rhinehart and Winston, 1973), 161.

22. Walter Isaacson, *Einstein: His Life and Universe* (New York: Simon and Schuster, 2007), esp. 138–39 and 189–92, on the deductive beginnings of both special and general relativity laws, and 116–18, on "Induction and Deduction in Physics," generally, which concludes with a brief discussion of Einstein's frustrations pursuing his theories empirically, causing him to concede, "'The longer and the more despairingly I tried, the more I came to the conviction that only the discovery of a universal formal principle could lead us to assured results.'" On his ultimate rejection of positivism, see 460–65. Born and Greene quotes are at 220, 223–24. Throughout Isaacson's book are aspects of Einstein's beginnings in, but movement away from, the positivism/empiricism of David Hume and Ernst Mach. Others have described Einstein as "a friend of logical empiricism and scientific philosophy," concluding that Einstein contributed as much to twentieth-century philosophy as to twentieth-century physics. See Don A. Howard, "Einstein's Philosophy of Science," *Stanford Encyclopedia of Philosophy*, http://plato.stanford.edu/entries/einstein-philscience/ (consulted on 6/21/2009). Einstein's 1905 special theory of relativity showed "that space and time did not have independent existences, but instead formed a fabric of spacetime." His (1915) general theory of relativity showed that the "fabric of space-time" was more than "a container for objects and events" (an allusion to Newton's bucket). Rather, "it had its own dynamics that were determined by, and in turn helped to determine, the motion of objects within it." Isaacson, *Einstein*, 223.

23. A. E. Taylor, *Elements of Metaphysics* (1903; New York: Barnes and Noble, 1961), 4, 6, 9–11; quote on 10; Henry J. Koren, *An Introduction to the Science of Metaphysics* (St. Louis: B. Herder Book Co., 1955), esp. 1–16; *The American Heritage Dictionary*, 2d college ed. (Boston: Houghton Mifflin Company, 1982), s. v.

"metaphysics," 790; "Metaphysics," *Stanford Encyclopedia of Philosophy*, http://plato.stanford.edu/entries/metaphysics/; and Gregory, *Scientific Materialism in Nineteenth Century Germany*, 18. Du Bois' own words, written late in his life, suggest much about his acceptance of metaphysics. He wrote in his autobiography of his evolving scientific education beginning at Fisk and then Harvard, where he studied the various "laws of the physical world." In Berlin he "began to grasp the idea of a world of human beings whose actions, like those of the physical world, were subject to law." See Du Bois, *The Autobiography of W. E. B. Du Bois*, 131.

24. I am obviously alluding here to Cornel West, *The American Evasion of Philosophy: A Genealogy of Pragmatism* (Madison: University of Wisconsin Press, 1989), esp. 138–50. John Higham had also reported that turn-of-the-century American intellectuals were timid when it came to discussions of "radical subjectivity," which was emerging in Europe. Rather, the new university professionals played it "safe" and avoided "radical experiments in art and philosophy." There is a very brief discussion of this in Lewis Perry, *Intellectual Life in America: A History* (Chicago: University of Chicago Press, 1984), 312–14. The point here is that Du Bois did not, in any way, evade philosophy, even if most American intellectuals did not notice. In fact, if one considers Koren's description of metaphysics in *An Introduction to the Science of Metaphysics*, esp. 8, it would be easy to conclude that Du Bois accomplished even more than I have indicated in the text. Koren describes metaphysics as incorporating theodicy, cosmology, (rational) psychology, philosophical anthropology, ontology, and epistemology. It is not difficult to see all of this in *Souls*. I have also used the words of Aldon Morris and Amin Ghaziani here, only slightly paraphrasing them, and for different purposes from theirs. They write that Du Bois "plunged headfirst into public sociology," with which I agree in regards to *The Philadelphia Negro* and the Atlanta University Studies. But in *The Souls of Black Folk*, Du Bois' "emersion" (to borrow a term, this time, from Robert Stepto) was not only in sociology, but also in philosophy. See Morris and Ghaziani, "Du Boisian Sociology: A Watershed of Professional and Public Sociology," *Souls* 7 (2005): 52; and Robert B. Stepto, *From Behind the Veil: A Study of Afro-American Narrative* (1979; Urbana: University of Illinois Press, 1991). For a critique of West's evidence of "evasion," see Robert Gooding-Williams, "Evading Narrative Myth, Evading Prophetic Pragmatism: Cornel West's 'The American Evasion of Philosophy,'" *Massachusetts Review* 32 (Winter 1991): 517–42.

25. A. E. Taylor acknowledged that mystics are, indeed, concerned with emotional issues rather than intellectual ones, but he also noted that "their philosophical method has invariably been scientific and rational." Taylor, *Elements of Metaphysics*, 14–15. A study that examines Du Bois' work in the context of mysticism (comparing it to William James's "psychical research") is Cynthia D. Schrager, "Both Sides of the Veil: Race, Science, and Mysticism in W. E. B. Du Bois," *American Quarterly* 48 (December 1996): 551–86. Although Schrager sometimes seemed to use "spiritualism" and "mysticism" similarly, she importantly saw Du Bois as having combined mysticism and positivism, she described the use of mysticism as having "radical potential," and she warned that unless "we find new strategies for reading the mystical register," we will simply miss much in scholarship like Du Bois' (555, 577). Keith Byerman

recognized both the empirical and idealist strands in Du Bois' work in *Seizing the Word: History, Art, and Self in the Work of W. E. B. Du Bois* (Athens: University of Georgia, 1994), viewing the two strands through different works—*Souls*, the idealist, and *Philadelphia Negro*, the empiricist. The rational/real, real/rational remark is more normally translated "what is rational is actual, and what is actual is rational" and comes from Hegel's "Preface" to *Philosophy of Right*. The phrasing is different still in Frederick Gregory, *Scientific Materialism in Nineteenth Century Germany*, 17, where Gregory writes "'Whatever is reasonable is real, and whatever is real is reasonable.'"

26. For a very useful study of the diverse ways Du Bois used this kind of science, including in his fiction, and his refutation of "brain science," see Maria Farland, "W. E. B. Du Bois, Anthropometric Science and the Limits of Racial Uplift," *American Quarterly* (2006): 1017–45. And see the second paragraph in n. 10, above. Hegel's detailed discussion of "the nervous system" and skulls is at *PS* §§327–46. About craniology, in general, Hegel concluded that skull "bumps" and "hollows" were scientifically useless and incapable of revealing anything scientifically (*PS* §338). A useful analysis of those aspects of Hegel's chapter is Alasdair MacIntyre, "Hegel on Faces and Skulls," in *Hegel: A Collection of Critical Essays*, ed. Alasdair MacIntyre (Garden City, NY: Doubleday and Co., 1972), 219–36.

27. Quotations from Fritjof Capra, *The Science of Leonardo*, 144, 148, 152. There are numerous possible interpretations of Hegel's ladders. But see *PS* §26 where Hegel insists that in the course of the journey to science (knowledge), "Science on its part requires that self-consciousness should have raised itself into this Aether in order to be able to live—and [actually] to live—with Science and in Science. Conversely, the individual has the right to demand that Science should at least provide him with the ladder to this standpoint, within himself." Although I might interpret Hegel too literally, there are many examples of this idea in *Souls*.

28. See Michel-Rolph Trouillot, *Silencing the Past: Power and the Production of History* (Boston: Beacon Press, 1995), esp. 74–82, where Trouillot discussed humanity's becoming, ostensibly, white: "Access to human status did not lead *ipso facto* to self determination" but to "*degrees of humanity*" (81).

29. As the discussion throughout this volume suggests, scholars have worked intensively to explain Du Bois' methods and to situate his work in a transnational intellectual world. In addition to already cited sources, Nancy Muller Milligan, "W. E. B. Du Bois' American Pragmatism," *Journal of American Culture* 8 (Summer 1985): 31–37, interprets Du Bois' effort as a blending of the "'method-oriented' pragmatism of [Charles Sanders] Peirce and the ethical 'justice oriented' pragmatism of [William] James" (31). The result, for Milligan, was a new "American Pragmatism" in which science/empiricism would lead to truth, which would lead to justice. But perhaps even more important here, although many early scientific materialists might not have called themselves metaphysicians, as Frederick Gregory notes, "materialism is a metaphysical position." See *Scientific Materialism in Nineteenth Century Germany*, x.

30. Isaacson, *Einstein*, 330, 448–54, and 458; Hume quotation from Walter Burkert, *Lore and Science in Ancient Pythagoreanism*, trans. Edwin L. Menmar Jr.

(Cambridge, MA: Harvard University Press, 1972), 20. Plato's quotations may be found at *PR*, 342c–e. For a copy of the original Hume statement, which includes extensive use of italics that I have silently removed, see David Hume, *Enquiries Concerning Human Understanding and Concerning the Principles of Morals*, 3rd ed. (1777; Oxford: Clarendon Press, 1975), sec. XII, pt. III, p. 165, §132. A useful discussion of Hume, not only as a historian and philosopher but as "a *philosophe*, a leader in the great eighteenth-century secularization of the intelligible universe," is J. G. A. Pocock, "Hume and the American Revolution," in *Virtue, Commerce, and History: Essays on Political Thought and History, Chiefly in the Eighteenth Century* (Cambridge: Cambridge University Press, 1985), 125–41, quotation on 126. And for a detailed discussion of the importance of dialectics in reaching the truth, see *PR* §§531d–534e. Walter Burkert suggests that this aspect of education (dialectics) is important for "push[ing] forward beyond the sensible world to true Being and thus to really exact knowledge" (*Lore and Science in Ancient Pythagoreanism*, 371).

31. Werner Marx, *Hegel's Phenomenology of Spirit: Its Point and Purpose—A Commentary on the Preface and Introduction* (New York: Harper and Row, Publishers, 1975), 73. Also see *Phenomenology*, §86.

32. The details on which this summary is based are in Hegel's section on "Spirit," or *PS* §§438–671.

33. Errol E. Harris, *The Restitution of Metaphysics* (Amherst, NY: Humanity Books, 2000), 77. This very issue of "abstraction" was ultimately taken up by the sociologists. See David Paul Haney, *The Americanization of Social Science: Intellectuals and Public Responsibility in the Postwar United States* (Philadelphia: Temple University Press, 2007). Harris provides an especially useful discussion of parts and wholes in *Restitution of Metaphysics*, 105–17. Robin George Collingwood (1889–1943) was a British philosopher and historian whose *The Idea of History*, published three years after his death, is a seminal work in the philosophy of history. Here, again, Gregory's distinction between "science" and "naked knowledge" (above) is important. Also consider Walter Burkert's report of Socrates's philosophical point that "true Being and . . . thus really exact knowledge" lay "beyond the sensible world." Burkert, *Lore and Science in Ancient Pythagoreanism*, 371.

34. Einstein is alleged to have said that he wanted to think like God, the rest was just detail. While the comment is obviously evidence of his "profound reverence for the harmony and beauty of what he called the mind of God as it was expressed in the creation of the universe and its laws," it is also the case (and especially important to this study) that in the comment, Einstein acknowledged his interest in the spiritual as much as the material, the real as much as the abstract. See Isaacson, *Einstein*, 20. And as egotistical as the oft-quoted line seems, to determine/discover "the laws of nature" has always been a goal of science. This was especially the case for eighteenth-century philosophers and the goal of natural science, which came out of natural philosophy by the latter part of the century. For an overview of this history, see Carl L. Becker, *The Heavenly City of the Eighteenth-Century Philosophers* (New Haven: Yale University Press, 1932).

35. Du Bois developed aspects of this idea in more detail in his *Autobiography*, 150–75, where he discussed "The Niagara Movement." In what appears to be an

extremely forthcoming discussion of his views on Booker T. Washington, the most salient issue (only briefly addressed in *Souls*) is that Washington's influence prevented people from developing and debating ideas (their own and others).

36. Of course, this general idea is central to Hegel's analysis. "The task of the individual is 'to elevate his singleness to his universal nature, to educate himself.'" Quoted in Werner Marx, *Hegel's Phenomenology of Spirit*, 31–32.

37. Julius W. Friend and James Feibleman, *Science and the Spirit of Man: A New Ordering of Experience* (London: George Allen Unwin, 1933), 12–17. Throughout this volume, Friend and Feibleman provided useful discussions on the fuzziness of the line between deductive and inductive evidence, ultimately concluding that the division between the "subjective and objective" is simply "untenable" (22).

38. Burkert, *Lore and Science in Ancient Pythagoreanism*, 20–21.

39. Although the quest for the good, the beautiful, and the true has been an important goal of philosophers for millennia, this characterization of it is based on Du Bois' words in the extraordinary "Program" that he designed, carried out, and wrote about for the solitary celebration of his twenty-fifth birthday. One part of the program has been heavily quoted, if not fully understood, for reasons that will be obvious.

> I rejoice as a strong man to run a race. And I am strong—is it egotism, is it assurance—or is [it] the silent call of the world spirit that makes me feel that I am royal and that beneath my scepter a world of kings shall bow. The hot dark blood of that black forefather—born king of men—is beating at my heart, and I know that I am either a genius or a fool. O I wonder what I am—I wonder what the world is—I wonder if life is worth the *Sturm*. I do not know—perhaps I never shall know: But this I do know: be the Truth what it may I will seek it on the pure assumption that it is worth seeking— and Heaven nor Hell, God nor Devil shall turn me from my purpose till I die.

Later, and less often quoted, the program continued:

> What is life but life, after all? Its end is its greatest and fullest self—this end is the Good. The Beautiful its attribute—its soul, and Truth is its being. Not three commensurable things are these, they [are] three dimensions of the cube—mayhap God is the fourth, but for that very reason incomprehensible. The greatest and fullest Life is by definition beautiful, beautiful,—beautiful as a dark passionate woman, beautiful as a golden hearted school girl, beautiful as a grey haired hero. That is the dimension of *breadth*. Then comes Truth—what is, cold and indisputable: That is *height*. Now I will, so help my soul, multiply breadth by height, Beauty by Truth & then Goodness, strength, shall bind them together into a solid Whole. Wherefore? I know not now. Perhaps Infinite other dimensions do. This is a wretched figure and yet it roughly represents my attitude toward the world.

Quoted in Beyerman, *Seizing the Word*, 4, 8. Note that in *The Autobiography of W. E. B. Du Bois*, 106–7, Du Bois' wording is slightly different.

40. Robert Gooding-Williams, *In the Shadow of Du Bois: Afro-Modern Political Thought in America* (Cambridge, MA: Harvard University Press, 2009), 128, sees "The Afterthought" as the end of the book rather than the song, and characterizes it as a pessimistic conclusion that leaves it to us to straighten out the mess that we have created. In my view, the book ends with the song (and is therefore a much more optimistic ending), and "The Afterthought" is truly an afterthought—almost a prayer, very much like most of Du Bois' characteristically sacred and secular (but not profane) meditations.

Although I have already pointed out that Shamoon Zamir's "'The Sorrow Songs'/'Song of Myself': Du Bois, the Crisis of Leadership and Prophetic Imagination," in *The Black Columbiad: Defining Moments in African-American Literature and Culture*, ed. Werner Sollors and Maria Diedrich (Cambridge: Harvard University Press, 1994), 161–62, relates Du Bois' use of the weary traveler to Blake's "The Mental Traveler," equally important here, Zamir also writes that in Blake's poem, "'the Babe' liberty is 'begotten in woe' and 'born in joy.' But the child is 'given to a Woman Old,' society, who nails him down upon a rock." Zamir continues with Foster Damon's characterization of the poem as "the formula of the history of the idea of Liberty," and its cyclical progression of birth, triumph, rejection, rebirth, etc. I concluded above that Du Bois' weary traveler is Liberty, but using Zamir's discussion of Blake adds to this in that the children in Du Bois' final song are, literally, children who were "begotten in woe"—slavery; "born in joy"—emancipation; but ensconced in an "Old" society—a backward-looking Jim Crow system. But because they are children, we must imagine their song as the suggestion of the rebirth of the cycle of consciousness's struggle for Liberty. And here, again, the example also reminds us of Du Bois' unequalled facility in the use of language and especially the metaphor.

INDEX

79–80, 89–97, 101; education of, 92;
collective journey of, 101–13. *See also*
Art: spiritual work of; Inner life;
Spirit; Striving
"The Conservation of Races," 161–62
Conservation of soul, 50, 162
Constitution: use in *Souls*, 20, 29, 31,
32, 33
Cooper, Anna Julia, 1. See also *A Voice
from the South*
Copernicus, 137
Cosmology, 151, 173; Plato's, 149;
Pythagorean, 149; definition of, 165;
human-centered, 173
Cosmos, 150; creation of, 149; ancient
views of, 166–67
Cotton Kingdom, 36, 40, 107
The Crisis, 14
Critique of Pure Reason, 10
Crummell, Alexander, 9, 48, 57, 75–99,
101, 112, 169, 171; and spiritual
striving, 27; and liberty, 34; spiritual
(religious) journey of, 76–89; as
prophet, 76–89, 97; wilderness
experience of, 82–87; temptations of,
83–86; and *Phenomenology of Spirit*,
90–97; spiritual (philosophical)
journey of, 90–97; and work, 96. *See
also* "Of Alexander Crummell"
Cuffe, Paul, 44
Cult: as race/nation, 117. *See also*
Pantheon
Culture, 19, 43; of acquisition, 23–24;
of New South, 23–25, 30, 34, 36,
57; sociological use of, 24, 66;
anthropological use of, 24, 193–95
(nn. 24, 27, 28); as lie, 30, 34, 36, 57;
gift of, 35, 172; black American, 56,
57, 112, 130, 152, 156; world, 67, 106,
109; and Talented Tenth, 68; as self-
alienated spirit, 109–10; false, 123;
African, 157, 158; spiritual, 172; as
substitute for mind/spirit, 228
(n. 9). *See also* "Kingdom of culture";
"Work, culture, liberty"

Curtain, Hegel's, 111–12. *See also* Veil

Darwinism, 64
Da Vinci, Leonardo, 159
De Anima. See *On the Soul*
Declaration of Independence, 32, 44,
196–97 (n. 37); use in *Souls*, 29–30,
32, 169; as "metaphysical claim," 30;
and natural law, 33
Deductive reasoning, 7, 150, 155, 157,
165. *See also* A priori synthesis
Delphi, 145
Demiurge, 142–46 passim, 153, 156, 173
Destiny, 79, 80, 82, 83, 86, 89; of race,
37, 61, 162, 163; and Crummell, 75,
76, 80, 85, 86
Dialectics, 63, 169. *See also* Aristotelian
dialectics; Du Boisian dialectics;
Hegelian dialectics
Dialogues, 142, 171, 174–75
Discord: in society, 7, 109, 167; in
nature, 110; in music, 137, 142, 147,
153. *See also* Harmony
DNA, 161
Double consciousness, 3, 7–8, 15–16, 18,
19, 34, 38, 40–41, 53, 122–23, 160; as
pathological, 41; as dialectical unrest,
94; as unhappy consciousness, 94,
122–23; and veil, 111–12; resolution
of, 145–46
Dougherty County, Ga., 52, 59, 96, 98,
107, 109, 123, 171
Douglass, Frederick, 1, 45, 48, 67
Dualism, 79. *See also* Unities
Du Bois, W. E. B., 159; as philosopher,
1, 12–13, 16, 25, 45, 46, 78, 80, 97, 99,
157–58, 163–66; as social scientist, 2,
163; in Berlin, 4, 5, 25; at Harvard,
4, 25; and Hegelian idealism, 4–5,
12–13, 164; and Bismarck address,
5; labeling of, 11–12; as "marginal
man," 12; biographical sketch of,
13–14; at Fisk, 25; critique of Booker
T. Washington, 25, 45–47; views
of social science, 37–38, 164, 166;

Freedom, 20, 93, 94, 102, 105, 117, 124, 163; quest for, 6–7; and liberty, 8, 11, 29–34, 38, 54, 122; as self-determination, 8, 30, 169, 170, 175; of consciousness (soul), 8, 174; loss of, 19–22; post–Civil War, 30–35; spirit of, 96, 163; and former slaves, 102, 121, 155; consciousness's quest for, 102–13, 125

French Revolution, 110, 173

Frenzy: Bacchic, 117; in black religion, 119, 120, 145

Frequency, 137–38, 140

Friedrich Wilhelm Universität, 12

Friend, Julius W., 173

Fugitive Slave Act, 81

Garrison, Lucy McKim, 139–41

Gates, Henry Louis, Jr., 76

"Gene me, gene me," 128, 129, 132, 133, 134, 150, 151, 157

General Theological Seminary, 84, 92, 93

George, Henry, 72

Ghaziani, Amin, 2

God consciousness, 130

Goethe, Johann Wolfgang von, 75, 144, 233 (n. 22)

"The good, the beautiful, and the true," 49, 50, 52, 175, 259 (n. 39)

Gooding-Williams, Robert, 18, 101, 156

Good Society, 62, 73, 74

Gospel: of Wealth, 9, 23, 72; of work and money, 22, 45; of pay, 106

Gould, Stephen Jay, 3

"Great Camp Meeting," 153

Greece, ancient, 22, 73; and World Soul, 40–41; government of, 71; and immortal soul, 89; and mythology, 148, 193 (n. 22); and science, 166; and customs, 170

Greekness, 162

Green, Beriah, 83

Greene, Brian, 165

Guardians, 63–64, 214 (n. 14)

"Guiding Hundredth," 61, 69–70. *See also* Talented Tenth

Haitian Revolution, 44

Hall, Stephen Gilroy, 12

Hampton Institute, 65, 138, 139

Harmonic rhythm, 142, 143

Harmony, 137, 142; and World Soul, 6, 8, 145, 151, 165, 175, 241 (n. 57); and soul, 54, 147; and morality, 110–11; in nature, 110–13; and Absolute Knowledge, 113; musical, 135–37, 140–42, 144, 152–53; and romantics, 142; and creation, 142–44; of universe, 142–44, 151, 152–53; as eternal, 144; and mind, 144; of spheres, 144, 151, 154–56, 158, 166–67; and Sorrow Songs, 153; as symbolic, 154–55; and theory, 245 (n. 80)

Harris, Errol E., 164

Hart, Albert Bushnell, 1, 161, 163, 164

Harvard University, 4–5, 12–13, 25, 62, 151, 161, 163, 164; and ideas about race, 253–54 (n. 10)

Hayford, Joseph Ephraim Casely, 41

Hegel, Georg Wilhelm Friedrich, 1–2, 4, 12–13, 90, 96, 98, 164, 165, 166, 167, 170, 173, 174, 176; and Africa, 6; and religion, 115–16

Hegel Club, 12

Hegelian dialectics, 38, 169

Hegelian idealism, 4–7, 9, 10, 11, 12, 80, 90, 101, 116, 161, 163, 164, 169, 170, 171, 172, 173. See also *Phenomenology of Spirit*; Philosophy: of spirit

Henderson, John, 27–28, 36

Heninger, S. K., Jr., 149, 152

Herodotus: and "Greekness," 162

Heroic Age, 47

Hertz, Heinrich, 137–38

Higginson, Thomas Wentworth, 138, 141, 145, 147, 149

"Higher aims of life," 45

Holt, Thomas, 17, 72

Hooper, W. D., 160
Horizon: A Journal of the Color Line, 14
Humanism, 115–16; civic, 33–34; atheistic, 115; Renaissance, 170
Hume, David, 168

Idealism, 1, 12, 90, 156. *See also* Hegelian idealism
"I Hope My Mother Will Be There," 132
Inductive reasoning, 7, 150, 157, 169
Industrial capitalism, 23, 169, 170, 173
Infinite knowledge, 131, 135, 151, 153, 174. *See also* Absolute Knowledge
Inner life, 39–40, 51, 53, 147; and Wagner, 250 (n. 106)
Interracial relations, 24, 33, 50, 52–53, 54
Intervals, 119, 135–36, 137, 138, 139, 140, 151; in Plato's creation story, 142–44
Invisible: communication with, 145
Isaacson, Walter, 164

James, Henry, 160
James, Jamie, 144, 145, 158
James, William, 1, 5, 62, 160, 164
Jesus, 77, 78, 81, 82, 83, 87
Jevons, J. Stanley, 146
Jim Crow car, 35–36
Jim Crow system, 64
Johnston, Ian, 136–37
Jones, John, 15, 34, 35, 54, 58, 59, 75, 112, 126, 171; and striving, 27, 34, 36; death of, 28, 34, 35, 36, 56, 58, 112; and liberty, 34; and development of soul, 54–59, 112, 169; and music, 55–58, 126, 134, 155; and Talented Tenth, 56; and fables, 58, 59, 75; as Socrates, 59; and Du Bois' dialectic, 169
"Josie," 23, 24, 36, 47, 48, 54, 60, 106, 171
Jubilee Hall, 125
Jubilee Singers, 125, 156

Kainz, Howard, 118
Kant, Immanuel, 10, 90, 101, 164
Kemble, Fanny, 138
Kepler, Johannes, 137
"Kingdom of culture," 36, 42, 130
Knowledge, 23, 128, 129, 130, 145, 150, 151, 156, 157; infinite, 51; immediate, 91, 110; as eternal, 116, 130; and Spirit, 128, 156, 172; as distinct from learning, 129, 130; as remembering, 148; love of, 149; and universal harmony, 151, 233 (n. 22), 248 (n. 96); and idealism, 156; black contribution to, 156, 172–73; and soul, 167; Plato's ways of knowing, 168; and World Soul, 172; and Crummell, 226 (n. 54). *See also* Learning
Krehbiel, Henry, 153

Labor, 51, 99; free black, 21–22; unwaged, 25; and self-determination, 74; and Crummell, 84; and Protestantism, 97–98; stolen, 108. *See also* Work
Land ownership: difficulty of, 24–25, 104–5; loss of, 104, 108–9
Lanier, Sidney, 128, 154
"Largo," 139
Lassalle, Ferdinand, 5
Law of heart, 106
Learning: as education, 19, 49, 54, 68, 69, 129, 130, 155, 157, 213 (n. 8). *See also* Knowledge
Leibniz, Gottfried Wilhelm von, 116, 119, 130, 144
Lewis, David Levering, 15, 22, 76–78, 89, 129
Liberty, 11, 19, 20, 26, 28–30, 32, 33, 38, 54, 107, 155; and freedom, 8, 11, 38, 54, 122; as focus of *Souls*, 26–35; and republicanism, 32; and Thomas Paine, 32, 197–98 (n. 39); and collective ambitions, 32–33; and civic humanism, 33–34; case

studies on, 34–35; and American Revolution, 44; and Cato, 198–99 (n. 40); and Blake, 260 (n. 40)

Life: knowledge of, 24, 50, 52, 90; preparation for, 52; philosophy of, 54; meaning of, 56, 59, 66, 75, 90, 98, 99; lessons, 58; essence of, 59; truth of, 79; ideals of, 159, 162; Soul's struggle for, 163; music as, 243–44 (n. 72)

Lippman, Edward A., 145

Living work of art, 117–19, 120, 123–25, 172

Lohengrin, 56, 58, 250 (n. 106)

Looking Backward, 72

"Lordship and Bondage," 5, 92–93, 96, 104, 154–55

Maconie, Robin, 131, 151

Man's Soul, 39

"March On," 132, 133

Marx, Karl, 96

Marx, Werner, 96

Marxism, 74

Master songs, 124–26, 132, 135, 171, 172, 231 (n. 16)

Material/spiritual worlds, 7–8, 10, 16, 38, 42, 52, 79, 112, 122, 144, 148, 152, 161, 162, 164, 166, 172, 175–76

Materialism, 45, 170

Materialists, 1, 32, 56, 163

Mather, Cotton, 97

Mediator, 95–96

Menand, Louis, 4

Metaphysical Club, 12

Metaphysics, 7, 38, 39, 113, 130, 135, 148, 154, 157, 161, 164, 165; Du Bois' use of, 7, 10, 11, 38, 130; and philosophy of religion, 9; and Declaration of Independence, 30; and music, 113, 135, 150, 155, 228 (n. 14); and Sorrow Songs, 150; and knowing, 157–58; and Aristotle, 165; as science, 165, 168; description of, 165, 256 (n. 24)

Middle class, 23–24; and Talented Tenth, 215 (n. 24)

Minor keys, 134

Minstrel, 117, 118, 119

Minstrelsy, 158

Missouri Compromise, 81

Mohammad, 78, 80, 82

Moon Illustrated Weekly, 14

Morality (will), 78, 109–11, 113; moral life, 44; moral imperatives, 44, 45; moral heroism, 47; moral objectives, 49; moral lessons, 58; moral view, 110; moral consciousness, 110–11

Morris, Aldon, 2

Moses, 77–88 passim

Moses, Wilson Jeremiah, 17, 41, 89, 97

Moton, Robert R., 138

Movement, 103, 112, 143, 153. *See also* Force

Multiple personalities, 42, 122. *See also* Double consciousness

Music, 3, 57, 115, 124, 131, 175; science of, 10, 130, 131, 135–42; as language, 10, 157; and religion, 53, 54–55, 57, 119–20; and John Jones, 54–59; Sorrow Songs, 54–59, 112–13, 131–46; Lohengrin, 56, 58; and spiritual striving, 57; and mathematics, 57, 135–37, 143–44, 152, 155; and culture, 57–58, 112–13; and harmony, 113, 119, 142, 144, 145, 152, 153, 158; cultural adaptation of, 113, 132–35, 144, 146, 149, 153, 155; and Romantics, 135, 142, 155; and metaphysics, 135, 158; relationship to soul, 135–37; and transcription difficulties, 138–42; and Creation, 142, 156; as spirit, 145; as communication, 148; as offering, 148; narrowing purpose of, 152, 158. *See also* Negro/new scale; Sorrow Songs

Musical epigraphs, 124, 131, 139, 156, 157

Shout, 53, 138, 145, 147, 149, 153, 156

Sigma Pi Phi. *See* Boulé

Single tax, 72

Skeptical consciousness, 93, 94, 104

Socialism, 50, 67, 72, 74

Social science, 13, 37, 38, 39, 130, 151, 161–62, 163, 164, 166, 168

Social world, 116, 233 (n. 22)

Sociology, 2, 3, 8, 11, 12, 22, 24, 25, 39, 40, 42, 58, 60, 62, 102, 161, 163, 164, 175; of South, 22–25; and liberty, 33. *See also* Du Bois, W. E. B.: views of social science

"Sociology Hesitant," 38, 60

Socrates, 47, 58–59, 136, 148, 154; and soul, 25, 44, 51; trial of, 51–52; and church, 53

Solomon, Robert C., 115–16, 131, 151

Songs, 176. *See also* Music; "New song"; "Of the Sorrow Songs"; Sorrow Songs

"Song of the Bride," 59

Sorrow Songs, 1, 9, 10, 55, 128, 132, 135, 139, 152, 153, 172; as spiritual, 10; as spiritual heritage, 10, 34, 56, 126, 155, 156, 157; as Absolute Knowledge, 10, 112, 113, 130–32, 144–49, 150, 152, 154, 155–56, 172; as liberty, 33–35; gift of, 35, 172, 200–201 (n. 43); and fundamental unities, 113, 158; and religion, 116–18, 119; as Absolute Art, 117–18, 119, 120; and collective consciousness, 125–26, 156; and World Soul, 126; evolution of, 132–33, 153, 155, 157–58; and sound, 138–39, 145; as epigraphs, 139; as new music, 140, 145, 153, 154; and creation, 142, 156; as real (actual), 144; and infinite, 145; repetition in, 149; and subdominant factors, 153–55; and harmony, 153–56, 157; new scale of, 154; compared to literary arts, 156; origins of, 156–57; and words, 156–57

Soul, 90; and striving, 3, 5, 6, 7, 8, 9, 16, 17, 18, 19, 20, 34, 36, 40, 41, 42–43, 45, 53, 54, 57, 59, 60, 131, 161; as focus of *Souls*, 3, 37–74; and knowledge, 5, 48, 148–56, 167, 170, 171; as sovereign, 8, 38, 40, 41, 50–51, 59, 155, 198 (n. 40); and double consciousness, 15–16, 41; conservation of, 19, 44, 50, 53, 54, 161–63; and potential, 25, 27, 80; meanings of, 25, 42; as consciousness/identity, 25, 42, 45, 55, 79, 112, 113, 120, 124, 148; and inner life, 38, 40, 53, 147; ancient descriptions of, 38, 51; work of, 42–44; characteristics of, 44, 45, 46, 48, 53–54, 56; development of, 45, 46, 49, 79, 101–13, 118–19, 145, 172–73; and education, 51, 52; and Greek traditions, 51, 60, 89; and essence, 59, 60, 79, 107, 135, 167; and immorality, 89; and language, 117; calculating, 119, 144; and nation, 121, 122; and music, 129; and metaphysics, 135–66; creation of, 142–44; and freedom, 163, 174, 175

The Souls of Black Folk: as work of philosophy, 3; as philosophy of history, 6, 7, 170; and metaphysics, 7, 9, 10, 11, 39, 130, 150, 161, 165, 167, 179–80 (n. 9); organization of, 8, 11, 18, 19–35, 101–28; Du Bois' review of, 38, 203–4 (n. 7); and *Phenomenology of Spirit*, 101–13; reactions to, 159–61; "Afterthought" of, 173–74. *See also* "Of Alexander Crummell"; "Of the Wings of Atalanta"

"The Soul's Music," 57

Sound: as Spirit, 134, 138, 140, 141

Spiers, Fiona, 72

Spinoza, Baruch, 37, 41

Spirit, 91, 92, 96, 97, 98, 104, 106, 109, 117, 118, 121, 122, 149, 152, 158, 161, 166, 167, 169, 172; philosophical meaning of, 25; as self-realization/ knowledge, 25, 44, 45, 48, 79, 90; "in potentia," 25, 80; necessary work

of, 43, 48; individual journey to,
89–97, 149; collective journey to,
101–13, 149; crisis of, 121; and art,
125–28, 131; as real/actual, 128, 152;
philosophy of, 128–46, 148, 149, 155,
156, 157, 166, 170–75; and sound,
134; in music, 134, 140, 141; and
Essence, 156, 167; as goal, 170
Spiritual: definition of, 10
Spiritualism, 166
Spiritual journey, individual: religious,
78–89, 99; philosophical, 89–97, 99;
collective, 101–13
Spirituals: as American music, 10, 34,
126, 155, 200–201 (n. 43)
Spiritual striving, 9, 15–36, 60, 90, 93,
166, 169; objectives of, 17, 19, 36,
170; as potential, 18–19; symbols of,
23; obstructions to, 25, 44; source
of, 40; as historical, 41, 43, 102–13;
necessity of, 43; and music, 57; and
purpose, 90; as soul/humanity, 102;
and education, 171
Spiritual work: of art, 119, 125–28, 171
Spiritual world. See Material/spiritual
worlds
"Steal Away," 132, 133, 155
Stirling, James, 115
Stoic consciousness, 93, 94, 104
Stroyer, Jacob, 145
Suffrage, 43, 102. See also Voting rights
Sundquist, Eric, 16, 28, 35, 56, 57, 132,
157
Supersensible world, 103
Superstition, 147–48
Swansong/swan's song, 58, 59
Swoboda, Philip J., 39
Sycophants, 43, 46, 49, 54, 169. See also
Assimilation

Tabak, D., 159–60
Talented Tenth, 2, 10, 22, 49, 56, 150;
and Plato's Philosopher Rulers, 8–9,
62–66, 67, 72; displacement of, 23;
and elitism, 47, 56, 61–62, 67, 71–73;

defined, 61; and Guiding Hundredth,
61, 69–70; theory of, 61–74, 167;
and leadership, 63–64, 66–69;
responsibilities of, 66–68, 71; and
elites, 67; membership in, 69–71; as
meritocracy, 73
Taylor, A. E., 165
Teleological process, 6, 119
Temptations, 27, 76, 77, 80, 82, 83–85,
90
Tennyson, Alfred, 54, 156
Tertium quid, 55, 102, 168
Thirteenth Amendment, 29
Timaeus, 142–43, 144, 145–46
Trouillot, Michel-Rolph, 168
Truth, Sojourner, 67
"Truth, Beauty, and Goodness," 49–50,
52, 93, 175
Tunnell, W. V., 61
Turner, Nat, 44, 46
Tuskegee Institute, 65, 75, 138. See also
Washington, Booker T.

Unchangeable being, 94, 95
Unconditioned universal, 103
Understanding, 103
Unhappy consciousness, 94, 95, 101,
104, 122
United consciousness, 94, 97, 148, 149
Unities: absolute spiritual, 107; of soul
and spirit, 156; of art and science,
158; fundamental, 158; of science and
religion, 158; and world historical
peoples, 167; of humankind, 168;
material/spiritual, 175–76
Universal difference, 103
Universe: harmony of, 152–53
University of Pennsylvania, 13, 163
Up from Slavery, 21
Uplift, 50, 66, 73, 93, 98

Vaudeville, 157–58
Veil, 3, 15–18, 87, 88; meanings of,
16–17, 18, 19, 87, 160; shadow of,
17; as Hegel's curtain, 111–12; and